P9-DTZ-832

BAD MEXICANS

ALSO BY KELLY LYTLE HERNÁNDEZ

MIGRA!
A HISTORY OF THE U.S. BORDER PATROL

CITY OF INMATES:
CONQUEST, REBELLION, AND THE RISE OF HUMAN
CAGING IN LOS ANGELES, 1771–1965

BAD MEXICANS

Race, Empire, and Revolution in the Borderlands

Kelly Lytle Hernández

W. W. NORTON & COMPANY
Independent Publishers Since 1923

For information about permission to reproduce selections from this book, write to Permissions, W. W. Norton & Company, Inc., 500 Fifth Avenue, New York, NY 10110

For information about special discounts for bulk purchases, please contact W. W. Norton Special Sales at specialsales@wwnorton.com or 800-233-4830

Manufacturing by Lakeside Book Company
Book design by Lovedog Studio
Production manager: Lauren Abbate

ISBN 978-1-324-00437-0

W. W. Norton & Company, Inc., 500 Fifth Avenue, New York, N.Y. 10110
www.wwnorton.com

W. W. Norton & Company Ltd., 15 Carlisle Street, London W1D 3BS

1 2 3 4 5 6 7 8 9 0

CONTENTS

Part 3: RUNNING DOWN THE REVOLUTIONISTS

Part 4: ¡TIERRA Y LIBERTAD!

BAD MEXICANS

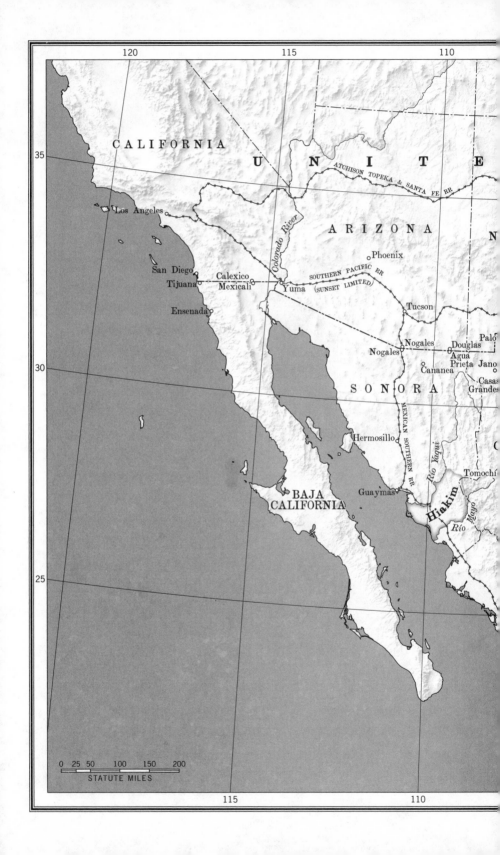

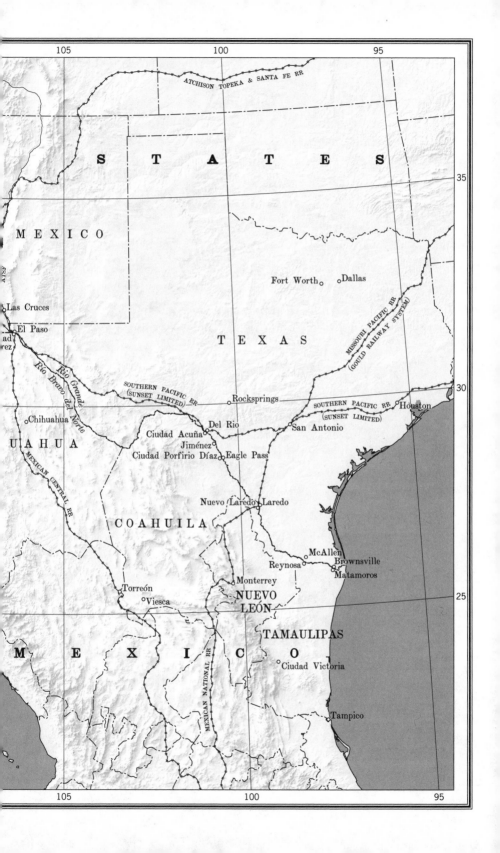

We Stand Between

THEY LIT THE PYRE AND WATCHED HIM BURN. ANTONIO Rodríguez, a twenty-year-old ranch hand, murdered a white woman, they said. White men from nearby farms formed a posse to track him down, while the other residents of Rocksprings, Texas, some four hundred of them, met at the edge of town and piled kindling at the base of a mesquite tree. The posse soon arrived, with a cowboy in the lead, dragging Rodríguez by a lasso looped around his neck. The mob laughed as they chained Antonio to the tree and doused him in kerosene. Someone threw a match and, thirty minutes later, when Antonio Rodríguez was dead, the residents of Rocksprings "returned quietly to town and business was resumed."[1] It was November 3, 1910.

Mexican American journalists in the U.S.–Mexico borderlands reported the grisly details of Rodríguez's murder, condemning it as an act of racial terror akin to the lynching of African Americans in the South. Newspapers in Mexico picked up the story. "Lynching is not practiced by the blonde 'Yankee' except upon beings whom, for ethnic reasons, he considers his inferiors," fumed the editors of the Mexico City paper *El Debate.* Another paper dubbed Anglo-Americans the "barbarous whites of the north," deriding them as the "giants of the dollar" but "pygmies of culture." "There is indignation among Mexicans here over this lynching," reported *El País.*[2]

By November 8, riots had erupted across Mexico. Targeting the considerable number of U.S.-owned businesses and homes, the protestors smashed windows and tore down American flags while chanting *"Mueran los yanquis!"* (Death to the Americans!)[3] The police arrested hundreds of people. In one case, officers drew sabers and descended upon a crowd, killing one man by stabbing him through the neck.[4] The protests continued, on the streets and in the press, prompting Henry Lane Wilson, the U.S. ambassador to Mexico, to issue a public warning: the United States government "will leave nothing undone" to protect U.S. citizens and property in Mexico.[5] It was a threat: the United States would invade Mexico if attacks on U.S. interests did not cease. The protests raged on. Ambassador Wilson decided to visit General Porfirio Díaz, the dictator of Mexico, to insist that he put a stop to the "anti-American disturbances."[6]

Porfirio Díaz had ruled Mexico for twenty-seven years. Seizing the Mexican presidency by coup d'état in 1876, the general had thrown open the doors of his country, handing out land and tax incentives to foreign investors. He also guaranteed pliant labor. Tens of thousands of U.S. investors rushed in, ranging from the Rockefellers to one-pick miners, making Mexico the first country where U.S. citizens made significant foreign investment. U.S. citizens soon controlled key sectors of the Mexican economy: railroads, oil, and mining. By 1900, they owned 130 million acres, amounting to one-quarter of Mexico's arable land.[7] By 1910, fully half of all money invested by Americans overseas—more than $500 million—went to Mexico.[8] And they expected President Díaz to protect their interests.

Díaz used foreign capital to industrialize the Mexican economy, often with little regard for the rights and wellbeing of Mexico's poorest citizens. When investors bought land claimed by Mexico's rural and Indigenous communities, Díaz dispatched soldiers to evict any stragglers or protestors. Most notoriously, when the Yaqui refused to be removed from their homeland, Díaz deported the rebel fighters, and their families, to labor camps in the jungles of southern Mexico.[9] When industrial workers protested the low wages and dangerous working conditions that prevailed at mines, mills, and factories, Díaz ordered troops to fire on the picket lines. In 1907, during a strike in Rio Blanco,

Díaz's troops killed at least fifty picketers on a single morning.[10] And, across Mexico, Díaz maintained a deadly mobile strike force, the *rurales*, to terrorize his regime's critics. The *rurales* killed more than ten thousand people during Díaz's rule.[11]

With Díaz in charge, investors brimmed with confidence. Even as protestors filled the streets of Mexico after Antonio Rodríguez's lynching, President Taft quipped to his secretary of state, "I cannot conceive of a situation in which President Díaz would not act with a strong hand in defence [sic] of just American interest."[12]

Still, the protests continued. After a week of conflict in the streets, Ambassador Wilson marched into the president's office in the National Palace to lodge a complaint. Díaz cut him off, informing the ambassador that he had already "given the press strict orders to stop any further comments on the anti-American demonstrations, and that one of the journals which had disobeyed these instructions, namely *El Debate*, had been suppressed."[13] When Wilson returned the next day, Díaz informed him that he had "given orders to the authorities of the whole Republic to act with the necessary energy to suppress any further agitation because of the Texas matter, and that if anything of the kind should happen again, those who participated in any demonstrations would be dealt with all the severity of the law."[14] The Mexican government, Díaz confirmed, would stamp out the protests and censor the press, and everyone involved in the recent "disturbances" would be "brought to account."[15]

But the root of the problem was not in Mexico, insisted Díaz. The problem was in the United States. There, across the border region, a large number of Mexicans were living in exile and openly planning a revolution against his rule. As Díaz put it, the riots in Mexico began only because two of those exiles, Francisco Madero and Ricardo Flores Magón, had "taken advantage of the unfortunate affair which happened in Texas to excite young students and men of the laboring classes in order to discredit the government."[16]

Francisco Madero, one of Mexico's wealthiest men, had been in the United States for just a few months. As recently as June 1910, he had run against Díaz in the presidential election, but Díaz had had him arrested on charges of "insulting the president and fomenting rebellion" and held him in custody until the voting was complete and victory declared, securing Díaz's seventh term as the president of Mexico.[17] Madero fled to Texas, where he committed his personal fortune to stockpiling guns and recruiting an insurgent army to force Díaz from power.[18]

Ricardo Flores Magón had been in the United States for six years, agitating for revolt. His followers, known as *magonistas*, had few resources. They were poor men and women, mostly miners, farmworkers, and cotton pickers, many of them displaced from Mexico when President Díaz gave their land to foreign investors.[19] They wanted their land back and they were willing to fight for it. For challenging his rule, the Díaz administration dubbed them "malos Mexicanos" (bad Mexicans).

By 1910, Ricardo Flores Magón and the *magonistas* had launched a series of attacks on the Díaz regime, including four armed raids. When Francisco Madero arrived in the United States and called for a mass uprising against Díaz's rule to begin at 6 pm on November 20, 1910, the *magonistas* vowed to join the fight. By November 16, when Ambassador Wilson met with President Díaz, armed men were mustering on the banks of the Rio Grande. Díaz told Wilson that a revolution was brewing and only the U.S. government could stop it. "Unless the American Government prevents these men from making an open revolutionary propaganda against the Mexican Government . . . a more serious disturbance might be expected," warned Díaz.[20]

U.S. authorities were already monitoring the situation. In Texas, federal agents tailed Francisco Madero, who, they confirmed, was acquiring trainloads of guns and smuggling them across the border. But, according to most U.S. authorities, Madero—a political reformer who was popular among Mexico's middle and upper classes—was not a threat to U.S. interests. After decades of corrupt elections, these wealthier Mexicans sought to oust Díaz from power and restore democratic rule, but they hardly questioned the economic arrangements of the Díaz regime. As Ambassador Wilson put it, a Madero administration would "do justice to American interests."[21] U.S. agents did not arrest Madero or his supporters, known as *maderistas*.

Ricardo Flores Magón and the *magonistas*, however, were a threat, because they sought a wholesale political and economic revolution. They not only demanded Díaz's ouster; they demanded a strict limit on foreign investment in Mexico, protections for workers, and the return of the land seized by investors during the Díaz era to Mexico's dispossessed rural and Indigenous communities. It was the *magonistas* who made "*¡Tierra y Libertad!*" (Land and Liberty!) the revolution's battle cry. This platform was intolerable to U.S. investors and the federal government they strongly influenced. U.S. authorities had been hounding the *magonistas* for years, ever since Flores Magón first arrived in the United States in January 1904.

Brilliant and ill-tempered, Ricardo Flores Magón looked more like a girthy professor than a gutsy revolutionary. On the pages of his Mexico City newspaper, *Regeneración*, Flores Magón named the Díaz regime a "dictatorship," daring to print a word no one else would.[22] "General Diaz has killed democracy," declared Flores Magón.[23] Moreover, he insisted, Díaz's economic policies had made Mexicans the "servants of foreigners."[24] Díaz had Flores Magón arrested numerous times, his printing press smashed by security forces. After fleeing to the United States in 1904, Flores Magón and his small circle of friends found themselves the target of a joint U.S.–Mexico counterinsurgency campaign.

The U.S. Departments of State, War, Justice, and Commerce and Labor committed dozens of agents, officers, soldiers, and officials, and enormous resources, to undermining the *magonista* revolt in the United States. The U.S. Marshals, the Bureau of Investigation (later the FBI), the U.S. Immigration Service, and the Arizona Rangers participated, too, as did police and sheriff departments across the country. The U.S. Postal Service played a particularly important role, providing Mexican authorities and agents with access to *magonista* mail, which allowed the counterinsurgency units to hunt down revolutionaries on both sides of the border. The Mexican government also hired a bevy of U.S.-based informants and spies, and likely paid off at least one U.S.

attorney with a diamond ring. In sum, U.S. agents were responsible for monitoring, tracking, arresting, imprisoning, detaining, deporting, and even kidnapping scores of Mexican revolutionaries in the United States, mostly in the borderlands, where the *magonistas* maintained a stronghold among the region's Mexican migrant workers.

Pressure on the *magonistas* was not limited to government authorities; the extralegal forces of white supremacy also rallied against them. Antonio Rodríguez, the man whose murder in Texas set off the conflagration in Mexico, may have been a *magonista*. He was a "revolutionist," whispered the residents of Rocksprings, Texas, after they lynched him. Rodríguez, they said, had not only killed a white woman, but was suspected of being one of the many *magonistas* known to be traveling the border region, raiding Mexican towns, spreading propaganda, recruiting fighters, and collecting guns for the coming revolt.[25]

Against this campaign of coordinated political suppression and racial violence, the *magonistas* persevered, outrunning and outsmarting the U.S.–Mexico counterinsurgency team. In 1904, Ricardo Flores Magón and the *magonistas* relaunched *Regeneración*, which they smuggled to tens of thousands of subscribers on both sides of the border. In 1905, they established a political party, the Partido Liberal Mexicano (PLM), to formally challenge Díaz's rule. In 1906, they built an army. By 1908, the PLM army had launched four armed raids on small towns in northern Mexico. The *magonistas* then began to cultivate the support of Anglo-American radicals, including the labor organizers Mother Jones and Eugene V. Debs, and others, instigating a series of political assaults that deeply wounded Díaz's political standing on the world stage. By 1910, the *magonistas* had primed Mexico for revolt.

Ricardo Flores Magón and the *magonistas* did not go on to lead the revolution's major battles. The PLM's ill-provisioned army lacked the resources needed to lay siege to Díaz. Flores Magón also lacked the will to shift from agitator to military general when the time came to fight, convinced that Mexico's aggrieved masses would spontaneously rise up and storm the dictator's palace once the PLM set the stage for revolt. He was wrong about that. Francisco Madero, Francisco "Pancho" Villa,

Emiliano Zapata, and others took the Mexican Revolution through its fighting phase. But it was Flores Magón and the *magonistas* who opened the road to revolution in Mexico. In so doing, they changed the course of history both north and south of the border.

The Mexican Revolution (1910–17) remade Mexico. In 1917, after seven years of fighting, Mexico adopted a new constitution that restored democratic rule, asserted public ownership of the subsoil, and increased protections for Mexico's poorest citizens, namely wage workers and communal landholders. Ultimately, most of the *magonistas'* demands were enshrined—although not enforced—in the 1917 constitution.

For their role in inspiring the revolt, Ricardo Flores Magón and the *magonistas* are widely remembered in Mexico. Historians have anointed them the "precursors" of the revolution. There are towns, streets, schools, statues, museums, libraries, and even a gym in Mexico named for Flores Magón and the other leaders of the movement: Juan Sarabia, Antonio Villarreal, Enrique Flores Magón, Práxedis Guerrero, and Librado Rivera. Radicals across Europe and the Americas continue to hold Ricardo Flores Magón in high esteem, because he never sacrificed his ideals. Until the day he died—some say he was murdered—in a dank cell at Leavenworth Penitentiary, Flores Magón was a rebel. In the 1940s, twenty years after his death, his body was re-interred in Mexico City's Rotunda of Distinguished Men (later renamed the Rotunda of Distinguished Persons), securing his place in Mexican history.

The Mexican Revolution also remade the United States. The years of fighting forced more than a million Mexicans to flee northward, which radically reoriented U.S. culture, politics, and society by cementing the pathways of mass migration from Mexico and giving rise to the first generation of Mexican Americans.[26] Not even the mass deportation/repatriation campaigns executed during the Great Depression could permanently reverse the flow.[27] By 1980, Mexicans had become the largest immigrant group in the United States, ending Europe's long dominance in the U.S. immigration story.[28] By 2010, more immigrants had arrived from Mexico than any other country in U.S. history.[29]

Today, Latinos, led by Mexican Americans and Mexican immigrants, constitute the largest non-white population in the United States. By 2045, the United States is projected to be a "minority white" nation, with Mexican Americans and Mexican immigrants driving the shift.[30] In other words, the 1910 Mexican Revolution is a seminal event in U.S. history: it changed who we are as a people.

Yet few people in the United States know much about the Mexican Revolution, and even less about the men and women who incited it. Typically, the extraordinary story of Ricardo Flores Magón and the *magonistas* is folded into the corners of Mexican American history, which itself is little known in the United States. History textbooks have had little to say on the subject, and until recently, legislators in Arizona all but banned the teaching of Mexican American Studies in K–12 classrooms.[31] Meanwhile, U.S. publishers and film producers persistently struggle to promote Latino voices, content, and experiences.[32] However, as historians of Mexico and the Mexican American experience have long made clear, you cannot understand U.S. history without Mexico and Mexicans.

The history of the United States as a global power cannot be told without Mexico. The U.S. government spent the nineteenth century charging across the North American continent, launching Indian wars, purchasing European empires, and invading Mexico, all in search of new lands for its white citizens to occupy. Boozed up on the fantasy of Manifest Destiny, the arriving Anglo-Americans dubbed themselves "settlers" and, backed by troops, fought to extinguish Indigenous claims to land and life in the region.[33] By the mid-nineteenth century, the U.S. settler state—also branded the "white man's republic"—claimed a massive strip of land from the Atlantic seaboard to the Pacific Coast.[34] The United States government and its settler citizens continued their territorial exploits—in Hawaii, the Philippines, Puerto Rico, and more—but they also began to seriously consider a new kind of expansion: economic and political domination without territorial acquisition. They began this form of expansion in Mexico, under the rule of Porfirio Díaz, buying land, extracting resources, and using labor without directly assuming control over territory or governance. Then, in 1904, President Theodore Roosevelt issued his corollary to the Monroe Doctrine, which asserted the right and responsibility of the United States to "exercise . . . international police power" wherever political or economic stability in the Americas seemed threatened. The Díaz regime picked up Roosevelt's "big stick," acting as a proxy state to enforce U.S. interests across Latin America.[35] In other words, the expansion of U.S. economic and political might was hatched in Mexico and, from there, projected across the Americas and, from there, around the world. Díaz's Mexico was the "laboratory" of U.S. imperialism.[36]

Relatedly, the rise of the American West cannot be understood without Mexicans. Foreign investment in Mexico triggered the rise of Mexican labor migration to the United States. Dispossessed in Mexico, millions of Mexicans first migrated within Mexico, to towns and cities, factories, haciendas, and mines in search of work. Then they began crossing the border, following the railway lines funded by investors to extract and export Mexico's natural resources. Across the U.S. West, Mexican migrants found plenty of work: on the railroads, in copper mines, lumberyards, farms, canneries, and more. By 1920, Mexican labor migrants comprised the American West's single largest low-wage labor force, driving the region's emergence as a global economic powerhouse.

But Mexico's labor migrants were not America's immigrants, and their arrival en masse at the beginning of the twentieth century opened a new field of race and inequity in the American story. Since the Mexican–American War (1846–48), Anglo-Americans largely regarded persons of Mexican descent in the United States as conquered, a mixed-race people slotted by Manifest Destiny to serve settler citizens and fuel their industries, or disappear. Migrating from job to job across the American West, Mexico's labor migrants built the region's industries while running headfirst into a web of white supremacy designed to keep them subservient. They confronted low wages, dangerous working conditions, segregation, and a racially-biased immigration enforcement regime, amounting to a system scholars describe as "Juan Crow."[37]

U.S. settler citizens expected Mexico's labor migrants to bow to the settler order. As Victor S. Clark, the first Anglo-American economist to study Mexican labor migration to the United States, explained in a 1908 report for the Department of Labor: "The Mexican laborer is unambitious, listless, physically weak, irregular, and indolent. On the other hand, he is docile, patient, usually orderly in camp, fairly intelligent under competent supervision, obedient, and cheap. If he were active and ambitious, he would be less tractable and would cost more. His strongest point is his willingness to work for a low wage."[38]

Victor S. Clark was wrong. Across the American West, Mexico's labor migrants struck for higher wages, challenged the tenets of Juan Crow, and even joined the *magonistas*. When they did, the consequences could be brutal. Historians William Carrigan and Clive Webb have documented that at least 547 Mexicans and Mexican Americans were lynched between 1848 and 1928. They estimate that thousands more were killed without record. Bodies were dumped in the Rio Grande to be swept into the Gulf of Mexico; corpses were left in the brush to be picked at by crows; bones were left on the plains to be buried by windstorms.[39] The 1910 killing of Antonio Rodríguez in Rocksprings, Texas, was the 448th such murder on record. No one was arrested. The coroner's report said Rodríguez's body was found "burned to a crisp, lying in the ashes."[40] A local judge ruled that "Rodríguez came to his death at the hands of parties unknown."[41]

The riots in Mexico that followed Rodríguez's lynching were not merely a protest against yet another incident of racial violence in the United States. They represented a rebellion against the unchecked power of U.S. citizens, namely Anglo-Americans, over Mexican lands and lives on both sides of the border. As one Mexican journalist put it, "We stand between the already special considerations that keep the yankee on Mexican soil and the degrading, cruel system faced by the sons of Mexico on the other side of the Rio Bravo [Rio Grande]."[42] Migration would provide no escape from their troubles. Fleeing Mexico by moving to the United States, the world's primary receiving country for immigrants at the time, only delivered Mexico's labor migrants deeper into the tangle. Or as W. E. B. Du Bois, the most trenchant scholar of race working at the time, might have put it, Anglo-Americans had cast a global "color line" encircling the lives of Mexicans living north and south of the border.[43] The *magonistas* were among the first to pose revolution as the only way for Mexico's dispossessed to truly change the conditions of their lives. Once it began, African Americans closely watched the Mexican Revolution—some even joined it—hoping the insurgents would snap the global color line.[44]

The rise of U.S. imperialism, the making of the American West, and rebellion against the color line are just three of the major themes in U.S. history that cannot be understood without Mexico and Mexicans. The *magonistas*, numbering no more than a few thousand men and women, many of them undocumented labor migrants, operated at the center of it all, tugging and thrashing at the era's interlocking cords of empire, capitalism, and white supremacy. Their primary target was not the United States, but their uprising, namely their insistence on winning "Land and Liberty!" in Mexico, imperiled the laboratory of U.S. empire. Their plan to redistribute land and nationalize industries directly threatened U.S. investors. Furthermore, if land in Mexico was redistributed, Mexican labor migrants might return to Mexico and remain there, denying industries across the American West access to a vital source of labor. As such, the *magonista* revolt threatened key sectors of U.S. society at the turn of the twentieth century. U.S. authorities, agents, and settlers mobilized to stop them.

In fact, the campaign to crush the *magonistas* opened a new chapter of policing in the United States. It was during the search for Ricardo Flores Magón and the *magonistas* that the U.S. Department of Justice established the Bureau of Investigation, later renamed the FBI. Stopping the *magonista* uprising was one of the FBI's first objectives. In the years ahead, the FBI would grow into a counterinsurgency superforce, suppressing a wide range of radical voices and movements, from the Red Scare to the Black Power movement.[45] In July 1908, just days after the *magonistas* launched their most deadly raid on Mexico, the FBI began its work by trying to stop them from inciting a revolution in Mexico that the United States could not control.

Despite their importance to the histories of both Mexico and the United States, the *magonistas* could have easily been erased from history. Within weeks of arriving in the United States, Ricardo Flores Magón and his friends knew they were being watched. In time, they figured out that agents for the Mexican government were stealing their mail. To thwart the counterinsurgency, the *magonistas* lived in hiding, spoke in code, and wrote in cipher. Whenever possible, they burned all evidence of their work. In battle, with their dying breaths, their bellies ripped open by bullets, they gasped out pseudonyms, covering their tracks to the grave. In other words, the *magonistas* intentionally left few records behind. But Porfirio Díaz, the dictator whom the *magonistas* charged with stealing everything from Mexicans—land, wages, lives, and sovereignty—stole the *magonista* story, too. His spies stole their letters, his agents cracked their codes, and his functionaries archived it all in Mexico City in the hope that the *magonistas'* tale would never escape, never be told. Despite this, the revolution the *magonistas* sought to incite was successful, and, for decades now, historians of Mexico and the Mexican American experience have plumbed the dictator's archive to tell their story.

Working in English and in Spanish, and even in code, several generations of scholars have been the caretakers of a remarkable history, tending to the *magonista* story like a fire in the night.[46] They traveled the world to interview *magonistas* and their friends and descendants, and to gather the extensive records documenting the many efforts to suppress their movement. They followed Flores Magón's trail, taking photos of everywhere he lived, worked, and hid. They chronicled the journeys of his friends and supporters. They published their findings in dissertations, articles, chapters, websites, and books. In Mexico City, Ricardo Flores Magón's great-grand-nephew operates a museum dedicated to the *magonistas*, and Professor Jacinto Barrera Bassols built an extraordinary digital archive which provides access to many of Flores

Magón's letters and other writings.[47] In other words, Porfirio Díaz did not smother the *magonista* revolt, and he certainly did not extinguish their legacy. A century on, a living library continues to tell their story.

Inspired and informed by that library, this book is about Ricardo Flores Magón and the *magonistas,* and the cross-border counterinsurgency campaign that failed to stop them. In particular, this book focuses on the U.S. role in the revolt and puts their uprising center stage in American history. The story begins in nineteenth-century Mexico, long before the insurgency began, with a poor, quiet boy from Oaxaca who would come to hold great power. In his power, which grew under the wing of U.S. empire, lay the origins of the *magonista* revolt.

Part 1

EL PORFIRIATO

CHAPTER 1

If We're Not Careful

P orfirio Díaz was just a child when he assembled his first gun and headed to the misty mountains surrounding the small city of Oaxaca to hunt for game. His family was hungry. Porfirio's father, José, had died in the cholera epidemic that swept Mexico in 1833, leaving his mother, María, with few resources to raise their seven children on her own.[1] Two of the children died, and María was unable to keep up the rent on the beautiful adobe inn she and José had run together. She gave up the keys and moved her kids from a bluff on the edge of town to a small house in the tannery district. The neighborhood had a constant stench. The house was likely simple: a few pieces of wood furniture and no glass in the windows, just canvas covering oversized holes in the wall. María barely made ends meet. She made *rebozos* (shawls), managed a tannery, and grew *nopales* (cactus pads) to sell at the local market. Her children worked, too. They sat with her at the kitchen table adorning *rebozos* and picked up odd jobs in town: tutoring, carpentry, and so on. Porfirio, her eldest surviving son, a quiet boy known to listen more than he spoke, proved the most clever and enterprising and bold. He learned how to cobble shoes, which he gave to family and sold to friends, and figured out how to assemble functioning guns from parts he found scattered and sold about town, detritus of the country's prior wars. With these guns he hunted for his family's meals.[2]

By the time Porfirio Díaz was born, on September 15, 1830, Mexico had been at war for decades and would be at war for decades more. The Mexican War of Independence (1810–21), a mass insurgency by Mexico's Indigenous, Black, and mixed-race majority, had ended the Spanish colonial era. However, a small faction of Mexicans, dominated by church leaders and *criollos* (the Mexico-born descendants of Spanish colonial authorities), held close to the habits of the colonial age. Believing in the deceit of race, the *criollos* and churchmen argued that a stable and prosperous republic was a racially stratified society, and expected that the Spanish colonial racial order, known as the *casta* system, would continue into the new nation. That system put them, Mexicans of European descent, on top of the social order, followed by *mestizos* (persons of mixed Spanish and Indigenous descent) and other mixed-race persons in the middle, with Black and Indigenous persons on the bottom. They also wanted to maintain a theocratic state. In a nutshell, the Conservatives wanted very little to change; they just wanted to crown themselves the new rulers of Mexico.[3]

Mexico's non-white majority refused to comply. Calling themselves Liberals, many of Mexico's Black, Indigenous, and mixed-race communities demanded that the status of "citizen" rank above all others, especially race, and insisted that the political and economic power of the church be subordinate to that of the state. But the Conservatives won control of the first constitutional convention. They made the Catholic Church the fourth branch of government and named a *criollo*, Augustín de Iturbide, the Emperor of Mexico. The Liberals took up arms, ousted Emperor Iturbide, and elected Vicente Guerrero, one of their most noted generals, the first Black president in the Americas. The Conservatives assassinated Guerrero, sending Mexico into a spiral of conflict, coups, and postcolonial chaos.[4]

Between 1830 and 1870, during the first four decades of Porfirio Díaz's life, the Mexican presidency changed hands more than fifty times as Liberals and Conservatives battled for control. Only two presidents ever finished their term. Some held the office for just a few weeks before the next coup d'état. Meanwhile, bandits seized control of the nation's roads. They robbed merchants of their cash, goods, and lives, and interrupted trade. Hunger deepened. Infant mortality soared. Life expectancy dropped. Disease spread. Mexico was in crisis.[5]

Taking advantage of the tumult in Mexican politics, the United States annexed the Mexican state of Tejas in 1845. Unsatisfied by the 172 million acres of new land, Anglo-American settlers, especially slaveholders dreaming of a cotton empire extending all the way to the Pacific, demanded more, prompting President James Polk to order the invasion of Mexico in 1846.[6] Troops soon stormed Mexico City and raised the U.S. flag over the National Palace, forcing Mexico to cede another 336 million acres—more than half of the country's remaining land. At the close of the war in 1848, U.S. treaty negotiators considered seizing even more land but, ultimately, decided that acquiring only Mexico's sparsely populated northern territory would balance the settlers' hunger for new real estate with their disinclination to incorporate a large number of Mexican people, whom Anglo-Americans generally disparaged as "mongrels" unfit for U.S. citizenship.[7] As John O'Sullivan, the journalist who coined the term Manifest Destiny, later warned, "the annexation of the country [Mexico] to the United States would be a calamity. 5,000,000 ignorant and indolent half civilized indians, with 1,500,000 free Negroes and mulattos . . . would scarcely be a desirable encumbrance, even with the great natural wealth of Mexico."[8] Senator Lewis Cass of Michigan agreed: "We do not want the people of Mexico, either as citizens or subjects. All we want is a portion of territory which they hold, generally uninhabited, or, where inhabited at all, sparsely so."[9] Drawn down the belly of the Rio Grande River and out west to the Pacific Ocean, the new U.S.–Mexico border was a 2,000-mile color line between what many Anglo-Americans regarded as "white" America and "mongrel" Mexico.[10]

Amid the upheaval of life and politics in nineteenth-century Mexico, María, a *mestiza*, tried to put her sons on a steady and secure path, sending Porfirio and his younger brother Félix to seminary in the hope that they would become priests.[11] As priests, their fate would be linked to that of the Catholic Church, the single largest institution in Mexico. During the colonial period, the Spanish Crown had granted large swaths of Indigenous land to the church. On that land, the church erected buildings and launched commercial enterprises, ranging from agriculture to textiles. The War of Independence ousted Spanish governors, but the Catholic Church retained most of its properties and its power. María, a devout Catholic herself, tried to insulate her boys within the walls of the church's enduring privileges. As priests, Porfirio and Félix would at least always have somewhere to live and something to eat.

Porfirio was not a strong student. He never learned to spell well, and his presidential archive is strewn with errors. A lifelong fitness fanatic, he preferred to spend his time working out.[12] When he got his hands on one of the first workout books to arrive in Oaxaca, he used it to build an improvised gym for himself and Félix.[13] The brothers also spent countless hours swimming in the local rivers.[14] When the United States invaded Mexico in 1846, Porfirio trained with a youth militia but was never sent to join the fighting.[15] Three years later, at the age of nineteen, just before he was due to graduate and begin his life as a parish priest, Porfirio, the young hunter and fitness fiend, dropped out of seminary and joined the Liberal faction in Mexico's ongoing domestic conflict. It was a decision that put him on the path to war, fame, and, ultimately, the presidency.[16]

Two men inspired Porfirio Díaz to join the Liberal faction. Professor Marcos Pérez, one of Mexico's leading Liberal intellectuals, taught at the Institute of Arts and Sciences in Oaxaca. When Pérez hired Díaz to tutor his son, Díaz began spending time in the Pérez home. There, he overheard Professor Pérez rail against the vestiges of Spanish colonialism in modern Mexican life, especially the unbroken power of the Catholic Church. Pérez, once a seminary student himself, noted Díaz's curiosity and began to mentor the young *mestizo* seminarian in the Liberal tradition.[17]

Pérez also introduced Díaz to Benito Juárez, the esteemed governor of Oaxaca. Like Díaz, Juárez had been born with little. An orphaned Zapotec boy from the mountains surrounding the city of Oaxaca, Juárez became the first Indigenous lawyer in Mexico and built a suc-

General Porfirio Díaz,
circa 1867.

cessful career representing Native clients while also entering politics, ascending from city council to governor in just a few years.[18] When Pérez took Díaz to meet Juárez at an opulent event held at the Institute, Díaz was mesmerized by their encounter. As he would recall many years later, Juárez spoke to the students "as friends, and as men who had rights," exhibiting a culture of "openness and frankness" to which the seminary student was not accustomed.[19] Roused to Liberalism by Pérez, Juárez, and their spirit of equity, Díaz quit the seminary and signed up for law school at the Institute.

He remained a poor student, preferring calisthenics to academics, but he was astute, charismatic, and determined, a cocktail of traits that made him a favored student. Pérez and Juárez kept him close. In 1853, when General Antonio López de Santa Ana—a legendary figure— ascended to power with the Conservatives, Díaz joined them in revolt.

No one man contributed more to Mexico's political tumult than the

Benito Juárez.

one-legged Santa Ana. More opportunist than ideologue, Santa Ana was a crafty military man who fought for and against the Spanish during the War of Independence, for and against Emperor Iturbide during his rule, and for and against the Liberals and the Conservatives thereafter. Willing to tack with the winds of power, Santa Ana seized and lost the Mexican presidency eleven times between 1833 and 1853.

In 1853, Santa Ana launched his final coup d'état. With the support of the Conservatives, he seized the presidency and then declared himself the Emperor of Mexico, naming himself *Su Alteza Serenísima* (His Most Serene Highness). The Liberal faction rebelled. Marcos Pérez penned stinging rebukes. Benito Juárez organized a guerilla army. Porfirio Díaz ventured into the mountains surrounding the city of Oaxaca to muster a unit of Zapotec Indians. He showed them how to assemble guns and taught them the military drills he had learned in his youth militia at the time of the U.S. invasion. He also built a gym, giving free membership to all men who vowed to fight and guiding them in exercises to improve their strength and stamina. Within the year, Juárez's Liberal army, supported by Díaz's Zapotec unit, removed General Santa Ana from office and seized control of the government.[20]

With Juárez at their head, the Liberals wasted no time in pressing Mexico toward the future they had imagined. In 1855, the Liberal congress adopted the Ley Juárez, ending the church's judicial privilege, which had protected the church and its personnel from civil and criminal prosecution in secular courts. In 1856, they adopted the Ley Lerdo, which banned corporate land ownership. In 1857, they elected Benito Juárez president and rewrote the constitution.

Drafted by Ponciano Arriaga, another leading Liberal of the era, the 1857 constitution ended the Catholic Church's status as the nation's official religion, guaranteed equal political rights to all men, banned corporate land ownership, and prohibited the president from running for reelection. The adoption of this constitution was the Liberals' proudest achievement. It infuriated the Catholic Church and the nation's Conservatives, triggering an explosive civil conflict which historians call the Reform War (1857–61).[21]

During the Reform War, President Juárez appointed Porfirio Díaz to serve as a captain in the infantry. Díaz proved to be a shrewd military strategist, commanding his troops in a series of unlikely victories, as when he lured better-armed Conservatives into a ravine, then buried them in a storm of rocks and boulders pushed from the cliff above by unarmed Zapotecs and *campesinos*. Noting the ingenuity and bravery of his old pupil, Juárez promoted Díaz to the rank of military commander and governor of Tehuantepec, a region of eastern Oaxaca famed for its hostility to outsiders as well as its internal ethnic divisions. In Tehuantepec, Díaz honed his gift for politics. He won compliance from local elites by retiring the practice of forcing village leaders to pay additional taxes to fund the war, but he also sowed dissension among them, creating space for himself to step in and resolve disputes. When patronage and arbitrage failed to win him loyalty, Díaz could be cruel. He slaughtered those known to harbor Conservatives, explaining the violence as unfortunate but necessary. "The human heart is guided more by fear than by any other emotion," he explained, "and so in order to demoralize the enemy, exemplary actions, carried out with energy and rigor, were indispensable even if they might be subsequently regretted."[22]

In the decades ahead, Díaz would often speak about the regret that follows violence. He would weep over the deaths of enemies and innocents alike. But he would slaughter all the same. As Benito Juárez later warned about his protégé, "If we're not careful . . . Porfirio could kill us while crying."[23]

When the Liberals won the Reform War in 1861, Juárez retook the presidency, determined to implement the Liberal vision for life in Mexico. But he soon learned how much the decades of coups, disease, invasion, and tumult had cost the treasury. Mexico was broke, drowning in $80 million of international debt. Juárez announced that Mexico would suspend payments on the debt for two years.[24] His goal was to buy enough time to establish a new tax and revenue system, allowing Mexico to pay off its European creditors without bankrupting the treasury. The debt moratorium proved to be a political disaster.[25]

Since the ousting of Emperor Iturbide, a small group of Mexican *criollos* had regretted the War of Independence. They had hoped that independence would allow a domestic elite of Mexicans of European descent to seize full political and economic control of Mexico, but with the rise of the Liberals, the nation's Indigenous, Black, and mixed-race majority upended their plan. For decades, Mexican *criollos* had visited the royal courts of Europe, begging a monarch to occupy Mexico, protect their properties, defend the Catholic Church, and enforce the colonial social order. They wanted a white empire to rule in Mexico.[26]

Few European monarchs wanted anything to do with the *criollos'* plan. Mexico was a political quagmire. Decades earlier, in 1823, the United States government had issued its Monroe Doctrine, vowing to protect any independent nation in the Americas from European colonization. Invading Mexico was thus tantamount to invading the United States. No one in Europe was willing to test the hemisphere's most powerful republic—no one except Louis-Napoleon Bonaparte, who, in 1848, seized the French presidency and convinced the French Congress to name him emperor. He titled himself Napoleon III, after his uncle Napoleon I, known as Napoleon the Great.[27]

Napoleon III dreamed of rebuilding the French empire in the Americas. The 1763 Treaty of Paris had forced France to cede most of its territories in North America. Then, in 1803, Napoleon I sold the sprawling Louisiana Territory to the United States, relinquishing France's last major North American holding. The next year, in 1804, enslaved Africans in the French colony of Saint-Domingue (Haiti) finished a decades-long revolt by killing off slaveholders, ousting French authorities, and declaring Haiti an independent republic. By the 1820s, the French Empire was effectively over.[28]

For years, Napoleon III "pored over maps of Mexico" while chain-smoking and plotting the resurrection of the French empire in the Americas.[29] While he waited for an opportunity to strike, Benito Juárez defaulted on Mexico's international debt. A few weeks later, the United States erupted in civil war. The timing seemed perfect: Juárez's debt moratorium presented a pretext to invade Mexico, while the Civil War lowered the protective shield around the Americas that the Monroe Doctrine had raised. "The situation in the United States is very favorable," Napoleon III observed from Paris.[30] In April 1862, with Union and Confederate forces battling at Shiloh and New Orleans, Napoleon III dispatched French troops to invade Mexico and recruited the Austrian archduke Ferdinand Maximilian Joseph Maria von Habsburg-Lothringen, a young royal with no country to rule, to serve as the titular head of the French invasion of Mexico. Napoleon III named the Austrian archduke Emperor Maximilian.

From the port of Veracruz, French troops marched across mountain roads and jungle paths to Mexico City. The Conservatives welcomed them at every stop. Juárez's guerilla fighters harassed them, but the better-provisioned French troops pushed on. By May 5, 1862, they had arrived in the town of Puebla, their last stop before Mexico City. Armed with little more than the old Brown Bessies left behind by U.S. troops during their invasion fourteen years before, General Díaz's Zapotec unit stopped them. French troops gathered on a small hill outside Puebla, their new guns glinting in the sun. At noon, the first French battalion stormed the main road into Puebla. Two further battalions attacked from the east and the west, raining cannon fire on the nearly six thousand Liberal soldiers pinned between them. Soon, only Díaz's unit was left, stationed in a church in the center of town. As French soldiers poured into Puebla, Díaz and his squadron burst from the church into hand-to-hand combat. Within minutes, 253 men were killed, 436 were wounded. But Díaz's troops kept fighting, for hours. A woman named Margarita Magón brought water to the fighters. Among them, she met Teodoro Flores, with whom she would later have three sons—who, in time, would become some of General Díaz's most vocal critics. But on this day, long before their boys were born, Margarita Magón and Teodoro Flores fought side by side with Díaz to stop the French troops from reaching Mexico City.[31] Eventually, the French forces were chased out of Puebla, closing the door to the Mexican capital. As the general in charge of the campaign later admitted, it was Díaz and his fighters who drove off the French troops *"con empeño y bizarría"* (with determination and bravery).[32]

The triumph at Puebla made Porfirio Díaz a legend. Proud officials in Oaxaca gifted him a massive ranch, La Noria; his family would never again live in poverty. The world marveled at the *mestizo* general who had led Zapotec fighters to victory against Napoleon's army. The victory is still commemorated: we call it Cinco de Mayo.

The Liberal triumph at Puebla reenergized the Mexican resistance. In 1867, Liberal forces ended the French occupation, humiliating Napoleon III and sending a stunned Maximilian to a firing squad and his wife, Empress Carlota, to a madhouse.

After ousting the French, Porfirio Díaz emerged alongside Benito Juárez as one of Mexico's most revered Liberal leaders, even though Liberalism was a rather loose concept for him. Whereas Juárez toiled over the finer details of Liberal philosophy and governance, often citing obscure laws and ancient texts in debates over the day-to-day architecture of equality, Díaz was more pragmatic. He derided Juárez's talmudic pondering as *"profundismo."*[33] Díaz had an agile, clever mind, but he preferred deeds to words. He would never be a strong public speaker. He spent a few unremarkable years in Congress, accomplishing little as a legislator. But, with nearly two decades of battlefield experience, he had become a ruthless tactician. His brand of Liberalism was bare-knuckled and broad: a belief in racial equality, a commitment to secularizing the Catholic Church, and a general defense of the Liberals' cardinal achievement, the 1857 constitution, beginning with its ban on presidential reelection, which allowed Díaz to challenge Juárez for the presidency.

In 1867, Juárez ran for his third term as the president of Mexico—a clear violation of the constitution. Díaz ran against him, with "No Reelection" as his campaign slogan.[34] But Juárez was too popular to unseat. Additionally, he had taken the precaution of replacing political opponents in key governorships, who in turn appointed *jefes políticos*, regional administrators, who appointed electors who voted in favor of Juárez. Díaz lost the election, having learned one final lesson from his mentor: political machinery can easily be manipulated to maintain political power. Díaz retreated to La Noria, where he married his twenty-one-year-old niece and experimented with his home-built munitions factory.

In 1871, Porfirio Díaz again challenged Benito Juárez, and again he lost. This time, Díaz responded to his electoral loss with an armed revolt. Throughout the revolt, Díaz spent much of his time in Brownsville, Texas, rallying political and financial support for his coup among Mexican exiles and U.S. industrialists. He tasked his brother Félix with leading the troops in Mexico. The military campaign quickly collapsed, especially as Félix failed to gauge how much Zapotec fighters in Oaxaca despised him for an incident that occurred the year before the revolt began, when Félix, while serving as governor of Oaxaca, participated in an attack on the village of Juchitán. After setting fire to the village and killing many of the men, Félix knocked down a wooden statue of the village's patron saint and, in front of the survivors, burned it.[35] With Félix at the helm of Díaz's troops, many Zapotecs chose to fight for Juárez. Villagers from Juchitán specifically targeted Félix.

When they found him, they shaved the skin from the soles of his feet and forced him to march several miles to his own execution, then cut off his feet before they killed him.[36]

Félix's gruesome murder shook his brother Porfirio; the two had always been close.[37] But Díaz kept fighting. When Juárez died a natural death in office, Díaz saw that he had no political choice but to call off the coup, and allowed Juárez's vice president, Sebastián Lerdo de Tejada, to take office without opposition.

Four years later, in 1876, when President Lerdo de Tejada ran for the office he had inherited, Díaz led another coup in protest at what he saw as Lerdo's reelection campaign. This time, he remained in Mexico to personally lead his supporters. Teodoro Flores and other veterans joined the insurgency, which Díaz called El Plan de Tuxtepec. The experienced comrades defeated the national army and forced Lerdo de Tejada from office, allowing Díaz to seize control of the federal government under the Liberal banner of "No Reelection." General Porfirio Díaz ruled Mexico with an iron fist for the next thirty-five years.

CHAPTER 2

Order and Progress

EARLY IN DÍAZ'S RULE, A GROUP OF MERCHANTS GROWING rich on smuggled goods resisted his efforts to suppress the bandit economy. Díaz, it is often said, ordered the local authorities to "kill them [the merchants] in cold blood."[1] It is an apocryphal story about Díaz's harsh rule, but even Díaz described his methods as "harsh to the point of cruelty."[2] Still, he had many supporters who objected neither to the bloodshed nor to his increasingly autocratic ways. After decades of civil war, two foreign invasions, countless epidemics, and generations of crippling debt, they were exhausted. As one of Díaz's defenders put it, "Rights! Society now rejects them. What it wants is bread. . . . We have already enacted innumerable rights, which produce only distress and malaise in society. Now let us try a little tyranny, but honorable tyranny, and see what results it brings."[3]

Under Díaz's "honorable tyranny," there were no more coups. No more invasions. The bandit economy was suppressed. Public health improved. Literacy rose. Electricity began to flicker on in the cities. During his more than three-decade rule, a period known as the Porfiriato, Díaz successfully brought what he called "order and progress" to Mexico. But it came at a cost.

Díaz draped his rule in a veil of democracy. In 1880, when his first four-year term was up, he stepped down and maneuvered his close friend, Manuel González, into the presidency. It was a puppet regime and everybody knew it, but Díaz had formally complied with the 1857

President Porfirio Díaz,
circa 1911.

constitution's ban on presidential reelection. In 1884, Díaz ran for president again, asserting that non-successive rule did not equate with reelection. He won the 1884 election and quickly convinced Congress to amend the constitution in order to allow for one consecutive reelection. In 1888, he was elected president again and then urged Congress to remove the constitutional ban on reelection entirely. Congress—a toothless body that Díaz called his "herd of tame horses"—yielded.[4] Meanwhile, Díaz fostered a cult of personality that positioned him to be drafted into candidacy by groups of adoring citizens, such as the Society of Friends of the President and the National Porfirian Circle.[5] As Díaz stated to a curated crowd at the start of his 1892 presidential campaign, "I do not expect, gentlemen, much less allow myself to presume that my fellow citizens will honor me with an electoral majority once again. I feel quite satisfied that I have fulfilled the sovereign mandate over two consecutive constitutional periods. But I would never fail to obey if another period were imposed upon me legally."[6] He won the next five elections: 1892, 1896, 1900, 1904, and 1910.

As the years passed, the election fraud grew increasingly bold. Ballot boxes went missing. Police lined up voters and directed their votes. Opposition candidates were jailed, or worse. Those who spoke out against Díaz's rule were subject to arrest, since Díaz had cajoled Congress in 1882 to broaden the definition of libel to include criticism of government authorities.[7] Díaz also dispatched the *rurales* to quiet dissenting voices. Armed and mounted, the *rurales* roamed the country, executing Díaz's enemies. They often shot their victims in the back, a technique permitted under the *ley fuga*, the law of flight, which the historian Paul J. Vanderwood describes as "Mexico's version of lynch law."[8] Díaz would unleash the *ley fuga* with a simple word: "severely." To punish offenders "severely," explains the historian Paul Garner, was Díaz's "euphemism for execution."[9] As many as 10,000 people died under declarations of the *ley fuga*.[10]

Violence, however, was rarely Díaz's first choice. He preferred rule by patronage, arbitration, and benevolence. Using the political scheme he learned from Benito Juárez, Díaz yoked nearly all political appointments to his person, so that his approval was required to win any public office in Mexico. "Candidates should be more or less friends of mine," he once said.[11] Among the most powerful positions in the Díaz regime was that of *jefe político*. Often reporting directly to Díaz, a *jefe político* was responsible for overseeing almost all areas of governance within a given jurisdiction: taxes, elections, police, jails, roads, and so on. *Jefes políticos* were not paid much but, in return for fixing elections, enforcing decrees, and impressing soldiers, Díaz granted them a rapacious and profitable autonomy. As the historian Alan Knight explains, *jefes políticos* in Chihuahua accumulated personal fortunes by fining *campesinos* for letting their burros sip from public streams. In Guanajuato, they fined Indigenous persons for entering town limits wearing the traditional baggy pants. In the Yucatán, they took endless kickbacks from plantation owners. In Sonora, they skimmed off land from *campesinos*. Everywhere, *jefes políticos* forced girls and women into various degrees of sexual slavery. The *jefe político* system, known as the *jefatura*, was one of the primary methods by which Díaz centralized political power. When the Mexican Revolution finally began in 1910, many fighters— men and women, mothers and fathers, husbands and wives and entire communities—took up arms to end the sexual abuses perpetrated by *jefes políticos.*[12]

Sitting atop the nation's political machinery, Díaz positioned himself as the final arbiter of everything, from local elections to labor strikes.[13] He woke every morning at 6 am and took a bath before dedicating several hours to answering correspondence and reading a number of newspapers, "sometimes noting with pencil some of [the] most strik- ing passages."[14] He followed this morning ritual with another round of letter-writing with his cadre of personal secretaries. Together, they replied to every letter that arrived in his office—more than one mil- lion of them recorded during his rule—without regard to class or race, using every one as an opportunity to settle a disagreement, solve a prob- lem, and, sometimes, to bestow a small favor or gift, such as a signed portrait of the president. As Díaz once put it, "even if an individual may appear to be useless (literally a corpse or a cadaver), that should not be a reason for us to be indifferent to the potential help he might give us . . . when it is a question of attempting to extend the influence of a party or campaign, every offer of help should be welcomed."[15] In homes across Mexico, a drawer held a letter from the president.

While building his political machine, Díaz used his second mar- riage to bury some of the nation's oldest political tensions. In 1879, his first wife (and niece) died after giving birth to their sixth child, a baby girl who died after taking just a few breaths. Only two of their children survived; the others died young, often in infancy, and almost certainly from congenital conditions. In 1880, Díaz met Carmen Romero Rubin at a party in the Mexico City home of the U.S. ambassador. The deeply religious daughter of a wealthy family in the Mexican north, she was seventeen years old, U.S.-educated, and European-descended. Smit- ten, Díaz asked her to marry him. She agreed, taking as her husband the fifty-one-year-old general, a poor son of a widowed *mestiza* from the southern state of Oaxaca. This domestic union symbolically united Mexico: young and old, north and south, poor and rich, *criollo* and *mestizo*, as well as church and state, as the old Liberal general conceded to a civil ceremony followed by a Catholic mass.[16]

Carmen also helped Díaz to smooth Mexico's relationship with its northern neighbor, which had been fraught ever since the U.S. invasion of Mexico. They honeymooned in the United States, visiting New Orleans, New York, Washington, DC, and St. Louis. Throughout the trip, Carmen remained at her husband's side, translating his words as they dined and chatted with Anglo-American elites. As Díaz's chosen biographer would later write, "the visit of Díaz and his bride to the United States at that time was the occasion of many notable demonstrations of American respect and admiration for the man who was beginning to be recognized in all civilized countries as the strongest, wisest, and most trust-worthy of Mexican leaders."[17] In their years together, Carmen tutored the old general in the aesthetics of Anglo-American power. She told him to stop spitting in public and taught him how to use a fork. One legend in Mexican history says that Carmen even encouraged Díaz to dab white powder on his bronze face, transforming the *mestizo* general from Oaxaca into a white president on the world stage.[18]

While his wife helped him retire domestic antagonisms and build bridges to U.S. elites, Díaz tackled the international debt that had long crippled the Mexican economy, dispatching agents to Europe to buy up Mexico's bad debts at a discount. It was a dubious step, frowned upon by global investors, especially those who lost money in the transactions, but Díaz's agents all but wiped out Mexico's debt, allowing him to begin filling the national treasury. His next step was to suppress Mexico's bandit economy, which was siphoning off millions in lost tax revenues. To this end, his methods were harsh. "We began by making robbery punishable by death and compelling the execution of offenders within a few hours after they were caught and condemned," Díaz later explained.[19] By the end of his first term, his law-and-order campaign had effectively ended smuggling, increased government revenues, and gained control of Mexico's foreign debt. The national treasury was finally registering more deposits than withdrawals.

Next, Díaz plugged Mexico into the global economy. To do so required investing in domestic infrastructure, beginning with an expansion of the railroad system to facilitate the movement of goods across and out of the country. In 1880, Mexico had fewer than 400 miles of railroad track. Most commerce still traveled by mules on bumpy wagon roads.[20] In contrast, the United States had recently completed a transcontinental railroad system with more than 93,000 miles of track stitching together markets from the Pacific Ocean to the Atlantic. Díaz knew that Mexico would never enter the global economy by mule train.

To grow Mexico's railroad system, he needed capital. To get it, he wooed international investors, beginning with the U.S. railroad magnates who had recently completed the transcontinental railroad.[21] At a meeting held at the Waldorf Astoria in New York City, he met with former president Ulysses S. Grant, the railroad baron Collis P. Huntington, and others to pitch a plan for U.S. railroads to extend their lines across the border, deep into Mexico.[22] Mexican legislators worried about building connections with the United States, the "colossus of the north," which might one day use those rails to, once again, invade Mexico.[23] But Díaz wrangled from Congress full executive authority over the negotiation and granting of railroad concessions.[24] With that power, he granted charters for the Mexican Central (El Paso to Mexico City), the Mexican National (Laredo to Mexico City), and Mexican Southern (Nogales to Mazatlán) railroads.[25] To spur construction, he prodded Congress to pass a land expropriation law that provided railroad developers with free access to any land that was without title or in tax arrears. Claims were processed fast. Residents had just nineteen days to vacate lands required by the railroads.[26] By 1890, the United States and Mexico were connected by international crossings at El Paso and Laredo. By 1910, foreign investors, led by U.S. citizens, had built more than 24,000 kilometers of track, a web of railroads spanning the country but mostly running north–south, tightly binding the U.S. and

Mexican economies.[27] The Rockefeller–Stillman clan headed up the Mexican Central Railroad. Jay Gould controlled the Mexican National. E. H. Harriman and the Southern Pacific conglomerate ran the Mexican Southern line. They were joined by Russell Sage, J. P. Morgan, the Guggenheim family, Grenville Dodge, Collis P. Huntington, Henry Clay Pierce, and others. U.S. investors controlled 80 percent of Mexico's railroad stocks and bonds.[28]

To encourage further investment in Mexican industries, Congress passed the 1883 Land Reform Law, which entitled survey companies to one-third of any untitled lands they located and surveyed. The remaining two-thirds could be purchased at auction. In 1893, Díaz lifted caps on the total amount of land any single survey company could acquire. Investors rushed in, fueling a frenzied land grab that remade Mexico. Millions of Mexicans, including 98 percent of Mexico's rural families and Indigenous communities, were left landless, while a small cohort of foreign investors grew wealthy.[29]

Mexican elites, also, seized the economic opportunities created by land reform. The Terrazas family, "the Rockefellers of Mexico," took control of more than 15 million acres, making the family's patriarch, Luis Terrazas, the "world's largest landowner and cattleman."[30] Alongside the Terrazas, a handful of other Mexican families benefited handsomely. The Maderos of Coahuila owned 7 million acres and were powerful enough to challenge both the Guggenheims and the Rockefellers, taking on the smelting monopoly run by the Guggenheims and the rubber monopoly operated by the Rockefellers.[31]

European investors rushed in, too, but U.S. citizens dominated the Mexican land grab.[32] As the historian Jason Ruiz has documented, Anglo-American investors, in particular, often described Mexico as their "treasure house" and believed that Mexico was the new and necessary frontier for Anglo-American expansion. "There no longer being any 'Great West' to which trade and travel may flow, it is believed that our country of the future lies in the South—the greater south— in Mexico, Central and South America," explained one travel writer.

According to the *Los Angeles Times*, a constant booster of U.S. investment in Díaz's Mexico, Mexico's "hidden riches" had been "wait[ing] for centuries for the aggressive force of the Anglo Saxon."[33]

Using the 1883 land reform law, William Randolph Hearst's father acquired 7.5 million acres of land and numerous mines. From Mexico, he extended his mine holdings into Latin America and around the world, but no other concentration of land or mining profits matched the family's holdings in Mexico. When Hearst inherited his father's holdings, he shoveled the family fortune into his U.S. media empire.[34]

Similarly, the Guggenheim family expanded their fortune in Mexico. Porfirio Díaz personally welcomed the Guggenheims to Mexico and granted them generous concessions: permission to build two smelters, the right to explore, exploit, and claim any mine anywhere in Mexico, and a bundle of giveaways that allowed the Guggenheims to grow their Mexican operations tax and duty free.[35] As Daniel Guggenheim later put it in a letter to the president, "these vast mining and smelting operations were begun under the solicitation and the most favorable supervision, regulations and laws of Mexico on behalf of my family." He described them as being "everything which I could desire."[36] The Guggenheim family, who subsequently took a controlling interest in the American Smelting and Refining Company (ASARCO), leveraging profits from their Mexican mines and smelters to do so, soon controlled the largest system of mines and smelters in North America.[37]

John D. Rockefeller's Standard Oil and Edward Doheny's Pan American Petroleum and Transport Company (Pan Am) dominated Mexico's petroleum industry. Doheny, a Los Angeles resident, controlled 85 percent of oil production in Mexico after a gusher near Tampico made him one of the richest men in the world. And almost every penny of Doheny's fortune was extracted from Mexico. In homage to the well of his fortune, Doheny decorated his Los Angeles mansion in Mexican style, with art and rugs and plants from south of the border.[38]

Cattle ranching, cotton farming, and timber were other industries with major U.S. investments and investors. J. P. Morgan owned 3.5 million acres in Baja California and controlled concessions of up to an additional 17.5 million acres across Mexico.[39] Edward Morgan was a lead investor in Los Corralitos, a 893,650-acre cattle ranch in northwestern Chihuahua.[40] The U.S.-based Palomas Land and Cattle Company acquired 2.5 million acres just south of New Mexico.[41] The Richardson Construction Company, based in Los Angeles, snatched up 993,650 acres of timberlands in Sonora.[42] Senator William Langer (R–North Dakota) owned 750,000 acres in Durango and Sinaloa.[43] The list of U.S. investors in Mexico reads like a who's who of robber baron America: Guggenheim, Rockefeller, Gould, Stillman, Morgan, Doheny, Huntington, Hearst, and more. But not every U.S. investor was an icon of prosperity. By 1902, 1,112 U.S. companies, involving 40,000 Americans, did business in Mexico to the sum of $511,465,166 of investment.[44] And, after surveying and snatching up massive claims, land developers sold off their holdings, plot by plot, to middling farmers who set up large but not massive operations. By 1910, 75,000 Americans lived in Mexico.[45] Mexico was "growing thick with Americans," joked some of them.[46] In sum, Porfirio Díaz oversaw an era in which tens of thousands of U.S. citizens laid claim to more than 130 million acres of Mexico, amounting to more than 27 percent of Mexico's arable land, and in which U.S. corporations and their executives came to dominate key industries in Mexico, led by railroads, mining, and oil.[47] In the process, they and the investor class dispossessed millions of people, leaving hardly 2 percent of rural Mexican families with land to till.[48] Still, they wanted more. As William Randolph Hearst put it, "I really don't see what is to prevent us from owning all of Mexico and running it to suit ourselves."[49]

U.S. investors saw Mexico as a satellite, a source of raw materials for U.S. industries and trade. They built mines, extracted petroleum, and invested in large agricultural enterprises. They did not invest in producing the basic food commodities Mexicans needed to live. While agricultural exports soared 200 percent between 1876 and 1900, food production for domestic consumption declined every year.[50] Corn and bean shortages made prices skyrocket. The average rural family struggled to earn enough to eat. The wages paid to laborers at the new farms, mines, and factories popping up across Mexico were not enough, especially when those salaries were paid in scrip and families were forced to shop at a company store (*tienda de raya*). As a teacher at a large hacienda in southern Mexico reported, most workers typically owed 400 to 500 pesos to the *tienda de raya* but only earned 2 pesos, or 15 cents, a day. The largely Indigenous workforce on the rubber and henequen plantations of the Mexican south always came up short at the end of the season. And if they tried to leave the hacienda before paying off their debts, they were hunted down by the *rurales*. Much like Black sharecroppers in the American South, scores of Mexicans in southern Mexico were trapped in debt peonage.[51] But exports soared.

Between 1890 and 1905, Mexico's copper output increased from 5,650 to 65,449 metric tons.[52] Lead, silver, zinc, and coal output also boomed.[53] Petroleum production soared from zero to more than 12 million barrels annually.[54] By 1910, Mexico was a critical node in the global economy. Mexican copper lit the world. Mexican petroleum powered its machinery. Mexican ore anchored skyscrapers from Paris to London. But trade with the United States dominated the Mexican economy: 75 percent of all exports headed to the United States.[55]

U.S. elites hailed Díaz for bringing this brand of "order and progress" to Mexico. The presidents of Stanford, Yale, Columbia, and the University of California variously described Díaz as "one of the ablest and most efficient rulers in any country within the last century," "a man of commanding ability," and "exactly fitted to the emergency of his times, [a man who] created out of chaos a government definitely suited to conditions." Andrew Carnegie described Díaz as "one of the greatest rulers in the world, perhaps the greatest of all, taking into consideration the transformation he has made in Mexico, for he is at once the Moses and the Joshua of his people." General Douglas MacArthur ranked Díaz among world leaders, placing the president of Mexico in a "small class" that included "Cavour, Lincoln, Bismarck, and Ito." William Jennings Bryan "rejoic[ed] in the progress that country [Mexico] has made under Porfirio Díaz." U.S. secretary of state Elihu Root delivered a toast to the president of Mexico: "As I am neither poet, musician nor Mexican, but only an American who loves justice and liberty and hopes to see their reign among mankind progress and strengthen and become perpetual, I look to Porfirio Díaz, the President of Mexico, as one of the great men to be held up for hero-worship of mankind." President Theodore Roosevelt dubbed Díaz "the greatest statesman now living."[56]

Not everyone agreed.

CHAPTER 3

Den of Thieves

I N 1901, THE TWENTY-FIFTH YEAR OF DÍAZ'S RULE, HUN-
dreds of Mexicans gathered for a conference at the posh Teatro de
la Paz in the historic silver-mining town of San Luis Potosí. On stage
sat Camilo Arriaga, the nephew of Ponciano Arriaga, the venerated
author of the 1857 constitution, which Benito Juárez, Porfirio Díaz,
and the Liberal faction had fought to make the law of the land. Arriaga
had rented the theater and called the conference. Broad-chested and
kind, he was a gregarious spirit, the sort of person who shook everyone's
hand and had a motley group of friends, even though his wealth always
set him apart. Born in 1862 in San Luis Potosí, he was the descendant
of Spanish colonists. Inherited riches from silver mining enabled him
to attend Mexico's elite schools and travel frequently to France, where
he attended engineering classes in preparation for taking his place in
the family business. But he was drawn to the gritty, bohemian world
of bookstores and cafés, and the writings of provocative European
intellectuals. Karl Marx's ideas about class struggle enchanted young
Arriaga, as did Mikhail Bakunin's rejection of all forms of hierarchical
power, including organized religion. Arriaga collected stacks of books
for his personal library. Whenever he returned home to Mexico, he
freely lent his books to his friends in San Luis Potosí. His copies of
Marx's *Capital* (1867) and Bakunin's *God and the State* (1882) circulated
among local reading groups.

Arriaga's early intoxication with insurgent philosophers might have

Camilo Arriaga.

remained a youthful exercise in rebellion had the family fortune buoyed him. But, by the 1890s, a series of recessions had scattered the Arriaga family holdings and rendered the young man a downwardly mobile aristocrat with a head full of new ideas. Slowly, he tested the waters of dissent.

A deputy to the national Congress, Camilo Arriaga held a minor position in Díaz's government. In the 1890s, he complained about the increasingly cozy relationship between the Catholic Church and the Díaz administration, an intimacy of church and state banned by the constitution. Díaz dismissed Arriaga from his position.[1]

Arriaga pushed on, leveraging his name, properties, and remaining cash to nourish a growing community beginning to question Díaz's rule. People gathered in his library to debate politics and philosophy. Among the first to join his reading group were Librado Rivera and Juan Sarabia.

Librado Rivera was a schoolteacher. A reserved, learned man with

Librado Rivera.

Juan Sarabia.

expertise in history and geography, he was often the quietest person in the room. His friends nicknamed him El Fakir for his ascetic manner. But Rivera listened carefully and was a deep thinker. He borrowed many books from Arriaga's library, preferring the most radical texts, especially early anarchist thinkers who challenged all forms of hierarchy and coercive power. Rivera was also determined, confident that any human could turn the page of history with the right ideas and enough mettle.[2]

Juan Sarabia was just seventeen years old when he met Camilo Arriaga. His father had died three years earlier, forcing him to leave school and take a string of low-wage jobs to stitch together a meager existence for himself, his mother, and his sister. He worked in a library, at a mine, and as a cobbler. Nothing paid enough. When he worked for the telegraph company, sending messages between San Luis Potosí and Zacatecas, he woke up before dawn, walked three kilometers to work, and labored ten to twelve hours before returning home. His pay was barely enough for the family's tortillas and beans—the diet of impoverished workers across Mexico. The Sarabia family slid from poverty to desperation when Juan was struck by pneumonia followed by smallpox. When he recovered, his face was permanently pockmarked and his memory alive with the pain of his family's deep hunger. But he had an indomitable spirit. After work, he would meet with friends, teenage boys standing on street corners under the crackling light of gas lamps, prodding one another about crushes, politics, and being broke. On his days off, Sarabia liked to joke around with his cousins Manuel and Tomás, playing pranks on one another. And he wrote poems, submitting a few of his pieces to the local press, where they captured the attention of Camilo Arriaga. Arriaga, always a risk-taker, offered the teenage Sarabia the position of editor-in-chief of *Renacimiento* (Rebirth), a newspaper he had just founded to press for social and political reform in Mexico. Sarabia took the job.[3]

About one year after the launch of *Renacimiento*, Arriaga contacted subscribers and other like-minded reformers across Mexico, inviting them to convene in San Luis Potosí for a five-day conference. His goal

Juana Belén Gutiérrez de Mendoza, circa 1914.

was to coordinate a national campaign for the separation of church and state and reform of the criminal justice system.

Among the few women to attend the conference was Juana Belén Gutiérrez de Mendoza. An autodidact from the mountains of Durango, she was the daughter of a landless rural blacksmith and, like many among the rural poor during the nineteenth century, she never knew her birthdate. But, by the age of twenty-four, Gutiérrez de Mendoza had been arrested enough times to earn one. As she once put it, "I am not certain but I have been told that I was born in San Juan del Rio, Durango on the snowy dawn of January 27, 1875. This piece of information must be very important, since it has been written down with painstaking thoroughness in court prison records, every time I have been there."[4]

The arrests began in the mountains of Coahuila where Gutiérrez de Mendoza lived with her husband, a miner, and had three children: two daughters and a son who died in infancy. While she raised the children, she became a vocal advocate for mineworkers. She sent letters to Mexico City newspapers, exposing the conditions faced by her husband and the other miners. The local mine company had her arrested and jailed. She was undeterred. Whenever she was arrested, she wrote, in capital letters, in the space for her name on the booking form: "SEDICIÓN–REBELIÓN" (sedition–rebellion).[5] By the time of the Liberal conference in San Luis Potosí, her husband had died and she had moved to Guanajuato, where she would soon launch *Vesper*, a feminist–anarchist magazine. She used the pages of *Vesper* to challenge "misery wages" for the nation's miners and rebuke men for failing to lead an effective movement for social reform in Mexico. "That is why we [women] have come to take your place," she chided.[6] Later, in 1911, Gutiérrez de Mendoza would join Emiliano Zapata's guerilla army and help to draft Zapata's revolutionary vision, "El Plan de Ayala." Until her death in 1942, she persistently demanded land for the poor, justice for the disparaged, and effective suffrage for all Mexicans, including women. At the 1901 conference in San Luis Potosí, Gutiérrez de Mendoza was still on her way to becoming one of Mexico's boldest voices, but she had already assembled a long rap sheet that made her infamous among Mexican activists and authorities alike.[7]

Lázaro Gutiérrez de Lara was another distinguished guest. The wavy-haired son of a prominent family from Monterrey, a manufacturing hub of railroads and smokestacks known as "the Pittsburgh of Mexico," historians have described Gutiérrez de Lara as "movie-star handsome with a compelling personality."[8] He could have charmed his way into the highest tier of Monterrey's business society to rub elbows with some of the world's richest men, including Daniel Guggenheim, who was then building a global mining empire headquartered in and around Monterrey. Or he could have shimmied into Díaz's inner circle, becoming one of his trusted experts, the *científicos*, who set social and fiscal policy and scooped up buckets of kickbacks. Before Gutiérrez de Lara even graduated from law school, his family's connections landed him a presidential appointment as a circuit judge in northern Mexico, near Hiakim, the Yaqui homeland. What he saw in Hiakim changed his destiny.

*Lázaro Gutiérrez
de Lara.*

Hiakim once spanned what is now the northern Mexican states of Sonora, Durango, Sinaloa, and Chihuahua, as well as the southwestern United States. By the 1740s, a series of violent conflicts with Spanish conquistadors, priests, and miners had hemmed the Yaqui into a much smaller territory. The Yaqui were determined to defend their remaining slice of Hiakim from further incursion. In 1876, just as Díaz was coming to power, an insurrectionary leader named Cajeme, "one who does not stop to drink [water]," led Yaqui fighters in expelling outsiders from Hiakim. But, as Díaz settled into his rule, U.S. investors identified the region as fertile for both agriculture and mining, and the Díaz administration moved quickly to open Hiakim to investors. In 1879, Díaz began giving away plots of Yaqui land. The Atchison, Topeka and Santa Fe Railroad acquired the permit and completed a track across Hiakim to connect the Mexican port of Guaymas, in Sonora, to the Sunset Limited connection in Deming, New Mexico. U.S. miners, traders, and agricultural developers soon followed.[9]

When the Yaqui opposed the incursions, federal troops arrived to dislodge them and their neighbors, the Mayo, from their homelands. Under Cajeme's leadership, Mayo and Yaqui fighters crushed the federal forces, sending them scrambling into retreat. Díaz sent agents to assassinate Cajeme. They harassed his family and torched his home, but failed to find him. The Yaqui leader responded by burning every ship in the Guaymas harbor and raiding haciendas, mines, and railroad construction sites.[10] When Díaz sent more than 3,000 troops to crush the Yaqui–Mayo uprising, they found Hiakim abandoned. Led by Cajeme, the Yaqui and Mayo had withdrawn to a newly-built fort in the dense forest along the Yaqui River. Inside El Añil, as they named the fort, behind a moat, a palisade, and two layers of tree-high walls, thousands of Yaqui and Mayo had stockpiled food, guns, and ammunition. It took the Mexican military more than a year to penetrate El Añil. In fact, they could not even figure out where the fort began and where it ended, as it was expertly concealed in the forest. It took soldiers a full day to reconnoiter just 40 meters of the fort's outer wall. Meanwhile, from parapets hidden in the forest canopy, Yaqui and Mayo sharpshooters picked off soldiers approaching the perimeter.[11]

With the bodies of federal soldiers littering the forest floor, Cajeme sent a note across battle lines, offering to stop shooting if the government's soldiers and settlers agreed to permanently retreat back across the Yaqui River, out of Hiakim. The government refused. The Yaqui and Mayo kept shooting. When government forces finally broke through, they found the fort all but abandoned. Thousands of Yaqui and Mayo had slipped away along hidden paths. Guerilla attacks continued throughout Hiakim until Cajeme was captured and executed by firing squad in May 1887.

After the death of Cajeme, many Yaqui agreed to become farmers and laborers, but they did not agree to sell off their homeland or to allow outsiders to settle in their territory. Regardless, President Díaz

auctioned off large plots and authorized railroad and mining companies to establish operations in Hiakim. When the Yaqui insisted that
the "whites and soldiers leave," Díaz's local governor warned, "if you do
not submit, I will proceed to pursue and punish you as you deserve."[12]
The Yaqui did not submit, and the punishment was harsh. Díaz dispatched nearly 5,000 soldiers to Hiakim with orders to round up and
forcibly expel the Yaqui from their homeland. Most were deported
south to the swampy Yucatán, where they were forced into debt peonage, making twine for export to the United States.[13]

Arriving in Sonora in 1896, Lázaro Gutiérrez de Lara watched as
the government's war with the Yaqui escalated into mass deportation,
a process so brutal that even members of the Díaz regime described it
as nothing less than a coordinated campaign of "extermination" and
"elimination."[14] Seeing Yaqui families being rounded up like cattle and
shipped off to the Yucatán, he quit his position as a judge and became
a defense attorney, challenging land claims made against the Yaqui by
investors carving up Hiakim for agricultural and mining operations.[15]
By the time Gutiérrez de Lara arrived at the 1901 conference in San
Luis Potosí, he, too, had been arrested multiple times and earned a
national reputation as a rabble-rouser.

MOST AMONG THE MEN and women who gathered in San Luis Potosí
had tasted Díaz's ire. Like Camilo Arriaga, they challenged Díaz's
reconciliation with the Catholic Church. Like Juana Belén Gutiérrez
de Mendoza, they questioned labor practices and ended up arrested,
imprisoned, or fired from jobs. Like Lázaro Gutiérrez de Lara, they
were trying to stop the dispossessions that made Mexico the "treasure
house of the world."[16] They did all this at a time when it was a crime to
publicly criticize the Díaz regime. Despite the risks, they gathered in
San Luis Potosí to discuss reform.

President Díaz almost certainly knew about the convention. Through
his extensive network of appointees and friends, news flowed like rivers
into his office at the National Palace. Arriaga had advertised the con-

ference in *Renacimiento,* and the local *jefe político* would have kept the dictator well informed. Just before the conference was set to begin, the 15th Battalion arrived in San Luis Potosí and began marching on the dirt streets surrounding the theater. The fifty-six conference delegates, and hundreds of other attendees, crossed the line, filing into the theater until the floor level and balconies were "filled to overflowing."[17]

Inside, Arriaga took a seat at a table on the stage and gaveled the conference into session. Then he stood and delivered a speech about the separation of church and state, a staple issue among the Liberals and a principle that even Porfirio Díaz had once championed. It was a safe way to begin the meeting. Over the next few days, poets and musicians performed. Antonio Díaz Soto y Gama, a young lawyer who, two years prior, had gone to prison for leading a protest and chanting "Death to Porfirio Díaz!," read from his dissertation, which detailed the vagaries of the *jefatura.* Juan Sarabia gave a passionate keynote address. Then Ricardo Flores Magón, a young journalist from Mexico City, took the stage.

Flores Magón was relatively new to politics, but he had gained quick entry into Mexico's dissident circles through his older brother, Jesús.

Jesús had been politically active since 1890, when Porfirio Díaz convinced Congress to alter the constitution in order to allow his perpetual rule. By 1892, he was at the center of a student movement in Mexico City. On May 17, 1892, he helped to coordinate a student march. As the students chanted "No reelection!," police swept through the streets arresting participants, including Jesús and his eighteen-year-old brother, Ricardo, who had tagged along.

The brothers were quickly released from jail, but Ricardo Flores Magón would always remember the arrest as the beginning of his career as a dissident. "The barrels of a couple of cocked revolvers touched my chest, ready to go off at my slightest move, thus cutting off my first attempt at public speaking," he would later write.[18] However, as Mexican historian José C. Valadés explains, he was not yet the man he would become. He was still "modest in life, modest in mind, [and] he was also modest in his actions," and he had yet to commit himself

Mugshot of Ricardo Flores Magón, circa 1903.

Jesús Flores Magón.

to politics. His rap sheet was nothing like those of others at the confer-ence. What he did have was a personal grudge against Porfirio Díaz.[19]

Jesús and Ricardo Flores Magón harbored deep animus toward the dictator. Their parents, Teodoro Flores and Margarita Magón, had met while fighting by Díaz's side in the Battle of Puebla on Cinco de Mayo, back in 1867. They never married, but they lived together as husband and wife and had three sons: Jesús (b. 1871), Ricardo (b. 1874), and Enrique (b. 1877). When Díaz seized the presidency, Teodoro Flores signed a loyalty oath and joined Díaz's troops on their victory march into Mexico City. When Díaz was sworn in as president, Margarita Magón and their sons joined him in Mexico City, expecting the new president to reward their years of loyalty. He did not.

Flores struggled to find work, leaving the family dependent upon his military pension. Then, one day, a bureaucrat cut him from the pension rolls, noting that he lacked proof of service in the military. Those papers had been lost during the French occupation of Mexico, when a Conservative neighbor set fire to Flores's home while he was away fighting in the Liberal army. As well as his military commission, Flores lost his first wife, his father, and his mother-in-law in the inferno.

Having fought by Porfirio Díaz's side during the Battle of Puebla, Flores reached out to the president when his pension checks were stopped. Díaz certainly could confirm his status as a veteran. But Díaz ignored the request, sending only a signed portrait of himself in return. The Flores Magón family spiraled deeper into poverty, bunking in two rooms of an old monastery owned by a friend on the southeast side of Mexico City.[20] The neighborhood was unpaved, unlit, and undrained. Sewage gurgled in every dent left by horses and carts. When Teodoro Flores died on April 22, 1893, the family hit bottom. Within days, they were evicted from their apartment. Margarita Magón searched for days for lodgings she could afford, trudging through the muddy streets. Finally, she found a place in the Arcos de Belem neighborhood, not far from the Belem Prison. One American journalist called the area "a microbic spot [which] should be avoided."[21]

Jesús helped his mother pay for the apartment until he was arrested a few weeks later. After completing law school, he had become a full-time lawyer and a part-time activist. With friends, he launched a journal, *El Demócrata*, which published articles about election law and the judiciary. Díaz largely tolerated this kind of grumbling. But in the spring of 1893, *El Demócrata* ran a series of articles about a recent uprising in northern Mexico, which the regime wanted to keep quiet.

Located just east of Hiakim, the small town of Tomóchic was home to several Yaqui and Mayo families seeking refuge from the *rurales* and the government's raids. There, they became faithful followers of a teenage *curandera* (healer) named Teresa Urrea. Teresita, as they called her, could cure cancer, blindness, stroke, paralysis, and more, inspiring thousands to flock to her home on her father's ranch in northern Sonora, Rancho Cabora. She became known as "the Saint of Cabora," healing an estimated 50,000 people, treating hundreds of thousands more. Teresita also spoke publicly on the issues harming the health of her followers, especially the land grabs that dislocated communities, spurred homelessness, exacerbated hunger, and fostered disease among the landless families arriving at her doorstep. Legend holds that Díaz considered Teresa Urrea to be the "most dangerous girl in Mexico."[22]

In 1892, when the parish priest in Tomóchic threatened to excommunicate Teresita's followers, the residents of Tomóchic ran him out of town and vowed their loyalty to her. Civil authorities tried to intervene on the church's behalf, but the residents of Tomóchic declared their town to be a sovereign community, independent of both the Catholic Church and the Díaz regime. Díaz dispatched a battalion of soldiers to Tomóchic and ordered that its residents be "quickly and severely punish[ed]."[23] The soldiers set fire to the town, incinerating every building and an estimated three hundred residents. According to the general who led the siege, the "enemy [had been] eliminated to the last man."[24] "They got what they asked for," said Díaz, offering counsel to a remorseful army general involved in the campaign. "No other result was possible without sacrificing your dignity and the authority which is the basis of social order."[25] The survivors from Tomóchic—including forty women and seventy-one children who surrendered before the inferno—fled into Hiakim and Mayo territory, to towns across northern Mexico, and across the U.S.–Mexico border. Teresita fled, too. In exile in the United States, she continued to provide healings and inspire small uprisings against the regime.[26] Díaz's astute minister of finance, José Yves Limantour, later sold the rich timberlands surrounding Tomóchic to the Wisconsin-based Cargill Lumber Company.[27]

When Jesús Flores Magón published the story of Tomóchic in *El Demócrata*, he was promptly arrested for criticizing military officials in the exercise of their duties as government authorities, a violation of the 1882 libel law. A judge sentenced him to nine months in jail.[28]

"You need to be brave now," Jesús wrote to his mother from jail. "You must understand that it is necessary to take risks to secure our sustenance, even if it means that there will be no food for now."[29] He encouraged his youngest brother, Enrique, just sixteen years old, to stay in school and continue his studies toward a prudent career: bookkeeping. And he found Ricardo, who had been working as a domestic servant while attending law school, a better job: as a printer's assistant. This is where Ricardo got his first peek at journalism. But Jesús continued to worry about Ricardo, whose grades were slipping—an unexpected turn for the young man whom fellow students described as "the most determined and daring of the [Flores Magón] brothers."[30]

By the end of 1894, Ricardo was falling into a phase Jesús described as *"un período muy borrascoso"* (a very stormy period).[31] He dropped out of law school and, for six years, he opened and closed a series of failed businesses, traveling across the sierras of Oaxaca and into the Valle Nacional and the Yucatán, selling ice to railroad companies and hauling bananas up north. Most of all, he spent his nights and days drinking, gambling, and carousing in brothels. It is said that during these years he learned about the underside of Díaz's economic development. He befriended women who sold sex to survive.[32] He met men and boys who got by on itinerant labor. He witnessed people being swept up in the anti-vagrancy dragnets set by the *rurales* and city police, then shipped down to labor camps in the Yucatán and across the Valle Nacional, where employers shackled convict laborers at night, fed them by trough in the morning, and worked them to death during the day. Those who managed to escape were tracked down by the *rurales* and returned to their employers for punishment. And, it is said, during his "stormy" years, Ricardo contracted a sexually transmitted infection that left him sterile.[33]

By 1899, the storm abated. Ricardo quit drinking and returned to his mother's apartment in Mexico City where he declared to Jesús, "Paper is an idol to me, and I think that it will soon be my great weapon."[34] The law school dropout who spent his early twenties carousing around Mexico was remaking himself as an intellectual. He dressed in black and sat in cafés debating politics, listening to music, and reciting his favorite poems. He picked up scraps of other languages, including English, French, Italian, Portuguese, Latin, and Nahuatl.[35] According to the historical anthropologist Claudio Lomnitz, Ricardo Flores Magón was a "bohemian" enraptured by "an urban life [combining] reading, writing, politics, and a somewhat dandified aesthetic."[36] Unlike Camilo Arriaga, he never traveled to Europe, but he encountered and read the Continent's most fiery writers in Mexico City's vibrant intellectual scene.[37] Works by anarchist intellectuals, such as the Russian anarcho-communist Peter Kropotkin, were among his favorites.

Kropotkin directly challenged the theory of social Darwinism that was popular at the turn of the century. Whereas social Darwinists believed that the concept of the "survival of the fittest" applied to humankind, Kropotkin argued that mutual aid and equity, not competition and hierarchy, were the basis of thriving societies. "Sociability is the greatest advantage in the struggle for life. Those species which willingly or unwillingly abandon it are doomed to decay," wrote Kropotkin.[38] The state, he argued, suppressed mutual aid and cooperation. As he put it, "the State and its sister the Church arrogate to themselves alone the right to serve as the link between men."[39] Instead of a state and church serving as the basic building block of society, Kropotkin advocated for communes regulated only by customs and voluntary agreements. There would be no police, no jails, and no punishment to enforce contracts in the anarchist society, only the common interest of free individuals joined together for a common purpose. To build this anarchist world, Kropotkin believed popular violence would be necessary. In particular, Kropotkin insisted that the dispossessed would have to seize and then abolish private property to free the means of production, including land, factories, seeds, and tools, so that individuals could have equal, unfettered access to the sustenance of life.

In time, Ricardo Flores Magón would declare himself an anarchist and become one of the world's most intrepid advocates for the total abolition of private property, the church, and the state.[40] He would go on to demand nothing less than the "annihilation of all political, economic, social, religious and moral institutions that comprise the ambient within which free initiative and the free association of human beings are smothered."[41] But, in 1900, he was just beginning to find his way as a political thinker. Seeing the change in his brother, Jesús invited Ricardo to join him and a friend in launching a new weekly newspaper.

In August 1900, Antonio Horcasitas and the Flores Magón brothers published the first issue of their new venture. They called the newspaper *Regeneración*, a title that imparted the editors' opposition to the Díaz regime by implicitly calling for a "regeneration" of the nation's commitment to the principles of the 1857 constitution: principles such as clean elections, a free press, and term limits. The editors published the journal from Jesús's law office, which was located in the Zócalo, Mexico City's central plaza, catty-corner to Díaz's office in the National Palace. They worked law cases by day and wrote articles by night.

At first, they were careful not to provoke Díaz. They emblazoned on the masthead that *Regeneración* was a *"periódico jurídico independiente"* (independent legal journal) with a limited editorial mission: "[to] seek remedies and, when necessary, to point out and denounce all of the misdeeds of public officers who do not follow the precepts of law, so that the public shame brings upon them the justice that they deserve."[42] In other words, the journal would denounce corruption in the Mexican legal system without ever punching up at Díaz.[43]

For the next four months, the editors published articles on the mis-

Regeneración,
December 31, 1900.

conduct of police, lawyers, and judges. Then, on November 30, 1900, on the eve of Díaz's sixth consecutive swearing-in ceremony, something changed. They published an article attacking monarchical rule in Germany—a thinly disguised assault on the Díaz regime. The editors never spoke about the change, but Horcasitas soon resigned, and the Flores Magón brothers ushered in the first major transformation in *Regeneración*'s editorial mission. On December 31, 1900, they rebranded *Regeneración* with an explicitly political mission, changing the paper's masthead to "periódico independiente de combate" (independent journal of combat). "Our struggle has been rude," wrote the brothers. "It has all the characteristics of a pygmy fight against titans. In this we have found ourselves at every step with the livid phantasm of political indifference, we have fought alone, without any arms but our democratic ideals, and without any shield but our deepest convictions."[44]

The switch won them loyal subscribers who promoted the newspaper and its ideas. Subscriptions rolled in from across Mexico and from Mexicans in the United States who wanted to "spread democratic principles among the popular masses."[45] Despite the risks, the Flores Magón brothers pressed on. Jesús was a well-connected and seasoned political agitator. Ricardo was young and confident, with a head full of sophisticated new ideas. Together, they rushed into 1901, promoting *Regeneración* as their vehicle for demanding fundamental political change in Mexico. "We will fight without rest," they declared, "until the achievement of our ideals, always thinking that those same ideals were those of our fathers of '57 sustained vigorously in the rostrum, in the book, in the press and in the battlefields."[46]

Camilo Arriaga took notice of the brothers' bravado and mailed them an invitation to the Liberal conference he was planning in San Luis Potosí. Ricardo made an impression from the moment he arrived. Attending a meeting at Arriaga's home, he stood in the library and pointed at a copy of the 1857 constitution—which had been drafted by Arriaga's uncle—declaring it to be a "dead letter." He eulogized the constitution, adding, "We'll have to take up arms to oppose Porfirio Díaz because the old man won't give up power voluntarily, and even if he wanted to, the clique that surrounds him wouldn't let him."[47] The bearish young man was thumping his chest for Arriaga, who was the standard-bearer of Liberal dissent. Arriaga admired his swagger but thought his extremism the mark of an unruly mind. As Arriaga later explained, many years after the two men had bitterly parted ways, "I never ceased admiring and liking Ricardo. But what a barbarian!"[48]

When Ricardo Flores Magón took the stage at the Teatro de la Paz, he likely wore bohemian garb: a baggy black suit with a crisp white dress shirt and a wide black tie. A mop of curly black hair flopped atop his chubby brown face, defined only by his dark, swollen, darting eyes. Confident, he projected his voice at the end of his speech, speaking aloud an idea that shot up to the rafters and shocked the nation's reformers. "The Díaz administration is a den of thieves!" he bellowed. Stunned, the attendees hissed. The nation's clearest voices for reform— Juana Belén Gutiérrez de Mendoza, Juan Sarabia, Lázaro Gutiérrez de Lara, Camilo Arriaga, and others—had all questioned this or that aspect of the Díaz regime: the mine owners, the crooked judges, the *jefatura*. But no one had disparaged the president's rule outright, and no one had questioned the legitimacy of his reign. To do so was a crime. The hissing grew louder, rushing from the rafters down to the stage as if to stuff the words back into Flores Magón's mouth. But it was done. Before anyone could fully imagine what those words would ultimately reap, he repeated the charge: "The Díaz administration is a den of thieves!" They knew what he meant. Porfirio Díaz was a thief: a thief of land, a thief of wages, a thief of life, a thief of democracy. Flores Magón met their caution by bellowing for a third time, "The Díaz administration is a den of thieves!" A few "ayes" peeked above the fog of caution, then the theater broke into stomping and applause.[49] Sitting on stage, watching the commotion, Camilo Arriaga looked out at the audience and wondered, "Where is this man taking us?"[50] But he already knew. Ricardo Flores Magón had torn the veil of legitimacy covering Díaz's long, harsh rule, and there would be no looking away, no turning back. Mexico was on the road to revolution.

CHAPTER 4

We Won't Be Silenced

Ricardo Flores Magón left the 1901 Liberal conference emboldened. A few weeks later, on March 7, 1901, a new
issue of *Regeneración* hit the streets of Mexico City. It was more daring than anything the Flores Magón brothers had published to date.
On page one, they criticized the mainstream press—subsidized by
Díaz—as a "social intoxicant that perverts public opinion, making
us think that our absolute monarchy is a democratic republic." They
charged Díaz with "doing away with the principles of democracy" by
"muzzling the press" and "imprisoning honest citizens whose republican ideas could not consent to Caesarism." And they named the Díaz
administration as "authoritarian and despotic."[1]

Inked on the pages of *Regeneración*, this inflammatory assault on the
regime radiated outward from the Zócalo, passing from hand to hand
on tramcars and buses and on the shoulders of paperboys hustling for
the day's meal. By noon, people throughout Mexico City would have
read the breach. By day's end, the editors' criminalized words would
have reached Puebla and the towns surrounding Mexico City. The next
morning, the paper would be delivered to readers as far away as San
Luis Potosí, Oaxaca, and then across the border to towns like Laredo
and El Paso, Texas, where displaced Mexicans clustered in search of
work. Everywhere they went, from the mines in Arizona to lumber
mills in Colorado to citrus farms in California, workers carried *Regeneración*. As one observer would later report, copies of *Regeneración*

were passed "from one town to another until they fell to pieces from use."[2] Few Mexicans—no more than 28 percent by 1910—were literate, but the strong oral tradition of sharing news by campfire and on soap-boxes, in cantinas, and in song helped spread *Regeneración*'s message.[3]

The March 7 issue was a stunning strike. By 1901, Díaz had ruled Mexico for twenty-five years, accumulating almost all political and economic power in his hands. The lapses of his rule, such as when the Yaqui refused to be moved from Hiakim or when the residents of Tomóchic declared their loyalty to Teresita, had been met with overwhelming force. But nobody talked about how the once Liberal leader had become an authoritarian. The official, state-supported press, such as *El Imparcial*, never printed articles that mentioned the elec-toral corruption, intimidation, graft, or bribes that secured Díaz's hold on power.[4] They reported on imports, exports, land surveys, and real estate sales—only the profits of "progress," never its costs and dam-ages. Even Filomeno Mata, a Mexico City journalist who was impris-oned more than thirty times for criticizing members of the president's administration, had never directly challenged Díaz. In fact, Mata was always careful to praise the president, looking to him as the only person who could fix problems within his otherwise valid administration. Just a few months earlier, the Flores Magón brothers, too, had been more restrained, cloaking their attacks in metaphors, criticizing individual misdeeds rather than the systemic corruption that flowed from Díaz's office. The March 7, 1901, issue of *Regeneración* offered no such cir-cumspection. The front page name-checked the president eleven times, referring to him as General Díaz, the "despot" and "autocrat," rather than by his preferred moniker, "Don Porfirio Díaz," the patriarch of the nation.

Díaz did not respond. On March 23, 1901, from their offices across the Zocalo from the presidential palace, the brothers published their next attack, a scathing exposé of an attempted rape by one of the pres-ident's men, a *jefe político* in the state of Sinaloa. The woman fought her attacker and escaped but could find no justice following the assault. She filed a formal complaint, but the local police refused to take action.

The article mapped the ways sexual violence had been woven into the architecture of Díaz's rule. Nearly every town in Mexico had its own version of this story. By publishing one woman's struggle for justice, the Flores Magón brothers hauled the most intimate pain of the Porfiriato to the surface of the national conversation. Díaz still did not respond.

The Flores Magón brothers ended March 1901 drilling into the anti-democratic nature of the regime, publishing articles attacking the *jefatura* as "insufferable."[5] They also circulated a manifesto issued by Camilo Arriaga, Juan Sarabia, Librado Rivera, and the other members of the Club Liberal Ponciano Arriaga, their affiliate in San Luis Potosí. The manifesto vowed to run a candidate in the 1904 presidential election.[6]

To that provocation, Díaz replied. A master politician, he declined to publicly rebuke the upstarts. Instead, he issued a rumor designed to discredit the Flores Magón brothers as "revolutionaries." It was a warning to the editors and their subscribers: Stop now or be punished as enemies of the state. The brothers confronted the rumor in the next issue of *Regeneración*: "We are not revolutionaries . . . [but] we will be if [Díaz's] tyranny doesn't stop."[7]

It was not long before police raided the office and served a warrant for the brothers' arrest, charging that they had insulted a public official, namely the *jefe político* in Sinaloa who was accused of rape and corruption. The brothers were booked into Mexico City's Belem Prison to await trial.

Belem Prison was located in one of the most impoverished areas of town, Arcos de Belem, just a few blocks from the apartment Ricardo still shared with his mother and younger brother, Enrique. Built by the Catholic Church during the colonial era—in 1683, to be precise—the facility had begun as an asylum for indigent women. After winning the Reform War, Benito Juárez and the Liberals had seized the property, repurposing the three-story building with a drippy basement as a jail. The top floor, known as the "Department of Distinction," was relatively clean and reserved for distinguished prisoners. Filomeno Mata had a personal cot delivered to the Department of

Distinction for his many terms there. When Jesús and Ricardo Flores Magón were jailed for participating in the 1892 anti-reelection march, along with dozens of other university students, they, too, had been held in the Department of Distinction. Belem's first and second floors were different. They were crowded with the thousands of men and women jailed each night in Mexico City, an estimated 85 percent of whom were picked up for public drunkenness.[8] Hundreds more were regularly jailed for violating an 1897 municipal law, the *ley contra rateros* (the anti-tramp law), which banned the poor from "smelling bad, begging, or appearing insolent."[9] In other words, the first and second floors of Belem were crammed with the city's impoverished, especially the flood of migrants who had been displaced from their homes by land surveyors, railroads, and mines. This group provided the everyday labor of the growing city, sweeping streets, hauling cargo on their backs, and so on. The upper classes disparaged them as "*leprosos*" and "*pelados*"—lepers, bums, beggars, and thieves. Even the official organ of the Catholic Church disdained the city's migrant poor, calling them "one of the most vile underclasses in the world, as dirty as it is insolent."[10]

Regularly arrested, migrants spent many days in the Belem deathtrap. Neither the facility nor the neighborhood had a sewer system and the swampy land had poor drainage. Under these conditions, typhus, influenza, and cholera outbreaks were mundane.

Ricardo Flores Magón described Belem as a "horrible prison," little more than "a fetid, wet, black dump" with "dark corridors . . . grimy stairs . . . [and] . . . a long hall whose roof we touched with our hands." Later in life, he recoiled when remembering how "I leaned my hands against the wall and withdrew in amazement: bloody spits decorated the walls."[11]

The worst area of Belem Prison was the basement. Sewage water regularly flooded the floors. The cells had no windows, no light. The toilets were holes dug into the damp ground, leaving pools of urine, feces, and vomit to curdle in each cell. Conditions were horrid, and yet, the solitary confinement cells seemed to be even worse. The

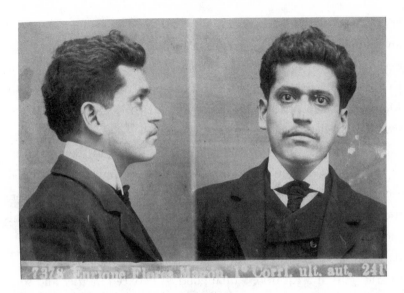

Mugshot of Enrique Flores Magón, circa 1903.

walls—thick, moist, and slowly decaying—exhaled centuries of mold. The imprisoned called the two solitary confinement cells "Hell" and "Purgatory."[12]

The Flores Magón brothers were held in the basement of Belem, but they refused to relent. They opposed Díaz's rule and harbored a personal rage against the president for his disregard of their father. On visiting days, they met with their younger brother, Enrique, whom they asked for help.

In 1901, Enrique Flores Magón was twenty-three years old and lighthearted. He mailed letters to his imprisoned brothers with the playful salutation *"queridos gordos"* (Dear Fatsos).[13] He registered his bicycle with a license plate that read "Porfirio Díaz" so that he could, in the words of historian Nicole Guidotti-Hernández, "ride the dictator over rough streets . . . metaphorically beat[ing] him into the ground."[14] Ricardo and Jesús affectionately called Enrique "Manito" (Little Brother).[15] But Enrique admired his older brothers and agreed to edit *Regeneración* while they were in jail. By June 1901, he was cranking out new issues of the journal, filled with articles drafted by Ricardo and Jesús. The basement of Belem did not tire the Flores Magón brothers as Díaz might have hoped; it provoked them. "The Díaz regime is an absolute monarchy, a military dictatorship. Citizens are slaves," they declared on the pages of *Regeneración* in June 1901.[16]

Fed up, Díaz sent emissaries to speak with their mother. By 1901, Margarita Magón had lived a long life. She had survived wars and invasions, epidemics and pestilence. And she had endured deep, grinding poverty. The president's emissaries found her and Enrique living in the family's rundown apartment in a swampy, unlit neighborhood. According to a memoir later published by Enrique, the dictator's men knocked at the door. Enrique answered and took the men to his mother's room, where she was lying in bed awaiting death. Just a few days before, she had dressed her weary body and gone to Belem Prison to visit Jesús and Ricardo, a final goodbye between mother and sons. The emissaries offered to release them immediately if she would convince them to stop publishing articles against the president. This was one of Díaz's standard methods—reaching out to cajole, convince, and co-opt the dissident Flores Magón brothers. They were highly educated and they could be useful to Díaz, employing their journalistic skills to support the regime rather than attack it.

But Margarita Magón had a few words of her own for President Díaz. She had not forgiven him for ignoring her husband's letters and forcing her family into poverty. According to Enrique, she looked at the president's men sitting beside her deathbed and chose her words carefully. She despaired at her sons' imprisonment—Ricardo, she must have known, had already caught an infection that left him permanently wheezy and nearly blind—but decades of bitterness welled in her throat. "Tell President Díaz that I choose to die without seeing my sons. And tell him this: I'd rather see my sons hang from a tree or a hanging post, than for them to retract or repent."[17] The president's emissaries left. That night, Margarita died with Enrique by her side. Three days later, a judge sentenced Ricardo and Jesús to two years in Belem Prison.[18]

Here it is important to note that historians question the veracity of Enrique's memoir. After Ricardo's death in 1922, Enrique spent the remainder of his life advocating for his brother to be lionized as "precursor" of the Mexican Revolution. Enrique's labor helped ensure that neither Ricardo Flores Magón nor the movement he sparked were forgotten. But Enrique's memoir is a tangle of fact and fiction. Whether Díaz's men ever knocked at the family's door, or whether Margarita Magón ever uttered such daring words, will never be known. As Claudio Lomnitz explains, "Like so much in Enrique's memoir, it is likely that this anecdote, too, is apocryphal."[19] But Enrique's story of his mother's deathbed protest suggests that he recalled Margarita Magón as supporting her sons in their opposition to the Díaz regime. What is clear is that Ricardo never forgave Díaz for keeping him from his mother's side when she was dying. "I could not give her a kiss nor could I hear her last words," he would later write.[20]

While Jesús and Ricardo were in jail, their friends in San Luis Potosí stayed active. Juan Sarabia and Camilo Arriaga continued to publish *Renacimiento*, forming partnerships with editors such as Pablo Cruz, as far away as San Antonio, Texas, who republished their articles.[21] Following another arrest in Guanajuato, Juana Belén Gutiérrez de Mendoza moved—with her daughters in tow—to Mexico City, where she continued to publish her anarcho-feminist journal, *Vesper*.[22] *Vesper* soon had a subscriber list of 8,000 and a steady crew of feminist journalists, including Elisa Acuña and Sara Estela Ramírez, a poet living in Laredo, Texas.[23] In July 1901, Antonio Díaz Soto y Gama gave a rousing public speech in which he lambasted Díaz for "betray[ing] democracy" and hollered that Díaz "holds the horseman's spur in higher regard than the hallowed constitution of '57, that spur which today lacerates his horse and tomorrow disembowels the people."[24] Díaz Soto y Gama was arrested a few days later and sent to Belem. In August, Enrique Flores Magón published a copy of his speech in *Regeneración*, and followed with a series of articles by his imprisoned brothers.[25] "We are fearless because the omnipotent power of the President does not frighten us. . . . We would be ashamed to be cowards," they wrote from Belem.[26] By October 1901, the imprisoned Flores Magón brothers were writing that "protest is a crime . . . so the people stay quiet . . . but we won't shut up . . . because we are neither cowards nor without honor (like the judges) . . . we attack high level officials and local officials, anyone. . . . For this reason, we attack President Díaz . . . we do not fear him."[27] Later that month, Mexico City police raided the *Regeneración* office again. This time, they seized the printing press, temporarily silencing the brothers.

The Liberals in San Luis Potosí issued another manifesto, charging Díaz with "despotism," criticizing the ongoing incursions in Hiakim, and proposing "the agrarian problem" as a theme for the next Liberal conference, which Arriaga was planning to host in February 1902.[28] While Arriaga made arrangements for the conference, Congressman Heriberto Barrón and Lieutenant Amado Cristo visited his home and asked to participate in the next planning meeting. Arriaga agreed, as both men had once been supporters of the Liberal movement in San Luis Potosí.[29] Maybe the congressman and army lieutenant were ready to become more active supporters of the Liberal cause.

On January 24, 1902, a few hours before the planning meeting was scheduled to begin at a local hotel, Arriaga noticed that as many as fifty policemen were gathered nearby. The *jefe político* stood with them. Still, attendees filed into the large salon. Among them sat Congressman Barrón and Lieutenant Cristo, next to an army sergeant from the 15th Battalion. Arriaga realized then that something was afoot. At 8:30 pm, he began the meeting cautiously by asking Julio Uranga, a member of his group, to give a speech about the Catholic Church. After Uranga spoke, Congressman Barrón stood up and shouted, *"Viva el General Díaz!"* Soldiers who had slipped into the audience disguised as farm laborers threw off their sombreros and serapes and began throwing objects at the stage. Barrón pulled out a small pistol and fired several shots into the ceiling. That must have been the signal for the policemen waiting outside, because dozens of them rushed into the hotel with guns drawn and began making arrests. Camilo Arriaga and Librado Rivera scrambled out a back door. Others rushed into the street. Twenty-five attendees, including Juan Sarabia, were taken to the local jail. Later that night, police raided Arriaga's home, ransacking the place and arresting Arriaga and Rivera. A few days later, a judge convicted Arriaga, Rivera, and Sarabia of "obstructing public officials in the exercise of their duty" and sentenced them to a minimum of one year in Mexico City's Belem Prison.[30] The 1902 Liberal conference never occurred.

At Belem, Arriaga, Rivera, and Sarabia joined Jesús and Ricardo Flores Magón in the basement. They were placed in separate cells, each with their own guard. Troops patrolled the streets outside.[31] Few people were allowed to visit the imprisoned writers. But inside Belem, the men were communicating through the walls. Juan Sarabia was in the cell between Jesús and Ricardo, and the three men developed a code using knocks. As the weeks passed, the men grew closer, surviving the mold, darkness, and pestilence together. They also discussed what they would do when released: how to write Díaz out of office. But, in these discussions, it must have been increasingly clear that Jesús Flores Magón was having doubts. When the brothers were released from Belem that April, Jesús got married, retired from dissident journalism, and devoted himself to his law practice. In the years ahead, he would provide his brothers with legal advice, while encouraging them to deescalate their direct confrontations with Díaz.[32] Ricardo and Enrique refused. For the rest of their lives, the Flores Magón brothers argued over politics. They "curs[ed] each other . . . vehemently," especially as Ricardo led Enrique and the nation's Liberals deeper and deeper toward outright armed revolt.[33]

CHAPTER 5

The Constitution
Is Dead

W HEN RICARDO AND JESÚS FLORES MAGÓN WERE RELEASED from Belem in April 1902, Ricardo had no means of publishing his inked assaults as their printing press had been confiscated by Díaz's men. Camilo Arriaga asked his friend Daniel Cabrera if Ricardo could take over his newspaper, *El Hijo del Ahuizote*, while Cabrera recuperated from an illness. Cabrera agreed.

Established in 1885, *El Hijo del Ahuizote* was a Mexico City journal that used political cartoons and satirical writing to discreetly criticize the government. As editor, Ricardo dispensed with such subtleties, lunging directly at Díaz and his administration. As the Mexican historian José C. Valadés explained, his articles in *El Hijo del Ahuizote* "began to injure the Díaz regime."[1] By September 1902, police had raided the offices of *El Hijo del Ahuizote*, seized all printing equipment, and arrested its new editors, Ricardo and Enrique Flores Magón.

Back in Belem, the brothers rejoined Arriaga, Sarabia, and Rivera, who had been there for eight months. A Díaz emissary visited the jail and offered to secure Arriaga's release in exchange for his silence. Most likely, Arriaga was targeted because it was his money and connections that subsidized the rebel writers. Eliminating his support would extinguish the firebrands. Arriaga declined, stating that if compliance was his key to his freedom, "it would be far better that I not go free."[2] He remained with his friends in the basement of Belem.

By January 1903, all the rebel writers had been released. Camilo

Santiago de la Hoz.

Arriaga and Juan Sarabia stayed in Mexico City, where they were joined by Sarabia's cousin Manuel, whom they called El Chamaco (the Kid). Librado Rivera (El Fakir) arrived, too. And Santiago de la Hoz, a fifteen-year-old poet from the Yucatán, made his way to the city. De la Hoz wrote with great passion, explained Ricardo Flores Magón. "His pen and his lyricism were his weapons . . . and he knew how to handle them without limit."[3] The group nicknamed him their *"juvenil luchador"* (young fighter).[4]

With Liberal partisans flocking to Mexico City, Arriaga purchased new equipment for *El Hijo del Ahuizote* and Juan Sarabia took over the editorship. Flores Magón focused on writing. For hours, he would crouch over his desk with his head so low that his eyes "almost touch[ed] the paper. . . . Then he would run, twisting with dancer curves, his small, thin, elongated letters" along the page, which was usually "on the back of the uncollectible bills of *El Hijo del Ahuizote*."[5] As one of their friends described it, "Though Ricardo Flores Magón was not the very smartest of the group . . . [he was] the prototype of the apostle. His

¡La Constitución ha muerto!

ends and means were absolutely incorruptible. . . . Flores Magón daz-
zled his comrades with his character of iron."[6]

On February 5, 1903, the third anniversary of the 1901 Liberal conference, Flores Magón and his friends met at the office of *El Hijo del
Ahuizote*.[7] Just a few blocks away, in the Zócalo, thousands of Mexicans
were gathering to watch the parade and fireworks celebrating Constitution Day. That afternoon, amid a flurry of festivities in Mexico City,
Santiago de la Hoz, Ricardo Flores Magón, Juan Sarabia, Enrique
Flores Magón, Manuel Sarabia, and others stepped onto the building's
balcony and unfurled a massive banner: "*¡La Constitución ha muerto!*"
(The Constitution is dead!) Someone snapped a photo from the street,
memorializing the writers' act of defiance in the heart of the city.

A few weeks later, Juan Sarabia published the photo alongside a cap-
tion reading: "We solemnly censure the assassins of the Constitution
who, as if in bloodstained mockery of the people they have scoffed,
celebrate this day with demonstrations of merriment and pleasure."[8]
He also published a series of manifestos, detailing the rebel writers'
increasingly confrontational stance. The first manifesto charged Díaz

with "having left the people in the saddest possible political orphan-
age, without a guarantee to protect them, a liberty to elevate them, or a
right to dignify them."[9] The next manifesto pushed explicitly into economic matters, attacking "the capitalist, the priest, and the high official, civilian or military" and "demanding that the proletariat be given
dignity."[10]

Typically, Díaz would have swiftly punished the writers, but he had
many fires to put out in the spring of 1903. Discontent was escalating across Mexico. On April 2, a march was held to begin a month-
long commemoration of Díaz's victory at the 1867 Battle of Puebla.
The march moved through the streets of Mexico City and ended at the
Zócalo, in front of the National Palace. Díaz stepped onto a balcony to
greet the adoring crowd, but the march quickly transformed into an
anti-reelection rally. Before Díaz knew it, the marchers were shouting
"Death to reelection!" Díaz stood on the balcony for a few minutes,
surveying the scene, before turning his back and disappearing inside.[11]
The next day, in the northern city of Monterrey, a reported 10,000
people marched in protest against the regime. For weeks, local students had been criticizing authorities for "not hear[ing] the complaints
of workers," and they had challenged the candidacy of General Bernardo Reyes, who was running for reelection as governor of the state
of Nuevo León.[12] General Reyes was quick to anger and instructed his
troops to open fire, killing fifteen marchers and arresting more than
eighty others.[13] Camilo Arriaga and Antonio Díaz Soto y Gama submitted a legal brief to Congress demanding that Reyes be sanctioned.
Congress, Díaz's "herd of tame horses," cleared Reyes of all wrong-
doing and accused Arriaga and Díaz Soto y Gama of filing a "false
accusation" against him. By the end of the month, Reyes was reelected
governor of Nuevo León. Fearing retaliation, Arriaga and Díaz Soto y
Gama fled to the United States.[14]

The massacre at Monterrey radicalized the Liberals in Mexico City.
For several weeks, they had been debating whether one of them should
oppose Díaz in the 1904 presidential election. Ricardo Flores Magón,

Juan Sarabia, and Santiago de la Hoz argued that someone from their group, most likely Flores Magón, should head a slate of candidates. Camilo Arriaga, Antonio Díaz Soto y Gama, and Juana Belén Gutiérrez de Mendoza disagreed, arguing that the Liberals would be accused of "personalism"—that is, advancing their personal interests above their principles.[15] Or, as Gutiérrez de Mendoza more forcefully put it, their goal was not to replace one man with another: "The fall of a tyrant is not the end of tyranny."[16] The writers fiercely debated the matter but, after the Monterrey massacre, they shifted to discussing the need for armed revolt and agreed to focus their attacks on both the regime's political corruption and its failed economic policies.[17]

In the April 11, 1903, issue of *El Hijo del Ahuizote*, the editors charged Díaz with making Mexicans the "servants of foreigners, who are the ones exploiting the wealth of our country."[18] Five days later, on April 16, police raided the newspaper's office, destroying the equipment and arresting everyone present for "contempt of public officials in the exercise of their duty." Among those arrested were Juan and Manuel Sarabia, Ricardo and Enrique Flores Magón, and Librado Rivera. They were released in late 1903. By then, the police had shut down *El Hijo del Ahuizote* as well as Gutiérrez de Mendoza's *Vesper* and nearly a dozen other small dissident papers across the country. Moreover, a Mexico City judge had issued an injunction prohibiting any newspaper in Mexico from publishing anything written by any of the writers arrested at the *El Hijo del Ahuizote* office on April 16, 1903. It was a gag order amid a political suppression campaign. The writers had nowhere left to publish their criticisms of the regime, but they were already at work on a new game plan. Camilo Arriaga and Antonio Díaz Soto y Gama were in Texas, preparing for the others to arrive. Juana Belén Gutiérrez de Mendoza and Elisa Acuña went first. Ricardo and Enrique Flores Magón and Juan Sarabia soon followed, taking the train from Mexico City to Laredo, the small U.S. border town where they had agreed to reconvene and relaunch their attack on Díaz.

To afford their train fares, Ricardo sold the only typewriter he could salvage from the "wreckage" at *El Hijo del Ahuizote*.[19] Díaz's detectives followed him to the station, where the three men slipped onto the Mexican National heading north. On board the train, Ricardo wondered aloud if they would be allowed to cross the border or if Díaz's "secret police" would send their descriptions to "one of the big North American companies with interests in Mexico." If those Americans asked their government to intervene, the dissidents might well be jailed again.[20] As they rode north to their fate at the border, the writers crossed the nation they planned to remake. In the Central Plateau, they passed the birthplace of the Mexican War of Independence, where Mexico's poor and racially marginalized led a mass uprising against the Spanish Crown, one of the most powerful empires the world has ever known. Then, as the train cut north through the mining districts of the Sierra Madre, they could see the smokestacks of gold and silver mines, almost all of them owned by U.S. investors. Even the train car in which they sat was owned by *norteamericanos*. The situation could have seemed hopeless.

In 1904, few Mexicans thought it possible to end Díaz's rule. General Porfirio was an astute politician and legendary general who had held the presidency for decades, and he was flanked by some of the world's most powerful men: British bankers, Anglo-American investors, even U.S. presidents. But the three dissidents were undaunted as the train creaked out of the mountains and accelerated into the borderlands. Here, in time, they would recruit an army to take down the Díaz regime.

Part 2

WE WILL BE REVOLUTIONARIES

CHAPTER 6

The Brown Belt

ICARDO AND ENRIQUE FLORES MAGÓN AND JUAN SARABIA
entered the United States at the port of entry in Laredo, Texas.
If U.S. border guards had been notified of their arrival, nothing was
done to stop them. In 1904, there were no fences, no concertina wires, no
floodlights, and no wall on the border. The Border Patrol would not be
established for another two decades. In 1882, Congress had passed the
Chinese Exclusion Act, which categorically prohibited all Chinese laborers from entering the United States. By 1904, epileptics, anarchists, convicts, prostitutes, "lunatics," "idiots," contract laborers, and the poor,
under the rubric of persons "liable to become public charges," were
also banned. The Immigration Service stationed a few armed guards
to watch for Chinese immigrants and other proscribed individuals, but
they rarely prevented Mexicans from crossing the border. In fact, federal law did not require the inspection of Mexican or Canadian border
crossers until 1907.[1] Chinese immigrants often tried to pass for Mexican, cutting their hair, donning serapes, and learning a few words of
Spanish. "*Yo soy Mexicano,*" they would say when stopped by an immigration inspector.[2] Even as land reform accelerated in Mexico at the
turn of the twentieth century, pushing tens of thousands of Mexicans
to seek work in the United States, U.S. authorities did little to stop
them. More Mexicans meant more workers, and more workers meant
more profits for the booming industries of the American West. Every
day hundreds of Mexican immigrants crossed the foot and wagon

International Bridge in Laredo, Texas.

bridge over the Rio Grande at Laredo without so much as a nod from U.S. border guards. In January 1904, the Flores Magón brothers and Juan Sarabia crossed with them, without record or inspection. They would soon be wanted men on both sides of the border.

The three men got to work the night they arrived. Paulino Martínez, a local journalist who had long supported *Regeneración*, had arranged for them to meet up with their old comrades at his home. Camilo Arriaga was there, joined by the feminist–anarchist journalists Juana Belén Gutiérrez de Mendoza and Elisa Acuña, as well as Juan's cousin Manuel Sarabia and the group's "young fighter," Santiago de la Hoz. The Villarreal Márquez brothers came from Del Rio, a small border town located about 100 miles upriver. In Del Rio, Crescencio and Francisco Villarreal Márquez edited two papers, *El Mensejero* (The Messenger) and *1810*, both of which republished articles from *Regeneración* and supported anti-Díaz activities in Mexico. Also in attendance was the twenty-three-year-old poet Sara Estela Ramírez, who, after reading *Regeneración* for the first time in 1901, had started a Liberal club in Laredo. Her father disapproved of her political activities but she persisted, establishing a feminist newspaper, *La Corregidora*, to publish her poetry and articles from *Regeneración*.[3] As she explained in the first letter she mailed to Ricardo Flores Magón, in May 1901, "Please count me in among your most devoted and enthusiastic supporters."[4] He wrote back and they began an epistolary relationship. They first met in person that night at Martínez's house, and Ramírez quickly emerged as a leader of the resistance.

Laredo was a gateway to south Texas, a scrubby region between the Rio Grande and San Antonio often referred to as America's Brown Belt, where Mexicans and Mexican Americans comprised (and still comprise) the majority population.[5] Spanish was more common than English, and life in south Texas reached toward Mexico. Most of the 450 Spanish-language newspapers published in the United States between the 1890s and 1930s were published in the Brown Belt and carried news from both sides of the border.[6] And thousands of Mexican labor migrants crisscrossed the region every day on their way to and from work throughout the southwestern United States. Their seasonal migration across the region, north and south of the border, was like a cord linking life, culture, and politics across the borderlands.

Historians estimate that 100,000 Mexicans immigrated to the United States between 1900 and 1910.[7] Most arrived in search of work. Dispossessed, hungry families pooled their resources, took out loans, and sold off valued possessions—a *burro*, a saddle, a crop of corn—to send their young, usually men, north in search of work.[8] U.S. employers and labor contractors (*enganchadores*) offered powerful incentives, offering to prepay railroad fares and provide housing and other living essentials, such as "beans, bacon, pots, and pans," with such advances to be deducted from future pay.[9] In other words, U.S. employers and *enganchadores* cranked open the spigot of Mexican labor migration to the United States. By 1910, Mexican workers were emerging as the dominant low-wage workforce across the southwestern United States, especially the border states.[10] Their labor drove the rise of the West's multimillion-dollar industries. By 1900, they comprised 70 to 90 percent of railroad track crew across the region.[11] By 1910, they were playing a leading role in hauling more than $34 million each year from Arizona's copper mines and $216 million from California's farms and mines, as well as $391 million generated from cattle, cotton, and crops in Texas.[12] All told, Mexicans did the lion's share of the seasonal and common labor needed to plant, tend, harvest, mine, and transport those goods to market. Invited and encouraged by U.S employers, Mexicans were building the twentieth-century American West.[13]

Few of Mexico's labor migrants had any intention of permanently settling in the United States. Up to 75 percent of Mexican immigrants to Texas returned home every year.[14] They came to the United States to earn money, while their hearts and dreams, their families and futures, remained in Mexico. What they experienced in the United States only affirmed their dreams of returning home.

After the Mexican–American War ended in 1848, white settlers expected easy access to the lands long occupied by Mexicans and Indigenous peoples. But Indigenous communities refused to disappear. The U.S. Army spent decades attempting to clear lands for white settlers, and the Apache, Comanche, and many others fought back. The so-called Indian Wars raged into the twentieth century. This prolonged and brutal effort to eliminate Indigenous peoples from the new American West unified the white settler republic, especially following the divisions of the Civil War.[15]

To clear Mexicans from the land, settlers used other tactics, beginning with debt. In Texas, the settler-dominated state legislature raised land taxes to a level that the region's cash-poor ranchers could not afford, forcing many Mexican landholders either to sell valuable parcels to finance tax payments or to slip into delinquency, which allowed sheriffs to auction off their properties cheaply.[16] When debt failed to force Mexicans from their land, lynch mobs often arrived.

Between the 1870s and 1920s, Mexicans and Mexican Americans across the American West, especially in Texas, were the targets of unchecked mob violence, an extra-legal system of racial terror geared toward opening up land and demanding Mexican deference to arriving

Lynching of Francisco Arias and José Chamales (Santa Cruz, California), May 1877.

Anglo-American settlers.[17] One of the earliest mass lynchings occurred near Corpus Christi, where Don Toribio Lozano, a well-to-do Mexican rancher with property on both sides of the border, frustrated Anglo settlers by consistently making his tax payments and refusing to sell his land. In 1873, while Lozano was visiting his estates in Mexico, a posse composed of white men from the nearby towns of Dogtown and Stonebridge raided his ranch and killed seven of his employees. Brothers Filomeno and Epifanio Rios were hung from the same tree limb. Jorge Rodríguez was hung from another branch of the same tree. The body of Blas Mata was found stiff, swinging nearby. Leonardo Garza and José María Reinas hung from a mesquite tree less than one hundred feet away. Vicente García swayed, alone, in a tree breaking from the brush just a few yards on. For more than a week, the seven corpses swung in the orchard until Lozano returned and cut them down.

Lozano spent two years seeking redress from local law enforcement, but no one was arrested. Finally, he gave up, sold his property in Texas, and returned to Mexico.[18] It was dispossession by lynch mob.

Even when land was not at stake, any perceived slight, "unknown reason," and unrecorded charge could stir a mob. In 1882, in Oatmanville, Texas, two men shot Augustin Agirer to death for taking their friend to court. In 1883, in Brownsville, Texas, just north of the Rio Grande, unknown persons for unknown reasons hung Silvestre García and then threw his body in the river. In 1895, San Juan Miguel was shot and mutilated with knives, then stuffed in a canvas sack and hung from a tree. On May 15, 1902, Ramón de la Cerda was "shot, dragged, beaten, and then buried" by a mob on a charge of theft. Four months later, in October 1902, his brother, Alfredo de la Cerda, was shot by the Texas Rangers on a charge of "protesting the Texas Rangers."[19] The Texas Rangers, a state-funded mobile strike force that operated much like the *rurales* in Mexico, were often implicated in the violence and would pose for postcards with the bodies of their victims. Mexicans called them *rinches*.

While attempting to clear the land of Indigenous peoples and subjugate Mexican and Mexican American residents, the settlers arriving in the borderlands ground white supremacy into everyday life. School, occupational, and residential segregation were common in the borderlands. Whites were managers; Mexicans were laborers. Whites lived in one neighborhood; all but the wealthiest Mexicans lived in another. Mexican children attended underfunded schools. In time, signs reading "No Mexicans Allowed" hung in shops and restaurants. Mexican American activists aptly dubbed these practices "Juan Crow."[20]

Juan Crow made Mexicans a racially marginalized workforce across the American West, creating a logic by which Mexicans were systematically paid less and treated worse than white workers. The Southern Pacific Railroad, for example, paid different wages based upon race. In 1908, Greek section hands made $1.60 per day, whereas Mexican section hands made $1.25 per day.[21] Employers often attributed their segregated compensation practices to what they described as the biological and cultural characteristics of Mexican migrant laborers. As one farmers' publication in California put it, Mexicans are "plentiful, generally peaceable, and are satisfied with very low social conditions."[22] But Juan Crow was the root of the inequities.

Juan Crow discouraged many Mexican immigrants from settling in the United States. Very few Mexicans became U.S. citizens in the early 1900s.[23] Every indignity was a reminder to save one's wages for a swift return home at the end of the season. But the story of one Mexican farmworker who dared to fight back captured the imagination of Mexicans on both sides of the border.

On the afternoon of June 12, 1901, Gregorio Cortez was resting on his porch, lying on his back with his eyes closed and his head in his wife's lap, when the county sheriff, William "Brack" Morris, pulled up in a horse-drawn surrey. Brack's deputy, Boone Choate, was at his side. The lawmen were following up on a tip that "a medium-sized Mexican with a big red broad-brimmed Mexican hat" had stolen a horse in the next county. Cortez glanced at the deputies before pushing his holster from its rest position on his belly to his right hip. "See what they want," he told his brother Romaldo, who walked out to the fence surrounding the small farmhouse set in a clearing. Leaning on the gate, Romaldo spoke briefly with the sheriff. "*Te quieren*" (They want you), he called back to his brother, who approached the gate but held back a few paces from the lawmen. Sheriff Morris asked, in English, if Cortez had recently traded a horse with a white man. Deputy Choate translated the question. "No," Cortez answered. Sheriff Morris then slipped open the gate and walked toward Cortez while instructing Choate to inform both men that they were under arrest for horse theft. "You can't arrest me for nothing," Cortez responded in Spanish. Choate, whose Spanish was elementary at best, mistranslated his words to mean, "No white man can arrest me." Sheriff Morris drew his gun. Romaldo hunched down and lunged at the sheriff who turned and fired, shooting him in the mouth. The sheriff then fired at Gregorio Cortez, but missed. Cortez, standing, as the legend says, "with his pistol in his hand," fired back, shooting Sheriff Morris in the right arm, sending the lawman to his knees. As Morris fell, he fired wildly. Cortez shot him again, hitting him in the left shoulder. Wounded in both arms, the sheriff struggled toward the gate, while Deputy Choate ran into the brush for cover, then fled back toward town. Cortez moved in close and shot the sheriff in the gut before picking up his brother and carrying him into the house.

The family made a hurried escape, washing Romaldo's face and packing their things before carrying Romaldo to the empty surrey out front and pulling away, leaving Sheriff Morris, not yet dead, lying at the gate. Morris crawled more than two hundred yards, out of the clearing and into the brush, where he collapsed and died. It would take a search party days to find his body.[24] Meanwhile, Gregorio Cortez took his family to a friend's house and fled, knowing a posse would soon be raised to hang him.

He traveled north, hoping to trick the search party. He walked 80 miles in forty hours, avoiding roads and cutting through the brush. He was still wearing the dress shoes and shirt he had on when the shooting began.

On the evening of June 14, he arrived at the home of his friend Martin Robledo, in González County. After dinner, they sat on the porch with Robledo's two eldest sons, Bonifacio (eighteen) and Tomás (sixteen), and their friend, a teenage boy named Sandoval. Robledo's wife and their two younger children were inside, getting ready for bed. Cortez slipped off his shoes.

But, while Cortez was trekking through the brush to the Robledo home, sheriff's deputies back in Karnes County had found and arrested his family, including the children. In jail and "under pressure," one of the family members told them where Cortez was heading. By the time he was slipping his shoes off on Robledo's porch, a posse of nearly two hundred men had encircled the house. They were drinking whiskey in the surrounding brush, waiting for the moment to attack.

The melee began when Sheriff Glover, mounted on a horse, charged out of the dark to confront Cortez, who had walked to the back of the porch. Glover took a shot and missed. Cortez shot back, killing Glover instantly and knocking him from his horse. Cortez jumped from the porch and ran barefoot into the brush where he ripped his vest into pieces, tying the strips around his feet, and took flight deeper into the brush, hearing the drunken posse shooting behind him. Robledo and his two oldest sons also fled. In hiding, they listened while the posse shot into the house where Robledo's wife, the two youngest children, and the teenage friend, Sandoval, remained. A bullet hit Sandoval. Another bullet ripped through the face of Henry Schnabel, a local farmer who had joined the posse. A few minutes later, when the posse stopped shooting, they found Glover and Schnabel dead and arrested the Robledo family as well as the wounded Sandoval. Before taking them all to jail, the posse strung a rope over a tree and wrapped a noose around the neck of Robledo's thirteen-year-old son, Encarnación. Demanding information about Cortez's whereabouts, they pulled and released the rope over and over again "until [Encarnación's] tongue protruded and life was nearly extinct." But "the boy [and the family] refused to talk."[25] When the posse tired of this game, they took Sandoval and the Robledos to jail and resumed the search for Gregorio Cortez.

For six more days, Gregorio Cortez lived on the run, eluding a posse as large as two hundred men on horseback. The governor of Texas put a $1,000 bounty on his head. The posse splintered into several groups that swarmed across south Texas, raiding homes, stringing up suspects, and harassing Mexicans. As one journalist put it, "reckless bands have scoured the southern portion of this state" in search of Gregorio Cortez.[26] On June 16, one Mexican was killed, another wounded, and five arrested, accused of being members of the "Cortez gang." There was no such gang—just one barefoot man on the run. On June 17, newspapers reported that another Mexican had been hung, another shot, another wounded, and another left with a fractured skull from the butt of a rifle. On June 18, three more Mexicans were killed, in separate incidents in separate counties.[27]

Cortez evaded arrest by cutting north and south, walking in circles and using herds of cows to cover his trail. After years of migrant

Gregorio Cortez
after his arrest.

labor in Texas, he knew the region well: its dry, stubby trees, its thorny brush, its dusty roads, its small encampments of Mexican *colonias*. And he was smart. He gained hours on a nearing posse by blindfolding a mare and coaxing her across an impassable river. The posse followed his tracks right up to the riverbank, where they lost his trail. Sometimes, a posse would get so close that Cortez, hiding in the nearby brush, could hear the men planning his capture. He always slipped away. Once, a posse came within feet of Cortez as he rested at the base of a cypress tree. While the men took a few moments to discuss their approach, he awoke to hear them talking. By the time they stepped out of the brush, he was gone, leaving just his hat behind. But on June 22, 1901, near Cotulla, not far from the border, Cortez stopped to rest at a friend's sheep ranch. The friend, eager for the bounty, turned him in. Lawmen arrived to take him to jail in San Antonio. Exhausted, he went quietly.

Jovita Idar at the La Crónica *office.*

No one expected Gregorio Cortez to survive the night. Two white sheriffs were dead, so was a member of the posse, and he had led the *rinches* on a humiliating manhunt across the borderlands. A lynch party was sure to arrive, to restore the balance of racial power in the borderlands. Cortez lived through the night but the danger persisted and Mexicans across the Brown Belt banded together to change what seemed to be Cortez's certain fate.

Jovita Idar, a young journalist based in Laredo, documented and decried the lynchings in the region, publishing articles in her family's weekly newspaper, *La Crónica*.[28] When a troop of Texas Rangers arrived at the office to destroy the printing press, Idar stood in the doorway, blocking the entrance. Rather than forcibly moving her aside, they left, but they returned the next day, early in the morning before Idar arrived, destroyed the building and the equipment, and arrested the morning shift workers.[29] But Idar's father had taught his children that they had an obligation to "fight for the Mexican people."[30] The Idar family kept the Cortez case front-page news and joined a network of Mexican and Mexican American journalists in forming an anti-lynching alliance.[31]

In San Antonio, the journalist Pablo Cruz publicly pressed both the U.S. and Mexican governments to stop the violence in south Texas. In particular, he criticized Porfirio Díaz for failing to protect Mexican citizens in the United States, writing that "the Mexican government turns a blind eye every time we speak of this or Mexicans assaulted in the United States. . . . It seems that the Mexican government does not care about the fate of its citizens on this side of the Bravo."[32]

Meanwhile, Mexico's migrant workers, few of whom could read or write, weighed in on Cortez's case by singing his tale. From cantina to campfire to *colonia* to porch to barrio, "The Ballad of Gregorio Cortez" burned like brushfire across the borderlands, chronicling the tale of a Mexican farmhand who disputed a false charge, defended his brother, killed white men, eluded the *rinches*, and lived to tell the tale. The song's popularity only grew as Cortez fought his case in court. Defended by a legal team paid by donations, he beat the original charge of horse theft, as well as the murder charges stemming from the deaths of Sheriff Morris and Henry Schnabel. A jury found that Morris had attempted an unauthorized arrest, and Schnabel, it was proven, had been shot by another member of the drunken posse. Following the path of his flight, each case took Cortez to a different county, putting the living legend on tour across the borderlands, stirring up hope for justice. Mexicans monitored the trial. They wrote, they read, they donated, they sang, imagining the day when a poor Mexican would win a fight against a more powerful foe. By January 1904, when Ricardo Flores Magón and the other rebel writers arrived in Laredo, Cortez had won every case but one, and Mexicans in the Brown Belt were eager to seize justice for one of their own.

CHAPTER 7

Send the Secret Police

A NTONIO LOMELÍ WAS PORFIRIO DÍAZ'S EYES AND EARS IN Laredo. As the consular representative for the Mexican government, it was his job to keep watch over Mexican citizens and interests in the region. On the morning of January 16, 1904, Lomelí was alarmed to discover that Ricardo Flores Magón and his friends had slipped into town when he read an interview given by Camilo Arriaga to the *Laredo Times* announcing their arrival: "Our clubs [in Mexico] where we spoke to the people have been broken up and our orators have been cast into prison. Our newspaper properties have been destroyed by the soldiery and the press of Mexico is now effectually gagged." According to Arriaga, the editors had relocated to Laredo to "continue our work in behalf of the liberties of our people."[1]

Lomelí rushed to the local Western Union office and sent a coded telegram to his boss, Ignacio Mariscal, Mexico's venerable secretary of foreign relations. "Mexican journalists Ricardo and Enrique Flores Magón, Camilo Arriaga, and Juan Sarabia arrived here with the objective, they say, of establishing in various American border communities opposition papers to promote their revolutionary propaganda." He neglected to note the arrival of the two women, Juana Belén Gutiérrez de Mendoza and Elisa Acuña. Regardless, Lomelí knew he needed help. "Send the secret police," he begged.[2]

President Díaz already had a man on the job. The local district attorney, John Valis, a.k.a. Juan A. Valls, was an old friend of his. Back in

1893, Díaz had asked Valis to head the Mexican consulate in Browns-ville. Díaz's consulates were little more than business offices, largely dedicated to securing U.S. investments in Mexico, and he liked to appoint U.S. citizens to head those offices and serve as pitchmen. Valis declined the Brownsville job and its "handsome salary" but joined the president's payroll, regularly providing "important and friendly ser-vice" along the border. In time, the two became friends.[3]

When the journalists from Mexico City arrived in Laredo talking about revolt, Valis was quick to respond. "I've been watching them since they arrived here," he wrote in a personal letter to Díaz. "I have been working against them and putting every possible obstacle in their way." Valis advised local Mexicans not to collaborate with the newcomers— advice that would have seemed like a threat coming from the local district attorney and a close friend of President Díaz. "You can know that I will not rest until these guys leave Laredo," Valis assured Díaz.[4] Díaz returned a short note of appreciation, expressing full confidence in Valis's ability to secure *"un seguro resultado"* (a secure result).[5]

The rebel journalists pressed on, throwing their efforts into raising enough money to relaunch *Regeneración*. As Enrique Flores Magón put it, they saved money for "paper, envelopes, and stamps" by putting themselves on a "diet of wild herbs and vegetables," which they picked around town.[6] On January 25, Lomelí reported that they were "writing day and night, carrying on a very extensive correspondence with people in Mexico and the United States [and preparing] a public manifesto, which will undoubtedly be political in nature and oppositional to our government, to be released on February 5."[7] Lomelí did not say how he had collected this information, but his intel was solid. The writers were planning the fourth Liberal Conference, to be held as a public event in downtown Laredo on February 5, 1904, Mexican Constitution Day.

The celebration began with a parade winding through the streets toward the main plaza, where the journalists hosted a marching band and festival. That evening, on the top floor of City Hall, they held a mass meeting attended by, in the words of an informant sent by Lomelí, *"una gran aglomeración de gente"* (a huge conglomeration of people).[8]

*Secretary of
Foreign Affairs
Ignacio Mariscal.*

The crowd listened to speeches against President Díaz, giving "enthusiastic applause [and] shouts."[9] Paulino Martínez delivered a rousing tirade while Ricardo and Enrique Flores Magón and Camilo Arriaga sat silently on stage beneath an altar to Benito Juárez, playing, in the words of the informant, "the role of victims of tyranny." Santiago de la Hoz and Juan Sarabia closed the evening with poems.[10] The meeting, which had been planned in Sara Estela Ramírez's home, was a success.

Lomelí was not impressed. As he explained in a telegram to Secretary Mariscal, the local Mexican population was "ignorant and turbulent . . . among them one always finds all kinds of support for movements oppositional to our government." Lomelí doubted that the journalists could mount any meaningful revolt among "ignorant" Mexicans of the borderlands, advising that "this little cabal merits only observation and vigilance, to see what happens and develops."[11] Secretary Mariscal disagreed.

Ignacio Mariscal had served as Mexico's secretary of foreign relations since 1885, having previously served as a congressman, a delegate to the Constitutional Congress of 1857, and a diplomat, always siding with the Liberals. Mariscal thrived in the world of diplomacy. He had a tactical mind and he was a confident, persuasive public speaker, able to mold any message to any audience. When the French invaded Mexico in 1862, President Juárez sent Mariscal to the United States to negotiate support for his administration. Mariscal quickly learned English and, once the Civil War had ended, he won U.S. recognition of the Juárez administration as well as shiploads of guns, dynamite, and everything Juárez's Liberal forces needed to drive Napoleon's troops out of Mexico.[12]

Decades of experience had taught Mariscal that a handful of rebels in the borderlands could upend the entire country. Benito Juárez had fought the Conservatives from his headquarters in New Orleans. Díaz had plotted coups from Brownsville. The Yaqui routinely attacked Mexican forces in Hiakim, then fled to sanctuary north of the border only to return and attack again. From exile in the United States, Teresita, the Saint of Cabora, inspired several of those attacks, including a deadly raid on the Mexican customs house in Nogales, Sonora, in 1896. Also during the 1890s, a journalist named Catarino Garza had led several raids against the Díaz regime from south Texas.[13] And now the rebel writers from Mexico City had arrived in Laredo, vowing to destroy the regime. Mariscal ordered a more proactive course.

On February 16, 1904, Mariscal instructed the Mexican ambassador in Washington, DC, to immediately inform the U.S. secretary of state that the journalists in Laredo were committing "punishable acts" by attempting to "disrupt public order in Mexico." Mariscal requested that federal authorities intervene as soon as possible to "impede their machinations," and perhaps even have them arrested.[14]

The secretary of state did not respond. At the time, federal authorities were unconcerned by a few Mexican agitators in the borderlands and unwilling to commit resources to shutting them down. Mariscal would have to manage the situation on his own.

The rebel journalists were building their network and growing more popular by the day.[15] The Idar family in Laredo supported the relaunch of *Regeneración*. So did Pablo Cruz in San Antonio, along with the editors of many of the Spanish-language newspapers in the region. People arrived from across Texas to meet with them, especially Ricardo Flores Magón. A Mexican American ranch owner named Aniceto Pizaña, in the Brownsville area, became a steady supporter.[16] But the writers themselves were divided by an increasingly rancorous dispute between Ricardo Flores Magón and Camilo Arriaga.

Arriaga was the standard-bearer of Liberal dissent in Mexico. Flores Magón was the movement's brash upstart. There had been tension between them since they first met, when Flores Magón stood in Arriaga's library, pointed to a copy of the 1857 Mexican constitution which Arriaga's uncle had drafted, and declared it a dead document. In 1903, the two men had clashed over tactics when Arriaga shot down the idea that someone from their group—likely, Flores Magón—should run against Díaz in the upcoming presidential election. In Laredo, the two men argued fiercely over leadership. It was a power struggle. Each saw himself as the head of the movement. They differed on politics, too, with Flores Magón the more militant of the two. By March 1904, their differences had reached breaking point.[17]

Sara Estela Ramírez tried to intervene, pleading with Flores Magón to make peace with Arriaga. "I have been sad and overwhelmed, Ricardo, with such mutual antagonism. I will tell you frankly that I am disappointed with everything, with absolutely everything. . . . I thought that there was unity and true fraternity in our group; I thought that there was in it a natural and exquisite harmony. . . . Each disappointment leaves a painful mark in my soul and—can you believe it?—there was even a moment in which I regretted participating in this intimate struggle with insufficient energy to fight against the perils that we set against ourselves."[18] She cautioned Flores Magón, who could be ruthless with his words in both political and personal fights, to soften his tone and find compromise. "I don't want to analyze the causes of your quarrels with Camilito. I believe you both are right and both are to blame," she wrote. But Flores Magón, a man who rejected compromise in politics, also refused concession in friendship, leaving Ramírez to despair, "We don't know how to forgive one another's shortcomings, to help each other out like true brothers. We criticize each other and tear ourselves apart instead of inspiring one another and mending our fences."[19]

By the end of March 1904, Arriaga had moved to San Antonio. Ramírez, Elisa Acuña, and Juana Belén Gutiérrez de Mendoza (with her young daughters in tow) joined him.[20] In San Antonio, the women published *La Corregidora* and restarted *Vesper*. When the U.S. Postal Service denied them bulk mailing privileges, Gutiérrez de Mendoza established a new paper, *La Protesta Nacional*, which she had postmarked from Saltillo, Mexico, to confuse U.S. and Mexican authorities.[21] Hoping to remain friends with Flores Magón, Ramírez reached out to him upon their departure for San Antonio. "I don't believe that my decision, absolutely spontaneous, will make me deserving of your enmity," she wrote. She was wrong. Historians have uncovered no record of Flores Magón replying to Ramírez's letter. When she died a few years later, in August 1910, on the cusp of the Mexican Revolution, a friend noted at her funeral that she had "found herself abandoned by her friends and struggled with this rejection."[22] Flores Magón remained in Laredo, plotting revolt. His brother Enrique, Juan and Manuel Sarabia, and Santiago de la Hoz stayed there with him.

In Laredo, the rebel writers knew that Lomelí, Valis, and other informants were attending rallies, following them to the post office, and reporting their movements to Díaz. Enrique Flores Magón noticed Mexican and U.S. police officers following him around town, hiding behind trees.[23] They ignored the surveillance until March 22, 1904, when Santiago de la Hoz drowned while bathing in the Rio Grande. As Ricardo Flores Magón would later write, young de la Hoz had "succumbed silently, drowned by the traitorous embrace of the murky murderous waters."[24] Brokenhearted by the sudden death of their "young fighter" and worried about police surveillance in Laredo, the remaining dissidents left town.[25]

They spent the next few months barnstorming the Brown Belt to build support for *Regeneración*.[26] Juan Sarabia was a powerful orator, and Ricardo Flores Magón was already notorious. During the tour, the last trial of Gregorio Cortez came to a close. In González County, a jury found him guilty in the murder of Sheriff Glover and sentenced him to life in prison. In the end, Cortez had lost, and Mexicans across the Texas borderlands were disappointed. Yet the saga had taught Mexicans in south Texas that they could fight back against posses, *rinches*, and lynch mobs, and stay alive. They did not give up. They still sang "The Ballad of Gregorio Cortez."[27] They donated their extra nickels and pennies to the journalists' cause.

The journalists raised $800, but they remained short of cash. Not only did they need enough funds to rent an office, buy a printing press, acquire ink and paper, and begin selling issues before they could seek the security of subscriptions, but the man to whom they entrusted their $800, to rent them an office, spent the money on his girlfriend. They were back to square one. Arriaga, despite his disagreements with Flores Magón, offered to help by asking his friend Francisco Madero for a donation on behalf of *Regeneración*. Madero sent $2,000 (approximately $50,000 in today's dollars).[28] In a letter to Flores Magón, Madero explained that he had always found the ideas expressed in *Regeneración* to be "congenial" to his own, and that he saw *Regeneración* as an important tool to advance the "regeneration of the Fatherland by arousing Mexicans in noble indignation against their tyrants."[29]

Madero's family had made a fortune during the U.S. Civil War, when Union forces closed southern ports, forcing Confederate cotton dealers to move their merchandise through Mexico. The Maderos facilitated the trade and invested their profits in buying up mines and haciendas in Mexico. With their 7 million acres of land, the Madero holdings included vineyards, factories, mills, and a string of haciendas that harvested everything from cotton to guayule (rubber) for export. Madero's father alone was worth more than $20 million ($529 million in 2021 dollars).[30] Madero himself had personal assets of more than $500,000 pesos.[31]

Francisco Madero was the eldest son and highly educated, having attended a Jesuit college as a child before studying in France and the United States. At UC Berkeley, he learned modern agricultural tech-

Francisco I. Madero.

niques and absorbed the Progressive Era's teachings about ameliorating social problems such as poverty. He returned home eager to modernize his family's business operations.[32] He brought new technology to Madero-owned cotton farms and paid higher wages and provided better housing for his workers than most of his competitors. A believer in homeopathy, Madero visited the homes of his workers to dispense herbs, tinctures, and other natural medicines. But it was his faith that took him into politics.

A spiritist, Madero believed that death was no more than a veil beyond which human eyes cannot see. He believed that human beings are immortal spirits temporarily inhabiting physical bodies in order to attain higher levels of intellectual achievement and moral improvement. Communicating with the dead guided him in key decisions in his life. Beginning in 1901, he claimed to receive daily visits from his brother Raúl, who had died in a fire at the age of four. Raúl advised Madero, he said, to practice self-denial and mortification of the flesh. Soon after, Madero became a vegetarian and a teetotaler. In 1903, when General Bernardo Reyes brutally crushed the Liberal protest in Monterrey, Raúl told Madero to enter politics. Madero established a club, Club Benito Juárez, to discuss politics with his friends. He also began to compete for local and state offices. Running without Díaz's blessing, he lost every election. In 1905, he ran for governor of the state of Coahuila and lost, again.[33] But his investment in the rebel journalists in Texas was paying off. With Madero's $2,000 and funds collected from Mexicans across south Texas, they successfully relaunched *Regeneración* from San Antonio.

CHAPTER 8

We Return to the Fight

S AN ANTONIO WAS A SEGREGATED TOWN. PROPERTY DEEDS prohibited Black and Mexican residents from living in white neighborhoods.[1] Black and Mexican children attended separate and underfunded schools. They also routinely lacked access to safe, clean, and secure housing. Many Mexican immigrants rented rooms in *corrales*, long warrens of one-room stalls, for which landlords charged 90 cents per week without a stove and $1.25 per week with a stove. At a time when Mexican farmworkers in Texas earned just 55 cents per day, the rent was too high, forcing many to build their own *jacales*, small huts made of earth and brush.[2]

But Mexicans in San Antonio also thrived in an ecosystem of their own, residing in a segregated enclave called Laredito. In Laredito, residents built small businesses that catered to their neighbors. Shoemakers, bakers, tailors, and butchers opened small shops. Women pushed food carts down alleyways and along the unpaved streets, selling tamales and *dulces* (candies). Paper boys hustled Laredito's four Spanish-language newspapers: *El Regidor, El Cronista Mexicano, El Latigo, La Fe Católica*, and *El Noticioso*.[3] Established Mexican American families retained a foothold in the middle, professional, and political classes.[4] And residents had recently landed a major blow against Juan Crow.

In May 1896, an immigrant named Ricardo Rodríguez walked into the federal courthouse in San Antonio to submit his application for naturalization. When the desk clerk asked him why he wanted to become a U.S. citizen, Rodríguez simply answered, "Because he lived here."[5] Before the desk worker could process the paperwork, two lawyers stepped forward to intervene, arguing that Rodríguez was racially ineligible to naturalize. They immediately filed a federal lawsuit designed to block Ricardo Rodríguez and, by extension, all Mexican nationals from becoming U.S. citizens. What followed was one of the most significant—but little known—court cases in U.S. history, *In re Rodríguez*, marking a watershed moment in the history of race and citizenship in the United States.[6]

In re Rodríguez began long before Ricardo Rodríguez tried to submit his application. Since the end of the Mexican–American War, white settlers in the American West had tried to limit the citizenship rights of Mexican Americans. As elsewhere, poll taxes and white primaries were popular disenfranchisement tactics. But Mexican Americans remained a powerful voting bloc in the Brown Belt, where an established political machine regularly turned out voters for the Democratic Party. The two lawyers who challenged Rodríguez's naturalization claim were Populists frustrated by this Democratic advantage. By the time they submitted their case, T. J. McGinn and Jack Evans had spent years trying to categorically disenfranchise all Mexican American voters, asserting that the U.S. Constitution did not guarantee the right to vote to all persons in the United States. They had a point. Across the United States, a patchwork of race, indigeneity, and gender restrictions limited the right to vote. As McGinn once asked an audience, if "a Mongolian is not a 'person'; an Indian is not a 'person'; a woman is not a 'person'; is an Aztec a 'person,' from the suffrage standpoint?"[7] Although his exclusionary logic was popular among whites in the region, the Democratic machine opposed his proposal and it subsequently failed.

In 1896, McGinn and Evans tried a new tack: suppressing the Mexican American vote by challenging the right of Mexican immigrants to become U.S. citizens. The Naturalization Act of 1790 had restricted the right to naturalize to "free white men." After the Civil War, the Fourteenth Amendment allowed formerly enslaved persons to become

U.S. citizens by extending the right to citizenship to persons of African descent. Therefore, by the 1870s, an immigrant had to be white or of African descent to become a U.S. citizen. In 1878, the U.S. Supreme Court ruled that Chinese immigrants were ineligible for naturalization. In 1880, a circuit court ruled that persons of mixed Indigenous and white parentage were also ineligible for naturalization. By the end of the nineteenth century, the road to U.S. citizenship had Black and white lanes only. Mexicans were neither.[8]

Sitting in the lobby of the federal courthouse in San Antonio in May 1896, McGinn and Evans waited to file a case to test the limits of the Fourteenth Amendment. When Ricardo Rodríguez arrived, they approached the desk clerk and asserted that Rodríguez, whom the press later described as a "peon type, very dark," was neither "a white person . . . nor of African descent, and is therefore not capable of becoming an American citizen."[9]

Led by the outspoken journalist Pablo Cruz, San Antonio's Mexican American residents funded a legal team to defend Rodríguez and, by extension, the right of all Mexican immigrants to become U.S. citizens. In the Treaty of Guadalupe Hidalgo, which ended the Mexican–American War, the United States government agreed to make citizens of all Mexicans living in the ceded territories. Rodríguez's lawyer argued that the treaty had set an inviolable precedent, holding open a special door to naturalization for persons of Mexican descent. On May 3, 1897, a federal judge agreed, ruling that the United States was treaty-bound to honor Mexican eligibility for U.S. citizenship. Won by Mexican Americans in San Antonio, most of whom were poor and living in a segregated area of town, *In re Rodríguez* transformed the story of race and citizenship in the United States. By 1952, when Congress ended racial barriers to naturalization, more than a million Mexican immigrants had entered the United States with the right to naturalize.

When Ricardo and Enrique Flores Magón and Juan and Manuel Sarabia arrived in San Antonio, they entered a community emboldened by the *In re Rodríguez* victory. Librado Rivera soon joined them. They rented a small house on the outskirts of Laredito and sustained themselves on black coffee and bread while working at a small wood table, using old soap boxes for chairs.[10] They were so broke that when Ricardo's good suit began to show the wear and tear of the constant work and travel, he covered the seat of his pants with patches. Embarrassed, he backed across rooms and stages rather than turn and expose his tattered slacks.[11] Regardless, the journalists were making progress.

Pablo Cruz likely welcomed them to town. Cruz's family owned several businesses in Laredito, including three newspapers. He made *El Regidor* the political organ and distributed it across the border region.[12] Cruz used the pages of *El Regidor* to blast the Díaz regime, especially its censorship of the press.[13] As he once editorialized, "[Díaz] fears the complete liberty the independent press could possess because they'll judge the acts of his administration."[14] Those acts, he wrote, included "extend[ing] concessions of great quantity to foreigners . . . [who] like a leech . . . will suck the last drop of blood from the nation."[15] He also republished articles from *Regeneración*. When the journal's infamous editors arrived in San Antonio, he built their network by helping to arrange for Ricardo Flores Magón and Juan Sarabia to speak at the city's 1904 Mexican Independence Day festival.[16]

Mexican Independence Day honors the day, September 16, 1810, when Father Manuel Hidalgo ignited the Mexican War of Independence. During the 1890s, as Díaz's rule turned perpetual, he and his followers pushed the festivities back to begin on September 15, Díaz's birthday, yoking the birth of the nation to the birth of its dictator. On September 15, a parade of marching bands and flower-laden carriages would flow down the main streets of Mexico City as President Díaz greeted a long line of supporters at the National Palace. (Except for Arnulfo Arroyo, who, on September 15, 1897, waited in line only to try to stab the president. Arroyo was murdered that night in his jail cell.) At 11 pm, Díaz, dressed in full general's regalia, would step onto the balcony and belt out "el Grito de Dolores," Hidalgo's battle cry.[17] For the next two days, every city in Mexico held rallies, marches, concerts, galas, firework shows, all orchestrated to celebrate Mexico's independence and its dictator.

As Mexicans migrated to the United States, they carried the festival with them, holding Mexican Independence Day celebrations in *colonias* across the southwestern United States. In San Antonio, Pablo Cruz led the organizing committee. He tended to use the event to poke at the president's rule.

The 1904 festival began on the evening of September 15, the president's birthday, with a torchlight procession from City Hall to San Pedro Springs Park. A brass band led the way through the streets, footpaths, and across short bridges to a large wooden stage. There, Cruz sat with members of the organizing committee, the local Mexican consul, Enrique Ornelas, and Ricardo Flores Magón. The band played the Mexican national anthem. Then, with hundreds of Laredito residents looking on and Consul Ornelas sitting just a few feet away, Flores Magón walked to center stage to speak on the meaning of independence in Mexico. No one recorded the speech, but we can imagine that, after months of barnstorming across south Texas, he delivered a refined yet spirited address, attacking the Díaz administration for its corruption of Liberal ideals. The next night, after another day of parades and bands, hundreds more showed up at the park, and it was Juan Sarabia's turn to take the stage. Again, no one recorded the speech. By 1904, Sarabia had been delivering anti-Díaz addresses and poems for years, and he likely stirred the crowd. Pablo Cruz had thus given the two exiles a significant platform to address the Mexican American community in San Antonio, and to make their case against Díaz.[18]

Consul Ornelas did not panic. He had been raised in San Antonio by his older brother, Dr. Plutarco Ornelas, who served as the Mexican consul in San Antonio for more than two decades. Ornelas grew up in the consulate and worked for many years at his brother's side. When Plutarco Ornelas was promoted to a post in San Francisco, Enrique was the obvious choice to succeed him. The train had hardly left the station when Enrique Ornelas began holding meetings with local power-brokers, drumming up new investments in Mexico.[19] Ornelas did not hesitate to put the journalists under surveillance, and when they held a rally a few weeks later, on October 18, 1904, Ornelas sent a detailed report to Secretary Mariscal of the mounting threat in San Antonio.

As reported to Ornelas by an informant, the rally was held at a Masonic hall and attended by more than 1,000 people. Local dissidents and the Mexico City journalists gave a series of animated speeches. Fearing a riot, the police stepped in whenever the chants and ovations seemed too fevered to be contained. When Ricardo Flores Magón spoke, naming Díaz "a coward, a traitor, a thief, a murderer, a bandit, a tyrant," the crowd, reported the informant, sprang into a stomping, roaring standing ovation, the "most excited" of the evening.[20]

Upon reading this report, Mariscal advised Manuel de Aspíroz, the Mexican ambassador in Washington, DC, that the journalists were "revolutionaries" who should be punished for "betraying the interests of their country . . . as soon as our authorities can find a way to do so."[21] Indeed, continued Mariscal, "I have reason to believe that they have already committed or will commit some punishable crime in the United States . . . please communicate these details to the Governor of Texas, so that he can prevent any harm that could come to the Mexican government by the machinations of these persons."[22] Aspíroz agreed, asking Mariscal to forward any further details. Mariscal instructed Ornelas to send all updates directly to the ambassador.

On November 5, 1904, the first issue of *Regeneración* from north of the border was published. The rebel journalists pulled no punches. "We return to the fight, as we always do after a blow," they wrote on the front page. "Tyranny has thrown us out of our country, forcing us to seek liberty on foreign soil . . . [but] our program remains the same. We will attack General Díaz . . . because he personifies a tyranny most hateful, most brutal, most fated in the history of our nation."[23] They published articles eviscerating Díaz, the governors of Nuevo León and Hidalgo, and consuls in the United States, castigating consular officials

Librado Rivera and Enrique Flores Magón in the
Regeneración *office in San Antonio, Texas.*

as "inept and indolent" for failing to protect Mexicans in the United States from violence and wage theft.[24] Ornelas mailed a copy of the issue to Ambassador Aspíroz.

The next week, on November 12, 1904, the journalists focused their criticisms on the new vice president, Ramón Corral, whom they said suffered from "incorrigible cretinism."[25] As governor of Sonora, Corral had played a leading role in the Yaqui War, orchestrating the capture and execution of Cajeme and overseeing the deportations to the Yucatán. Corral had a disagreeable personality, making him generally disliked across Mexico, which, historians say, is precisely why Porfirio Díaz picked him to be vice president.[26] No one would oust Díaz while Corral was heir to the throne. But the journalists went after both the president and his heir, threatening a clean sweep of the regime. Again Consul Ornelas mailed the issue to Ambassador Aspíroz.

On November 19, the third issue of *Regeneración* from San Antonio ran a headline article entitled "Porfirio Díaz Is Not the Nation." "Tyrants have always tried to appear divine," began the article, which challenged Díaz's efforts to depict his rule as natural, inevitable, and sacred, in, for example, the recent Independence Day festivals. "By virtue of their [divinity]," it continued, "despots have never allowed, nor do they allow themselves [nor their rule] to be discussed," because when rule is divine any revolt against the man is a revolt against the nation and against the divine, too. The editors cut through the illusion, arguing that "the nation cannot be a man like Díaz, who scourges, extorts, [who is so] violent, oppressive." Díaz, they said, might call them "bad Mexicans" for challenging his rule, but in fact, they wrote, they were patriots and Díaz was a traitor to the nation.[27]

It was not long before an armed man broke into the *Regeneración* office and attempted to stab Ricardo Flores Magón in the back. Enrique tackled the man. They rolled and grappled into the street, where police broke up the fight. Believing that Díaz had sent the man, the rebel writers packed up and left town. Two months later, they were publishing *Regeneración* from St. Louis, Missouri.[28]

CHAPTER 9

What I Believe

W HY THE MEXICO CITY JOURNALISTS CHOSE ST. LOUIS
is not known. Few Mexicans lived in the city, and the year
before they arrived St. Louis had hosted a world's fair that amounted to
a national tribute to white supremacy and U.S. imperialism. Nineteen
million spectators visited the fair, touring an "ivory city" with anthro-
pological exhibits on communities displaced or dominated by U.S.
territorial expansion. The exhibits described these cultures as "back-
ward," "conquered," "unfit," and "disappearing." One of the most popular exhibits was the Apache Village, where young Apache men and
women were confined to a boarding school while Geronimo, the once
fearsome warrior, posed for souvenir photos with tourists for a nickel.[1]
Each photo was a trophy of white settler conquest in the American
West. Not far away, twenty "purchased" Africans were commanded to
dance and sing for passersby. One of them, a young man named Ota
Benga, was later transferred to the Bronx Zoo where Madison Grant,
the popular Anglo-American eugenicist later praised by Adolf Hitler,
kept him on display in a cage. The most visited exhibit was the Phil-
ippine Reservation, which held one thousand Filipinos imported from
the newest U.S. territory. Throughout the fair, which historian Walter
Johnson describes as the "largest human zoo in world history," ambu-
lances stood by to carry away overheated spectators who fainted during
the white imperial bash.[2] When Ricardo Flores Magón and his friends
arrived, St. Louis was still awash in the fair's afterglow.

Antonio I. Villarreal. Mugshot taken at El Paso County Jail in 1906.

Slipping into town in February 1905, the journalists rented a small apartment where they were soon joined by the Villarreal family from Nuevo León. Sisters Teresa and Andrea Villarreal were militant liberals and strong public speakers. They would become some of the movement's most public figures, drumming up press and giving speeches across the United States. Their brother Antonio, a former literature professor, was still rebuilding his life after a four-year prison stint in Mexico. In 1901, he had killed a man in a duel, which, some said, was occasioned by a literary dispute. Duels were rarely prosecuted in Mexico at the time, but Villarreal was an active member of the local Liberal Party and had been writing articles against the Díaz regime. He was arrested, prosecuted, and imprisoned for murder. When released, the Villarreal siblings and their father, Próspero, moved north to join the Liberal editors in exile.[3]

The local Mexican consulate seemed not to notice the Mexican exiles' arrival, allowing them time to write without interference. As usual, Ricardo Flores Magón led the initiative, as the director of *Regeneración*. Juan Sarabia was the editor-in-chief and Enrique Flores Magón was the manager. Camilo Arriaga, Librado Rivera, Manuel Sarabia, and others wrote articles, provided office support, collected the mail, and found day jobs to keep the paper afloat.

In his free time, Juan Sarabia liked to go to the circus. Manuel Sarabia liked to meet women. So did Antonio Villarreal, who liked to crack jokes, but only when Ricardo Flores Magón was out of earshot. Rivera, who brought his wife and two young children to St. Louis, spent time with his family. Ricardo Flores Magón just worked. Veins throbbed on his furrowed brow as he pounded out article after article on the typewriter, smoking cigarette after cigarette. According to a spy who would soon infiltrate the operation, all of the exiles in St. Louis were "fanatic," "resolute," and "good journalists," but Flores Magón was the "most dangerous" of them all and "capable of anything." As the spy warned, Flores Magón was *"el alma de todo,"* by which he meant "the soul of the revolution," and he wrote as if he "had no time to lose," with every thought on Mexico, "suffering Mexico." When his handler asked, "And if Ricardo Flores Magón was to be arrested and put in prison for many years, what would happen?," the spy replied, "It would all end."[4]

On February 25, the journalists released the next issue of *Regeneración*, blasting Díaz, "the relentless tyrant," for chasing them so far from home. As usual, they vowed to continue their fight.[5]

Flores Magón made time for one kind of pleasure in St. Louis: radical politics. Giving the lie to the recent world's fair's veneer of white unity, the white working class in St. Louis routinely launched strikes against business owners. The Socialist Party of America had a chapter in every ward in St. Louis. Eugene V. Debs, the fiery labor organizer who repeatedly ran for president on the Socialist ticket, often spoke in the city. And Emma Goldman, the "Anarchist Queen," also regularly visited St. Louis, which the internationally renowned Spanish anarchist Florencio Bazora called home. Flores Magón dove into the St. Louis scene, becoming friends with Goldman and Bazora.[6]

There is no record of the conversations between Emma Goldman and Ricardo Flores Magón in these years, but the essay Goldman soon published, "What I Believe" (1908), outlining her views on anarchism, provides a glimpse into their discussions.

In "What I Believe," Goldman described anarchism as a political philosophy dedicated to the pursuit of absolute individual liberty. She identified anarchism as "a process rather than a finality. Finalities are for gods and governments, not for the human intellect." The key principles of anarchism, according to Goldman, were the abolition of private property, the state, the church, and militarism. She also defended free speech as a sacred human right. "I believe that free speech and press mean that I may say and write what I please. This right, when regulated by constitutional provisions, legislative enactments, almighty decisions of the Postmaster General or the policeman's club, becomes a farce," she wrote. And she regarded anarchism as the "only philosophy of peace, the only theory of the social relationship that values human life above everything else," arguing that it was the organized violence of the state that drove some anarchists to use violent means. Most anarchists at the turn of the century would have agreed with Goldman on these points. But, unlike most of her fellow travelers, Goldman applied anarchist theory to sexuality and gender relations, rebuking heteronormativity and the institution of marriage. "Marriage," she wrote, "is often an economic arrangement purely, furnishing the woman with a lifelong insurance policy and the man with a perpetuator of his kind or a pretty toy. That is, marriage, or the training thereto, prepares the woman for the life of a parasite, a dependent, helpless servant, while it furnishes the man the right of a chattel mortgage over a human life."[7] Goldman understood that she was living in a nation hostile to her philosophy. In 1903, Congress had banned anarchists from immigrating to the United States. Goldman published "What I Believe" in order to speak her truth, even if it put her at risk of deportation.

It is likely that Emma Goldman discussed her anarcho-feminist philosophy with Ricardo Flores Magón when they met in St. Louis, and that their conversations affirmed or advanced Flores Magón's own journey toward anarchism.[8] He, too, would reject marriage as an oppressive institution that "placed the wife under the custody of the husband."[9] And he would urge women to join the revolution as armed combatants. "She does not come with roses or caresses; she comes with an axe and a torch," he published in November 1910, on the eve of the Mexican Revolution.[10] Yet, as the work of the historian Gabriela González and the theorist Emma Pérez has made clear, Flores Magón's radicalism did not challenge traditional gender hierarchies.[11] Despite years of working with anarcho-feminists ranging from Juana Belén Gutiérrez de Mendoza to Emma Goldman, Flores Magón and his circle of male friends tended to relegate revolutionary women to secondary roles.[12] "Your duty is to help man," explained the men in "A La Mujer," an article addressed specifically to revolutionary women.[13] "To be there to encourage him when he vacillates; to stand by his side when he suffers; to lighten his sorrow; to laugh and to sing with him when victory smiles."[14]

Still, it would be years before Flores Magón publicly detailed his own political philosophy, leaving historians to debate what he believed, and when, as he made the shift from militant liberalism to anarchism. What the archive does make clear is that, as early as 1905 in St. Louis, his circle of friends began to note his increasingly radical talk. If disputes over leadership had caused tension back in Laredo, Flores Magón's drift toward anarchism opened a rift within the group. Juan Sarabia, Manuel Sarabia, and Camilo Arriaga were socialists—they rejected capitalism but embraced the state. In fact, they imagined the state as the primary instrument for dismantling capitalism and managing a shared economy. But Flores Magón spoke more and more in anarchist terms. "There is not a single government that can benefit the people against the interests of the bourgeoisie," he wrote in a private note to his brother Enrique.[15] Camilo Arriaga was uncomfortable with the new direction in Flores Magón's thinking. The two men had argued for years over tactics and leadership. Now, in St. Louis, they battled over goals. Should they seek to replace the Díaz regime (socialism), or dismantle the state altogether (anarchism)? With Flores Magón beginning to demand the total abolition of capitalism and the state and Arriaga insisting on a more moderate path, their differences became irreconcilable.

Seeking compromise, Arriaga and Juan Sarabia asked Flores Magón

to "tone down" his views when writing for *Regeneración*.[16] He agreed
to do so, but only because he believed he could build a broader base
of support for anarchist principles without explicitly naming them as
such. "We [will] continue to call ourselves liberal in the course of the
revolution, but in reality we will spread anarchy and carry out anarchic
acts," he privately explained to a friend and Enrique, who, ultimately,
followed his brother into anarchist politics.[17]

Flores Magón kept his promise. Between 1905 and 1911, the articles
he selected to appear in *Regeneración* stuck to the socialist creed. On
the pages of *Regeneración*, the journalists demanded labor rights: "It
is perfectly just, that the worker demands for his labor any price that
seems reasonable to him, and that he refuses to serve anyone who does
not pay him that which he considers himself entitled."[18] They harshly
criticized organized religion as an instrument of oppression: "Heaven is
a childish invention of all those who have an interest in humanity being
exploited and oppressed. Hoping to go to heaven, stupid crowds allow
tyranny and mistreatment, because, according to the friars, he who suffers most has a better right to have the heavenly doors opened to him."[19]
And they besieged capitalism, even raising the issue of land redistribution. But the articles said nothing about the abolition of private property or dismantling the state. Moreover, the articles routinely attempted
to mobilize national pride to bring about economic reforms—an idea
that would be anathema to any committed anarchist. As Flores Magón
editorialized in September 1905, "The absurd division of territory that
exists in Mexico [creates] the fact that a few men are owners of the
land, while millions of people lack not only a patch of land to cultivate
or a plot to build a *jacal* [hut]." The solution, he suggested, would not
require the abolition of the state. "A just division of land," he explained,
was necessary to "make our country strong because its citizens would
be happy, because everyone would enjoy their rights as citizens, and we
would not suffer sadness or desperation."[20]

Yet, even as Flores Magón toed the line, the debate between socialism and anarchism widened the rift between him and Arriaga. By
May 1905, Arriaga left St. Louis. Or, as Flores Magón put it in a letter

to his brother Jesús, *"Camilo no está con nosotros"* (Camilo is not with us).[21] This time, everyone in St. Louis stayed with Flores Magón, even though several shared Arriaga's concerns about his anarchist turn.

Having nearly exhausted his inheritance, Arriaga moved back to San Antonio, where, in the words of historical anthropologist Claudio Lomnitz, he "drift[ed] . . . in an aimless exile. Penniless, depressed and dispirited."[22] Arriaga would later return to Mexico and, ultimately, join Juana Belén Gutiérrez de Mendoza and others in ousting Díaz and rebuilding Mexico, but, for now, he was lost and probably a bit stunned by his removal from the helm of the Liberal movement. Flores Magón threw salt on the wound, announcing Arriaga's departure from the group with a blistering article in *Regeneración*. He blamed the split on Arriaga, whom he described as wasting the group's "meager resources," making "extraordinary purchases" and refusing to live the frugal life of a revolutionary in exile, and branded him "a traitor to the cause."[23] But exiling and disparaging Arriaga did not thin the ideological lines beginning to splinter the group, which would go on to split into socialist and anarchist factions. In time, Flores Magón would lash out at all who refused to follow him on the road to anarchism.

In St. Louis, the Flores Magón brothers, along with Librado Rivera, Juan Sarabia, Manuel Sarabia, and the Villarreal family, cranked out weekly issues of *Regeneración* to nearly 20,000 subscribers. The Díaz regime soon stepped up its efforts to stop them. By September 1905, Mexican authorities had successfully convinced the U.S. Postal Service to deny second-class postal privileges to *Regeneración*, forcing the rebel writers to pay full freight to distribute their journal in Mexico. The costs were prohibitively high for a small newspaper dependent upon subscriptions from workers and *campesinos*. They responded by smuggling *Regeneración* into Mexico, shipping it in hollowed-out Sears canisters and recruiting migrant workers as couriers. Couriers ran many risks in the process. *Rurales*, it was said, arrested Mexicans for uttering the name "Magón" anywhere south of the border.[24] *Regeneración*, after all, was the only paper that dared to name the Díaz regime a dictatorship. Despite the danger, one migrant worker stuffed copies of *Regeneración* beneath his shirt and distributed it on his travels because, as he put it, Ricardo's words "lit a dream within him that could not be extinguished."[25]

The journalists also established a political party, the Partido Liberal Mexicano (PLM). The PLM's stated objective was to reestablish democracy in Mexico by challenging Porfirio Díaz in the 1910 presidential election. The journalists in St. Louis comprised the PLM's leadership team: La Junta Organizadora del PLM. Ricardo Flores Magón was the president. Juan Sarabia was vice president. Antonio Villarreal, secretary. Enrique Flores Magón, treasurer. Librado Rivera and Manuel Sarabia were *vocales*, which the historian W. Dirk Raat translates as "voting board members." Together, they vowed to lead a movement to remove Díaz from power *"por todos medios"*—by any means necessary.[26]

Within two weeks of establishing the PLM in St. Louis, the local Mexican consul, Miguel E. Diebold, had convinced the St. Louis County sheriff to raid the office of *Regeneración*. With Diebold looking on, the sheriff and at least two deputies arrested Juan Sarabia and Ricardo and Enrique Flores Magón on a charge of defamation and libel for an article they had printed about Manuel Esperón y de la Flor, an old friend of the president's and a *jefe político* in Oaxaca. According to the article, Esperón y de la Flor had amassed a personal savings account of more than $18,000 by assessing punitive fines on workers and residents. Anyone who complained was either drafted into the armed services, arrested, or had their property seized. The article described Esperón y de la Flor as "the Horse of Attila, sowing destruction wherever it went."[27] The article also insinuated that Esperón y de la Flor offered sex with his wife in exchange for favors from the governor of Oaxaca. Esperón y de la Flor and his wife had traveled from Oaxaca to St. Louis to press charges against the three men at President Díaz's request. As deputies hauled the journalists off to the county jail, the sheriff stuck around to help Diebold confiscate papers and seize the printing press.

The files carried back to Diebold's office that day were the Díaz regime's first seizure of Junta records north of the border.[28] By 1909,

Diebold would amass 3,000 stolen letters.[29] The Mexican consuls along the border would capture even more, giving the regime a clear view of La Junta's networks and activities. What Diebold read alarmed him.

La Junta was receiving two hundred letters a day: correspondence from labor organizers across Mexico and the United States, with a heavy concentration in the borderlands; journal subscriptions from laborers, *campesinos*, and even from Mexico's more moderate dissenters, such as Francisco Madero. La Junta was also secretly building a network of revolutionary cells, called *focos*, to prepare for armed revolt. "We want a republic in which all Mexicans will be free and happy. We already know: to achieve this [outcome] the only remedy is revolution, and it will take all of our efforts to incite a popular uprising," explained La Junta in a flood of letters mailed to thousands of *Regeneración* subscribers, whom they encouraged to establish *focos* and correspond directly with La Junta.[30] Subscribers soon confirmed the founding of at least forty PLM *focos*, mostly in the borderlands of south Texas and Arizona. Thumbing through the stacks of seized letters, Diebold realized that the PLM was more than a political party. It was an instrument of armed insurrection.

As long as Ricardo Flores Magón was locked up in the county jail, silenced and unable to raise the $500 bail, the specter of revolution in the borderlands seemed an abstraction. But PLM supporters soon raised enough money to bail the three men out of jail. It is likely that Francisco Madero provided at least part of the bail money, as Flores Magón sent him a letter thanking him for wiring a $900 money order. "You cannot understand how grateful we have been for your invaluable service and the sincere debt of gratitude that we owe you," he wrote.[31] The journalists then jumped bond, fled St. Louis, and began living on the run. President Díaz issued a $20,000 bounty for Ricardo Flores Magón's recapture.[32]

Traveling under pseudonyms, the three men headed north to Canada, staying for a time in Toronto before settling in Montreal. Sending and receiving mail under the name Antonia Méndez, Flores Magón worked as a day laborer and spent his evenings writing dozens of articles, which he mailed to the *Regeneración* office in St. Louis. He also dispatched hundreds of personal letters, asking supporters and subscribers for their input on a platform he was writing for the PLM.

Back in St. Louis, Librado Rivera and the Villarreal sisters rebuilt the *Regeneración* office, while Manuel Sarabia and Antonio Villarreal departed for the border to recruit PLM members and *foco* leaders.[33] Wherever they went, Sarabia and Villarreal found PLM members who, like them, were broke and hungry and struggling to organize. With Ricardo Flores Magón on the run and the *focos* in disarray, the PLM was sputtering. But, on June 1, 1906, a labor strike at an American-owned copper mine in Cananea, Mexico, forced La Junta to declare war on the Díaz regime.

CHAPTER 10

Cananea

STANDING ON THE VERANDA OF HIS HOME, A TWO-STORY mansion set upon a bluff in the craggy mountains of Cananea, William C. Greene, pot-bellied and hellbent on making a fortune in Mexico, could peer down onto the streets of his company town. He already knew that trouble brewed in Ronquillo, the ramshackle barrio in the canyon beneath his mansion where the Mexican miners lived. At the recent Cinco de Mayo festival, the miners had invited Lázaro Gutiérrez de Lara to speak. By 1906, Gutiérrez de Lara had been living in the area for years, stirring up trouble for men like Greene by filing legal cases for the local poor, fighting the deportation of the nearby Yaqui, and generally championing the Liberal cause. Standing on a large wooden platform before a crowd of more than one thousand, Gutiérrez de Lara encouraged Ronquillo residents to establish a Liberal Club. The Liberals, he said, would help them protest the pay cut recently announced by Greene's mining company, the Cananea Consolidated Copper Company, known as the 4Cs. From June 1, 1906, the Mexican miners' pay would drop to three pesos per day, while the Anglo-American managers would be given a pay raise to five U.S. dollars per day. Esteban Baca Calderón, a popular Ronquillo resident and miner, approved Gutiérrez de Lara's call for political action, appealing to the Cinco de Mayo crowd that it was time to "teach the capitalist that you are not beasts of burden—the capitalist who in every way and everywhere has displaced us with his legion of blue-eyed blondes."[1]

Since the festival, 4Cs managers had reported a constant buzz among the miners. Secret meetings in Ronquillo. Hushed conversations in the mines. Copies of *Regeneración* being passed among the workers.[2] Greene suspected that agents for the Western Federation of Miners (WFM), one of the most radical labor unions in the United States, "had been through the [Cananea] mines inciting the Mexicans."[3] His suspicions were correct.

For years, the WFM had been organizing a series of crippling strikes across the American West. Committed to a philosophy of "industrial unionism," which required organizing laborers across traditional barriers, including the color line and international boundaries, the WFM actively recruited Mexican miners, on both sides of the border, into their ranks.[4] Knowing that mine owners might use violence to suppress strikes, the WFM leadership encouraged members to form rifle clubs "so that . . . we can hear the inspiring music of the martial tread of 25,000 armed men in the ranks of labor."[5] And the WFM demanded more than "bread-and-butter" issues, such as higher wages and better working conditions. In 1901, the union declared its purpose to be "a complete revolution of present social and economic conditions." On these grounds and with such tactics, WFM members launched a series of strikes that spread across Colorado in 1903 and 1904.[6] In 1905, the WFM was a founding member of an even more radical organization, the Industrial Workers of the World (IWW), whose manifesto declared: "Universal economic evils afflicting the working class can be eradicated only by a universal working class movement."[7] By early 1906, the WFM had entered southern Arizona, signing up members from the towns of Bisbee and Douglas. In particular, they targeted the Copper Queen Mining Company, owned by Greene's friend James Douglas.[8] Now, WFM agents were entering Mexico disguised as itinerant workers, lending support to the Mexican miners in Cananea as they prepared to confront Greene over the recent wage cut. Even worse, according to Greene, it was rumored that Manuel Sarabia, a leading member of the PLM, was in town.[9] The PLM, Greene knew, was determined to end the Díaz regime, which had approved Greene's purchase of nearly one million acres of land in Sonora, given him generous tax exemptions, and waived a federal ban on foreigners owning land within 100 kilometers of the border. Thanks to Díaz's generosity, not only had Greene built Mexico's largest mining operation and fifth largest company, but he had launched a swirl of subsidiary businesses, including a railroad, a lumberyard, and a cattle ranch, and he was expanding his operations into Chihuahua. If the WFM and the PLM began riling up his miners, the whole machine might collapse.

The rumors were true. For months, Manuel Sarabia had been traveling across the borderlands, north and south of the line, recruiting subscribers for *Regeneración* and establishing *focos*. He swung through Ronquillo during the spring of 1906, touching base with Antonio de Pío Araujo, an early PLM loyalist in the area, as well as Esteban Baca Calderón and others who had recently established a labor union, La Union Liberal Humanidad, which doubled as a PLM *foco*.[10] From his veranda on the bluff, Greene never saw Sarabia, nor did he have any evidence of what Baca Calderón and the others were up to, but he rightly sensed a labor strike forming among the shacks of Ronquillo.

The 4Cs was in no position to weather a strike. Greene, once a middling bean farmer in Arizona, had built the company with loans, stock offers, and dividends. By 1906, it was drowning in debt, and Greene had been fighting off corporate takeovers for years. The Amalgamated Copper Company, led by the Rockefellers and Henry Rogers of Standard Oil, repeatedly tried to acquire the 4Cs, using bear raids and whisper campaigns to drive down the value of its stock. Four times Greene beat back the Amalgamated Copper Company. Then, in January 1906, mine inspectors reported that the quality of the ore was declining. Greene would need to make a massive capital investment if he wanted to continue to extract copper from the Cananea rock. In February 1906, the 4Cs board of directors warned Greene that they would not approve another stock issue. There would be no easy infusion of cash to modernize equipment. In May, mine managers informed him of rumors that the miners were preparing to strike. Greene knew a strike could crush him.

Greene imposed a curfew to keep crowds of Mexicans from gathering on the streets, but he could not stop their chatter. On May 31, 1906, when his mine manager reported several boxes of dynamite missing from the Oversight mine, where Baca Calderón worked, Greene decided it was time to prepare for a confrontation. That night, around 10 pm, Greene sent an urgent telegram to William Brophy in Bisbee, Arizona, the general manager of the Copper Queen company store, imploring him to keep the store open for a late-night shopping spree. Brophy agreed, more than willing to help an old friend; back in the 1890s, when Greene was just a local farmer, he had sold Greene's beans at the Copper Queen, and he had been an early investor in Greene's prospecting ventures south of the border. Greene ordered his conductor to pull his private railroad car up to his mansion on the bluff, and then to charge full speed to the border. Greene arrived in Bisbee near midnight and went directly to Brophy's store, where he purchased every gun in the place, including ninety-eight rifles and twenty pistols, plus 5,000 rounds of ammunition, mostly the explosive "dum dum" bullets designed to expand upon impact, ripping a target's flesh. With this arsenal, Greene rushed back to Cananea, arriving at 4 am, and distributed the guns and ammunition to "our most reliable men." He then went home and tried to get some sleep, wondering "if I had made a fool of myself as everything was quiet."[11]

One hour later the strike began. At 5 am on Friday, June 1, 1906, Esteban Baca Calderón and about twenty members of La Union Liberal Humanidad gathered at the portal to the Oversight mine. Baca Calderón and the strike leaders wore their best clothes—dress shirts with slacks and church shoes and sombreros—to signal their intention to negotiate as workers rather than fight as revolutionaries. As miners arrived for the 7 am shift, the well-dressed strike leaders persuaded the men to shut down the mine.

By 8 am, two thousand miners had joined the strike and delivered their demands to Arthur S. Dwight, the general manager of the 4Cs. They demanded a pay raise from three to five pesos a day, an eight-hour workday, and the opportunity to become managers. Dwight called the demands "absolutely absurd" and refused to meet with the strike committee.[12]

The strikers pushed up the chain of command, sending a copy of their demands to Greene's home. Still exhausted from his midnight run across the border, Greene got up and read the demands, and agreed with his general manager that the demands were frivolous. While his secretary finished typing up his formal reply to the workers—"I have examined your communication . . . appears to me to be without foundation . . . instigated by persons . . . contrary to the prosperity and well-being of the workers"—Greene got into his car and headed down the hill to Ronquillo, confident that he could convince the workers to return to their posts.[13]

Greene was a hustler. Born in Wisconsin to a Quaker family with deep Anglo-American roots, he counted General Nathanael Greene of the American Revolution and the founder of Cornell University among his kin. In his early twenties, Greene had struck west, professing, "If I don't make a fortune, you'll never see me again."[14] By 1880, he was prospecting in the minefields near Tombstone, Arizona. He found nothing. In 1881, Apaches raided his camp, taking everything he owned, including four horses, one mule, one burro, two saddles, one pistol and two rifles, and burning his tent down. They raided another of his camps in 1883 and another at the end of the year. In a fourth raid, in 1886, they took six horses. Greene would later falsely claim that, during these years, he beat back Apache raid parties enough to earn himself the moniker "Colonel." According to his unfounded boasts, Geronimo himself once attacked Greene's camp but ran away in fright when Greene charged directly at the famed Apache warrior. "You were too brave to be killed. You ran straight toward us," Geronimo said, according to Greene. This was all bluster. In fact, Greene anointed himself "Colonel" in New York City when he went north seeking investors for his mines in Cananea. Taking an apartment at the Waldorf Hotel, where he could bump into some of Wall Street's most vaunted men, including Charles Schwab and Francis Stillman, Greene wore a ten-gallon hat and promoted himself as the Indian fighter turned Western entrepreneur who had acquired the richest copper mines in the world.[15] He just needed investors to uncork a fortune from Cananea. Stillman and dozens of others ploughed money into Greene's operations.

When the miners from Ronquillo delivered their demands to Greene's home, he was confident. He had hustled his way into a mining fortune. He had beaten back bear raids by one of the most powerful mining consortiums in the world. And he had convinced the world that he had bested Geronimo. Moreover, his "most trusted men" were well armed. A couple hundred Mexicans demanding a better deal did not shake Greene. So he walked out of his home and got into his Packard, one of four luxury automobiles he kept in Cananea, and drove down the dirt road to Ronquillo to speak with the men.

On Ronquillo's Calle Principal, Greene found hundreds of miners milling about. He parked his Packard and walked around, shaking hands and telling the men not to listen to the agitators.[16] Go back to work, he advised, explaining that the 4Cs paid the highest mining wages in Mexico.[17] Cocksure, he climbed back into his Packard and chugged up the hill. It was 11 am.

Some of the strikers went home, but Esteban Baca Calderón stuck around, mocking Greene's visit to Ronquillo and his efforts to talk the strikers back to work. Greene did pay the highest mining wages in all of Mexico, but the real value of those wages was plummeting by the day; the cost of living in Mexico jumped 200 percent between 1900 and 1910. Meanwhile, those nominally high wages were paid in company scrip, little strips of paper called *boletos* with Greene's face stamped on them. The scrip, of course, was only good at the company store, which charged a 30-40 percent markup on its products. Paying workers in scrip was illegal in Mexico, but President Díaz, whom Greene counted as a friend, steadily overlooked the violation, just as he overlooked the ban on foreigners owning land within 100 kilometers of the border.

By 2 pm, the strike was back on and Baca Calderón gathered the strikers for a march. Their plan was to shut down all Cananea mining operations until Greene agreed to negotiate.

By 3 pm, more than two thousand miners, many joined by their families, were walking double-file up the road to La Mesa, the American enclave.

Set behind Greene's mansion on the bluff above Ronquillo, La Mesa had a cemetery, park, school, church, bank, business offices, stores, saloons, a municipal building, and brand-new housing for Cananea's Anglo-American workers and their families. It was a world apart from Ronquillo, where Mexican miners and their families lived in homes slapped together from company trash. While La Mesa offered a view of rocky mountain slopes cut with ribbons of green smoke drifting from the smelter below, in Ronquillo the ribbons of smoke rained speckles of lead. When an American doctor visited Cananea in June 1902, he found that 138 people had died in the last six months, almost all of them Mexican and almost all from "disease of the pulmonary tract."[18] The march to La Mesa was about more than just low wages; it was about the social consequences of poverty and poor housing in Ronquillo, and the barriers faced by Mexican miners and their families trying to improve their conditions of life.

Baca Calderón led the marchers up the hill to La Mesa, past Greene's seven-chimney home to the lumberyard, where the strike leaders planned to call for the workers inside to join the strike. When they arrived, brothers George and Will Metcalf, from Santa Barbara, California, were standing guard with a four-inch fire hose unwound at their feet. George, the yard manager, was armed with a rifle. Someone had alerted him to the march, giving him just enough time to run home to grab arms. The strike leaders stepped forward and asked to speak with the workers inside. George Metcalf, known to be an "impatient," "arbitrary," and unpopular man, told them to leave or be sprayed with the fire hose. They ignored him and called to the men inside. The Metcalfs hosed them down. The strikers rushed the gate, pushing the Metcalfs aside. During the scuffle, someone—probably George Metcalf—began firing, and within five minutes three miners were dead. The Metcalfs were dead, too, each with a miner's candlestick jammed into his back. And the lumberyard was on fire, building into an inferno that burned through the night. Americans standing at the border, 40 miles away, pointed at the sky glowing orange to the south and knew that something was very wrong.

With the lumberyard on fire behind them, the strikers picked up their dead and continued to march across the bluff toward city hall, where they expected to demand justice for the men who had been killed. They walked into an ambush by Greene's "most trusted men." As León Díaz Cárdenas, a member of the strike committee, later explained, "They were near the hall when, at the crossing of Chihuahua Street and Third Street, a discharge of firearms opened bloody wounds of flesh in the proletarians. Six men fell dead, among them a child of less than eleven years. The massacre, coldblooded and premeditated, had begun. . . . The workers, indignant as they were, could not repel the aggression. Unarmed, they replied to the shots with curses and stones, sustaining a desperate and unequal contest."[19]

The marchers scattered, running back to their homes in Ronquillo in search of safety. Greene's men followed, shooting indiscriminately and killing more than three dozen residents.

As gunfire pinged on the slopes of Cananea, Dr. J. W. Galbraith, who worked as both Greene's company doctor and the U.S. consul in Cananea, panicked. From his office on the bluff, Galbraith tapped out a series of desperate telegrams to U.S. authorities. "Send assistance immediately to Cananea, Mexico. American citizens are being murdered and property dynamited and we must have help," he wrote to Elihu Root, the secretary of state. When a reply was slow to arrive, Galbraith contacted Root's office again: "Imperative that immediate assistance be rendered to American citizens at Cananea, Sonora, Mexico." Breaking protocol, Galbraith even reached out directly to the secretary of war with the following message: "A general insurrection at Cananea. Mexicans against Americans, and all others. Several Americans killed. . . . We must have protection. Can you render immediate assistance?" Galbraith's telegrams, all of them hysterical, factually incorrect, and soon to be reprinted in newspapers from Tucson to New York, told a tale of white U.S. citizens being slaughtered by Mexicans. Greene doubled down on this tale, with a series of telegrams to friends north of the border warning of a "race war" breaking in Cananea and begging for their help. In the border towns along the Arizona–Sonora divide—Bisbee, Naco, Douglas, and Tucson—people thronged the streets and collected their guns, debating how best to protect American lives and property in Mexico. In Bisbee, angry men looking to form a "minuteman" company armed themselves with "carbines, shotguns, small bore rifles and the more dangerous and effective models of the latest design."[20] They would not stand by as Cananea burned.

By 6 pm, the U.S. secretary of war had dispatched troops to the border but warned them not to cross without authorization, wanting to avoid an international incident if Díaz opposed the incursion—which Díaz did. Sensitive to Mexican fears of another U.S. invasion, Díaz insisted that Mexican troops handle the situation and immediately sent *rurales* under the command of Emilio Kosterlitzky to Cananea.

Emil Kosterlitzky was born in Russia, where he joined the navy, but he deserted his post in Venezuela and made his way to Mexico where he altered "Emil" to "Emilio" and enlisted in the army. Soon, his name was synonymous with the Díaz regime. As the historian Samuel Truett explains, "No Mexican evoked the police power of the state more famously than Lieutenant Colonel Kosterlitzky."[21] Stationed in northern Mexico, Kosterlitzky first came to Díaz's attention tracking down Apache fighters. By 1890, he was commanding the *rurales* stationed in Sonora, where it was his job to make the region safe for investors. Mostly, he tracked down horse thieves and rebel Yaqui, often reporting that the regime's antagonists had been simply "disposed of." Mexicans dubbed him "the mailed fist of Porfirio Díaz."[22]

In June 1906, Kosterlitzky was in Hiakim, wrapping up the government's deportation campaign. When he received the call to Cananea, he and his men left immediately, but the nineteen-hour ride meant that they were not expected to arrive until 7 pm on Saturday, June 2.

Greene was not satisfied. Almost all of the shooting had been done by his men and was over by sunset, but he wanted immediate protection for himself and the white U.S. citizens in Cananea. Therefore, into the night of June 1, while the streets of Cananea were quiet and the lumberyard burned, Greene phoned his friends north of the border for help. One of them put him on the line with Captain Tom Rynning of the Arizona Rangers.

The Arizona Rangers had been established just a few years before. Modeled on the Texas Rangers, the Arizona Rangers roamed the territory asserting Anglo-American dominance. But at a time when U.S. investors were buying up large tracts of land just south of the border, neither Anglo-American property, lives, nor interests halted at the border, and "Colonel" Greene was quick to demand that Captain Rynning and the Arizona Rangers mount up. "Hell is popping here and every American life is in danger," he hollered into the phone and, just before the line was cut, Captain Rynning heard him plead: "For God's sake, Tom, get a few hundred armed men together and burn the railroad track up getting here before we're all wiped out . . . they're rushing us steady and we can't stick it out a lot longer."[23]

Captain Rynning, an experienced soldier of U.S. expansion, had been a Rough Rider with Theodore Roosevelt in Cuba before he became a Ranger in the Arizona Territory. Rynning chose to ignore the War Department's nonintervention order and recruited 279 men from the streets of Douglas to ride south to Cananea. Two Black men, former cavalrymen known as Buffalo Soldiers, volunteered for Rynning's vigilante brigade, but Rynning declined their offer to fight. Greene had raised the specter of "race war" and Rynning feared the "mixing [of] breeds in that kind of jam."[24]

In the early morning hours of June 2, Rynning and his men, whom he called his Bronco Army, struck south toward Cananea. Knowing that armed men operating under the direction of a U.S. government official could not lawfully enter Mexico without authorization, Rynning called the governor of Sonora, Rafael Izabal, and struck a deal. Izabal, often derided as "the American governor of Sonora" for his unabashed support of U.S. investors in the state, was distressed and panicked by the telegrams flooding out of Cananea. He was also powerless. Captain Rynning and his Bronco Army were already across the border, and Izabal could not stop them from riding to Cananea.

Instead, he met Rynning's Bronco Army just south of the border and deputized them into the Mexican military. Under Izabal's orders, Rynning and the Bronco Army rode south as fast as possible, storming into the mining town at 11 am.

When the Bronco Army arrived, Cananea was quiet. The inferno still burned in the lumberyard, but the shooting had long been over. The strikers were mourning the dead and Greene's "most trusted men" had retreated to the bluff. Noting the calm, Governor Izabal told Captain Rynning and his men to return to the United States, but, rather than depart, Rynning posted snipers on nearby hills and ordered his men to take up defensive positions around the mines and railroad trestle at the edge of town.

With the Bronco Army standing guard, Kosterlitzky on the way, and the Mexicans in Ronquillo in shock and mourning, Greene left the security of his mansion to address the miners. As he had done the day before, he drove down the dirt road in his open-top Packard and parked in the middle of a crowd. But this time, Greene did not leave his car. With his left foot on the front seat and Governor Izabal sitting in the back, Greene lifted his arm and lectured the workers. "You Mexican people all know me well," he began. "I have been a poor man myself. Some of you were my friends then, and all of you know that I have acted always honestly and fairly with you. When I have been able to pay you $3.50 for your work, I have gladly paid it. But a man cannot pay more than he makes. I cannot pay you five dollars at this time. The revenue from the mines would not permit it." "Yes, all that is true, but why doesn't the company pay the Mexicans the same wages they pay the Americans?" muttered one of the miners. Greene ignored the question and drove back up the hill.[25] The workers did not follow. At least forty of their friends, relatives, and neighbors were dead. Their strike was over.

That night, Kosterlitzky and his men charged into Ronquillo and arrested the strike leaders. The arrival of yet another armed posse added to the chaos. Kosterlitzky ordered Rynning and his men out of town. Rynning stalled for a few hours and then left, but confu-

*Rynning's Bronco Army stands guard while William C. Greene
lectures miners the morning after the 1906 Cananea strike.*

sion persisted. When Lázaro Gutiérrez de Lara's brother heard that
he was in prison, he implored President Díaz to let him go. Díaz
sent a telegram inquiring about Gutiérrez de Lara's condition and
the authorities in Cananea interpreted it as a release order. Gutiérrez
de Lara walked out of jail and fled north across the border, where he
soon connected with La Junta. Without powerful families or friends
to plead their cases to the president, Baca Calderón and the other
strike leaders remained in jail. Governor Izabal recommended that
they be publicly executed, but Díaz's vice president, Ramón Corral,
intervened, worried that this would only inflame protests.[26] Instead,
the men were summarily sentenced to fifteen years in prison. Baca
Calderón was released from prison in 1911, after which he became a
general in the Mexican Revolution and later governor of the state of
Nayarit.

The strike at Cananea hardly lasted a day. Yet in the weeks, months,
and years ahead, the story of Cananea was like a small shifting of the
seabed that leads to a tsunami on the shore. On Wall Street, the chaos

in Cananea caused 4Cs stock to tumble. Trading of all Mexican-based stocks ground to a halt, as U.S. investors worried about the security of their lives and properties in Mexico. Mexican citizens began to question Díaz's omnipotence.

For many Mexicans, Díaz's rule had always been a devil's bargain. After Mexico's chaotic nineteenth century, they traded democracy for "order and progress." But they never traded their sovereignty. Still, to protect U.S. lives and property, Captain Rynning and his Bronco Army had invaded Mexico and neither President Díaz, Governor Izabal, nor Kosterlitzky and his *rurales* could stop them. *"Invasión del territorio nacional por tropas norteamericanos"* (Invasion of Mexican Territory by North American troops) was the headline in Mexico City's *El Tiempo*.[27] The incursion by the Bronco Army made many wonder if Díaz's development strategy had put Mexico at risk of another full-scale U.S. invasion. Would U.S. guns inevitably follow U.S. dollars? And if the Díaz regime could not stop a few hundred half-drunk vigilantes from Arizona, it could not be counted on to stop an army. Ricardo Flores Magón hit the regime particularly hard, quickly issuing a circular that charged Díaz with "ask[ing] that the feet of foreign legions enter our territory and trample our brethren." Now, he insisted, it was time for Mexican citizens to "convert apathy into enthusiasm and fear into rage" by rising up against the dictator who forfeited Mexican sovereignty.[28] Like Flores Magón's blasphemous "den of thieves" speech, which tore a hole in the rhetorical shroud protecting Díaz, the strike at Cananea shredded Mexican citizens' belief in the regime's ability to protect them.

La Junta had neither called nor led the strike at Cananea, but Porfirio Díaz held them responsible for inspiring it and all the questions it raised about the limits of his power. As Kosterlitzky explained in a report submitted to Díaz on the night he arrived in Cananea, "Gutiérrez de Lara is the principal leader of the revolt aided by . . . writers of that filthy scurrilous sheet [*Regeneración*]."[29] His men had found copies of *Regeneración*, as well as letters to and from La Junta, including a letter signed by Ricardo Flores Magón, in the homes of the strike leaders.[30] Greene, who hired Pinkerton detectives to investigate the uprising and track down everyone involved on both sides of the border, told Díaz that Manuel Sarabia had been in Cananea as late as ten o'clock on the morning the strike began. When Díaz spoke with the U.S. ambassador on Monday, June 3, just two days after the strike, he attributed the problems in Cananea to La Junta in St. Louis, whom he condemned as "those Mexican anarchists."[31]

La Junta did not deny their involvement with the strike. In fact, they boasted and even inflated their role, claiming Cananea as the beginning of their armed uprising against the Díaz regime. In a manifesto issued on July 1, 1906, La Junta vowed to turn the strike into a full-blown revolution within one year.

Díaz was determined to stop the PLM revolution before it could start. He ordered his henchmen "not to rest" until they "crush[ed] that St. Louis crowd."[32]

CHAPTER 11

No Alarm in Mexico

"Hundreds Killed in War of Americans and Mexi-cans," was the story William Randolph Hearst splashed across his media empire the morning after the Cananea strike.[1] Nearly a decade earlier, in 1898, the diehard expansionist had run a series of false stories similarly inflammatory and jingoistic; the resulting frenzy had prodded President McKinley to declare war on Spain (and its territories). After ten weeks of conflict in Cuba, during which Theodore Roosevelt and his Rough Riders made their name, the United States seized Spanish claims in Puerto Rico and the Philippines, just as Hearst had hoped.[2] In 1906, Hearst hungered for Mexico, too. His family already controlled more than one million acres in Mexico, but Hearst was beginning to dream of a day when the United States would fully dominate Mexican lands.[3] He used the chaos in Cananea to try to prod an invasion. "Forty-five American miners killed and more than twice that number wounded and dying, fifty Mexican miners and four policemen killed and many more wounded," reported Hearst's *San Francisco Examiner.* "The town is burning, the citizens are fleeing for their lives to the hills, stores are being looted and machinery being dynamited. . . . This, in brief, was the situation at Cananea at 6 o'clock to-night." The only hope for calm, reported the *Examiner,* were the "American and Mexican soldiers . . . rushing in from across the American line and from the interior of Sonora."[4] The next day, Hearst papers reported that "order was restored soon after the arrival of the American volunteers, 500 in number, under the command of Captain Tom Rynung [sic]."[5]

Hearst continued his invasion-mongering throughout the summer of 1906. He ran stories about Mexico teetering on the brink of a race war, an anti-American revolution that would oust Díaz from power, strip U.S. investors of their property, and even threaten U.S. lives. Several other major media outlets joined him. *Harper's Weekly* ran a special report, "The War Peril on the Border." "Clouds of war are beginning to gather on the southern border of the United States," cautioned the article, which reported that there was a "long list of outrages, anti-american riots, assassinations of Americans in Mexico and demonstrations connived at by secret anti-American societies."[6] And, the author warned, "the first grand blow" was scheduled to begin on Mexican Independence Day, September 16, 1906.[7]

Reports of an Independence Day revolt worried U.S. investors, large and small. As the economic historian Mark Wasserman explains, tens of thousands of investors had turned to Mexico "in search of their personal pots of gold at the end of the rainbow. To many dreamers, Mexico was the land of opportunity. From the wealthiest, sophisticated investors to the most scraggly prospectors, they sang the praises of the possibilities."[8] Reports of revolt in Mexico made their investments seem frighteningly shaky. If investors got too scared, they might take flight, pulling, stalling, or canceling new investments, which would not only sap "order and progress" in Díaz's Mexico but devalue all foreign investments. Díaz and his supporters launched a counteroffensive in the U.S. press, insisting that all was well in Mexico.

Harrison Gray Otis of Los Angeles took the lead. Owner and publisher of the *Los Angeles Times*, Otis loudly rejected all reports of unrest in Mexico, dismissing such claims as "yellow journalism" and the fabrication of "fake newspapers . . . printing their miserable lies."[9] "The Hearst sheets and other yellow rags have had a war between the United States and Mexico raging, or about to rage. . . . No person of common sense believed the trash, of course," reported the *Los Ange-*

les Times, which, for months, blamed the reports on "fakers . . . very fond of working off their fake tales of horror—of Yaqui 'uprisings' and other gory happenings—upon greenhorn newspaper reporters and upon greenhorn yellow editors."[10] According to Otis, who owned nearly one million acres in Baja California, U.S. investments in Mexico were safe. "The idea of a 'war with Mexico' is utterly preposterous and utterly silly," exclaimed reporters in the *Los Angeles Times.*[11] "Relations between the two countries were never more friendly than they are today. No possible cause nor excuse for war exists. . . . As for American investments in Mexico, there is no doubt that they are safe under the protection of President Díaz and his government."[12]

Díaz's supporters backed this position with regular reports on U.S. investors thriving in Mexico. Colonel Greene showed up in New York City with a bullish swagger on the prospects of the 4Cs. As the *New York Times* reported on August 7, 1906, "It was a dog days market on the curb yesterday . . . except for the flurry in Greene Consolidated Copper, business was at a standstill."[13] Similarly, the *Los Angeles Times* reported, Edward Doheny was expanding his operations and "furnishing thousands of barrels of oil to the Mexican Central Railway for use in the oil-burning engines and in sprinkling the roadbed."[14] Epes Randolph, president of the Cananea, Yaqui River and Pacific Railroad, and chief of all other Southern Pacific extensions into Mexico, reported that great progress was being made in extending the railroad from Guaymas. "A gigantic bridge is being constructed across the Yaqui River at Torin," and soon the connection would allow investors to "tap the coal fields of the Yaqui and Pacific Railroad."[15]

Meanwhile, Díaz assured U.S. investors that he would allow no harm to come to them or their investments. "The Americans need have no fear of being banished from this country," promised Díaz in a public dispatch to the U.S. Department of State. He continued, "and I propose taking immediate actions to suppress attacks upon foreigners. A few executions of the leaders will put an end to any persecutions by Mexicans and summary work will be made of every person found guilty of crime."[16] A few days later, Díaz delivered on this promise, crushing a strike by the League of Mexican Railway Employees. Henry Clay Pierce, an oil baron and chairman of the board of the Mexican National Railroad, thanked President Díaz for his personal intervention and issued the following statement of confidence in the Díaz regime: "This authoritative announcement of the policy of the Government is very important to industrial enterprises in Mexico and is the best evidence possible that foreigners and their property are fully safeguarded by the strong arm of the Mexican Government."[17] The *New York Times* followed suit, reporting that "Díaz took a very firm stand in dealing with the strikers, making it clear to them that the interest of foreign investors in Mexico would be fully protected."[18] Harrison Otis's *Los Angeles Times* cheered Díaz for forcing the "unionist strikers [to] bend knees for mercy."[19]

But Díaz knew better. While his supporters published tales of calm and control, Díaz was receiving private reports that Mexico was, in fact, a tinderbox of discontent.

Just days after the strike at Cananea, Díaz sent a friend on a "confidential mission" to travel across Mexico investigating political conditions.[20] That friend was the writer Rafael de Zayas Enríquez, who, for decades, had championed Díaz's rule and helped to steer the president's press corps and public image, justifying Díaz's perpetual rule as "the necessary consequence of more than sixty years of internal revolution."[21] Díaz wanted to know if Cananea was an isolated incident or the forerunner of more revolts to come. Beginning in Veracruz and ending in northern Mexico, Zayas Enríquez interviewed Mexicans of every description: old, young, urban, rural, poor, rich, *mestizo*, Indigenous. In two batches, on July 17 and August 3, 1906, he mailed an exhaustive report to Díaz, a report which he suspected would rankle the autocrat. Writing with "the frankness of an old and tried member of your party, who has never served directly or indirectly any government but yours," Zayas Enríquez delivered an unvarnished appraisal of political conditions across Mexico.[22] "It would be a great mistake to suppose that the present movement is confined to the working classes," he wrote. "On the contrary, it is widespread, including directly and indirectly all classes of society."[23] And, he continued, "discontent reigns in almost every state."[24] The uprisings in Cananea and elsewhere, he warned, were merely "forerunners" of larger revolts to come.[25] As Zayas Enríquez explained, the list of complaints against the Díaz administration was long. "There is a considerable discontent over the immovability of many of the public officials and employees of the Government; irritability on account of the abuse practiced by some, perhaps by many of them; impatience on the part of those who think that they are justly entitled to hold high public positions, and who place all their hopes on a change of administration, even if it be only a partial change." Zayas Enríquez reported that citizens wanted both labor and land reform. These last two items were urgent, Zayas Enríquez wrote, because while "[i]t is certainly true that although the condition of the laborer is bad, that of the peon is infinitely worse."[26] With so many complaints mounting against the regime, dissident journalists had endless fodder for their newspapers. "They find a great number of readers," Zayas Enríquez informed the president.[27] And whereas Díaz often suppressed negative reporting, Zayas Enríquez advised that attacking dissident journalists "is the greatest mistake of all. Every persecuted editor will in that way be raised to the rank of a Martyr to Liberty; and the hero of the dungeon usually becomes, sooner or later, the hero of the barricade."[28]

Díaz did not accept his friend's advice. While the regime's favored journalists flooded U.S. newspapers with reports of peace in Mexico— "conditions are normal in Mexico," "No alarm in Mexico," and so on—Díaz dug in against La Junta, determined to thwart the uprising rumored to be scheduled for September 16, 1906.

Díaz turned to U.S. ambassador David E. Thompson for help. Like Díaz, Thompson had been born into poverty. In 1854, at the age of thirteen, he left home in Nebraska to work on the railroad. By the 1880s, he was an executive on the Burlington Line and accumulating a small fortune by investing in Mexico's expanding railway system. In 1900, when a census taker asked Thompson his line of business, he simply replied, "capitalist."[29]

Thompson first visited Mexico in 1876, the year Díaz became president, and soon returned as an investor. Over the years, Thompson bought two plantations in the state of Veracruz, invested in Mexico's railroad boom, and played a central role in what historian William Schell calls the "Tropical Mafia," a loose cabal of American investors who duped scores of U.S. tourists into buying unseen plots of land in southern Mexico.[30] The con usually involved Díaz, as the Tropical Mafia escorted well-to-do tourists to the National Palace or Díaz's summer retreat, Chapultepec Castle, for a private moment with the president, who would regale them with stories from his years as a general in the isthmus of Tepeyac, offering personal tips on which plots to buy. The Tropical Mafia sold millions of worthless, swampy acres to tourists recruited by Thompson and beguiled by Díaz.[31]

By 1906, Díaz and Thompson were old friends. The men were both 33rd degree Masons and members of the Mexico City Masonic lodge. When the Thompson family was in Mexico City, which was often, the two families dined together. Mrs. Thompson and Mrs. Díaz were friends, and each was significantly younger than her spouse. And Thompson knew Díaz's most protected secret. Nearing eighty years old, he was beginning to lose his hearing. His mental faculties were slowing. His competency was slipping. He still kept an active schedule and remained the formidable centrifuge of Mexican political life, but close advisers noted the president's decline.[32] A word unheard. A look too long. A shaking finger; a trembling hand. In these years of decline, David Thompson was Díaz's eyes and ears and most trusted adviser on one of the most important pegs of his rule: friendly relations between the United States and Mexico.[33]

In January 1906, President Roosevelt appointed Thompson U.S. ambassador to Mexico. He needed a man whom Díaz trusted. Two years before, in 1904, Roosevelt had announced an addendum to the Monroe Doctrine (1823), known as the Roosevelt Corollary, which asserted that the United States had an international right to intervene across the Americas "if it became evident that [a country's] inability or unwillingness to do justice at home and abroad had violated the rights of the

United States or had invited foreign aggression to the detriment of the entire body of American nations."[34] Roosevelt wanted Díaz to take primary responsibility for enforcing the policy in Central America: to stand ready to dispatch Mexican troops to do America's bidding. But Díaz openly opposed the Roosevelt Corollary, arguing that it would lead to a U.S. invasion of Mexico.

While briefly serving as ambassador to Brazil (before he was run out of the country under allegations of corruption), Thompson had secured a promise from the Brazilian administration to implement the Roosevelt Corollary across South America. Roosevelt thought that Thompson, Díaz's good friend, would be able to gain similar concessions from the Mexican state.

Roosevelt was right. Thompson took up his post in March 1906 and soon convinced Díaz to intervene in a series of civil wars and boundary disputes roiling Central America. In return, Thompson convinced the Roosevelt administration to take up one of Díaz's political priorities: suppress *Regeneración*, capture Ricardo Flores Magón, and thwart any pending revolt from north of the border.[35] As Thompson put it to Secretary of State Elihu Root, *Regeneración* was a "slanderous" journal, which made "attacks upon the private and public life of Mexican officials."[36] Writing for his friend, Thompson informed the Department of State that it was "President Díaz['s] . . . wish that our government could through some process end the possibility of the publishers of this paper from continuing their evil work. . . . I venture to suggest that if these men could be dealt with . . . the President would feel a deep gratitude."[37] Thompson also wrote that the paper was "not only intended to awaken a dormant spirit of revolution of the people of this country, but it is decidedly antagonistic to foreigners, especially Americans. . . . There is no doubt that the constant publication of articles inciting the Mexican people to hate its government . . . have been instrumental in bringing about the above mentioned disturbances [at Cananea]," wrote Thompson.[38] In other words, to protect U.S. interests south of the border, U.S. authorities needed to take action north of the border.

Throughout the summer of 1906, the U.S. government followed

Thompson's advice and escalated its response to the PLM. On July 5, Secretary of State Root forwarded copies of *Regeneración* to the U.S. attorney general with the following note: "the [State] Department would be glad to have your advice as to what measures, if any, can be taken against the newspaper in question."[39] The U.S. attorney general instructed the U.S. district attorney for eastern Missouri, David P. Dyer, to investigate *Regeneración* and its editors. Perusing copies of *Regeneración*, Dyer had an idea: the provisions of a new federal law, the Alien Immigration Act of 1903, categorically banned anarchist immigrants from entering the United States. Clarence Darrow had challenged the law all the way to the Supreme Court, arguing that banning and deporting immigrants for their political beliefs violated constitutional protections for freedom of speech. The Supreme Court disagreed.[40] Therefore, if authorities could prove that Ricardo Flores Magón was an anarchist, "it seems that he can be deported," Dyer explained.[41]

The attorney general approved this course of action but needed a detective to gather a body of evidence against Flores Magón. At the time, the Department of Justice did not maintain a police force, but the Treasury Department had two: the Secret Service and the U.S. Marshals. As was then the custom, the attorney general asked to borrow an agent from the Treasury Department, and Secret Service agent Joe Priest, based in San Antonio, was assigned to assist Dyer in gathering evidence against the editors of *Regeneración*.[42]

Priest began by reading back issues of *Regeneración*, but could not find any proclamations of anarchism. Flores Magón's beliefs on the subject remained a private matter; he did not talk about them publicly, and he certainly did not publish the full scope of his thoughts. On the pages of *Regeneración*, he called for the end of the Díaz regime but stopped short of calling for the abolition of the state. He called for land redistribution without calling for the abolition of private property. He had kept his promise to Camilo Arriaga and Juan Sarabia to "tone down" his views when writing for *Regeneración*.

Lacking evidence of anarchism on paper, Priest interviewed Mexicans in San Antonio about the PLM and heard dangerous chatter. He wrote to his supervisors that La Junta was planning an uprising for September 16, 1906. Pinkerton detectives hired by William C. Greene to hunt down Ricardo Flores Magón reported similar rumors. By July 24, the Department of State had received numerous warnings that Mexican workers were planning a revolt against U.S. investors in Mexico. Acting secretary of state Robert Bacon sent a telegram to the U.S. ambassador in Mexico City, David Thompson, warning that "there is an organization among Mexican workmen, especially in the northern part of Mexico, whose purpose is to cause the expulsion of foreign workmen from that country, and that the 16th of September next is set as the time when the expulsion is to begin. . . . You will bring the matter to the attention of the Mexican government and suggest preventive measures be taken to protect the rights of American citizens, as persons and property may be endangered by the alleged combination."[43]

Mexican spies in the United States confirmed these reports. After Cananea, various members of the Díaz regime had dispatched undercover agents north to infiltrate PLM *focos*. Pretending to be a disgruntled *campesino*, a soldier named Adolfo Jiménez Castro successfully infiltrated the *foco* in El Paso, Texas, and won the confidence of its leaders, who invited him to a secret meeting scheduled for September 2 at a small store downtown.[44] To Jiménez Castro's surprise, members of the famed Junta were there. Antonio Villarreal, Juan Sarabia, and Ricardo Flores Magón led the meeting, sharing their plan to raid Ciudad Juárez. The attack would begin with two hundred armed men dynamiting the customs house and attacking city hall and the police station, where they would release the imprisoned. Then, the raiders would commandeer a train to Chihuahua City, blowing up bridges along the way. In Chihuahua, the fighters would attack the national bank, the mining bank, and the homes of local aristocrats, including that of Luis Terrazas, the world's largest landowner and cattleman.[45]

Jiménez Castro alerted his commander about La Junta's plans. The commander alerted Díaz. Díaz alerted Ambassador Thompson, who passed the word to U.S. authorities. By September 4, U.S. marshals and local police were combing the streets of El Paso in search of Ricardo

Flores Magón. They kicked in doors and tailed suspects but found no trace of him. However, authorities in Douglas, Arizona, stumbled onto an alarming hub of PLM activities.

Established in 1901, the town of Douglas began as a smelting camp for Phelps Dodge mines in Bisbee. Soon other companies built a series of smelters in Douglas, which is located on the border just across from Agua Prieta, Sonora. By 1906, Douglas was smelting more than 61 million pounds of copper annually and was home to a few thousand people, mostly smelter employees, many of them Mexican immigrants.[46] In the summer of 1906, an informant alerted Antonio Maza, the local Mexican consul, to the fact that "a group of Mexicans in town" were planning to raid the Agua Prieta customs house. According to the informant, "in a house on Avenida de Ferrocarril [Railroad Street], several [Mexican] men gather with illicit purposes" and "talk about ways to get guns, cut telephone lines and steal horses."[47] Maza wondered if the men were *magonistas* or, in his word, "*revoltosos*" (revolutionaries).[48]

Working with the Arizona Rangers and U.S. immigration authorities, Maza conducted "an effective surveillance" and convinced the local U.S. attorney to issue arrest warrants for the two men believed to be the group's ringleaders, Bruno Treviño and Abraham Salcido.[49] Treviño had been in Cananea on June 1, making him an instant suspect. Salcido also had a history of labor organizing in the region. In fact, he had just returned home from Arizona Territorial Prison in Yuma, having served two years for his role in leading the infamous 1903 Clifton–Morenci strike, in which approximately 2,000 Mexican miners had shut down mines across southern Arizona, only to see their picket line broken by a downpour of biblical proportions. The ensuing flood drowned nearly fifty people, mostly miners.[50] When the waters receded, Salcido was arrested and convicted of inciting a riot. Upon his release from prison, Salcido returned to the mines and joined the PLM *foco* in Douglas.

The Douglas *foco* was one of the most active. Some three hundred members from both sides of the border, many of whom had participated in the Cananea uprising, held twice-weekly meetings at the

Half-Way House, a restaurant on the border. Led by Salcido and Tre-viño, the Douglas *foco* spent the summer of 1906 gathering guns and planning the raid in Agua Prieta, to be followed by a raid on Cananea. But just days before the uprising was scheduled to begin, they were arrested on the orders of a man named George Webb.

George Webb was Chief U.S. Immigration Inspector in the Arizona Territory. His primary duty was to prevent Chinese immigrants from entering the United States in violation of Chinese exclusion laws, and to that end he supervised a team of eighteen Mounted Guards who patrolled the Arizona backlands.[51] Rounding up Mexicans, rebels or otherwise, was not one of his duties, but Webb was well aware of U.S. interests in Mexico and offered to help track down *magonistas* within his jurisdiction. As Webb put it, "A large percentage of the inhabi-tants of the Mexican interior are United States citizens, who have vast amounts of capital invested there, and many of them have their families with them; and the matter of this embryonic revolution affects Amer-ican interests very seriously."[52] His first stop was the mining camps in the Patagonia Mountains, where he rounded up Treviño and others. Then, on the evening of September 3, he led a team of immigration inspectors and Arizona Rangers, including Thomas Rynning, in a coordinated raid across Douglas, kicking in doors and seizing twelve men, including Abraham Salcido, plus "125 rifles, eighty-five revolv-ers, 25,000 rounds of ammunition, 100 pounds of dynamite, 200 caps, [and] 10,000 feet of fuse.[53] The officers also seized PLM and IWW propaganda, a small archive of letters, and ten flags, at least one flag made of red silk and wrapped in white lace.[54] Captain Rynning kept the guns but turned the flags and letters over to Consul Maza, who sent everything to Mexico City for inspection. The letters, some penned by Ricardo Flores Magón, confirmed plans for a revolt in Agua Prieta and Cananea.

The reports from El Paso and the arrests in southern Arizona made international news. Newspapers as far away as Germany printed the story.[55] Mexican government agents in Washington, DC, again lobbied the acting secretary of state, Robert Bacon, who promised to do "everything possible" to get a "good result."[56] In particular, he promised to support a new libel suit against Ricardo Flores Magón, agreeing that the case was a strategy to "quickly shut down *Regeneración.*"[57] A few hours later, the Mexican ambassador walked into Secretary Bacon's office, wanting to confirm that the U.S. government was prepared to suppress *Regeneración* and the PLM. Bacon confirmed the government's position. By September 6, President Roosevelt had put the Departments of War, Justice, Commerce and Labor, and the Treasury on high alert, ordering all U.S. authorities to "go to the utmost limit in proceeding against these so-called revolutionists."[58]

Despite the U.S. government's involvement, Díaz and his supporters continued to deny reports of unrest in Mexico into September 1906. Across the Brown Belt, Mexican consular officials admitted that "bandits and bad Mexicans" affiliated with the PLM were circulating "various proclamations" but insisted they were in control of the situation. "Total tranquility and unlimited confidence reins in our Government," wrote the consul in Eagle Pass, Texas.[59] Ambassador Thompson publicly claimed that any report of "anti-American feeling" and "an organized revolution" was false. He described Cananea as nothing more than a "small labor riot" and assured the U.S. investing community that "if there should be any local disturbances they will be handled rightly by the Mexican government. Such a thing as a general uprising is not to be seriously considered."[60] Daniel Guggenheim and William Greene co-signed an editorial printed in the *New York Herald* entitled "American Property Safe in Mexico."[61] That same day, the St. Louis County sheriff again raided the *Regeneración* office. The office was nearly empty, containing just some printing equipment, dirty dishes, and stacks of paper. The sheriff seized everything but the dishes, shuttering *Regeneración.*[62]

But, as Mexican Independence Day neared, Ricardo Flores Magón remained at large, stoking panic among investors. On Wall Street, all trade in Mexican securities had screeched to a halt by September 14, 1906. As a reporter for the *Mexican Herald*'s New York bureau put it, "the investing public is disturbed by the reiterated rumors printed in

American papers regarding a threatened anti-foreign movement and revolutionary outbreak. If trouble of any kind develops, no matter how comparatively trivial, the large interests which thus far have been able to keep the market of Mexican securities steady in the face of rumors should find it difficult if not impossible to hold up prices through the heavy selling movement which will be bound to follow."[63]

As September 15 dawned, investors anxiously awaited news from the border. The morning press forecasted that "today will reveal whether yankees are safe in Mexico" and "if nothing happens to the foreigners in Mexico, Díaz will have added another leaf to the laurel to which his unparalleled rule of this strange nation entitles him to."[64] Stationed in Cananea, Kosterlitzky and his *rurales* waited for the local inferno to reignite. On the Arizona border, Rynning's Rangers patrolled the line. In Ciudad Juárez, Mexican troops remained vigilant. Along the length of the Texas–Mexico border, U.S. troops were prepared to fend off armed men trying to invade Mexico. Just south of the border, clusters of Mexican troops kept watch, waiting for armed *magonistas* to charge.

As night arrived and the Independence Day celebrations began, fireworks exploded in the sky over Mexico and Mexican *colonias* in the United States. Along the border, U.S. and Mexican soldiers listened for gunfire amid the bursts. In Mexico City, soldiers and *rurales* patrolled the streets, waiting for a revolt, while Díaz kept his usual birthday schedule, greeting well-wishers at the National Palace before stepping onto his balcony to belt out "el Grito" before crowds of cheering Mexicans below.[65] The evening ended peacefully, as it had for decades, with parades, fireworks, and Porfirio Díaz in charge. The next morning, Mexican stocks surged on Wall Street, none more than the Cananea Copper Company, which gained 3¼ points by day's end.[66] The panic was over. The *magonistas* had not attacked. But Mexican Independence Day was not the date the PLM had been preparing for.

CHAPTER 12

Send Five Dollars for the Machine

WHILE CANANEA BURNED, RICARDO FLORES MAGÓN WAS writing letters from his hideout, a small apartment in Montreal, Canada. For weeks, he had worked odd jobs by day and spent evenings hunched over his typewriter, pounding out correspondence with *foco* leaders across the United States and Mexico, gathering their thoughts for a PLM party platform. Suggestions poured in. Set term limits. Guarantee voting rights. Establish a minimum wage. Prohibit child labor. Require workmen's compensation. Eliminate debt servitude. End Chinese immigration to Mexico. Expand public education and make attendance compulsory. Make churches pay taxes. Enforce the national ban on foreigners owning land within 100 kilometers of land borders, 50 kilometers of the coastline. Return land to dispossessed Indigenous and traditional landholders. A special provision was proposed for the thousands of Mexicans living in the United States: repatriate them at the government's expense and give them land to cultivate. In all, Flores Magón received enough suggestions, and added a few of his own, to craft an expansive, fifty-two-point platform.[1]

The 1906 PLM platform, if enacted, promised to fundamentally redistribute political and economic power in Mexico. For Flores Magón, however, the platform was a compromise, a constellation of what he called "timid reforms."[2] Personally, he would have demanded more, committing the PLM to pursuing the total abolition of private property as well as church and state. He also likely disagreed with the platform's proposed ban on Chinese immigration. Many Mexicans in the early twentieth century held strong anti-Chinese sentiments, believing Chinese immigrants to be racial outsiders and strikebreakers and often arguing that banning Chinese immigration would improve conditions for Mexican workers.[3] Flores Magón, however, believed that all the world's workers, regardless of race, gender, or citizenship, should claim the means of production.[4] On the matter of racism, he would later declare, "Capitalism foments racial hatred so that the peoples never come to understand each other, and so it [empire] reigns over them."[5] In 1906, however, he was still cloaking his convictions, letting the PLM platform reflect the broad sweep of demands mailed to him by *foco* members and *Regeneración* subscribers.

Once the platform was ready, the PLM rushed to release it, hoping to leverage the outrage following the strike in Cananea. On July 1, 1906, they began moving 750,000 copies across the borderlands. Crescencio Villarreal Márquez distributed copies across Coahuila. Antonio de Pío Araujo took copies to the mining camps. Antonio Villarreal crossed the border to hand-deliver copies across northern Mexico.[6] In Texas, California, and Arizona, Mexico's migrant workers passed the manifesto from hand to hand. In Mexico City, Modesta Abascal, one of La Junta's most dedicated distributors, made sure all of her contacts received the platform. They carried PLM propaganda across central Mexico, down into Oaxaca, and up into the mountains of Morelos to a village leader named Emiliano Zapata, who had recently begun subscribing to *Regeneración*.[7]

By mid-July, President Díaz had a copy in his hands. He gave it to Ambassador Thompson, who sent it to the Department of State, the U.S. attorney general, and even President Roosevelt, insisting that the United States help Díaz crush the PLM. They all agreed. Meanwhile, William C. Greene's Pinkerton detectives were on the case. Together, U.S. and Mexican authorities began building a cross-border counterinsurgency team charged with throttling the PLM revolt before it could begin. They watched the *Regeneración* office in St. Louis. They paid informants. They planted spies. They concocted lawsuits. But the team failed to crack La Junta. They could not get access to actionable or reliable information. They did not know that Ricardo and Enrique Flores Magón and Juan Sarabia had escaped to Canada. They did not know that Crescencio Villarreal Márquez had recruited 250 members from both sides of the border to join the *foco* based in Del Rio, Texas. The only fact the counterinsurgency team thought they had uncovered—that the revolt would begin on Mexican Independence Day—proved to be false, perhaps even a distraction planted by PLM members themselves.

Into the fall of 1906, while the counterinsurgency team scrambled after them, La Junta was drafting battle plans and recruiting an army. As Ricardo Flores Magón explained in a letter to Villarreal Márquez and other *foco* leaders: "We will attack from 20 locations—Laredo, Douglas, El Paso—and so on. The idea is to have many men ready to attack on both sides of the border."[8]

Across the borderlands, *foco* leaders pledged to raise an army. From El Paso, León Cárdenas wrote, "I know well that this campaign is going to bring us serious difficulties, the wrath and vengeance of Mexican authorities, but it doesn't matter because we will beat them all. . . . We are at the doorstep of combat and we will be courageous, even if for this we only leave our children to remember our stand, if luck so orders it."[9] "I am ready to die to overthrow the tyrants," testified Ancelmo Velarde.[10] "The few of us who can get together will be at the orders of a commander," guaranteed Rafael Valle.[11] "In this district, my friends can raise at least two towns," promised another.[12] By September 1906, enough men had pledged to fight that La Junta established a PLM army and distributed military credentials to the soldiers. They called themselves the "gladiators."[13]

La Junta also spent the summer of 1906 soliciting support from two opposing groups: Yaqui fighters and Mexican soldiers. The Yaqui had valuable experience fighting the Díaz regime. La Junta appointed Javier Guitemea, a member of the *foco* in Douglas, Arizona, to "confer with the Chief or with the Chiefs of the Yaqui tribe in the state of Sonora, Mexico, and . . . enter into arrangements with said chief or

PLM army credential.

chiefs to effect an armed uprising against the dictatorship of Porfirio Díaz."[14] Such efforts, bolstered by the PLM's vow to return expropriated lands to Indigenous communities, won the support of at least two Indigenous men who would become influential PLM militants: José María Leyva (Yaqui) and Fernando Palomárez (Mayo). Leyva had been named in honor of Cajeme.[15] Palomárez—trilingual in Yoeme, Spanish, and English—had been organizing miners in the Hiakim borderlands since at least 1902. As the historian Devra Weber has documented, Palomarez made sure to leave what he called "a trail of powder" wherever he went, a reference to the incendiary ideas and plans of the PLM.[16]

La Junta also hoped that disgruntled Mexican soldiers would join the revolt, sending dozens, if not hundreds, of manifestos and recruitment letters to members of the military, promising promotion and higher wages should they choose to fight with the revolutionaries. Ricardo Flores Magón was so bold as to send recruitment packages directly to military commanders stationed at the National Palace. "Permit us to share with you a copy of the PLM Platform," he wrote to Captain Francisco Lacroix at the Palace:

In this platform, you will note the following facts: In Mexico today, secretly organized under the leadership of La Junta, the PLM is determined to soon achieve its legitimate, honorable, and beneficial goals. . . . Our Party is already well organized across the country and counts among its members people of every social class, which gives our movement a truly popular character. . . . Conflict between the people and the tyrants is inevitable; the irrepressible confrontation between those who demand liberty, political rights, better working conditions, sovereignty . . . and those who desire despotism, misery, shameful submission to foreigners, general ignorance, ruinous loans, and other infamies that only benefit the entitled. . . . Before the uprising begins, before we lift the popular flag, we thought it important to address the honorable men in the military, and call your attention to the justice of our cause so that you will have time to meditate on . . . your position as patriots and as Mexicans in the coming battle. In the coming battle, the people will fight for the general good, for the liberty of all, for national honor; the dictatorship, on the other hand, only fights for its petty and personal interests; for the power it has abused for thirty years; to maintain the wealth that the oppressors have accumulated by rape and crime, to maintain foreign supremacy over Mexicans, to extend the reign of oppression and injustice. . . . We truly hope that you join us. If you accept this invitation, please send us a short note letting us know how many men and arms you can raise for the revolution."[17]

It was a risk, reaching out to the military. But Díaz underpaid and overworked his troops. La Junta hoped to find recruits among both officers and enlisted men.

Several Indigenous leaders, from the Popoluca in Veracruz to the Tarahumara in Chihuahua, joined the PLM army, but few Mexican soldiers broke rank. In the end, most of the PLM fighters were *cam-pesinos*, miners, and migrant laborers of the borderlands. Some were farmers, railroad workers, and more skilled tradesmen. A few were journalists, business owners, and members of the middle class. As Flores Magón described the men on the PLM muster roll, "they do not have prestige . . . they just have hearts ready to sacrifice."[18]

Those who brought their hearts to the struggle rarely brought guns and bullets. Most PLM soldiers were too poor for such goods, requiring La Junta and *foco* leaders to spend countless hours begging for guns and ammunition. As Flores Magón wrote to a potential supporter, "the desperation that grips the community is so significant that even the groups that do not have guns are eager to join the fight . . . armed with just rocks and clubs." But it would be a mistake to fight without guns, warned Flores Magón. "If we are to risk our lives, we must arm ourselves," he wrote, requesting donations for guns.[19]

But La Junta had few connections to persons of means. There were no deep pockets to provision the PLM army. Arriaga's friendship with Francisco Madero had secured a major loan to relaunch *Regeneración*, but Flores Magón had exiled Arriaga from the group and criticized him in print. Now, when Crescencio Villarreal Márquez tried to reach out to Madero on behalf of La Junta, Madero quickly rebuffed the request for financial support. "It is still not time to mount an uprising," wrote Madero to Villarreal Márquez. Villarreal Márquez sent Madero additional requests for funds to purchase guns and ammunition for the PLM's coming revolt, but Madero held that dissidents in Mexico should wait for a "constitutional opportunity," such as the next presidential election, to unseat Díaz, advising the PLM to work within the "limits" of the political process. Revolt, in the words of Madero, was "anti-patriotic" and had "no plausible pretext."[20] Moreover, he explained, Flores Magón had crossed a line by "insulting everyone, especially Camilo Arriaga [and] la Señora."[21]

By "la Señora," Madero was referring to Juana Belén Gutiérrez de Mendoza, who had long challenged Flores Magón's *personalista* approach, exemplified by the fact that La Junta was floating his name as a leading candidate to run for president against Díaz. She believed that ideals trumped individuals and pushed the rebels to advance a set of ideas rather than a slate of candidates. Flores Magón hit back, publishing in *Regeneración* that she was a lesbian living with her lover, Elisa Acuña. As Flores Magón put it, the relationship between Gutiérrez de Mendoza and Acuña amounted to "a quarrel with Nature, which has so wisely created the two sexes," rendering the two women "depraved and odious beings."[22] It was a calculated public outing designed to shame and alienate Gutiérrez de Mendoza, but it did not work. Liberals in Mexico continued to value her voice, while she refused the shame and launched a counterattack, publishing articles in *Vesper* that accused Flores Magón of mishandling donations and growing suspiciously close to Anglo-American labor organizers. Still, the outing deepened the rift between Flores Magón and Madero. A spiritist vegetarian who practiced herbal medicine and meditation, Madero refused to support the irascible, intemperate tenor of Flores Magón's attack on Juana Belén Gutiérrez de Mendoza and his revolt against Díaz.

Even without major financial support, the PLM army established brigades across the border region, with some detachments as far away as Veracruz. Everywhere, PLM fighters were eager for battle. From Canada, Flores Magón urged them to wait for all of the *focos* to be ready. "The more the revolution is dispersed, the harder it will be for the despotism to subdue," he wrote to the *foco* in Douglas.[23] Indeed, his only military strategy was a kind of prepared spontaneity. He believed that a mass uprising would naturally follow a singular but well-designed PLM raid, like a chain reaction of insurgency rolling across Mexico. So he advised the Douglas *foco*, and others, to wait until more groups were ready to join them: "There are forty revolutionary branches throughout the country resolved to take up arms, but not all the groups count with sufficient arms."[24]

By September, the PLM army was almost ready. It was time to coordinate battle plans. On September 2, 1906, Ricardo Flores Magón and Juan Sarabia arrived in El Paso for a two-hour planning meeting— the meeting attended by Adolfo Jiménez Castro, the Mexican soldier working undercover among the rebels. Prisciliano Silva was there; he was the leader of an armed rebel group in El Paso. Vicente de la Torre, J. Cano, and Rafael Rembao were there; they were veterans of past anti-Díaz uprisings. César Canales was there; "a man of few words [but] quick decision," he was a journalist from Nuevo León who had once tried to mount a series of raids into Chihuahua.[25] Antonio de Pío Araujo was there; he had been in Cananea on the day of the strike and had since moved to Douglas, where he was a founding member of its *foco*. He was also one of the PLM's most able gun-runners, collecting and stashing what he called *dulces y escobas* (candies and brooms)— guns, ammunition, dynamite—across the border region. Allies kept *dulces y escobas* under floorboards, in caves, and in many other hiding places. Crescencio Villarreal Márquez was there; he led the *foco* in Del Rio, one of the largest *focos* along the border. Lauro Aguirre was there, too; whenever revolt was in the wind in Mexico, Aguirre was always nearby. During the 1890s, he had backed the Teresita movement against the Díaz regime. When Teresita was banished to the United States, he followed and continued to support various attacks against the Díaz regime from El Paso. When the *Regeneración* journalists arrived from Mexico City, he had provided them support, letting them stay at his home, publishing PLM material in his journal, and so on. At this meeting, with a Mexican government spy listening in, they spoke in loose code, laying out plans for attacking Ciudad Juárez and other border towns. After the meeting, Flores Magón immediately left town, returning to Canada to prepare for the impending revolt, while Juan Sarabia headed south to Ciudad Juárez to recruit rebel fighters. The others fanned out across the borderlands to prepare the PLM army. Adolfo Jiménez Castro reported everything he heard to his commander.[26]

The Jiménez Castro report triggered a mass search for PLM fighters in the borderlands, but only the *foco* leaders in Douglas were arrested. More than one dozen units remained operative and PLM fighters pressed on, collecting *dulces y escobas* and preparing to fight. By September 8, La Junta had distributed to each *foco* "General Instructions for Revolution." An English translation of the instructions, made by Mexican authorities for their U.S. counterparts, reads as follows:

1. From the moment that each revolutionary group receives the present instructions, it shall prepare and be ready to uprise (in arms) when so ordered by the Junta, which may happen from one moment to another . . . if they do not do so . . . the guilty shall incur the punishment of death. . . .

2. If the outbreak in Cananea, which is expected any moment, takes place, all and each one of the revolutionary groups shall equally uprise without further notice from the Junta.

3. If the outbreak does not take place at Cananea, but shall happen in another place and initiated by members of the Liberal Party, all and each one of the revolutionary groups shall equally uprise without further notice from the Junta.

4. Should the Junta or several of its members or only one of them fall into the hands of the Mexican Government or into those of the United States Government . . . all and every one of the revolutionary groups shall immediately uprise in arms, as the fact of the apprehension of one or several of the members of the Junta, will signify that the Government has taken papers and data compromising the cause of the Revolution. . . .

5. If nothing foreseen in the foregoing clauses happens, the Junta will then fix the date for the general uprising . . . the Junta will be careful in advising by telegraph those who are to uprise, in the following terms, to wit:

   a. When a group must uprise immediately, the Junta will address it in a telegram as follows, "Send money for the machine." . . .

   b. In case the uprising should be at a determined date, the Junta shall address a telegram to all the groups in the following terms: "You shall receive the machine on the —— day. (Here the day of the uprising will be inserted.)"

   c. When a group is at a point of being discovered by the Government and fears its attack or attacks, address the following telegram . . . "Anita is seriously ill, advise family."

6. Upon the uprising of each group it shall act as follows:

    a.   It shall issue and circulate profusely a proclamation [and] secure funds and whatever other elements that are necessary . . . ; give in all cases receipts for the amounts and whatever taken, which receipts must be honored at the triumph of the revolution.

    b.   Be inflexible with the authorities, at least with the principal ones who have caused the greatest harm to the people and committed the greater crimes. They will be subject to court martial, if there is time for it, and if there is not, the tyrants will be shot down without formation of cause.

    c.   Confront the Government forces with visible superiority over them . . . it is better that when a place is once conquered to execute its authorities and appoint from the people new authorities.

    d.   The revolutionaries must go to another point, securing more men and elements until they constitute a respectable force.[27]

These instructions were almost certainly written by Ricardo Flores Magón. By design, they lacked clear military organization or strategy. The refusal to centralize authority over the fighters or control their actions was a stock tactic in what anarchists call "spontaneous revolt," the insurgent process by which the working class would seize control of their lands and lives through shared individual action without creating new forms of hierarchy, authority, or control. Spontaneous revolt is an essential part of the anarchist process because, as the anarchist scholar Noam Chomsky puts it, "the spontaneous actions of popular forces [are needed to] create new social forms in the course of revolutionary action."[28]

With Flores Magón's loose instructions in one hand and the PLM's

1906 platform in the other, PLM soldiers waited for the signal to revolt. Disproportionately poor, most of them worked as they waited. They mined. They planted. They hauled. They picked. They waited.

As Mexican Independence Day approached, newspapers on both sides of the border began reporting that both Mexico and the United States were standing ready to crush their uprising. U.S. and Mexican troops were on the border. Arizona Rangers patrolled the line. Kosterlitzky and his *rurales* waited in Cananea. U.S. Marshals kept watch in El Paso while Pinkerton detectives staked out the PLM headquarters in St. Louis. Mexican police clustered in Ciudad Juárez. Agent Joe Priest listened for chatter on both sides of the border. As one of the gladiators noted, "The dictator's surveillance is widespread in the borderlands."[29] The fighters laid low.

When the PLM uprising did not materialize on September 15 or 16, Díaz and his supporters read the silence as evidence of victory. But the regime was making a tactical mistake. Despite the odds, the PLM army had not folded. They were waiting for the signal to fight.

On September 21, 1906, La Junta sent a telegram to Crescencio Villarreal Márquez in Del Rio: "Send five dollars for the machine." Villarreal Márquez knew exactly what it meant: five dollars, five days.[30] He alerted Juan José Arredondo, a fifty-six-year-old widower who lived on a hacienda just south of the border.

Juan José Arredondo had once been a captain in the Mexican military but lost his position when Díaz reorganized the army. He had also once occupied a small plot of land but lost it when Díaz allowed moneyed international surveyors to claim untitled land in Mexico. Dispossessed and unemployed, Arredondo's family spiraled downward. Arredondo wound up sharecropping on Hacienda de Victoria, a massive estate owned by Gerónimo Treviño, who had used Díaz's land reform laws to lay claim to more than 5 million hectares of land.[31] After his wife died, Arredondo's children left to find work in Texas. Arredondo spent the remainder of his life fighting to reclaim some portion of his land and status. When his friend started a PLM *foco* in the nearby town of Jiménez, Arredondo joined.[32] The PLM's promise to oust Díaz and return land to the Indigenous and *campesino* communities brought him to the fight. Working with Villarreal Márquez in Del Rio, Arredondo gathered guns and recruited sixty fighters. Most recruits were mature men like Arredondo, who maintained a long list of grievances against the Díaz administration. Arredondo's army of the dispossessed—sharecroppers, cotton pickers, and migrant workers— was ready to strike when La Junta's telegram arrived.

CHAPTER 13

The Jiménez Raid

O<small>N THE EVENING OF</small> S<small>EPTEMBER</small> 25, 1906, <small>THE MAYOR OF</small> Jiménez, Mexico, heard a rumor: armed men were planning a raid on the small border town. He put the municipal police on guard and went to bed. Around midnight, two policemen rapped on his bedroom window: dozens of armed and mounted men were just outside of town. Mayor Ismael Rodríguez waved off the policemen and returned to bed, saying that they would head out to arrest the men in the morning. Two hours later, the policemen woke him again, reporting that "some suspicious men on horseback" had just ridden into the plaza.[1] The mayor's brother soon appeared, warning that the men in the plaza were talking about robbing the mayor's store and locking up local authorities. This got his attention. The mayor fled his home, sneaking to his father-in-law's house a few doors down, where he hoped to hide until the armed men departed. But the raiders executed their plan perfectly. By 8 am, Mayor Rodríguez had been locked in the jail. By noon, PLM fighters had declared Jiménez free from the rule of Porfirio Díaz.[2]

The raid began when sixty PLM fighters rode into Jiménez just after midnight on September 26. Most of them were armed. With Juan José Arredondo at their head, they occupied the central plaza and, from there, struck out into the side streets to arrest local authorities. According to the city treasurer, Presentación Flores, a PLM fighter knocked on his door at 4 am. When Flores asked who was there, the fighter began to "violently push" at the door.³ When Flores refused to open it, the fighter left. In the quiet of the early morning, Flores could hear gunfire nearby. A few minutes later, he heard horses' hooves and men shouting just outside. The men began shooting and threatening to chop down his door with an ax if he did not open it. When Flores peeked out, several PLM fighters grabbed him and marched him across the plaza to City Hall, where Arredondo informed him that he was now a prisoner of the PLM and required to hand over every peso in the treasury. Another PLM fighter, Calixto Guerra, took Flores to the treasury and watched as he opened the safe and pulled out a bag containing $108.50 (pesos) in silver. Flores handed over the bag and Guerra wrote him a receipt, explaining that the PLM would return the funds to the people of Jiménez once their revolution removed Porfirio Díaz from office. Guerra then took Flores to the jail and locked him up.⁴

There, Flores encountered the local revenue agent, Vicente Garza Paz, who told a similar tale. He too had been violently woken at 4 am by knocks on the door. Outside, he heard familiar voices: those of Jiménez residents Marcario Arreola and Juan Casillas. When he opened the door, Arreola and Casillas, both on horseback, informed him that "by order of Mr. Juan José Arredondo they were going to take him to the City Hall so that he could turn over the funds of the Collector's Office." At first, Garza Paz said he would not go because "it was not the office hour yet." Arreola and Casillas insisted, letting Garza Paz know he could come voluntarily or be taken by force. Garza Paz picked up his keys and went with them. Along the way, Garza Paz could hear "many shots in the direction of the Plaza." He would later learn that most of the shooting had occurred at the store owned by the mayor, where PLM fighters shot open the door and took every gun and bullet in the place. It was a meager haul: just one shotgun, one pistol, and several rounds of ammunition. But the PLM fighters needed every gun and bullet they could find. At City Hall, Arredondo ordered Garza Paz to open the customs safe. Finding only $15 (pesos) and suspecting that Garza Paz had hidden state funds, the PLM fighters "examined the books of account" until they were "finally satisfied" that $15 (pesos) was all Garza

Paz had to hand over. Calixto Guerra handed him a receipt and promised that, when the revolution was successful, all public funds would be returned to the people of Jiménez. Guerra then locked Garza Paz in the town jail.[5]

By mid-morning, Arredondo and the PLM army had nearly completed their mission: they had seized all available funds, guns, and ammunition, and local authorities were in jail. They had also slaughtered a cow to procure some meat for the next leg of their journey. All that remained was to declare Jiménez free from Díaz's rule. So, the PLM army performed a liberation ceremony. About two hundred curious residents joined them, having slowly come out to the plaza to inquire about the ruckus. PLM fighter Telesforo González climbed the steps of the city hall. At twenty-five years old and standing six feet tall, González was one of the youngest and tallest of the fighters. He read aloud "A La Nación," a proclamation prepared by La Junta and signed by Ricardo Flores Magón for this moment:

In legitimate defense of trod-upon liberties, of infringed rights, of the dignity of the country trampled upon by the criminal despotism of the usurper, Porfirio Díaz; in defense of our honor and of our lives threatened by a government that considers integrity a crime and smothers in blood the most legal and peaceful attempts of emancipation; in defense of justice, outraged without respite by the handful of brigands that oppress us, we rebel against the dictatorship of Porfirio Díaz and we will not put down the weapons we've taken in hand with complete justification until, united with the Mexican Liberal Party, we've made triumph the program promulgated on July 1 of the current year by the Organizing Junta of the Partido Liberal [PLM].[6]

González continued to recite the "excesses of the dictatorship," including the "violations of electoral rights," suppression of the free press, and the invasion of Mexican territory by foreigners. When González finished, the PLM fighters stepped forward, one by one, to sign the proclamation.[7] Then Arredondo announced that the PLM army was moving on to liberate another town. By 3 pm, they were gone.[8]

Once the PLM army had left, someone opened the jail doors and set the imprisoned officials free. The mayor called the nearest military post: an army fort in Ciudad Porfirio Díaz (now called Piedras Negras), located just 30 miles away. Several detachments of Mexican soldiers and *rurales* rode off in pursuit. Squads went north and south in a fevered search for the raiders.

After leaving Jiménez, Arredondo led his troops to Hacienda de Victoria to rest and recruit more fighters. The owner, or *hacendado*, Treviño, was on a European vacation with his family, leaving the workers in charge. Like Arredondo, many of them held grievances against the Díaz administration. In fact, many had only recently arrived at the hacienda after losing a long, bitter legal battle and being evicted from their homes in the nearby towns of Rosales and Gigedo.

At the close of the Spanish colonial era, the Liberal Party had redistributed 87,800 acres of Spanish mission lands to the Pausane and Tapajuaya Indigenous communities, who established the towns of Rosales and Gigedo. Later, President Díaz personally confirmed their land titles. Yet several of the region's wealthiest families, including the Maderos, contested the titles and hired influential lawyers to sue the residents for restitution. Díaz reneged on his support and ordered the governor of Coahuila, Miguel Cárdenas, to convince the residents of Rosales and Gigedo to cede their titles in exchange for guaranteed access to land and water. The residents refused and negotiations were held in May 1902. Somehow, Cárdenas convinced the shareholders' lawyer to grant him power of attorney in the negotiations, and, without the residents' approval, he settled the case in favor of the wealthy complainants. Infuriated, the shareholders rejected the deal and refused to leave. Ultimately, Cárdenas had police drive the residents of Rosales and Gigedo from their homes, sending many to the nearby Hacienda de Victoria in search of shelter and work.[9] Their grievance burned all the hotter given their long struggle for autonomy and Díaz's Janus-faced promise.

In 1905, Dimas Domínguez, a local dissident who had been running opposition candidates against Díaz's cronies in the region, had established a PLM *foco*. Many of the dispossessed from Rosales and Gigedo joined, drawn by the PLM's promise to return land to the Indigenous and *campesino* communities uprooted by Díaz. [10] When Domínguez and his friend Juan José Arredondo, a neighbor at Hacienda de Victoria, began recruiting soldiers for the PLM army, nearly one dozen men from Rosales and Gigedo—mostly fathers with their sons—signed up to fight. For them, armed revolt was the next phase of a land struggle their families had been fighting for decades.

Arredondo hoped his PLM fighters could rest safely at Hacienda de Victoria, among their families and neighbors—that no one would turn them in. But someone did call the authorities, bringing soldiers and *rurales* to the barn where the PLM fighters had laid over to feed their horses.

In a coordinated attack, soldiers and *rurales* quietly posted themselves around the barn and waited for the PLM fighters to emerge. Then they opened fire. As Arredondo later recalled, "just as we passed through the streets they fired and charged without crying, 'Who goes there?' A few shots came from our party. We could not resist on account of the surprise. . . . Not all of the fighters were armed and so they all scattered in different directions."[11] Except for one: PLM fighter Antonio Villarreal was killed in the firefight. A resident of Jiménez, Villarreal was one of the young men who had been recently evicted from Rosales. A proven dissident, he had led his neighbors in resisting their eviction by filing a lawsuit in the Mexican Supreme Court. He was also an active member of the *foco* in Jiménez, and had joined the PLM army and accepted a commission from La Junta to travel, clandestinely, between Coahuila, Sonora, and Chihuahua recruiting fighters.[12] The soldiers buried him where he fell, but his father arrived the next day to disinter his son and bury him in Jiménez. When he uncovered the body, he found his son's hands bound with rope, suggesting that he had not died in the firefight at all. Rather, his father believed, Villarreal had been captured alive and executed.[13]

Also killed that night was one of the *rurales*, Patricio González.[14] Several bullets hit González in the right forearm, with the most significant damage done by a seven-centimeter bullet that ripped across the underside from just beneath the elbow crease to the wrist, fracturing the bone and tearing open an artery. After the shooting stopped, soldiers carried González to Jiménez, where physicians were unable to stop the bleeding. The next morning, at 7 am, González was pronounced dead from a "most abundant hemorrhage" at the wound site.[15]

After the gunfight, nearly every government agent in the region began looking for the PLM fighters. Díaz ordered that the rebels were to be found and killed. If the agents in Coahuila failed to do this, Díaz would no doubt remove Governor Cárdenas from office.[16] For the next several days, PLM fighters across Mexico attempted to incite similar attacks. In Acayucan, Veracruz, Hilario Salas (Mixtec) led two hundred PLM fighters in an ambush of government forces but they were quickly routed.[17] In reprisal, the regime made mass arrests and laid siege to several villages. Meanwhile, the Jiménez raiders hid in the mountains and took zigzag paths toward the border, trying to evade *rurales* and soldiers along the way. Arredondo and two other fighters finally arrived at the border on September 30, at a spot near Eagle Pass. He knew the crossing well, having often taken this route to visit his daughter in Del Rio. At "about day light; early in the morning; about 6 o'clock," Arredondo later testified, he and the others crawled out of the brush near the riverbank and quickly constructed a two-stick raft to carry them across the Rio Bravo to Texas.[18] All but three of the Jiménez fighters made it across the border. Díaz had no intention of letting them escape his wrath.

Part 3

RUNNING DOWN THE REVOLUTIONISTS

CHAPTER 14

Something Unusual

E MILIO KOSTERLITZKY AND HIS MEN ARRIVED AT THE BOR-
der after dark and waited for hours at the obelisk marking the
international boundary between the towns of Nogales, Sonora, and
Nogales, Arizona, known as Ambos Nogales. Curious residents
formed a crowd. Kosterlitzky's arrival meant that Díaz's fist was about
to strike. By midnight, hundreds of people had gathered around the
rurales, while others looked on from a safer distance. The people of
Ambos Nogales sensed that "something unusual [was about] to occur,"
as one local reporter put it.[1] They were right. They were about to witness U.S. authorities force a group of PLM fighters across the border
and into the custody of Kosterlitzky. It would be the first mass deportation of Mexicans from the United States.

At the dawn of the twentieth century, deportation was a new but
powerful practice in the United States. Amid a brutal anti-Chinese
movement among white settlers in the American West, Congress had
invented deportation when it passed the 1882 Chinese Exclusion Act,
the nation's first deportation law, which authorized federal authorities
to arrest, detain, and forcibly remove any Chinese laborer who entered
the country after 1882. In 1891, Congress approved the deportation of
all noncitizens who entered or remained within the United States in
violation of immigration restrictions. Until the 1920s, Chinese immigrants were the principal targets of the nation's emerging deportation

regime, followed by the poor, the unwell, and otherwise maligned, disparaged, and "undesirable" immigrants.

Meanwhile, as Chinese immigrants were being rounded up, detained and removed from the country, the Supreme Court issued a series of rulings, known as the Chinese Exclusion Cases, which made deportation one of the least democratic practices in modern American life. In *Chae Chan Ping* (1889), the Supreme Court ruled that Congress maintains what is called "plenary power" over stopping noncitizens from entering the United States, which means that Congress can pass laws and set rules to limit immigration without judicial review. In *Fong Yue Ting vs. United States* (1893)—a ruling that, to this day, remains a bedrock precedent of U.S. deportation practices—the Court extended this unchecked power to allow those already living within the nation to be forcibly removed. In other words, the Court created a realm of governance within the United States to which the Constitution did not apply. As the Court put it in *Fong Yue Ting*: "The provisions of the Constitution, securing the right of trial by jury and prohibiting unreasonable searches and seizures, and cruel and unusual punishment, have no application [to deportation]." In 1896, the Court tripled down on the federal government's "absolute and unqualified" power over deportation, ruling in *Wong Wing vs. the United States* that noncitizens in deportation proceedings could be detained without regard to the Fifth Amendment, which protects persons in the United States from the deprivation of liberty without due process.[2]

Unhinged from the rights and protections inscribed in the Constitution, immigration authorities routinely rounded up and detained Chinese immigrants for months, sometimes years, while conducting extensive investigations and background checks. Before the U.S. Immigration Service opened the Angel Island Immigration Station off the coast of California in 1910, most Chinese immigrants were indefinitely detained in a warehouse in San Francisco. In other words, by the early twentieth century, deportation had been forged into a procedure of extraordinary federal power. However, in 1906, this emerging regime was still in its infancy. In fact, the federal government deported fewer than 1,000 immigrants annually until the 1920s, amounting to just .01 percent of the one million immigrants who entered the country every year.[3] And, to be clear, the power of deportation was rarely used against Mexicans, who were generally allowed to cross the border at will during the early twentieth century. But, following the raid at Jiménez, U.S. immigration authorities tapped their extraordinary power to deport "undesirable" immigrants to force PLM fighters back into Mexico for punishment.

The first such deportations occurred in the Arizona–Sonora borderlands. When the Jiménez raiders escaped across the border into Texas, Mexico's secretary of foreign relations, Ignacio Mariscal, reached out to U.S. authorities to coordinate an international manhunt. The Díaz administration wanted the Jiménez raiders, and anyone who had helped them, extradited; they also wanted Ricardo Flores Magón, as well as every member of La Junta. While U.S. authorities and Mexican operatives began scouring the borderlands, they bore down on PLM members already in custody. These were the men of the PLM *foco* in Douglas, Arizona, who had been arrested during the raids orchestrated in early September by Chief Immigration Inspector George Webb.

Webb's first target was Abraham Salcido, who was reviled by local authorities for his role in the 1903 Clifton–Morenci strike. Webb quickly appointed a Board of Special Inquiry—a three-man panel of immigration officials—to formally request a deportation warrant from the Commissioner General of Immigration. The secretary of labor signed the order, and Webb promptly transported Salcido to the border, where he was handed over to Mexican authorities for prosecution. Deporting the other *magonistas* in Webb's custody was not so easy.

A half dozen of the *foco* members in Webb's custody were Mexican Americans or Mexican immigrants with impeccable paperwork documenting their lawful entry into the United States. The secretary of labor ordered Webb to release all U.S. citizens and documented immigrants, while the other PLM members in Webb's custody hired lawyers and fought their deportation.

In a series of hearings, Webb grilled the six PLM members remaining in his custody, searching for any violation that would subject them to deportation. "Where were you born?" he asked. "In Mexico," they all answered. "Were you ever convicted of a crime in Mexico?" he continued, hoping that the immigration ban on previously convicted persons might apply. "No," they each replied. "When did you come to the United States?" he probed. This question was important because, until 1917, there was a three-year statute of limitation on deportation for all but Chinese immigrants. Regardless of how a non-Chinese immigrant had entered the country, three years of residence in the United States without incident automatically upgraded the person's immigration status to legal and lawful. All of the immigrants in Webb's custody had entered within the last three years. Webb had found his opening. If he could prove that they had not complied with the administrative requirements for lawful entry, such as passing a health exam or paying an entry fee, they would be subject to immediate forced removal from the country. "Did you make application of Immigration Officers for admission?" he pressed. "No," and "I didn't know that such a thing existed," they all answered.[4] "Did anyone stop you on the line?" he continued. Again, their answers were similar: "No, I did not see any Officers"; "I thought I saw two inspectors but they did not say anything to me"; and so on.[5] Like most Mexican immigrants during the early twentieth century, they had crossed without question. In turn, they had not taken a medical exam or paid the entry fee. With this common omission on record, Webb followed the perfunctory process of asking the Commissioner General of Immigration for his stamp of approval on their deportation warrants and was shocked when the warrants were denied, the Commissioner stating that the men had "apparently entered because [of the] inattention [of the] immigration officers to duty. Have them medically examined and report results."[6] Webb protested. This is "a very serious thing . . . these parties have been stirring up strife," he explained to the Commissioner.[7] The PLM uprising, he continued, "is a matter that affects not only the Mexican government, the government of a friendly nation, but seriously endangers the lives and properties of a great number of Americans and other foreigners and their families who are now in Mexico."[8] Managing U.S.–Mexico relations was not his job, yet Webb took the liberty of urging the immediate deportation of all PLM members in his custody as a "deterent [sic] to others of a similar class and thereby conserve the peaceful and friendly relations now existing between the United States and Mexico."[9] The Commissioner General ordered Webb to just do his job and get the medical exams completed.

Webb filibustered for weeks, knowing that if the men in his custody passed the medical exams they would be released and allowed to remain in the United States. Meanwhile, he sent more letters and protests to his bosses in Washington, lobbying the Commissioner General to approve the deportations. The U.S. Attorney in Arizona, J. L. B. Alexander, weighed in, providing a statement in support of Webb's campaign. "I am clear and convinced that all of the above named persons entered unlawfully into the United States," wrote Alexander. "They all appear to be criminals and the facts show that they have devoted nearly their whole time to plotting a revolution against their own government. . . . Their [sic] are certainly undesirable people . . . such people should not be countenanced and permitted to remain in this country."[10] The Commissioner General did not budge. Having heard rumors that PLM fighters would be assassinated if forced back to Mexico, his own boss, the U.S. secretary of commerce and labor, had concluded, "to deport is to execute" and supported him in delaying any decision on deportations pending completion of the medical exams.[11]

Three days after the Jiménez raid, the Commissioner General abruptly reversed his position and, without explanation, issued a blanket deportation order for all of the PLM fighters in Webb's custody.[12] Webb enforced the order without delay, recruiting a team of immigration officers and Arizona Rangers to transport the detainees to the border. He also coordinated with Mexican officials.[13] Vice President Ramón Corral emphasized "the utmost importance of returning the deportees into the custody of Mexican authorities."[14] Secretary Mariscal concurred, stating that "The Mexican government has a significant interest in this deportation."[15]

U.S.–Mexico border obelisk in Ambos Nogales.

On October 3, 1906, Webb's deportation team pulled Bruno Treviño, Carlos Humbert, Leonardo Villarreal, Gabriel Rubio, Lázaro Puente, and Luis García from their cells at the Tucson County Jail. Before they left, Puente mailed a letter to his toddler son. Expecting to be assassinated in Mexico, he wanted his son to know that he had lived nobly, not as the *bandido* that the Díaz regime was sure to brand him. "I am a victim of the hatred and persecution of prominent people," he explained.[16] Webb's team boarded with their prisoners on the next train to Nogales. Near midnight, the train pulled into the station. Webb's team handcuffed the men and marched them to the border, about one block away.

As they approached the obelisk marking the boundary between the United States and Mexico, the residents of Ambos Nogales began pushing and jostling the officers, trying to get a look at the prisoners marching between them with their heads down. The crowd had been waiting for hours and wanted to know what was going on. When the officers finally shoved through the crowd, Treviño, Humbert, Villarreal, Rubio, Puente, and García looked up and saw Kosterlitzky and his *rurales* lined up just south of the obelisk. A local journalist recorded their reactions. The men "made frantic pleas to be released ... in sheer desperation the men began to struggle and attempt to escape," he reported.[17] Webb's team shoved the panicked men across the border into Kosterlitzky's custody. Within moments, the *rurales* had the PLM members cuffed, chained, and marching south toward Hermosillo, where they were scheduled to be tried for "treason against the Mexican republic."[18] A few days later, rumors began to circulate that some of the men had been killed by firing squad.[19]

CHAPTER 15

The Death of
Juan José Arredondo

W HEN IT CAME TO TRACKING DOWN THE JIMÉNEZ RAID-
ers, the Díaz regime prioritized finding their leader, Juan
José Arredondo. They wanted to make an example of the man the
U.S. press dubbed the "dean of the revolutionists."[1] Under pressure,
the governor of Coahuila personally arranged for Arredondo's capture,
hiring a south Texas judge, James G. Griner, to coordinate his arrest
and extradition.[2] Griner got to work immediately, signing arrest warrants and recruiting nearly every sector of U.S. law enforcement in the
Brown Belt to find Arredondo and the rest of the Jiménez raiders. The
U.S. Customs Service, the Immigration Service, the U.S. Marshals,
and the sheriff of Val Verde County joined the manhunt.

Griner's interagency task force tracked Arredondo to Spofford, a
small railroad junction about 40 miles from the border. Arredondo's
daughter and grandchildren lived on a ranch in the area. The sheriff, a
customs inspector, and an immigration agent found Arredondo walking on a dirt road near the ranch. When they approached, Arredondo
admitted who he was and what he had done. He did not resist arrest,
and the officers took him to jail in Del Rio.[3]

The task force soon arrested nine other raiders, and the Mexican
government filed extradition cases against all of them.

Extradition is the formal process by which a person in one country is surrendered to another country for criminal prosecution. The
process is usually regulated by treaty, and political crimes are typically

excluded. In other words, a person can usually be extradited for murder but not for participating in an armed revolt against a government. The first U.S.–Mexico extradition treaty was signed in 1861, as the United States descended into civil war. Many U.S. slaveholders wanted Mexico to extradite all Black persons who had successfully fled enslavement— at least 3,000 before the 1850s—and, despite the political chaos of the times, Mexico had consistently refused to return the runaways. Already at war with the Confederacy, President Abraham Lincoln signed an extradition treaty that excluded all political acts, including the self-emancipation of enslaved persons.[4]

Judge Griner had his doubts about the Mexican government's extradition strategy. Not only were the *magonistas'* infractions political, but when the Mexican government first filed its extradition requests with the state of Texas, the cases were assigned to a judge in Del Rio whom Griner described as "detrimental" to the interests of the Mexican government.[5] Griner wanted the cases transferred to a new judge in a different district. But the clock was ticking.

U.S. law gives foreign governments just forty days to present evidence in extradition proceedings, in order to prevent extradition proceedings from turning into indefinite detention. Arredondo and the Jiménez raiders in custody in the Del Rio jail were scheduled to be released on November 20, 1906, if credible evidence against them was not submitted. Griner advised the Mexican government to route new extradition warrants through the Department of State, but the process moved slowly. On November 19, the eve of the raiders' release, Griner was still scrambling to move the hearings. That afternoon he took a final gamble, boarding the late train to San Antonio to secure federal arrest warrants. Before leaving Del Rio, he telegraphed the following note to Consul Enrique Ornelas in San Antonio: "Am leaving this evening train_important matters relative your Government_must have complaints filed before seven o'clock tomorrow morning. Have U.S. Commission [have] our US Marshal ready to wire sheriff here to hold Prisoners_my train will reach your city about one am tonight_meet me or wire where I can see you tonight."[6] Ornelas wired back with instructions. When Griner's train pulled into San Antonio at 1:15 am, he walked to Ornelas's office, where a U.S. Commissioner was waiting with a new set of federal arrest warrants.[7] Griner took the early train back to Del Rio, arriving just in time to step into the courthouse a few minutes before 9 am. When the Del Rio judge terminated the extradition hearings and set the raiders free, Griner handed the new warrants to two U.S. Marshals, who rearrested the men. This time, the raiders would face extradition in a federal court in San Antonio.

The move to San Antonio reset the extradition clock. Griner now had forty more days—until December 30—to make the Mexican government's case against Arredondo and the others in custody. He advanced the Mexican government's contention that, on September 26, 1906, Juan José Arredondo had led a brigade of bandits in robbing, kidnapping, and murdering the residents of Jiménez, Mexico. To prove that the Jiménez raid was a criminal and not a political act, and thereby covered by the extradition treaty, Griner called several witnesses. A resident of Jiménez testified that the raiders had stolen one of his cows and slaughtered it. Mayor Ismael Rodríguez recounted how the raiders took guns and ammunition from his store.[8] Captain Bermea of the *rurales* told of the shootout at Hacienda de Victoria: "I was assaulted from several directions by armed people, and the result was that one of my men, Patricio Gonzales, was killed."[9]

The raiders' lawyer easily proved that political intent had motivated the raid. He put Arredondo and the others on the stand, prompting each man to explain why they had participated. Described by the local press as the "aged leader of the Jiménez raid," Arredondo testified in a "straightforward manner, in a husky or rather gruff voice," taking his time to explain that he had once been a captain in the Mexican military but, by 1906, he had turned against the Díaz regime, joining a "secret club" linked to La Junta in St. Louis and volunteering to lead a PLM battalion against the president.[10] The Jiménez raid was the culmination of their plans. Crescencio Villarreal Márquez, who had not participated in the raid but admitted to planning and coordinating the attack from his home in Del Rio, provided the most pointed testimony. "The purpose of this movement was to get the towns to uprise. It was to overthrow the government of General Porfirio Díaz," he testified.[11] Their attorney also read sixty-two letters into the record, mostly strategic correspondence between Crescencio Villarreal Márquez and Ricardo Flores Magón.[12] By the time all of the letters were entered into the record, the U.S. Commissioner saw the Jiménez raid for what it was— a political act, with Arredondo in the lead—and refused to extradite the accused. As the Commissioner put it, "An offense was committed at Jiménez, Mexico, September 26, 1906, and [evidence] connects the prisoners with that offense," but "the offense committed was of a political character and I order the prisoners discharged from custody."[13]

On January 5, 1907, Juan José Arredondo and the Jiménez raiders walked out of the San Antonio courthouse. That night, hundreds of PLM supporters gathered in a local park to celebrate their release.[14] But Arrendondo did not join them. Upon leaving the courthouse that afternoon, an immigration inspector had arrested Arredondo for unlawfully entering the United States. It was a setup. As Consul Ornelas explained in a telegram to Secretary Mariscal, "I was able to arrange to have him arrested for deportation."[15] A few weeks later, a local Board of Inquiry recommended deportation, describing Arredondo's "undesirability" as an immigrant. As one of the members put it, the Jiménez raid was "for the purpose of robbery" and clear evidence of his "undesirability as an alien to be admitted to the United States."[16] But, without comment, the Commissioner General of Immigration refused to approve the deportation. Arredondo was allowed to return home to Del Rio, where, in the words of a Mexican operative charged with monitoring *magonista* activities in the region, Arredondo threw himself back in with "the seditious doings of a few bad Mexicans on the border of this country."[17] By March 1907, Arredondo, Villarreal Márquez, and the others had established a new *foco* in Del Rio. They were holding late-night meetings, gathering guns, and recruiting fighters from across the Brown Belt. "The situation on this border is more serious than you know and requires special treatment," warned the Mexican consul in Eagle Pass.[18] He also suggested finding a "remedy" that would not involve "inept" U.S. agents, who had proven unable or unwilling to secure Arredondo's return.[19]

Two months later, Arredondo disappeared from Del Rio and turned up in a jail just south of the border. Mexican authorities said that he had crossed the border and surrendered himself, offering to identify *magonistas* in exchange for immunity. A spree of arrests followed. Within days, seventeen PLM affiliates were rounded up.[20] As Antonio de Pío Araujo noted, "There have been many arrests in México."[21] Arredondo, however, was not provided immunity. He was convicted of an unstated crime and imprisoned at the San Ulua Prison. By summer, he was dead.

La Junta bickered over the fate of Juan José Arredondo. Had their trusted comrade really turned against them? Some thought the arrests in Mexico were certain evidence against him. How else could the Mexican government have found so many of their friends so quickly? "Juan José Arredondo betrayed the cause. There is much demoralization in the movement because of his bad action," wrote Antonio de Pío Araujo, who was nearly arrested at a safe house in Mexico City.[22] Ricardo Flores Magón dismissed such thoughts, insisting that "we consider Arredondo to be one of the most loyal [PLM fighters]."[23] As for the arrests, Flores Magón suggested that someone close to La Junta was supplying the Mexican government with valuable intel. "Don't leave any papers out on your tables and don't let anyone peek at our communications," he advised all members of La Junta. "Tear up our envelopes so no one knows where our letters come from."[24] But Tomás Sarabia, Manuel's brother and Juan's cousin, was coming to another conclusion. With most PLM leaders hiding or traveling through the borderlands on gun runs and recruitment trips, La Junta routed their letters via central hubs, and Sarabia was their San Antonio communications operative, keeping an up-to-date list of everyone's address so he could receive and forward mail accordingly. Recently, he had noticed that the mail passing through his hands often arrived "*violada*" (violated), as he put it.[25] Someone was opening PLM letters, prompting him to wonder if someone was reading their mail and if this was how La Junta and PLM members on both sides of the border were being hunted down. Sarabia was correct. By 1907, agents of the Díaz regime had successfully penetrated the U.S. postal system.

CHAPTER 16

The Dead Letter Office

B ASED IN ST. LOUIS, AARÓN LÓPEZ MANZANO WAS THE PLM's first correspondence officer. Young and energetic, Manzano did his job well, making sure letters to and from La Junta reached their final destinations. He visited the St. Louis post office every day, sometimes twice a day, ferrying the armloads of PLM letters that coursed through the veins of the U.S. postal system. It was difficult work. Every member of La Junta used at least one pseudonym and their letters passed through at least five couriers before arriving in St. Louis. Sometimes they wrote in code.[1] Manzano—affectionately known as Mr. Apple, since his surname means apple tree in Spanish— kept track of the couriers, codes, circuits, and pseudonyms, making sure every letter stayed on course.

After the Jiménez raid, the Mexican consul in St. Louis, Miguel E. Diebold, quickly realized that stopping La Junta required breaking their correspondence chain. Staking out the post office, he learned that Mr. Apple was responsible for moving La Junta's mail through St. Louis, although he did not know how the system worked. Diebold first asked an immigration inspector to investigate Mr. Apple's status: could he be deported back to Mexico? He could not. Mr. Apple was a lawful immigrant. Could Mr. Apple be extradited? He could not. There were no documents connecting Mr. Apple to any crimes in Mexico. Running out of ideas, Diebold hired a private detective named Thomas Furlong to aid him in "pursu[ing] and dispers[ing] the PLM Junta."[2]

Thomas Furlong, from his book Fifty Years a Detective: 35 Real Detective Stories *(1912).*

Thomas Furlong began his spy career during the Civil War. Plain-looking and tubby, he traveled throughout the Confederacy collecting intelligence for the Union. After the war, Furlong was elected police chief in a Pennsylvania mining boom town and, from there, he built a secret police force for one of the nation's least popular robber barons, the railroad magnate Jay Gould. As historian Kerry Seagrave puts it, Furlong built Gould's secret police into a "force of thugs" trained to protect financial assets and crush labor organizing along Gould's 10,000 miles of track, including the extensive Missouri Pacific Railroad Line headquartered in St. Louis.[3] By the turn of the twentieth century, Furlong had established his own private detective company.[4]

Based in St. Louis, the Furlong Secret Service Company never rivaled the much larger, better established Pinkerton Agency, and Furlong's name did not become synonymous with American spycraft. But Thomas Furlong always imagined he could build the nation's premier detective agency and aspired to be the nation's Sherlock Holmes, a nickname actually given to one of his first employees, William J. Burns.[5] He spent his career as the scrappy spyman in St. Louis hustling contracts from the Pinkertons and seeking bigger opportunities at every turn. He solved murders, found missing kids, chased down train robbers, and so on, always looking for the next hot case. In October 1906, Consul Diebold dropped by Furlong's office, offering the opportunity of, in Furlong's words, "running down the revolutionists."[6] Furlong grabbed the gig. In time, Furlong would describe it as "the most difficult, as well as one of the most important, cases I have ever handled."[7]

Furlong began by putting everyone affiliated with the PLM in St. Louis under twenty-four-hour surveillance. At the time, few of them remained in the city. Ricardo and Enrique Flores Magón and Juan Sarabia were on the run. Antonio Villarreal was in the borderlands recruiting fighters. Only Manuel Sarabia and Librado Rivera had stayed in town, along with Mr. Apple, the Villarreal and Rivera families, and Trinidad Saucedo, a mysterious woman whom historians identify as the girlfriend of one of the Flores Magón brothers. Furlong assigned agents to follow them all. Fearing arrest, Rivera refused to leave his apartment, and Sarabia took to sneaking around town, trying to shake Furlong's men. After running into a Furlong agent lurking in a dark alleyway, he left town, too.

Furlong also assigned agents to monitor the post office. They watched Mr. Apple drop off and pick up letters, always waiting to see if Ricardo Flores Magón himself would show up. With that same hope, Pinkerton spies hired by William C. Greene also hung about the St. Louis post office, pestering postal workers for information. The postmaster became so frustrated by the spies lurking about the building and bothering his staff that he sent a message to the local U.S. Marshal, imploring him to coordinate with the Mexican consul. "So many inquiries and visits have been made and are being made by private detectives alleging to be in the employ of other private individuals in Mexico, or some branch of the Mexican Government, that these people [*magonistas*] have been and are continually being apprised of the desire for the apprehension of some of their number," wrote the postmaster. "It is simply a case where 'too many cooks spoil the broth' and I think that your office, this office, and the Mexican Consul, Mr. Diebold, had better be let alone to work the matter out."[8] Consul Diebold soon showed up at the postmaster's office with a special request.

Diebold asked the postmaster if he and his agents could intercept all PLM letters arriving at the St. Louis post office. The postmaster refused, explaining to Diebold that interfering with mail delivery was a federal crime. It was a felony for anyone but the addressee to open mail. But the postmaster was sympathetic to Diebold's request, so he advised him to seek an exception from the U.S. Postmaster in Washington, DC.[9] Diebold telegrammed this advice to Balbino Davalos, the new Mexican ambassador to the United States. Two days later, Davalos showed up at the office of the U.S. Postmaster, George B. Cortelyou.[10]

Cortelyou was in charge of the world's largest communications system.[11] Established by the Post Office Act of 1792, the U.S. Postal Service had a broad remit—everything from encouraging the free press by offering low postage to newspapers, to connecting the nation by mandating that the U.S. Post Office create roads to serve all existing and emerging communities. With the presumed exclusion of enslaved or Indigenous communities, these two provisions guaranteed that all white towns as well as the frontiersmen and families already pushing the boundaries of the young nation's territory would have a shared information and communication system that bound them together and to home.[12] As the nation—and its colonial outposts—expanded, the postal system grew and grew.

Everywhere U.S. settlers went, the U.S. Post Office swiftly followed: beyond the boundaries of the original thirteen colonies into the Ohio Territory, through the Louisiana Purchase, up along the Oregon Trail, and across the Mexican cession.[13] Following the Spanish–American War, the U.S. military government in the Philippines began issuing new stamps and controlling the mail system. The U.S. Post Office seized the Hawaiian postal system in 1900. And so it continued. By the turn of the twentieth century, the rise of U.S. empire had made the U.S. Post Office a global communications powerhouse. Its more than 76,000 post offices moved more than 15 million letters every year, reaching every corner of the continental United States and its expanding territories. Even the smallest of towns, hamlets, and pit stops had postal service. And the service was swift. Once the transcontinental railroad connected the continent, the U.S. Post Office began processing letters and packages on board trains, allowing mail to be delivered at an ever-quickening clip.[14]

Moreover, the U.S. postal system was cheap. An individual could send a first-class letter for just a few pennies, depending on how far it would travel. Newspaper publishers received an even better deal, paying just one penny per pound of paper regardless of distance. And, in 1902, when the Post Office established its Rural Free Delivery system, the nation's most far-flung settlers began receiving mail service directly to their homes. In the borderlands, rural routes delivered mail everywhere from *colonias* to farmhouses to towns.[15] In southern Arizona, some mining camps could count on receiving mail twice daily.[16]

Established in part as the communications engine for Anglo-American conquest and industry, the routes were leveraged by rebels and dissidents for their own purposes. During the antebellum period, abolitionists mailed material into South Carolina. Slaveholders burned the mail.[17] Birth control advocates routinely defied and challenged the 1873 Comstock Law, which prohibited mailing contraception, or information about it, across state lines.[18] By 1906, the PLM had tapped the U.S postal service, too. They used the second-class rate to cheaply mail *Regeneración* to subscribers across the borderlands and they used penny postage to send letters—hundreds and hundreds of letters—setting up *focos*, recruiting fighters, planning raids, and so on.

Following the Jiménez raid, Ambassador Davalos showed up at U.S. Postmaster Cortelyou's office to see what could be done to track down the *magonistas* via the U.S. postal system. Cortelyou, a career diplomat and confidant of President Theodore Roosevelt, took the unscheduled meeting and listened carefully as Davalos explained the urgency of seizing all PLM letters passing through the St. Louis post office. The *magonistas*, as Ambassador Davalos put it, were revolutionaries hell-bent on disrupting peace and commerce in Mexico. Given the extent of U.S. investments in Mexico, Davalos emphasized that the capture of the *magonistas*' leader, Ricardo Flores Magón, would benefit both countries. Postmaster Cortelyou informed Davalos that intercepting the mail would constitute a federal crime but called into the room his second-in-command, Chief Inspector William Vickery. Vickery took Davalos to his office to talk.[19]

Vickery advised Davalos of two provisions: first, that a U.S. Marshal could arrest any person who collected mail not addressed to them, and second, that any letter left undelivered or uncollected for more than thirty days was a "dead letter." Uncollected letters were forwarded to the dead letter office in Washington, where experts would try to decipher the addressee or return the letter to sender. But, Vickery noted, before any of the PLM's uncollected correspondence left St. Louis, the local postmaster could allow a Mexican agent to open, read, and copy—but not seize—it. In other words, the U.S. Post Office offered a legal workaround that would enable the arrest of Mr. Apple and allow agents of the Mexican government to review the PLM's mail.[20] Davalos left Vickery's office and telegrammed the news to Diebold in St. Louis, where, within a week, he, Furlong, and the local U.S. Marshals' office had concocted a sting operation.

With the approval of the local postmaster, U.S. Marshal William L. Morsey planted in the PLM's post office box a letter addressed to a man named Señor D. Cacilio Romo. Morsey and Diebold then waited for Mr. Apple to arrive. When Mr. Apple pulled out a stack of letters, including the letter addressed to Señor D. Cacilio Romo, another marshal, W. W. Noll, stepped forward. "Are you Mr. Romo?" he asked. When Mr. Apple replied, "No," Noll arrested him and booked Mr. Apple into the St. Louis County Jail.[21]

Mr. Apple's arrest was a major setback for the PLM. Not only did it effectively shut down the PLM's correspondence system in St. Louis but, after thirty days, the PLM letters piling up at the post office were pronounced "dead" and made available for Diebold and Furlong's team of detectives to copy. Furlong used those letters to track down *magonistas* on both sides of the border. Having tracked Ricardo Flores Magón—code names Caule, Benjamín, and Rafael—to a small apartment in Montreal, he jumped on a train and found the Flores Magón brothers living above a restaurant, doing common labor by day and writing letters by night. He put them under surveillance, but while he waited for the Mexican government to submit extradition papers to the Canadian government, the brothers noticed the spy and fled the city.[22]

Furlong expanded his search. By November 1906, he was receiving copies of PLM letters intercepted in post offices across the United States. They were not all dead letters. Most of them had been intercepted upon arrival at the post offices in Los Angeles, El Paso, St. Louis, and Chicago. When Mexican authorities asked Furlong how he was able to gain such immediate access to *magonista* mail, Furlong refused to answer. All he would say was that "These letters were . . . intercepted by one of my men who is stationed . . . for that purpose," and he strongly advised Mexican authorities to keep his access to the U.S. mail system "strictly confidential," warning that "if the manner in which this information came into our possession were mentioned or known to persons who are doubtless friendly to the cause in which we are engaged, but who are not as deeply interested in the result as you and your Government are, they might, I fear, make trouble for good and loyal men who have been, and are rendering us valuable assistance in this matter, and if so, it would be almost impossible for us to keep track of the guilty parties."[23]

Most likely, Thomas Furlong and his agents, including post office plants, were bending if not breaking U.S. federal law by intercepting mail. Nevertheless, the strategy worked. La Junta did not know it yet but, following Mr. Apple's arrest in November 1906, they no longer enjoyed the element of secrecy or surprise. Worse, Furlong and his men began using tips, clues, and addresses gleaned from their letters to chase them across the United States, Canada, and Mexico.

Furlong's agents opened the envelopes, copied the letters, and then returned the letters to the postal system, hoping the *magonistas* would not notice that their correspondence was being monitored. The copied letters arrived at Furlong's office within days, by the bundle, sometimes suitcases, amounting to what Furlong described as "material enough to cover reams of foolscap."[24] Furlong studied each one, then passed it along to Consul Diebold, who sent all the letters to Secretary Mari-

PLM code key.

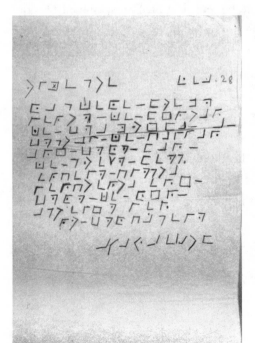

Coded letter sent from Antonio de Pío Araujo to Aarón López Manzano, on February 28, 1907. The letter was seized by the Furlong Secret Service Company and sent to Ignacio Mariscal's office in Mexico City. Along with other rebel correspondence, this letter is now archived at Mexico City's Acervo Histórico Diplomático, which is located at Avenida Ricardo Flores Magón #2.

scal's office in Mexico City.[25] Today, the PLM letters stolen by Furlong's men are bound, catalogued, and archived in the U.S. Embassy Collection in Mexico City's Archivo Histórico Diplomatico de la Secretaría de Relaciones Exteriores. These letters remain some of the best evidence historians have to piece together the PLM revolution brewing in the borderlands. For Furlong, every PLM letter contained a clue. An address. A name. A plan. But Furlong had to decipher the evidence.

As early as the summer of 1906, La Junta began writing in ciphers and codes, assigning each letter in the alphabet a symbol or using euphemisms for key words. ("Five dollars" was "five days," for example, in the letters sent before the Jiménez raid.) They also used pseudonyms and passed each letter through different couriers to hide its origin and destination. The *magonistas* could spend hours drafting a single coded letter. Ever cautious, the PLM correspondence directors, Mr. Apple in St. Louis and Tomás Sarabia in San Antonio, often recoded the letters as they passed through their hands.[26] After reviewing some of the first letters to be seized in St. Louis, Consul Diebold noted how difficult it was going to be to track down the *magonistas*. "They have recently adopted a code system that makes it very difficult for us [the Mexican government] to follow all of the persons of interest and discern one from another," he complained.[27] And they changed the code frequently. Sometimes they used ciphers—symbols for letters. Sometimes they used codes—switching up letters in a consistent pattern. Sometimes they used codes within ciphers. Furlong persisted. He decoded and deciphered the letters, finding the patterns, listing the pseudonyms, and mapping the hot spots where La Junta seemed to be hiding or gathering.

CHAPTER 17

We Knew His Whereabouts Continuously

L IBRADO RIVERA WAS ARRESTED IN HIS APARTMENT ON
October 31, 1906, during a sting coordinated by Consul Diebold, U.S. Marshal Morsey, Thomas Furlong, and the St. Louis Police
Department. Two undercover detectives entered the apartment dressed
as gas company employees. Pretending to check the pipes and appli-
ances, they were searching the apartment when, toward the back, they
saw a man ready to jump out a window. They rushed the man, pulled
him back into the apartment, and demanded to know his name. Rivera
lied, giving his name as Herbert Koro and claiming to be an immigrant from Argentina making some extra money by helping with
chores. The police believed his cover but Diebold, who was waiting
outside, asked Morsey to take the man into custody for further investigation. Lacking grounds for arrest, Morsey called the local immigration inspector and asked him to place a hold on "Koro," who was
booked into the St. Louis Hospital for a health evaluation, a process
that would give Morsey plenty of time to investigate his identity.[1]

Rivera was held incommunicado for eleven days in the St. Louis
Hospital. Feeling isolated, he was relieved to see a man named Sanders, who had briefly worked as a printer's assistant at the *Regeneración*
office, walk into the general ward. Rivera asked Sanders to sit by his
side and proceeded to spill everything he knew about La Junta. What
Rivera did not know was that Sanders was on Furlong's payroll. That
evening, Sanders confirmed Rivera's identity and wrote a detailed

report of their meeting.[2] The next day, Rivera was transferred to jail, where he would be detained pending the outcome of an extradition request from Mexican government. Two days later, Mr. Apple joined him, following his arrest at the post office.

With Librado Rivera and Mr. Apple in jail, Diebold had an idea: he asked if Marshal Morsey or Thomas Furlong could just send Mr. Apple "across the border without any further legal requirements."[3] In other words, the consul proposed an international kidnapping. A few days later, Morsey quietly put Rivera and Mr. Apple on a train heading south. Morsey would likely have succeeded in what may have been an extraordinary rendition attempt except for the fact that the Villarreal sisters persuaded the St. Louis press to cover the story, forcing Morsey to abort the mission about 70 miles south of the city. The men were returned to St. Louis for their court proceedings: Rivera for extradition, Mr. Apple for illegally receiving mail.

The U.S. Commissioner quickly dismissed Rivera's extradition case, as the Mexican government had provided no evidence that he had committed an extraditable crime in Mexico. Rivera went home, gave a few interviews to local reporters, and then, fearing another arrest, went underground.[4] The Díaz regime offered $2,500 for his recapture, dead or alive.[5] When a judge released Mr. Apple on bail, he, too, went on the run.[6]

Furlong tracked them down, using the letters being opened and transcribed by his agents stationed at post offices across the United States.

"We knew his [Rivera's] whereabouts continuously from the time he left St. Louis," boasted Furlong.[7] By January 1907, Furlong had tracked Rivera to Texas, where he had connected with the PLM gun-runner Antonio de Pío Araujo, whom Mexican and U.S. operatives identified as using a string of pseudonyms and code names in PLM correspondence, including German Riesco, Moran, Axayacatl, Arcuijo, Cipriano, Emilio Bello, Charles Watson, Emilio Aceval, Joaquin B. Calvo, Alberto M. Ricaurte, Luis F. Carlo, A. G. Hernández, and "El Provisional."[8] In a letter Araujo mailed at 3:30 am from Waco, he wrote about how busy he had been collecting *dulces y escobas* for a raid on

Matamoros, just across the border from Brownsville.[9] He had already stashed fourteen carbines, 1,600 cartridges, and sixty sticks of dynamite in their provisional barracks under the floorboards of an old ranch house outside of Del Rio.[10] There was another stash in a cave about 10 miles away.[11] "The hour of vengeance is near," wrote Araujo. "The revolution will not wait another month. We go to victory, or death."[12] While waiting for Flores Magón to issue the signal to attack, the fighters looked for work in and around Del Rio.[13]

But Flores Magón never sent the signal. He nixed the Matamoros raid, writing, "It's my opinion that we should not begin the movement. We need to first notify our comrades throughout the Republic of the Instructions that you already have, so they can prepare themselves, so they can be ready to fight . . . and when enough of us are ready, then we will begin the movements at once at all points."[14]

With the Matamoros raid on hold, Rivera began moving about with no clear pattern, mailing increasingly desperate dispatches from isolated locations. Under the pseudonym Leonel, he wrote from Denver, "I am on the verge of being apprehended. I leave here tomorrow morning. Do not write anymore. I still do not know if I can escape."[15] He then walked 33 miles through rain and snow, arriving in Colorado Springs with his feet "full of sores." All he could afford to eat was a cup of coffee and a bit of bread. *"Esto es todo"* (That's it), he added. Alone and broke, and worried that spies were following him everywhere, he begged his friends to send him funds to survive, explaining that he could not look for work: "If you have a peso or two, send me whatever you can."[16] Pennies and dollars arrived from comrades across the United States and Mexico.[17] Still, in May 1907, Rivera reported that he was in as desperate a situation as could be imagined, *"sin dinero, perseguido, y sin trabajo"* (without money, pursued, and without work).[18] Although he was starving, Rivera, the quiet teacher from San Luis Potosí, refused to give up, remaining committed to the PLM and its cause.

Rivera's wife felt differently. Back in St. Louis, Concepción (Conchita) Rivera had given birth to their third child, a girl named Teresita. Whenever possible, Rivera mailed her money, which she shared with

*Concepción
(Conchita) Rivera.*

the other PLM families in the city. Manuel Sarabia, Tomás Sarabia, and Ricardo Flores Magón also sent money to the families in St. Louis, and the women evenly split every dollar that arrived. But it was never enough. As she struggled to feed her children, Conchita Rivera's letters to her husband grew increasingly tense. "I make a dollar or two every week, but the work tires me and the baby won't let me be," she wrote.[19] She wanted him to know how difficult her life was without his help. "You should know that you left me in disgrace with my children. . . . I am suffering without respite," she continued. She was thinking about returning home to Mexico without him, she wrote. "I want you to understand that I cannot live here, let me leave, there it will be easier for me to raise my children. I am confident that they [government officials] will not harm me."[20] She had already consulted Rivera's mother on the matter, and his mother agreed. "Son, it is time for you to quit all this with your ideas [of revolution], for yourself, for your poor wife, for your innocent children, and your inconsolable mother," she wrote in a blistering letter from Mexico.[21] "[We have] already suffered so much and what have you gained? Not much. Think about it. What if something happens to you [God forbid], if your enemies catch you, what will happen to your family, to your unfortunate children . . . your inconsolable wife . . . and your mother who already suffers from your capriciousness. No, son, think about it good and figure out how to escape the clutches of Porfirio Díaz."[22] She wanted him to quit the campaign against Díaz, but Rivera chose to stick with the PLM and kept moving, staying one step ahead of Furlong's men.

Furlong also tracked Mr. Apple, who, after jumping bail, headed to Mexico to recruit more PLM fighters. On his way, he stopped in San Antonio to train Tomás Sarabia as the PLM's new chief correspondence officer. While there, he mailed a letter to his mother, asking for money for the next leg of his journey. Furlong's men intercepted her reply. "Dearest son, I want to help you but I cannot because we are very poor," she wrote, adding a few words of caution to her son: "Be careful because these are very delicate times."[23]

With nothing more than a pistol and four dollars in his pocket, Mr. Apple left San Antonio for the city of Monterrey in the Mexican state of Nuevo León, arriving on April 24, 1907. From there, he sent a letter, under the code name Foca, warning his comrades, "we're screwed," because there was "heavy surveillance" in Mexico and two of their closest contacts in Monterrey had been arrested.[24] Not knowing who to turn to for support in Monterrey, he wrote to Tomás Sarabia in San Antonio, asking him to send, in code, information about whom he could contact for a job and support. He also instructed Sarabia to "not send me any other papers, just the ones I've told you to" and "tear up my letter after you read it."[25] Mr. Apple was sure he was being watched. Then, his letters stopped. One week, two weeks, three weeks passed. When Sarabia did not hear from him, he wrote to his brother Manuel, asking, "What has happened? Was he captured?"[26] One month later, Mr. Apple finally made contact. "I was betrayed in Monterrey," he wrote from Belem Prison.[27]

Using the PLM letters intercepted by his agents at the San Antonio post office, Thomas Furlong had tracked Mr. Apple to Monterrey. On the afternoon of April 29, 1907, when Mr. Apple went to collect his mail at the Monterrey post office, a man waiting in the lobby slipped in behind him and quietly grabbed him by the arm. It was Furlong.[28] Another man grabbed his other arm. It was Sanders, the print shop assistant/spy who had betrayed Librado Rivera. An hour later, Mr. Apple was in jail and Furlong was in his hotel writing a letter to the Mexican ambassador to the United States, explaining that not only had Mr. Apple been captured but "a number of valuable papers were found on his person including his Commission as General Delegate signed by Ricardo Flores Magón as well as the code key and numerous names of co-workers."[29] The key, he promised, could be used to run down Flores Magón and the rest of La Junta. "I firmly believe," wrote Furlong, "that if permitted with the services of three operatives and myself from now on that I could land them all in Mexican prisons within the next sixty days."[30]

In jail, Mr. Apple talked with dozens of other PLM members, most of whom had also been tracked down and arrested after having had their mail intercepted. Soon after, he was transferred from Monterrey to Belem and from there to San Ulua Prison in Veracruz. On May 22, 1907, he smuggled a letter out to Tomás Sarabia, warning him to "not send letters through the mail because they are all stolen and they take copies of them and later send them on to their destination."[31] Three weeks later, he smuggled another letter out of jail to Jesús María Rangel, a trusted friend and PLM fighter in Waco, Texas. "All our letters are being violated . . . this is how they have learned so many of our secrets," he explained, urging Rangel to "change your address as quickly as possible and tell the same to Labrada [Tomás Sarabia] and all of our friends."[32]

For Manuel Sarabia, the warning arrived too late.

CHAPTER 18

The Kidnapping of
Manuel Sarabia

A FTER LEAVING ST. LOUIS, MANUEL SARABIA WENT TO Chicago to hide out. Thomas Furlong tracked him there. While awaiting instructions from the Mexican government, Furlong assigned an agent to get close to Sarabia. On January 15, 1907, the agent reported, "I have been keeping track of Manuel Sarabia . . . most of this time I have been in company with him, taking our meals together, etc. . . . I have his confidence I believe as much as anyone can have and hope shortly to get his entire confidence."[1] Sarabia, however, was cautious. He used an alias, Sam Moret, and, as the agent recounted, "He is very careful in writing his letters, as he always goes to his room and does not let me see them. He is also very careful not to open his letters in my presence."[2]

Sarabia left Chicago in March 1907, heading to the border to recruit more PLM fighters and establish more *focos*. He stopped in Indian Territory (Oklahoma) to make contact with Mexican miners in towns such as Dow and McAlester, and in May he arrived in southern Arizona. Secretary Mariscal had recently ordered all Mexican consuls in the border region to use "vigilance" and be on the lookout for "bad Mexicans."[3] Working in and around Douglas, Sarabia noted the increased surveillance, led by Chief Immigration Inspector George Webb, who was helping Mexican consular officials to interrogate "various suspicious Mexicans" and investigate the immigration status of suspected *foco* members.[4] By June, he felt Díaz's men closing in on him. "I'm in a dangerous place," he wrote to Antonio de Pío Araujo.[5] By the end of the month, he had been kidnapped.

On June 30, Sarabia went to the train station in Douglas to drop a letter in the mail car. As he later reported to the *International Socialist Review*, a "red-faced man, who had been watching me from the opposite side of the street," followed him. As he sped up to drop his letter into the moving train car, the man rushed across the street and grabbed him by the shoulder. "I stopped, suddenly, facing him, amazed at the affront. Then he questioned me in a menacing voice: 'Can you speak English?' I replied curtly, 'Certainly—but what business have you with me?' 'You're under arrest—that's all,' was his harsh answer."[6] When Sarabia demanded to see an arrest warrant, the man, an Arizona Ranger named Samuel Hayhurst, unsheathed his revolver, pressed it to Sarabia's chest, and forced him to walk to the jail, where the Mexican consul, Antonio Maza, was waiting. Maza had already contracted with a Pinkerton agent and a city marshal named Dowdle to guard Sarabia. Around 11 pm, the three men, along with a local constable named A. J. Shropshire, handcuffed Sarabia and removed him from his cell. Sarabia sensed danger. When the officers hauled him outside toward a parked car, he decided to run. "Ducking suddenly under their arms, I dashed down the street," he recalled. "Like two dogs after a cat, they pursued me, and before a dozen yards were passed, I felt one's hand upon my shoulder and with a jerk, I was lying upon the ground. I arose, panting and hatless, the two holding me firmly between them as I walked slowly back to the automobile." But Sarabia was not done fighting. "As my breath came back so did my determination to resist," he wrote, and he recalled hollering out, over and over, "Help, friends, I am being kidnapped—I have committed no crime. My name is Sarabia, Manuel Sarabia, help!"[7]

Then, one of the officers "pulled a handkerchief from his pocket, rolled it into a ball and, with a brutal thrust, pushed it into my mouth. I was gagged. My cries stopped. Between the two powerful men, I was lifted and pushed, struggling at every inch, into the open side of the big automobile." The officers closed the curtains in the car, blindfolded Sarabia, and drove to the border, accompanied by the new head of the Arizona Rangers, Harry Wheeler. In 1917, Wheeler would coordinate the mass arrest and removal of striking miners from Bisbee, Arizona, in a now infamous event known as the Bisbee Deportation. On June 30, 1907, Wheeler aided and abetted the international kidnapping of Manuel Sarabia. At the border, Wheeler stood with Maza, Dowdle, and Shropshire, forcing a struggling Sarabia across the border. Blindfolded, Sarabia could hear a posse awaiting him. "A familiar jingle struck my ear . . . —bridles and spurs—the *rurales*!" he recalled, before one of them ripped off his blindfold, revealing Emilio Kosterlitzky mounted with ten men surrounding him. There was nowhere to run. Kosterlitzky instructed his men to toss Sarabia over the back of a mule, "as a sack of potatoes," and bind his feet with rawhide beneath the mule's belly. Bound and gagged, Sarabia was kicked and carried for eighteen hours to the prison in Hermosillo, where he was held incommunicado.[8] Consul Maza wired Secretary Mariscal that Manuel Sarabia had been apprehended and successfully returned to Mexico.[9]

It had been a busy day in Douglas. Early that day, local miners had held a large rally. Some of the nation's leading labor organizers had attended, including Mother Jones. A miner walking within earshot of the jail that evening heard Sarabia yelling and ran to the hotel where Mother Jones was staying. Mother Jones would later tell the United States Congress that the miner "burst into the room very excited. He said, 'Oh Mother, they have kidnapped Sarabia, our young revolutionist.' . . . He was flushed and almost incoherent. I said, 'Sit down a moment and get cool, then tell me your story.'"[10] The man told Mother Jones all about Manuel Sarabia, La Junta, the PLM's support of the strikers at Cananea, and their determination to protect workers in Mexico. Based upon the screams, the miner surmised that Sarabia had been kidnapped and was facing a lawless extradition to Mexico. Mother Jones told the miner, "Get all the facts you can, get them as cor-

rect as you can and immediately telegraph to the governor. Telegraph
to Washington. Don't stop a moment because if you do they will murder him."[11] That night, the miners delivered to Mother Jones the facts
she had asked for. Sarabia had been kidnapped. U.S. officers aided the
kidnapping. Emilio Kosterlitzky had seized him at the border, and his
life was in danger. Mother Jones was inclined to believe the tale as,
just the year before, Pinkerton agents in the employ of mining companies had kidnapped three officials of the Western Federation of Miners
(WFM)—William "Big Bill" Haywood, Charles Moyer, and George
Pettingbone—and spirited them across state lines for prosecution in
Idaho.[12] She immediately wired the governor of Arizona and President Roosevelt. She and the WFM spent the next few weeks leveraging their platforms to educate U.S. journalists and labor leaders about
the PLM and the complicity of U.S. authorities in Díaz's cross-border
counterinsurgency efforts. As she explained, "Sarabia had incurred the
hatred of Díaz and the forty thieves that exploited the Mexican peons
because he had called Díaz a dictator. For this he had served a year in
Mexican jails. He came to the United States and continued to wage the
fight for Mexico's liberation. Díaz's hate followed him across the border
and finally he had been kidnapped and taken across the Mexican border at the request of the tyrant."[13]

Mexican authorities disclaimed any knowledge of the kidnapping, calling the story "pure fabrication."[14] But Mother Jones kept the
pressure on until U.S. audiences and authorities took issue with the
notion of a foreign government undertaking a kidnapping on U.S.
soil. By July 5, the U.S. attorney general had ordered the U.S. attorney
for Arizona, J. L. B. Alexander, to investigate, while Captain Harry
Wheeler of the Arizona Rangers quietly slipped into Mexico to negotiate Sarabia's safe return.[15]

On July 12, Wheeler returned to Douglas with his prisoner. Sarabia's return cut short further inquiry into how high the plot reached,
allowing the Díaz regime to lay the blame on Consul Maza, who was
arrested and charged with kidnapping. The U.S. attorney concluded

that local authorities had acted alone, meaning that there was no reason for the Department of Justice to investigate further.[16]

The next month, U.S. officers and agents working at the behest of the Mexican government attempted another kidnapping. This time the target was Ricardo Flores Magón.

CHAPTER 19

El Alma de Todo

FOLLOWING THE JIMÉNEZ RAID, MEXICAN GOVERNMENT officials and their allies publicly maintained that Ricardo Flores Magón and the PLM posed no threat to the Díaz regime, that the so-called *magonistas* in the United States were nothing more than a bunch of crooks and swindlers, tricking poor Mexicans into sending them money by promoting false solutions to imaginary problems. Across the United States, Mexican consuls fed journalists this story. "Ignorant Natives . . . deceived into contributing large sums to correct imaginary wrongs," wrote the *Galveston Daily News*.[1] "Mexican Revolution for Revenue Only," began an article in the *Arizona Republican*.[2] In St. Louis, Consul Diebold submitted a letter to the editor of the *St. Louis Globe–Democrat* declaring La Junta to be "swashbucklers . . . men of no influence whatever, devoid of social standing, humble, impecunious, hungry adventurers and fugitives from justice," while assuring readers that "there is no revolution imminent in Mexico. The country is prosperous, the people perfectly contented and happy and the government is established upon solid bases, and capital finds there safe investment, which fact is substantiated by the $500,000,000 American dollars invested in Mexican mines, agriculture, and industrial enterprises."[3]

Nonetheless, at the highest levels of the Díaz regime, the PLM uprising was treated as a serious threat to national security. As Enrique Creel, one of Díaz's closest advisers, put it in a letter to Vice President Corral: "Whatever comes to pass, we must persevere for months and

Enrique Creel.

years, if it is necessary, and spend whatever is required, until we capture Ricardo Flores Magón and the other leaders, because that is what the public good demands and what our patriotism demands."[4] President Díaz agreed, naming Creel the Mexican Ambassador Extraordinary and Plenipotentiary to the United States and authorizing him to take charge of finding Flores Magón and the *magonistas*.[5]

Enrique Creel was as determined as President Díaz to track down Ricardo Flores Magón and crush the PLM. Known as "the Mexican J. P. Morgan," Creel was Mexico's leading banker, owning or investing in banks in six Mexican states.[6] His largest holding, Banco Central Mexico, was Mexico's second largest bank, intimately tying Creel's personal wealth to the regime's well-being. Creel was also the son-in-law of Luis Terrazas, one of Mexico's wealthiest men, and contributed mightily to the Terrazas family's economic dominance. As the historian Mark Wasserman explains, Creel was "second-in-command" over the enormous Terrazas holdings.[7] Moreover, Creel, the bilingual son of a Mexican woman and a U.S. consular official, was the primary intermediary between U.S. investors and President

Díaz. For hefty fees, he brokered the meetings and deals that delivered the most beneficial terms for investors in Mexico. So favored were Creel's services that the U.S.-owned Mexican Central Railway paid Creel $50,000 (pesos) a year just to sit on its board.[8] Deeply invested in the Díaz regime, Creel worked hard to protect it, and prioritized the search for Ricardo Flores Magón.

Flores Magón had been living on the run for nearly a year, since jumping bail in St. Louis in March 1906. There had been rumored sightings of him everywhere from Texas to New York to Canada to California, but whenever the regime dispatched operatives to investigate, he disappeared. In Texas, one operative believed "that there is no question . . . that Ricardo Flores Magón is in or very near Del Rio, but I have been unable so far, due to the fact that practically the entire Mexican colony is in sympathy with these people, to get any definite information as to where he is exactly located."[9] Thomas Furlong tracked him to Montreal and had him under surveillance, but he slipped away before the Mexican government could submit a viable extradition request. By December 1906, when Creel took charge of the regime's cross-border counterinsurgency strategy, the search for Flores Magón had notched a series of missed chances and near catches. Creel, too, got close, when he thwarted a PLM raid on Ciudad Juárez.

La Junta had been planning a raid on Ciudad Juárez for months. Juárez was Mexico's portal to the United States, its leading trade partner. Every year, millions of dollars in copper, coal, cotton, steel, timber, and more flowed over the bridge that hung across the Rio Grande between Ciudad Juárez and El Paso. Whereas the raid on Jiménez had been a short fight in a remote town, a raid on Juárez would deliver a humiliating blow to Díaz's claims of peace and security in Mexico. Flores Magón hoped that a PLM raid on Juárez would be a bold enough move to trigger an uprising across the country. But the regime knew the PLM was coming.

After the Jiménez raid, the regime blanketed the borderlands with spies and informants, trying to anticipate the PLM's next move.[10] Intel on *magonista* activities flowed across government desks from the border to the National Palace. One of the most alarming reports came from the *jefe político* in Ciudad Juárez, who warned that Ricardo Flores Magón was rumored to be traveling the borderlands and "activating a rebellion." In particular, he reported, there was a high level of "rebel activity" in and around El Paso, where *magonistas* "work actively and with much malice and there is no doubt that they are distributing negative propaganda across the borderlands."[11] It was being said that nearly one thousand PLM fighters were gathering in El Paso, ready to storm Ciudad Juárez. Determined to protect Mexico's primary portal to the U.S. market, President Díaz ordered five hundred soldiers to Juárez, where they prepared for the *magonista* strike.[12]

On the evening of October 19, 1906, Juan Sarabia and his childhood friend Zeferino Reyes guided a small contingent of armed PLM fighters across the bridge between El Paso and Ciudad Juárez. Once in Juárez, Reyes took the lead. He knew the city well and, as a soldier in the Mexican Army, he was the most experienced in military maneuvers. Behind Reyes, the small contingent of PLM fighters crept down the wide, dusty road toward the jail. The plan was to release political prisoners and then, with reinforcements, attack Juárez. But when the PLM fighters burst into the jail, they were swarmed by soldiers and police officers, who took them into custody and charged them with treason. Reyes, it turned out, was one of Díaz's spies, and had led the PLM fighters into a trap. The raid on Ciudad Juárez was over before it began.[13]

Thwarting the raid was a major victory for the Díaz regime, proving that the regime stood ready to crush the uprising. Moreover, as Juan Sarabia was the vice president of the PLM, his capture marked the first arrest of a Junta leader. And police found in his possession one of La Junta's most guarded documents: a list of *Regeneración* subscribers, including names and home addresses.[14] Creel instructed the Juárez police to strike out across town and round up *magonistas* in the Juárez area. He then sent a copy of the list across the border to El Paso, where Thomas Furlong, U.S. Marshals, and the El Paso Police Department raided the homes of *Regeneración* subscribers. By morning, a dozen *magonistas* were in custody—plus, Furlong had a few tips on where to find Ricardo Flores Magón. They raided Lauro Aguirre's home, searched a hotel, and ransacked an office located above a bar called the Legal Tender Saloon—all presumed to be PLM hideouts. At the Legal Tender Saloon, they got close to nabbing Flores Magón. He and Antonio Villarreal had been nearing the building when Villarreal sensed something amiss and told Flores Magón to wait at the corner while he checked the building. Villarreal was arrested on site. Flores Magón escaped.[15]

Creel's team spent days combing the streets of El Paso for the man known as "*el alma de todo.*" But it was useless: "*fué inutil* [sic]," explained the *jefe político* from Juárez, who had crossed the border to aid the search.[16] Flores Magón was gone. Creel was furious. Díaz offered a $20,000 bounty for Flores Magón's capture.[17]

After a short respite in Los Angeles, Flores Magón traveled constantly to evade arrest. Up to Canada. Down to San Francisco. Over to Texas. The extant historical record does not tell every place he went, but he later recalled these months as frantic: "The secret service of two nations pursued me from one place to another, from city to city."[18] Meanwhile, Juan Sarabia, Antonio Villarreal, and dozens of PLM fighters and subscribers were in jail on both sides of the border, following the thwarted Juárez raid.

In Mexico, Juan Sarabia and the Juárez raiders were tried for treason. President Díaz wanted their prosecution "to leave an impression."[19] While their cases unfolded, they were held in the Allende Jail in Chihuahua City. An old stone stockade, the Allende Jail had two large galley rooms and twelve isolation cells, named for the months of the year. The hottest cells had summer names: June, July, August. The coldest cell was called December. In hourly bursts, the guards swapped Sarabia between cells, cycling his body through the seasons. The sequence always ended the same way. Near midnight, a blindfolded Sarabia was led into the jail courtyard to the sound of clanking swords and clacking rifles. Then silence fell, and only the crackle of oil lamps could be heard. In the noiseless void, the guards pulled their triggers on empty cartridges. Sarabia never knew if he would be executed or not. As this torture proceeded, daily, for two months, he got sicker and sicker. The tubercular infection that would, ultimately, kill him, in 1920, was slowly clogging his lungs.[20]

By the time Juan Sarabia's sentencing hearing began on January 8, 1907, he was notably slower and skinnier, his voice raspier, but his spirit was unbroken. When given the opportunity to tell his side of the story, he stood and spoke with eloquence.

The courtroom was packed. Several supporters and onlookers had regularly attended the trial, but the day before the sentencing hearing, two thousand workers had gone on strike at the textile plants in Rio Blanco, protesting low wages, poor working conditions, and the exorbitant prices charged at foreign-owned company stores.[21] News of the strike spread quickly. A local PLM organizer seized the energy of the strike to encourage people to take the risk of publicly supporting the PLM by attending Sarabia's hearing. Creel assigned soldiers, *rurales*, and police officers to patrol the courthouse and the surrounding streets. The crowd came, regardless. When Sarabia entered the courtroom, they cheered his name. The soldiers beat people in the throng and the judge canceled the hearing. The next morning, soldiers escorted Sarabia back to the courthouse, where an even larger crowd awaited his arrival and cheered his name. The judge ordered silence and, over a persistent din of hisses and murmurs, Sarabia rose from his seat and spoke in his defense. "Not with the humiliation of a criminal but with the honor of an honest man, I defend myself against the many absurd charges I face," he began, before delivering a lecture on the history, legitimacy, and urgency of the PLM revolt. From small sheets of paper, penned between seasons in jail, he delivered what became known as his "Menace to Authority" speech, railing against censorship and the conditions of labor in Díaz's Mexico. As he spoke, Díaz's soldiers were arriving in Rio Blanco, shooting down the strikers and ordering residents to toss the corpses into train cars. Scholars estimate that between fifty and two hundred people were killed.[22] No one in the courtroom knew of the massacre unfolding in Rio Blanco but, in the context of similar atrocities across Mexico, Sarabia proudly confessed to being a revolutionary. He admitted to being a leader of the PLM, a signatory to the PLM's 1906 platform, and a soldier in the PLM's revolutionary army, actively working to overthrow the current regime. "The facts are true," he admitted. But, as he reminded the court, according to Article 35 of the 1857 constitution, "it is a prerogative of the Mexican citizen to take up arms in defense of the Republic and its institutions." Sarabia closed by upholding the legitimacy of revolt in Díaz's Mexico:

> Was the rebellion in which I took part directed against a legal and democratic government, or against a violating despotism of the republican institutions? . . . It is well known . . . in Mexico we do not live under a constitutional regime and that neither electoral suffrage, nor public liberties, nor the independence of the powers of the Nation, nor anything that constitutes the Democratic institutions exist in our homeland under a government that has governed our destinies for more than a quarter of a century . . . in Mexico there is no more law than the will of General Díaz. . . . General Díaz disposes of our homeland at his whim, appoints the officials of popular election, invades the sovereignty of the States, is an arbiter of all matters, and exercises, in short, an absolute power. . . . The town is a nullity, the Republic a sarcasm, the institutions a corpse. . . . The government against which I intended to revolt is a dictatorship that violates the republican institutions and, therefore, I did not commit any crime with my acts of rebellion, but rather exercised a right well defined by the Supreme Code of what should be the Mexican Republic.[23]

As expected, the judge handed Sarabia the most severe punishment possible: seven years and two months in prison plus a $1,300 (peso) fine. The others received between two and five years in prison. When, a few days later, they were transferred to prison, a crowd arrived to witness the proceedings. Creel had ordered soldiers to line the streets between the jail and the train station. The people stood behind the soldiers shouting *"Viva!"* as Juan Sarabia and the Juárez raiders walked by. When he heard of the crowd's cries, Ricardo Flores Magón wrote to Juan's cousin Manuel Sarabia, "The people are on our side. The public sympathy that has accompanied our Charalito [Juan Sarabia] is the best sign that they understand our mission, and that it is good, honest, and just."[24] To Díaz, he wrote, "If Juan Sarabia dies in jail we will kill you." He signed the threat with his favorite penname "El Scorpio" (The Scorpion).[25] From St. Louis, Andrea Villarreal seconded the threat, giving an interview to the local press in which she declared, "If Juan Sarabia perish [sic], the Liberal Party will kill Díaz."[26]

At the train station in Chihuahua City, the Juárez raiders were boarded in cattle cars, locked in day and night until Enrique Creel arrived. When he arrived the next evening, he boarded a passenger car on the same train, and they departed for Mexico City. Once in the capital, Creel headed for the National Palace, where he confirmed Sarabia's capture to the president. A few hours later, Díaz came down to the station to personally dispatch Sarabia to San Ulua Prison in Veracruz, where he spent the next three years.[27]

As Sarabia and the Jiménez raiders faced prosecution in Mexico, Antonio Villarreal faced a series of charges in the United States. First, the Mexican consul in El Paso, Francisco Mallen, asked U.S. authorities to charge Villarreal with violating the U.S. Neutrality Act for his role in supporting the Juárez raid. But, since the attack had not materialized, Mallen feared that Villarreal would be released on bail and would skip town.[28] So Mallen switched strategies, asking Ambassador Davalos to submit formal extradition proceedings against Villarreal. When the extradition process stalled, Davalos and Mallen scrambled to find some way to keep Villarreal in custody and force him back to Mexico. "They are trying to screw you, and that's that," wrote Flores Magón, who, though he was in hiding, managed to get a letter smuggled to Villarreal as he awaited his fate in the El Paso County Jail.[29] As the clock ticked, Mexican authorities remembered the "Douglas strategy" and began scouring U.S. immigration law for a hook to yank Villarreal back to Mexico. They found one.

According to U.S. immigration law, former convicts were categorically prohibited from entering the United States. With a felony record for the literary duel he'd won a few years earlier, Villarreal had entered the United States in violation of U.S. immigration restrictions, making him a deportable immigrant. On February 25, 1907, two U.S. immigration officers removed Villarreal from his cell and walked him toward the international bridge. On the other side of the river, Mexican authorities were waiting to take him into custody. The plan was for Mexican officers to load him onto a train to be quickly spirited away from the border.[30] Officers stood guard all along the river, in case Villarreal attempted to run or the *magonistas* tried to free him. But, on the way to the bridge, Villarreal asked the immigration officers if they could stop by the Western Union office so that he could send a telegram to his family, letting them know he was being deported and that he would be home soon. The officers agreed. While they waited in the street, Villarreal jumped out a back window and disappeared. A few weeks later, he joined Flores Magón on the run.[31]

Using stolen letters, Thomas Furlong tracked Flores Magón's movements everywhere he went. In January 1907, the agent who had befriended Manuel Sarabia in Chicago picked up steady correspondence between Sarabia and someone named Rafael Escarcega at 1429 Weyse Street, Los Angeles. Believing this to be a code name for Flores Magón, Furlong and Sanders rushed to Los Angeles. They got within feet of nabbing him.

Arriving by train on January 12, Furlong and Sanders walked directly to Weyse Street, a short dirt road near the train tracks, which Furlong described as "entirely occupied by Mexicans in poor circumstances."[32] Furlong and Sanders watched the house, but two white men loitering on the street of a Mexican neighborhood sparked "immediate suspicion." So they retreated and reached out to the local police for help. Two Mexican American detectives, Tomás Rico and J. F. Talamantes, were put on the case. With Rico and Talamantes on board, Furlong rented a room in the building directly behind the Weyse Street house. From there, Furlong, Sanders, Rico, and Talamantes could take turns peering into the backyard. As Furlong described the stakeout, he could stand just twenty-five feet from the house's back door and "plainly observe all who entered and left . . . without being seen by anyone."[33]

Monitoring the house was made easy by the fact that it did not have interior plumbing. All occupants had to use the "closet" in the yard, which sat directly below Furlong's window. When, after a few days, the agents had not seen Flores Magón visit the closet, Furlong concluded, "Magón was not stopping at this house as he surely would have made his appearance at least once to go to the closet in the rear if for nothing else." Still confident that the house was a link in the PLM chain, Furlong devised a plan. On January 18, around 10 am, he planted officers around the Weyse Street house—in the rented room, on the street, and one even climbed into a tiny shed along the side of the house—and then sent to the house a letter addressed to Señor R. Escarcega. A PLM adherent named Modesto Díaz answered the door. When the letter carrier insisted that Mr. Escarcega sign for the letter, Díaz said that he was not there but he would send his brother to fetch him. "The brother came out of the house and started on a run down Weyse Street to the corner of Ann where he turned East and entered No. 201 Ann Street," Furlong later recounted to Creel. At the Ann Street house lived a young man and his widowed mother.[34] The young man, Mr. Escarcega, rushed to Weyse Street to collect the letter. Furlong's agents followed. Escarcega signed for the letter and returned home. Thinking Flores Magón must have been waiting inside the Ann Street home to receive the letter, Officers Rico and Talamantes forced their way inside, but they found neither Flores Magón nor the letter Escarcega had just signed for. When pressed for answers, Escarcega said he had slipped the letter to a man on the street before returning home. Escarcega took the officers back outside and pointed out the man to whom he had given the letter. Rico and Talamantes approached the man, demanding to know where he had taken the letter. The man "absolutely refused" to answer. Frustrated, Rico and Talamantes arrested the Díaz brothers, Modesto Díaz's wife, Mr. Escarcega, and the man on the street.[35]

At the LAPD station, the officers put the men and Mrs. Díaz in separate rooms and grilled them as to Flores Magón's whereabouts. Nobody broke. Modesto Díaz said he "would die first," and his wife refused to answer any of the officers' questions.[36] When the Mexican consul arrived and took over the interrogations, he advised Mrs. Díaz that "the parties for whom this mail was intended were irresponsible adventurers and were hum-bugging the people by getting money from them and making false representations etc. and that they were doing wrong by shielding such people," but Mrs. Díaz was immovable, deflecting their questions with *"energía y viveza"* (energy and liveliness), wrote Consul Antonio Lozano to Creel. After two days of questioning, Modesto Díaz seemed to break, telling the consul that his contact was a man named Cárdenas in El Paso. Finally, the officers released Díaz, his wife, and the others, but Díaz's tip was a lie. "Everything Díaz said was a lie," Consul Lozano had to admit.[37]

The Weyse Street sting had failed, but Furlong and his team were getting close and Furlong knew it. According to a letter Furlong later intercepted, Flores Magón admitted to Manuel Sarabia that he had barely escaped capture that day in Los Angeles. "He does not know how he escaped," as Sarabia put it.[38] Legend has it that Flores Magón escaped the Weyse Street raid by jumping out of a window and, wearing a dress, disappearing into a crowd of women on the street.[39] To protect his whereabouts, La Junta shut down almost all communication with him while he moved more often.[40]

Until Antonio Villarreal joined him, sometime in March 1907, Flores Magón was alone. "I don't know how I'll fare now : . . I don't have anything here, not one friend. The vagabond's life is a sad one," he wrote.[41] With Villarreal's arrival, he at least had a friend.

The two men had not known each other long before they began living on the run together. They had not known each other in Mexico; Villarreal and his family had joined La Junta in St. Louis in 1905. Nevertheless, the Villarreal family had thrown themselves behind the PLM.

Antonio's father, Próspero, sold newspapers on the street to help raise funds, and the Villarreal sisters, Teresa and Andrea, became spokeswomen for the cause. They gave fiery speeches and fielded journalists' questions, helping to keep the PLM in the news, which became especially important after most members of La Junta went underground. In St. Louis, Villarreal had worked for *Regeneración*, doing office work and writing articles. Villarreal, a socialist, and Flores Magón, an anarchist, must have debated politics, but it was Villarreal's actions to protect *"el alma de todo"* at the Legal Tender Saloon in El Paso that forged a brotherhood between the two men. As Flores Magón wrote in the letter he had had smuggled to Villarreal in the El Paso County Jail, "You saved me. . . . If you hadn't told me to wait at the corner near the cantina, they would have caught me, like a defenseless drunk. . . . Now I have become famous. Everyone thinks I am so crafty. The truth is that if you had not been there, I would have been captured. Don't you see? You know that my eyes are bad. I'm a slow walker and too trusting. Defects like these, and others, make me unable to save myself for/ from myself." Flores Magón thanked Villarreal for his loyalty and his friendship: "I embrace you, my brother," he signed the note.[42]

When Villarreal joined Flores Magón on the run, their conditions did not improve much. With a bounty on Flores Magón and a deportation order on Villarreal, they had to move constantly and furtively. Too scared to be seen in public, they did not work, leaving them dependent on money sent by their supporters, most of whom could only afford a few cents or dollars at a time. "We are broke," wrote Flores Magón.[43] "We don't have more than two cents, and not a friend at hand."[44] Unable to buy enough food, Flores Magón and Villarreal reported "a dogged hunger," eating just enough to keep them from standing in line at public soup kitchens. "With such hunger one does not want to write," Flores Magón complained, saying he felt "faint, frail, and irritable.[45] He virtually stopped writing, both letters and articles. Although Thomas Furlong had failed to capture him, his efforts stifled Flores Magón's pen, sheathing his greatest weapon. On the other hand, the less Flores Magón wrote, the harder he was to track.

With Ricardo Flores Magón and Antonio Villarreal living in deep hiding, Furlong had few leads. But, in May 1907, Flores Magón's letters began to ping once again across the PLM correspondence chain. The arrest of Juan José Arredondo forced him to intervene in an internal debate raging among the PLM leaders. Some called Arredondo a traitor, believing the Mexican government's claim that Arredondo had walked across the border to turn himself in and inform on other fighters in exchange for immunity and a job. Others said Arredondo had been duped or kidnapped. The debate bred bad feelings and suspicion, and Flores Magón pleaded with the PLM leaders not to turn on one another. "We cannot yet confirm that Arredondo is a traitor. Perhaps he drank too much in the company of spies, it is known that he liked to drink, and when he was drunk and when he could not tell what was going on, he was taken to Mexico. This version [of events] is very possible," he urged.[46] By June 1907, Furlong had intercepted enough of Flores Magón's letters to trace him back to Los Angeles.

LOS ANGELES WAS A good place for Ricardo Flores Magón to hide. Whereas fewer than five hundred Mexican immigrants lived in Los Angeles in 1890, an estimated 25,000 lived in the city by 1910. Every day, more Mexicans arrived in Los Angeles, taking up residence near the railroad and on the east side of town. They found work in the region's booming industries: agriculture, transportation, bricks, oil, and domestic service. Their labor was building the town into a city. Although local employers had actively recruited Mexican workers to the city as a "cheap" and "docile" workforce, Mexicans in and around Los Angeles proved rebellious. In 1903, for example, nine hundred Mexican track workers formed a union and went on strike for higher wages. That same year, Mexican agricultural workers not only went on strike but also rejected an offer of affiliation with the American Federation of Labor, which had demanded that the Mexican workers exclude Japanese coworkers from their union as a condition of joining the federation. In 1905, after receiving notification of the establishment of the PLM, an active core of Mexican radicals in Los Angeles formed a *foco*. That same year they also played a leading role in establishing a local of the Industrial Workers of the World. Thus, a busy core of Mexicans living and working in Los Angeles were politically engaged and experienced organizers in radical movements.[47]

By July 1907, Flores Magón was not just hiding in Los Angeles; he was making Los Angeles the new headquarters of the PLM. He worked with Modesto Díaz to reboot the old PLM organ *Regeneración* under a new name: *Revolución*. When *Revolución* hit the streets of Los Angeles in June 1907, Furlong sensed that Flores Magón was nearby. He was right. La Junta had been wandering the West since fleeing St. Louis in 1905, but they convened in Los Angeles during the summer of 1907 to support the launch of *Revolución* and plot the next round of raids. Furlong was determined to stop them.

Furlong and the Mexican consul, Antonio Lozano, hired a secret agent named C. H. Schwartzmann, a Mexican citizen living in Los Angeles. The son of a German father and a Mexican mother, he spoke German, Spanish, and English. For $12 per week plus a $500 reward when Flores Magón was captured, Schwartzmann agreed to infiltrate the local *foco*. He hung out in a bookshop owned by a PLM adherent, Rómulo Carmona, and attended open meetings. He never worked his way into the PLM's inner circle, but he won a measure of trust from Modesto Díaz who, by mid-July, spoke too loosely in front of him, leaking plans for a new raid in September.[48] Furlong's agent at the post office confirmed Schwartzmann's intel, catching a letter from Flores Magón to a PLM squadron leader in Texas, which read: "It's time to start the movement. We are going to do everything possible because it will be in September . . . keep secret what I say . . . keep it secret so word doesn't get out and allow the enemy to prepare."[49] By early August, Furlong's agents were intercepting increasingly alarming correspondence. Antonio de Pío Araujo reported preparing for an attack on Matamoros.[50] And the Sarabia brothers, Tomás and Manuel, warned their mother that they might soon die while participating in a general uprising, a "*grito de rebelión*," in Mexico.[51] They wanted their mother to be prepared for their deaths as well as for any vengeance the dictator might take upon their families.[52]

Furlong was confident that another PLM raid was coming, and soon, and that the only way to stop it was to capture Ricardo Flores Magón. Furlong assiduously tracked every PLM letter processed at the Los Angeles post office either to or from one of Flores Magón's aliases. He quickly realized that most of those letters were carried in an envelope addressed to or from one woman: María Brousse.

María Brousse was the only woman among the founding members of the Los Angeles *foco*. She was always at the center of PLM activities in Los Angeles, running the local correspondence system, and when Flores Magón first arrived in Los Angeles and needed a hideout, she invited Mexico's most wanted man into her home, which she shared with her husband and teenage daughter, Lucia (often called Lucy).[53] Flores Magón moved around a lot, coming and going from her house, but he and Brousse grew close. In his eyes, she made her name as a "gladiator" by smuggling dynamite to Chihuahua City to free PLM fighters—perhaps Juan Sarabia—from jail, though the plan fell apart when the men involved failed to show up. She also pledged to kill Porfirio Díaz and Theodore Roosevelt should La Junta ever issue assassination orders. When several PLM men expressed the opinion that Brousse was reckless, Flores Magón chided them: "I regret the differences in regard to María . . . this unjust calumny only makes me feel the more warmly toward her. . . . She is ready to execute any commission. . . . She is prepared for any excursion no matter how dangerous. She does not inquire if she will be in danger of death. She simply gives herself to the cause. Such self-abnegation is not to be found among our brothers."[54]

It did not take long for Flores Magón to fall in love with her. "If there is anything sacred and sincere in me," he swore, "it is the love that I have for you as a woman and for the revolution as an ideal. María and the revolution: that is what fills my heart."[55] Brousse loved him back. "You are in my heart and my thoughts. I embrace you with all

Ricardo Flores Magón and María Brousse (de Talavera).

of my soul and I kiss you the same," she replied.[56] By the time of his arrest, she had left her husband and the pair had committed to spending the rest of their lives together as a common-law couple, as neither of them, both anarcho-feminists, believed in the institution of marriage. Ricardo informally adopted Lucia as his stepdaughter. She called him "my sweet father."[57]

In August 1907, Thomas Furlong did not yet know the nature of Flores Magón's relationship with María Brousse, but he did suspect that she was the person moving his mail. He assigned agents to watch her carefully. Soon, they saw her coming and going from a small house she rented from an African American real estate agent working on the outskirts of downtown. Furlong and his agents staked out the house, which was set back from the street on a deep lot.[58] By August 21, Furlong was confident that Flores Magón was hiding inside. "Have found and have under surveillance Ricardo Flores Magón," he wired to Enrique Creel, asking for "help and instructions."[59] Creel arrived in Los Angeles two days later to oversee a top-secret plan to capture Ricardo Flores Magón. Emilio Kosterlitzky arrived, too. They told the local press they both just happened to be in town on vacation.[60] However, for weeks, the Mexican government had been hatching a plan to coordinate the capture of Flores Magón "by indirect methods and not in an official manner."[61]

The attempted kidnapping of Ricardo Flores Magón began at 4 pm on Friday, August 23, 1907, and involved private agents and public officers, including Furlong, Sanders, another Furlong agent, and LAPD detectives Rico and Talamantes. The agents surrounded the house and then burst in through the back door, finding Ricardo Flores Magón as well as Librado Rivera and Antonio Villarreal inside. The operatives lunged at the three fugitives, who refused to submit. In a brawl that lasted nearly an hour, the Junta leaders and agents thrashed one another, breaking dishes and chairs before their struggle tumbled into the front courtyard. There, Flores Magón dropped to the ground bloody and unconscious. Rivera and Villarreal were simply too tired to fight on. Among them, they had "a few teeth knocked out, bruised faces, and black eyes," as Furlong later recalled.[62]

When a surrey and a horse-drawn coupe sped up to the house, Rivera began to fight again, but Furlong choked him and dragged him into the surrey. Talamantes and Rico crammed Flores Magón and Villarreal into the coupe, tying them down with ropes drawn through the windows. Rico climbed in behind them, sitting on Villarreal's lap and shoving his boots into Flores Magón's chest. Villarreal bit the back of Rico's neck. When Flores Magón regained consciousness, he began kicking at Rico's chest. Rico pressed himself harder against the fighting men. When the driver began to pull away, Talamantes hopped onto the running board, grabbing Flores Magón by the hair.[63]

The fracas incited passersby to form a crowd. The neighborhood was largely industrial, with dirt streets and a heavily Mexican population. Members of the crowd recognized the men and began chanting for their release. With witnesses all around, Furlong abandoned what was most likely a kidnapping plan and directed the arrest team to the local jail. The crowd followed. By the time Furlong's team pulled up to the jail, several hundred Mexicans were standing in the street cheering for the PLM. Detectives Rico and Talamantes rushed the men inside. Into the night, Mexicans milled about on the street lifting up shouts of support for the men inside. "We can sustain their lives and avoid their deaths with the community's exuberant exaltation," explained one of their supporters.[64]

In the end, Flores Magón was not forced back to Mexico, as the crowd of Mexicans on the streets of Los Angeles thwarted the kidnapping attempt. Regardless, Creel rejoiced at the news of his arrest. After years of searching, Ricardo Flores Magón, *el alma de todo*, was behind bars. Or, as the *Los Angeles Times* wrote in seeming delight, he had been dragged through the city by Thomas Furlong and his men, kicking and screaming like a "clawing cat."[65] Creel remained in Los Angeles for a few weeks, coordinating a legal strategy that would keep Flores Magón in prison as long as possible because, he and many others hoped, "it would all end" with Flores Magón locked away behind stone and steel.[66]

While Creel was in town, the city's elite celebrated the health of U.S. investments in Mexico. Parties on yachts and in ballrooms were held almost every night. Edward L. Doheny threw the biggest gala of all.

Doheny had made his first million dollars in and around the tar seeps of Los Angeles. Then he invested in Mexico. In 1904, his drillers hit a major gusher, which poured out thousands of barrels per day and kicked off Mexico's oil boom, with Doheny's company, Mexican Petroleum of California (MPC), producing an estimated 85 percent of Mexico's oil.[67] What Doheny did not own, Standard Oil did. Together, they ran a near monopoly of the Mexican petroleum industry. Doheny's Mexican investments made him the single largest independent oil producer in the world.[68] After Flores Magón's arrest, Doheny opened his bottomless bank account for a celebration described as "without parallel in local history."[69] In particular, he convened forty of L.A.'s most prominent men to celebrate Creel and the health of Díaz's Mexico. Held at the Hotel Alexandria, the most luxurious hotel in town, the opulence of the evening awed Doheny's guests. When the doors of the banquet hall swung open, they stepped into a "fairyland."[70] The walls were latticed with the colors of Mexico: green vines, red flowers, and white lights. Clusters of asparagus grass hung from the ceiling, a canopy of wispy green. At the center of the hall, a banquet table in the shape of an ellipse surrounded a freshwater lake filled with goldfish and lined with carnations. Three fountains stood at the center of the lake, intermittently spouting flutes of red, green, and white. Lanterns glowed above the lake. Creel was overcome with emotion. "For the first time in my life I am at a loss for something to say," he said, calling the displays "magnificent . . . as if they were brought by the angels of heaven."[71] Into the night, Doheny's guests feasted on caviar and sherry and other delicacies, praising Creel and raising toasts to President Díaz. But the PLM threat was far from over.

CHAPTER 20

The United States vs. Ricardo Flores Magón

I**T WAS NEARLY MIDNIGHT WHEN ANSELMO FIGUEROA KNOCKED** on Job Harriman's door. They knew one another from the local Socialist Club. Harriman let him in and listened as Figueroa, an active member of the PLM *foco* in Los Angeles, explained why Harriman, a criminal defense attorney and one of the nation's most prominent socialists, should take the case of the three Mexican men arrested that afternoon. The jailed men, he said, were political prisoners captured as part of a cross-border counterinsurgency campaign to stop a revolution from starting in Mexico, and a revolution in Mexico would strike a blow against U.S. capitalists. Without Díaz, U.S. investors such as the Rockefellers, the Guggenheims, William Randolph Hearst, and Edward Doheny would no longer be able to make and multiply their fortunes in Mexico. Without the profits they extracted from Mexican land and labor, this who's who of U.S. capitalists would have fewer resources at the ready to suppress the U.S. labor movement. In this way, the fate of the U.S. labor movement was bound to the success of a revolution in Mexico.

Harriman understood the stakes. Harrison Gray Otis, owner of the *Los Angeles Times* as well as nearly a million acres of land in Mexico, was a leading figure in the local Merchant and Manufacturers Association (MMA), which was driving an "open shop" campaign in Los Angeles at the time. If that campaign was successful, labor unions would effectively be prohibited from organizing workers in the city. In

Job Harriman.

turn, the nation's socialists, joined by many labor unions, were locked in battle against Otis and the MMA in Los Angeles. The PLM uprising was a threat to a significant portion of Otis's wealth. Harriman took the case.

Job Harriman had grown up in a religious family and, as a young man, became an ordained minister. But he soon had doubts, ministering to a congregation whom he described as praying and confessing at church but living otherwise "immoral lives ... [taking] advantage of their neighbors."[1] He left the church. Alienated from friends and family, he felt as if he was "a strange man in a strange country" but he continued his studies in history, literature, and philosophy, and, in so doing, underwent what he described as an "intellectual re-formation." In time, he read *Capital* by Karl Marx. "I read it and read it and read it again, and marked it and compared passage with passage, and tried to find a way through his irresistible logic," recalled Harriman about Marx's theory of the capitalist exploitation of labor and the need to redistribute the means of production. Soon, he became a traveling speaker for various socialist causes, bringing a fire-and-brimstone style to sandlots and soapboxes across the country. He whipped up crowds with dreams of utopia and parables of capitalism's contradictions.[2] By the 1890s, Harriman was a nationally recognized figure who counted Eugene V. Debs, Emma Goldman, Samuel Gompers, and Mother Jones among his friends.[3] In 1900, Harriman even ran for vice president of the United States, alongside Debs, on the Socialist Party of America ticket. When they lost, Harriman disappeared from politics for a while. Years of travel had battered his health, causing tuberculosis to flare. Hoping that dry air would heal his lungs, Harriman, along with his wife and their child, took a wagon into the desert where they lived in penury in a tent, subsisting on donations from friends. By 1905, Harriman's health had improved and the family returned to Los Angeles, where Harriman threw himself back into socialist politics and rebuilt his legal practice, taking on civil rights and labor cases.[4] With just a weekend to prepare the PLM case, Harriman and his law partner, A. R. Holston, also a prominent socialist, arrived at the courthouse on the morning of Monday, August 26, 1907, ready to defend Ricardo Flores Magón, Librado Rivera, and Antonio Villarreal, as well as Modesto Díaz, who had also been arrested.

The prosecution team was ready, too. The search for Flores Magón had lasted more than a year, spanned three nations, and covered more than 100,000 miles. In that time, a small army of officials had joined the manhunt. Since January, the Mexican consul, Antonio Lozano, had been working with local and regional officials to find his hideout, including the LAPD and the Los Angeles County sheriff, who offered to apprehend Flores Magón personally, for a fee.[5] With the fugitive finally in custody, the Los Angeles district attorney, John D. Fredericks, volunteered to argue the case. Enrique Creel hired two local attorneys, Horace H. Appel and Donald Barker, to assist him. Oscar Lawler, the U.S. attorney for southern California, was also on hand to aid the prosecution. And Thomas Furlong vowed to stay with the case until the very end—when either the Mexican government successfully extradited Flores Magón and the others back to Mexico or had them imprisoned in the United States for as long as possible.

On that Monday morning, the defense and prosecution teams waited as Flores Magón, Rivera, Villarreal, and Díaz were escorted to the courthouse from the city jail, located one block away down Broadway, within the LAPD headquarters. PLM supporters lined the route. Little girls in white dresses scattered red carnations along the street, into the courthouse, through the hallways, into the courtroom, and up to the defendants' table, everywhere the prisoners might step. The crowd cheered as the four men shuffled by, shackled, under armed guard, and on a path of petals. The courtroom was packed with more supporters, and once the prisoners were seated at the defendants' table, men in the crowd began reaching across the bar to shake their hands. Mothers lifted their children so that the rebels could "pat them on the faces."[6] More than twenty LAPD officers lined the room.

When the judge began the proceedings, Job Harriman filed a habeas corpus petition, arguing that Flores Magón, Villarreal, Rivera, and Díaz had been arrested without cause and detained without charge, and that the whole affair was being directed by the Mexican government. District attorney Fredericks struggled to counter the claim: Detectives Rico and Talamantes had neglected to file charges when they arrested the men, and H. H. Appel, one of the attorneys hired by the Mexican government, was sitting at the prosecution table, whispering into Fredericks's ear. The judge granted Fredericks one day to develop his response to Harriman's petition and remanded the men back to jail.

The next day, when they returned to the crowded courtroom, shuffling and shackled, their route was again carpeted in red flowers. Harriman began the hearing by putting Flores Magón on the stand. Still bruised from Friday's brawl with Furlong and his men, he went to the witness box, turned to face the crowd, and sat down. With Flores Magón and his injuries on display, Harriman held the stage, challenging the men's arrest on technical grounds. In front of the bruised revolutionary, Harriman and Fredericks debated the facts surrounding the arrest and the relevant precedent regarding warrantless arrests. Harriman won, convincing the judge that the arrests were warrantless and even suspicious, seeming to stem from a botched kidnapping effort. Detectives Rico and Talamantes rushed out of the courtroom and down the block to LAPD headquarters, where they hastily filed "resisting arrest" charges against Flores Magón, Rivera, and Villarreal. By the time they returned, the judge had released Modesto Díaz from custody, but he agreed to remand the other three on the fresh charges.[7]

The next morning, Harriman fought the new charges, arguing that "the prisoners had a perfect right to resist arrest, when that arrest was made without warrant."[8] Harriman won this argument, too. But the judge remanded the three men to jail again, this time on the presumption that legitimate warrants or charges were forthcoming and if the men were released, they would abscond.[9] Flores Magón, after all, had jumped bail in St. Louis the year before. Villarreal was still subject to deportation. Rivera had no outstanding warrants or orders but had been living underground since his release from custody in St. Louis.

With the three men remaining in custody, Creel worked with his legal team to figure out what charges to file. There was no clear path forward. To date, all the Mexican government's efforts to extradite *magonistas* had failed, suggesting that any further attempt would also fail. The Department of Commerce and Labor was refusing to deport Villarreal.[10] Flores Magón could not even be extradited back to Missouri to stand trial in the libel cases filed against him by both Manuel Esperón y de la Flor and William C. Greene, as libel was not an extraditable offense. Without new charges, Creel knew that Harriman would soon find a way to compel the judge to release the men. Desperate, he filed extradition charges, aided by U.S. attorney Lawler.[11] According to the petition, the three men had stolen $25 and murdered a John Doe in Jiménez, Mexico, on an unknown date.[12] The charges were bogus and Creel knew that the men would not, ultimately, be extradited, but subjecting them to extradition proceedings gave his team forty days to strategize another way to have them either returned to Mexico or imprisoned in the United States.

At the highest levels of the U.S. and Mexican governments, officials had already been discussing how best to prosecute *magonistas* captured in the United States. Back in March, following the failed attempts to extradite Juan José Arredondo and the Jiménez raiders, Ambassador Creel enlisted the help of his old friend John Foster, a former secretary of state, in convincing the State Department to press every relevant branch of the federal government, from the Department of War to the Department of Justice, into suppressing the *magonista* threat. As Creel explained in a fourteen-page rant to Foster, "A few Mexicans have declared themselves enemies of General Díaz's administration . . . carrying on a highly harmful propaganda which is in complete conflict with the good relations that exist between the peoples of Mexico and of the United States." Of course, Creel added, Ricardo Flores Magón and his followers were on a fool's errand. Their movement, he wrote, was "fantastical and highly ridiculous; it has not found and never will find any support among the people of Mexico who are content with the administration of General Díaz and fare well under the sound and prosperous regime it has mapped out." Still, Creel wanted Foster to convince the Department of State to help suppress the *magonistas*, as the rumblings of revolt were causing "alarm . . . that there may be danger in Mexico of some subversive movement [and] this might be seriously prejudicial to the credit of the Mexican Government, which has maintained peace for over thirty years, and might cause disquietude among American citizens who have invested capital in Mexican enterprise and many of whom live in Mexican territory." In the end, Creel explained, the interests of the U.S. and Mexican governments were aligned against Ricardo Flores Magón. "The work of Flores Magón and his associates," he explained, "is aimed very directly against citizens of this country . . . to arouse a feeling of hatred for Americans, making them believe that the agreements, contracts, and conventions which the Government has concluded in favor of Americans, who have invested in Mexico a capital of over five hundred million dollars, are exorbitant, undue, and without legal foundation."[13]

Foster responded quickly, advising Creel and Mexico's secretary of foreign relations, Ignacio Mariscal, that the Mexican government should abandon extradition and deportation proceedings. Neither strategy had been successful. Moreover, forcing the men back to Mexico could appear "improper," making the targets seem to be "victims of political persecution."[14] Foster recommended that the Mexican government instead urge U.S. officials to prosecute *magonistas* for violating the U.S. Neutrality Act, which prohibited all persons from using U.S. soil to "set afoot" any military expedition against a foreign government with which the United States was at peace. Violating the U.S. Neutrality Act, carried a penalty of a maximum $3,000 fine and up to three years in prison. Creel, Mariscal, and President Díaz agreed with this new approach.

Creel reached out directly to the secretary of state, Elihu Root, urging him to convince the Department of Justice to round up and prosecute Ricardo Flores Magón and his followers for violating the U.S. Neutrality Act by instigating the Jiménez raid.[15] The secretary of state supported the strategy, sending a letter to the U.S. attorney general, Charles Bonaparte. "Our relations with Mexico are exceedingly friendly," explained Root to Bonaparte. "That is of great importance to the U.S. as well as to Mexico that they should continue so, and that it is a serious injury to this country to have its territory used as a base of operations for men plotting not only revolution but assassination against President Díaz and asking whether it is not practical to take legal proceedings against the offenders."[16] Bonaparte agreed, instructing U.S. attorneys as follows: "It is the desire of this Department that the most careful investigation be made of this matter and that every effort be taken to prevent the use of our territory for the firing out of armed expeditions against Mexico. . . . Please investigate the matter in the most careful manner possible."[17] In other words, by the time Flores Magón was arrested in Los Angeles, the secretary of state and the U.S. attorney general had already joined the case against him. All the U.S. government needed was evidence that he and the others had violated the U.S. Neutrality Act by setting afoot an armed assault on a friendly, neighboring nation, i.e., Mexico.

With Flores Magón, Rivera, and Villarreal detained in jail for bogus extradition proceedings, Creel's legal team lined up all of the U.S. authorities who would be needed to prosecute them for violating the Neutrality Act. Lawler assured Creel that the local U.S. attorney's office would do everything possible to win their conviction. As Lawler reported to U.S. attorney general Bonaparte, "All of the Mexican officials have been repeatedly assured that we were at their service and would not proceed with any local prosecution unless such steps were desired by them."[18] Consul Lozano sent Lawler a $500 watch as thanks for all of his help on the case.[19] Donald Barker, one of the attorneys for the Mexican government already on retainer, reached out to Los Angeles district attorney Fredericks to get him on board with the plan. Fredericks agreed to transfer the case to federal authorities and guaranteed that "every effort will be made and influence used to accomplish the [Mexican government's] object[ive]."[20] With U.S. authorities from Washington to Los Angeles on their side, Creel's team had cleared the path to prosecute the three men under the Neutrality Act. *United States vs. Ricardo Flores Magón* would bring down onto the revolutionaries the full force of the U.S. government, with Mexican authorities providing assistance in the background.

U.S. district attorney Lawler revealed the plan at the final extradition hearing in mid-October 1907. By then, the three men had been detained for more than forty days, and Mexican officials had yet to submit any credible evidence against them.[21] Expecting them to be released from custody, hundreds of Mexicans gathered at the courthouse for the hearing. When the revolutionaries arrived, once again shackled and shuffling on a red carpet of carnations, the men in the crowd lifted their hats and hollered huzzahs. Children released little balloons into the air, each with the names of the accused carefully written on it: Magón–Villarreal–Rivera. Deputies rushed the men past the crowd and into the hearing room, where a U.S. Commissioner was waiting.[22]

The hearing moved quickly. The Commissioner dismissed the extradition case, freeing the men from custody. But before they could leave, Lawler stepped forward to charge the men with violating the Neutrality Act, citing evidence from U.S. attorney J. L. B. Alexander in Arizona linking the men to Tomás Espinosa, a member of the PLM *foco* in Douglas, who had recently been convicted of violating the act for his role in planning the Douglas *foco*'s thwarted raid on Agua Prieta and Cananea. The evidence that had been used to convict Tomás Espinosa largely consisted of the numerous letters he had written to and received from PLM adherents in the Arizona–Sonora borderlands while planning the raid. At the personal request of Ambassador Creel, U.S. attorney Alexander returned to that bolt of letters and searched for any evidence linking Flores Magón, Villarreal, and Rivera to Espinosa's case. "As you know, the Mexican government is very much interested in the punishment of certain criminals who have been doing mischief on the frontier. . . . I beg you to cooperate in every possible way on behalf of justice and of the good friendly relations which exist between the two countries," explained Creel in a telegram to Alexander.[23] Alexander found a series of letters sent between Rivera, Villarreal, and Flores Magón and members of the Douglas *foco*. The clinchers were letters from Flores Magón mailed shortly after the Cananea strike, discussing the price of guns and declaring the following: "Are our compatriots at Cananea disposed to be respected? If they are, it is imperative for them at the earliest possible moment to arm themselves. As long as the populace is undecided to fight with the same weapons that despotism uses on them, nothing can be done. The Government is so infamous that men without arms are assassinated, but men with weapons it dreads. Therefore, we must make it tremble and furthermore we must demolish it, the wrong must be cut down at the root."[24] With this evidence in his hands, Alexander wrote to U.S. attorney general Bonaparte that he was ready to file federal charges against Ricardo Flores Magón, Librado Rivera, and Antonio Villarreal for helping to plan the Agua Prieta raid: "There is no doubt in my mind but that upon the removal of these three persons to Arizona, the evidence in my possession will amply warrant their convictions for violation of the neutrality laws."[25] Bonaparte approved Alexander's request to pursue the case and sent arrest warrants to Lawler in Los Angeles. When the men were released from custody on the bogus extradition hold, a U.S. Marshal took them back into custody, and the Commissioner set bail at $5,000 each (roughly $140,000 in 2021 dollars), an amount recommended by attorneys Barker and Appel because it would "preclude the release of the prisoners . . . as it is very unlikely that they will be unable [sic] to raise that amount of money or secure satisfactory bondsmen."[26]

With Flores Magón, Villarreal, and Rivera back in jail, Creel's legal team searched for any additional evidence linking them to the Douglas *foco*. A special emissary from Mexico City dropped off a suitcase of Furlong's copied letters at U.S. attorney Alexander's office in Phoenix.[27] It was a risky move, since many of the letters had, likely, been illegally acquired, but Creel was determined to see the men sentenced to several years at the Arizona Territorial Penitentiary in Yuma, a hot and decrepit stone heap where Mexican authorities expected Flores Magón's health to fail and his lungs to finally collapse. As Consul Lozano put it, "in the Yuma Penitentiary they will have to work, like all of the prisoners, breaking rocks and constructing new buildings at the Prison, work so hard, in high temperature, that in no time it breaks even the strongest and most desperate men."[28] The plan was cynical: lock up Flores Magón for as long as possible in Arizona where, it was hoped, he would die in prison, taking his revolt with him to the grave. It was also a solid plan.

In jail, Flores Magón was already complaining about his poor health. "I am very sick," he wrote to María Brousse.[29] "They cannot deny me liberty on bond because it would be the same as assassinating me," he insisted.[30] The jail doctor did not agree, so Flores Magón asked Brousse to find a private physician to examine him. The physician concluded that Flores Magón had severe bronchitis and might die if left in jail. The jail doctor reexamined him and still disagreed, noting that he had a persistent cough and had lost twenty-five pounds while in jail but that these concerns were not significant enough to compel his release.

As the jail doctor put it, Flores Magón's only problem was the "great quantities of brown paper cigarettes" he smoked constantly.[31]

For Creel's gambit to succeed, Flores Magón, Villarreal, and Rivera would have to be transferred from California to Arizona for prosecution. Job Harriman was determined to stop the transfer. In a series of legal maneuvers that dragged on for more than a year, Harriman blocked, challenged, and stalled the federal warrant to transfer the cases. But, in March 1909, after nineteen months of wrangling, Harriman's tricks and delays had run their course. A judge ordered the men removed to Arizona. Worried that PLM fighters might attack the transfer party, Furlong led a small army of marshals, spies, and guards in following their train to Arizona, where U.S. attorney Alexander successfully prosecuted the three men for violating the Neutrality Act. In May 1909, a judge sentenced them to fifteen months in the federal penitentiary in the Arizona Territory. The Díaz administration was thrilled with the outcome. Ricardo Flores Magón was on his way to prison and, quite possibly, his death. Consul Arturo Elias, from Tucson, bought U.S. attorney Alexander a $475 diamond ring for his "important services . . . in the matter of the revolutionaries."[32] When Alexander tried to refuse the ring, Elias told a courier to leave it on his doorstep anyway.

As hoped, Flores Magón's health steadily deteriorated in Yuma. His eyesight weakened. His lungs throbbed. He vomited often.[33] A year and a half into the sentence, one of his friends reported that "Ricardo is very sick, he is suffering with nervous prostration and bilious disorders, and has been transferred to the hospital; but his condition will not better there, even if he does not get worse, for the climate in Yuma is exceedingly hot. Our unfortunate companion is a mere shadow of what he was a year and a half ago."[34]

But Flores Magón did not die. And, while he was away, the PLM revolt only grew as new leaders rose to challenge the regime.

Part 4

¡TIERRA
Y LIBERTAD!

CHAPTER 21

The People's Cause

Práxedis Guerrero was an unlikely *Magonista*. The blond scion of a wealthy Mexican family, he had grown up on a sprawling hacienda in Guanajuato. Affectionately called Prax by his friends, he was handsome, popular, and an excellent equestrian. But, when he was sixteen years old, he ran away, wanting to experience a different life. For several months, he worked in a beer factory and a smelter before his mother persuaded him to come home. He finished school, worked in his family's various businesses, and joined the Second Reserve, a citizen militia force organized by General Bernardo Reyes, Díaz's loyal minister of war. By age nineteen, Guerrero was a second lieutenant in the Reserve's cavalry. But, as liberal dissent grew in Mexico, Guerrero grew curious. He read Camilo Arriaga's newspaper from San Luis Potosí as well as *El Hijo del Ahuizote* from Mexico City. He even began reading some anarchist texts. He was a wealthy young man with a position in the Mexican military, but he possessed an independent streak and a curiosity about radical ideas. Would he support the Díaz regime or the insurgency against it?[1] In the end, as Guerrero explained to his mother, his "heart and brain rebelled against social conditions that made some men masters and others slaves."[2]

Guerrero, whose surname means warrior in Spanish, took his first step toward the Liberals in April 1903, when General Reyes ordered troops to shoot at protestors in Monterrey. Following the Monterrey Massacre, Guerrero resigned from the militia and returned full-

*Práxedis Guerrero
as a teenager.*

time to his family's business ventures until September 1904, when he renounced his family's wealth and headed to the United States to live as an itinerant worker. Manuel Vázquez, an orphan boy from the hacienda, joined him, as did Francisco Manrique, Guerrero's best friend from a neighboring estate.[3] When they crossed the border together in 1904, Guerrero declared, "Tomorrow I will leave, perhaps forever, Mexican soil."[4]

After crossing the border, Guerrero chose to wear only the simple clothes of Mexico's migrant laborers, usually overalls and *huaraches* (sandals). He never ate more than he could afford to buy with his wages, becoming a vegetarian for "humane reasons."[5] He penned love poems to his mother. "Only your memory fills my thoughts, Mother of mine! If I die, the last sigh that escapes my bosom will go to you, the last name that my lips pronounce will be yours," he wrote to her.[6] "My God! My God! Don't forget my Mother!" he exclaimed while migrating from the fields of Texas to the lumberyards of Colorado to the docks of California, before settling in the mines of southern Arizona.[7]

When he reached Arizona, his letters home stopped. Cristobal Espinosa, a family friend, had a chance encounter with him in the mining town of Morenci, and reported to his mother that Guerrero was living a dangerous life—that he had become involved with disreputable groups and was not well liked by his boss. She begged him to return home. Guerrero refused. As he put it, Espinosa "is witness to my life as a worker; he can say that he saw me in a humble room, in company of Francisco Manrique, who, as you know, came with me; he can say that he saw me blackened by smoke, dirty, and full of oil, but he can never say that he saw me doing something bad."[8]

What Guerrero did not tell his mother was that he had started a labor union, Obreros Libres, and that he was rooming with Manuel Sarabia, whom he had met when Sarabia swung through town during a PLM recruitment tour. The two men quickly became friends. Guerrero is "my pal . . . a fighter who knows no fear . . . and I am honored to call him my brother," as Sarabia once put it.[9] In May 1906, Guerrero, Manrique, Sarabia, and six of their friends founded a PLM *foco* in Morenci.[10] Two days after the strike at Cananea, Guerrero led the Morenci *foco* in mailing $22 and the following note to La Junta: "Social reform and political reform of Mexico are the ideals for which we are now and will always be ready to sacrifice our energies. The people's cause is ours."[11] Ricardo Flores Magón sent the Morenci *foco* a welcome letter. "The union grows stronger every day both in the Mexican Republic and in the south[western] region of the United States where thousands of compatriots reside," he told them, promising that Mexicans on both sides of the border would soon be ready to "claim with the necessary energy what is denied to us: freedom and well-being."[12]

Guerrero and Flores Magón began a personal correspondence. Their early letters are lost but, by the time Furlong's men tapped their line in September 1906, Flores Magón was referring to Guerrero as "*querido amigo*" (dear friend) and Guerrero had become one of Flores Magón's most trusted confidants. He was one of the few people who knew Flores Magón's final address.[13]

We do not know what drew the two men to each other. They may have noted a shared spirit in their correspondence. In time, Ricardo and Enrique Flores Magón, Librado Rivera, and Práxedis Guerrero would all declare themselves to be anarchists, setting them apart from the other PLM leaders. Or, perhaps, Ricardo Flores Magón and Práxedis Guerrero recognized each other as master propagandists. Both were gifted writers. Whereas Flores Magón's specialty was the diatribe, Guerrero had a punchy, poetic style. Rather than writing long, exhaustive screeds listing Díaz's wrongs and naming his sins, as Flores Magón relentlessly did, Guerrero focused on printing up short pamphlets with lyrical calls to action. His first pamphlet, published while he was working on the docks in San Francisco in 1905, was called "Alba Roja" (Red Dawn).[14]

After Flores Magón was arrested in Los Angeles, Guerrero and Manuel Sarabia, along with Francisco Manrique and Manuel Vázquez, journeyed to Los Angeles to help publish *Revolución* and plan the next raid. In Los Angeles, they joined a vibrant political community committed to supporting the PLM.

Los Angeles was home to a large PLM *foco* as well as a Spanish-speaking division of the Socialist Party of America. Mexicans and Mexican Americans dominated the IWW's Los Angeles chapters, and participated in industrial and agricultural labor unions across the region.[15] The Union Federal Mexicana (UFM), for example, launched a major strike against Henry Huntington's Pacific Electric rail system in April 1903, encouraging seven hundred Mexican laborers to walk off the job and demand a significant wage increase.[16] The local socialist club supported them. Huntington refused to pay the increase, even though he boasted of having the money to do so. As a spokesman for Pacific Electric told the *Los Angeles Times*, "Mr. Huntington proposes to run his own affairs and can in no matter accept union dictation."[17] The LAPD swooped in, beating and arresting the strikers. Undaunted, they walked off the job again the next week. Teresita Urrea, who happened to be in town during one of her popular healing tours through the U.S., led what the *Los Angeles Times* described as a "crowd of Mexican women" in a march to the railroad tracks in support of the strikers.[18] In the end, the Union Federal Mexicana lost the strike, but they had established the first labor union for Mexican railroad workers in the United States, forged collaborative relationships with U.S. socialists, and emboldened Mexican immigrant political action by seeding an oppositional culture that walked out on low wages and marched against police violence. There would be no turning back. Mexicans in the United States, and their descendants, would increasingly become central players in the region's workforces, unions, and political communities.[19]

At the center of Mexican politics in Los Angeles was Rómulo Carmona's bookstore, La Aurora. La Aurora was a popular hangout for Mexicans in Los Angeles looking to discuss everything from politics to technology. Carmona carried almost every newspaper from Mexico as well as science books, dictionaries, religious texts, and leftist journals from around the Spanish-speaking world.[20] He was also a PLM partisan. He vowed to "defend the liberal ideal of protest . . . until the last moment of my life . . . permanently protesting with my words before the enemy, I loudly yell Long Live the Social Revolution!"[21] He made *Revolución* easy to find on the racks and kept the store open late into the evening for PLM members who worked by day—paving streets, picking crops, canning fruit, tending children, and so on, doing the daily labor of the growing city—to have a place to hear and debate the news arriving from Mexico. Carmona even briefly hid Ricardo Flores Magón when he first came to Los Angeles after fleeing the arrests in El Paso in October 1906, and later hid Enrique Flores Magón when he arrived in town following his brother's arrest.[22] While hiding out in Carmona's care, Enrique likely began a romantic relationship with Carmona's sixteen-year-old daughter, Paula, who was also active in the PLM.[23] Paula Carmona wrote one of the movement's feminist manifestos, "Que Luchen" (Let Them Fight), in which she urged Mexican mothers to join the fight against Díaz: "Those who have a family must fight oppression and exploitation so that their children do not become slaves."[24] It is possible that when Furlong's men raided the Weyse Street house in January 1907, it was Paula Carmona who helped

Ricardo Flores Magón to escape through a back window and into a crowd of women. Eschewing the institution of marriage, Enrique and Paula committed to being life partners. By 1912, they had three children together.[25]

Los Angeles was also home to a restless group of Anglo-Americans eager to support the revolt in Mexico. The socialist lawyer Job Harriman led them to the fight. In particular, Harriman brought his friends from the local socialist party to meet Ricardo Flores Magón during visiting hours at the Los Angeles County Jail. In broken English, Flores Magón explained to Harriman's friends why the PLM was fighting to end the Díaz regime. As one of Harriman's friends later recounted, Flores Magón "awakened" him during those jailhouse meetings, teaching him that Porfirio Díaz was not the benevolent ruler he was so often feted to be. Rather, Díaz was a dictator and Mexico under Díaz was a country "with neither constitution nor laws in operation."[26]

After a similarly rousing jailhouse meeting, Harriman's friend John Murray signed on to support the prisoners and their cause. A slightly-built blond man with a bushy mustache, Murray hailed from an elite New York family (Manhattan's Murray Hill neighborhood was named for his kin). Plagued by tuberculosis, he moved to northern California, where he married and had two children. But in the early 1900s, inspired by the writings of Leo Tolstoy, Murray renounced his inheritance, divorced his wife, and moved to Los Angeles, where he became active in union politics and the Socialist Party. By 1907, he was editor of the Los Angeles-based newspaper *The Socialist*. In his writings and work, Murray demonstrated a rare commitment to building an interracial labor movement at a time when the largest labor unions in the United States were strictly segregated and unapologetically committed to winning higher wages and better working conditions for white men only. Murray advocated for workers to unionize across racial divides and devoted himself to improving the wages and working conditions of the region's most vulnerable and lowest-paid laborers, namely Mexican miners and farmworkers. He was one of the socialists most actively involved in the UFM strike against the Pacific Electric rail system.[27]

A socialite named Elizabeth Darling Trowbridge also supported the PLM. As a child, she had never fit the mold of her highbrow Boston family. "The girl refused to become a debutante, nor would she conform to the expected standards," remembered one of her friends.[28] As a student at Radcliffe, she joined the Socialist Party and, upon graduation, spent her time and money on the poor, for which her mother "threatened to have her committed for insanity."[29] At the age of twenty-nine, she arrived in Los Angeles on a vacation with her widowed mother. At the end of the trip, her mother returned to Boston but Elizabeth Trowbridge did not, claiming that California's warm weather was better for her health. Perhaps exasperated by her unconforming, unmarried, unruly daughter, Mrs. Trowbridge agreed to let her remain in Los Angeles with her inheritance. She moved in with family friends P. D. and Frances Noel. Although Noel was a banker, he and his wife, a suffragist and labor organizer known as the "most eloquent woman speaker of Southern California," were also members of the local Socialist Party.[30] Trowbridge soon became involved in radical politics and joined the Noels, Job Harriman, and John Murray, as well as the young socialist couple John Kenneth Turner and Ethel Duffy Turner, in forming a support group for the PLM. The historian Claudio Lomnitz dubbed their group the "Mexican Cause."[31]

The Mexican Cause served as Harriman's research unit and supported the publication of *Revolución*. Trowbridge bankrolled their efforts, renting an office space downtown, which they called the Western Press Syndicate.[32] She bought equipment, covered salaries, paid for research trips, and deposited money into an account for Job Harriman to use in the prisoners' defense.[33] In return, the Mexican Cause gave Trowbridge the unconventional, purpose-driven life she had been searching for. She admired La Junta, who had sacrificed so much for their principles. Of Ricardo Flores Magón, she wrote, "The two chief characteristics of the man are his perfect mastery over self, and his courage and devotion in the cause of the oppressed."[34] Of Manuel Sarabia, whom she would marry, she wrote, "[He is] a man of education, refinement, and intelligence. . . . His smile was singularly winning."[35] For

Ethel Duffy and John Kenneth Turner.

her new life and chosen family, Trowbridge dedicated her inheritance to supporting the revolution in Mexico, cutting checks and handing out petty cash.[36] Her resources sustained much of the PLM's operations in Los Angeles. For the Rivera family, her support was a lifeline.[37]

When Librado Rivera fled St. Louis in December 1906, his wife, Conchita, struggled to make ends meet and threatened to return home to San Luis Potosí. Rivera was determined to stay with La Junta. The couple were arguing over the matter when, in August 1907, their baby daughter, Teresita, suddenly died. Conchita grieved alone in St. Louis while Librado stayed in hiding with Ricardo Flores Magón in Los Angeles. A few weeks later, Creel's net finally closed in and the men were arrested. Despondent, Conchita Rivera bought a ticket to Laredo, intending to cross over to Mexico and return home to San Luis Potosí. But when she went to a bank to pick up money her family had wired to her, the attendant asked her unnerving questions: "Where are you coming from? Where are you going? What are you going to do? Where do you live?" She saw police standing guard in front of the house where she had rented a room for herself and her children to stay the night. Scared, she decided to return to St. Louis. On her way to the train station, a man attacked her and her children at knifepoint. What happened during the attack she did not say, but she continued to St. Louis and then headed to Los Angeles, where she arrived destitute and depressed with two hungry, frightened children in tow.[38] Elizabeth Trowbridge gave her a job, paying her to cook for the Mexican Cause as well as the PLM leaders who were flooding into town.

Following his brother Ricardo's arrest, Enrique Flores Magón arrived in Los Angeles from Canada. Lázaro Gutiérrez de Lara came from Mexico. Antonio de Pío Araujo, the PLM's top gun-runner, came and went from Texas, collecting more *dulces y escobas* along the way. Manuel Sarabia, Práxedis Guerrero, Francisco Manrique, and Manuel Vázquez arrived from southern Arizona. They all worked side by side with local *foco* members as well as the Mexican Cause to publish *Revolución* and support the legal campaign to free the men in jail.

On Sundays, the team often met at either the Noel or the Turner house for a meal. Guerrero usually showed up in tatters. "Guerrero refused to buy himself a new suit of clothes, saying that the Cause needed the money more than he," recalled John Kenneth Turner. "I remember the first time I invited him to supper at my home. He glanced down a little shyly, a little sadly, at his clothes, then, scorning a bourgeois apology, he shrugged his shoulders and said: 'All right.'"[39] On holidays, especially September 16, Mexican Independence Day, the friends played music and danced. Even in these times of celebration, Guerrero, who was otherwise the most lively party guest, rarely ate more than a few beans. "I could not tolerate rewarding myself with better food when millions of human beings do not at this moment have a piece of bread to place in their mouths," he once explained.[40]

The rebels worked and played while Creel's men lurked at the edges. "The spies began to follow us through the streets," reported Ethel.[41] Furlong's agents staked out the downtown office and put María

Brousse and others under twenty-four-hour watch. U.S. and Mexican authorities at every level sought to concoct reasons to arrest them. Or, as Guerrero more poetically put it, "[A] threat hangs over us; a starving pack of hounds besieges us, waiting for the moment to sink its fangs in. Today, tomorrow, at any hour, in whatever place, we might succumb."[42]

Lázaro Gutiérrez de Lara was the first to be snatched. Hoping to stomp out the prisoners' defense committee, for which the charismatic Gutiérrez de Lara easily raised funds, Secretary Mariscal personally requested he be extradited to Mexico. According to Mariscal, Gutiér-rez de Lara had committed a "robbery on <u>blank</u> day on the <u>blank</u> month of 1906 in the <u>blank</u> state of the Republic of Mexico."[43] It was a vague accusation, but enough to have Gutiérrez de Lara detained for forty days while evidence against him was gathered. Harriman argued his case, demanding his friend's release, especially as the for-tieth day approached and the Mexican government had yet to submit any details or evidence of the alleged robbery. When Creel's attorney, Donald Barker, warned the local Mexican consul, "The period of forty days now running, it will certainly be difficult to hold this man any longer in prison," the consul amended the extradition request to accuse Gutiérrez de Lara of stealing four dollars' worth of wood back in 1903, when he was a lawyer in Cananea.[44] When the consul realized that $25 was the minimum for extradition, he upped the charge to $28 of stolen wood.[45] With such maneuvers, Mexican authorities kept Gutiérrez de Lara in jail for months, until Harriman won his release on January 9, 1908.[46]

By then, Manuel Sarabia had also been arrested, charged with vio-lating the U.S. Neutrality Act for sending letters of support to the Douglas *foco*. And Modesto Díaz was rearrested on January 14, when LAPD officers stormed *Revolución*'s printing office, and held him on charges of criminal libel for calling Detectives Rico and Talamantes "dogs" and "hirelings" of the Díaz regime.[47] He quickly made bail, but was arrested again. He made bail again, and was arrested once more. The arrests of Manuel Sarabia and Modesto Díaz finally closed *Revolución* in March 1908. A few months later, Díaz died in jail.[48]

With *Revolución* silenced and Ricardo Flores Magón, Antonio Villarreal, Librado Rivera, and Manuel Sarabia in jail, Enrique Creel was confident that the *magonista* threat was over. He began winding down his counterinsurgency team in early 1908 by reducing Furlong's contract. Furlong pushed back, claiming that there was still work to be done. In particular, the leaders of La Junta needed to be securely transferred to Arizona for prosecution. Creel kept Furlong on payroll but at a reduced rate until that had been accomplished. Cutting back his surveillance operations, Furlong and his agents stopped monitoring the women coming and going from the jail.[49] It was a tactical mistake.

María Brousse visited the jail often. The guards listened to everything she and Flores Magón said in the visiting room, but at least the lovers were able to hold hands. The chance to touch seems to have been intoxicating. "I am tired of suffering from the deprivation of love. Also, I think you will be my best medicine, because without you, I am dead," Flores Magón once wrote to Brousse in a letter that was seized, copied, and saved by Furlong's men.[50] "Soon I will take care of you so that you will be well. I will be your medicine. We will cure ourselves of the sickness that consumes us both," she replied.[51] Sometimes, when the visiting room was closed, she and Lucia would pass by Flores Magón's cell on the street below. He awaited these moments. "Tell me what time you normally pass by so I can be ready," he wrote to Lucia, or as he called her, "my dearest Lucia."[52]

Twice a week, one of the two women dropped by the jail to pick up Flores Magón's dirties and drop off his cleans. Conchita Rivera did the same for her husband. It was a womanly service that, if Furlong's men had been watching more closely, they might have found suspicious.

Not everything Flores Magón wanted to say and not everything he needed to hear could be shared in the presence of guards. So Brousse used the laundry system to smuggle notes. In the seams of his clean underwear, she sewed tiny letters from herself, Lucia, and PLM members. He picked them out and in their place sewed notes composed on tiny slips of paper in his perfect penmanship. She would return to the jail a few days later to pick up his dirty clothes and hidden correspondence.[53] In this way, the women kept the PLM movement alive by defiantly connecting its jailed leaders with members across the borderlands. Furlong's men did not catch the ruse until it was too late.

One day in June 1908, Elizabeth Trowbridge and Ethel Duffy Turner met Brousse in front of the jail, all wearing long skirts. Together, they walked inside and asked to meet with Flores Magón, Villarreal, and Rivera in the visiting room. They all shook hands before sitting at a table in a corner. Trowbridge faced Rivera. Turner faced Villarreal. In the middle, Brousse faced Flores Magón. They began chatting about "trivial things" without taking their attention from the guard pacing the room. When the guard turned his back, Brousse dropped her purse on the floor, with the top gaping open. When she bent down to pick it up, the other two women waved their long skirts to conceal her hands. As Turner later recalled, "with one quick movement, María took the edges of a paper Ricardo passed [beneath the table] . . . and in the next moment, the paper was in her purse."[54] She closed her purse and put it back by her side. They continued chatting for a bit, then the women left the jail, heading in separate directions. Knowing what they had done, Turner and Trowbridge felt like they were "floating" down Broadway toward the office.[55] Brousse walked to a PLM safe house, where she handed the packet to Práxedis Guerrero. That evening, he left for the Texas border. As always, he was accompanied by his friends Francisco Manrique and Manuel Vázquez. They carried with them the packet smuggled out of the jail: Flores Magón's orders for the next PLM raid.

CHAPTER 22

An Attempt to Precipitate
a General Disturbance

THE ATTACK BEGAN ON JUNE 25, 1908, IN THE SMALL
town of Viesca, Coahuila, more than 300 miles from the border,
near the city of Torreón, where President Díaz had backed a "capricious and cruel" *presidente municipal*, Tomás Zertuche Treviño, for
years.[1] Led by Benito Ibarra, president of the local Liberal Club, the
local PLM *foco* had been preparing for months. "One by one they collected weapons for the group: one day it was a pistol, another a carbine. They slowly furnished themselves with ammunition," wrote
Práxedis Guerrero, who later interviewed the raiders for an article in
a later reboot of *Regeneración*.[2] According to that account, Ibarra had
convened one hundred PLM fighters just outside Viesca, where they
ripped up railroad tracks and tore down telegraph wires. Then they
rode into the town plaza shouting, "*¡Abajo la Dictadura! ¡Viva el Partido
Liberal!*" (Down with the dictatorship! Long live the Liberal Party!).
Their first target was the home and office of Zertuche, who had heard
rumors of the impending attack and "fled terrified" earlier that day,
leaving a minor official in charge.[3] The local police put up a brief but
tepid defense, in which two officers were killed and Ibarra's son was
wounded. The PLM fighters soon controlled the town. They released
prisoners from the jail and read aloud the 1906 PLM platform, then
took horses from Zertuche's stable and grabbed money from the public safe, riding out of town on June 26 toward Matamoros, the next
target on Flores Magón's plan. Zertuche returned to Viesca swearing

to deliver "severe punishment."[4] Nearly three dozen residents were promptly arrested, including José Lugo, who had not participated in planning the raid but took up arms and became a vocal supporter during the uprising. As their summary hearings unfolded, resulting in long prison sentences for most and the death penalty for Lugo, Zertuche had the telegraph wires fixed and notified the nearest military garrison of the attack. Soldiers intercepted the rebels en route to Matamoros. In a gunfight in the desert said to have lasted hours, a police chief was killed and a PLM fighter was captured. The remaining rebels escaped, taking flight in separate directions, vowing to meet up later and finish the attack on Matamoros. However, the gunfight had depleted their ammunition, effectively ending the raid on Matamoros before it could begin.[5]

The Viesca raid shook President Díaz. He dispatched 1,000 soldiers to the area and called a special session of the cabinet to discuss the "conditions" on Mexico's northern border.[6] And although his top advisers, including U.S. ambassador Thompson, were privately describing the raid as "revolutionary movements" and "an attempt to precipitate a general disturbance," Díaz directed Vice President Corral to publicly brand the Viesca raiders *bandidos* (bandits).[7] In a statement provided to the Associated Press, Corral dismissed the political thrust of the raid, stating, "For over a score of years the Republic of Mexico has been absolutely free from bandit raids or uprisings similar to the disgraceful affair which occurred at Viesca yesterday. For that reason we will mete out stern measures to these criminals in order that they and the world may know that the days of the bandit in this country have passed."[8]

But the raiders were not bandits; they were insurgents. Corral knew it. Creel knew it. And Díaz knew it, too. The regime had been arresting PLM fighters in Mexico for weeks, including a survivor of the Tomóchic uprising of 1896.[9] And the El Paso Police Department had warned them about the uprising before it began.

On June 24, 1908, the eve of the attack on Viesca, El Paso police raided the home of Prisciliano Silva. Neighbors had complained about seeing men moving guns in and out of a house at all hours of the night.

Expecting to find "thieves or smugglers," police tossed the house, searching for guns and any stolen or smuggled merchandise. They found four Mexican nationals, including Prisciliano Silva and his son Benjamín, with guns hidden under mattresses, boxes of ammunition, and what the local Mexican consul later described as "a lot of revolutionary correspondence, making clear that it was their plan to disturb the peace on the Mexican border."[10] The El Paso Police Department arrested the men. Well aware of the *magonista* threat in the region, they also picked up Lauro Aguirre, who seemed to be implicated in the plan, and handed over the seized letters to the Mexican government. The Mexican officials who hunkered down to decode the letters slowly pieced together a vast and coordinated PLM siege planned for the borderlands. They telegrammed a warning to Ambassador Creel and President Díaz, but it was too late. By June 25, the PLM fighters on their way to battle had already mailed their last letters to their loved ones. "I believe that when this letter arrives in your hands, your friend will be where fate decrees. . . . It is midnight and at 4:30 am only God knows what luck we will have . . . and although some friends have lost hope, I have faith in God that we will triumph. . . . Goodbye for now. Your friend. We will see each other again someday," wrote PLM fighter Leocadio B. Treviño.[11]

With men like Treviño ready to die for the cause, Mexican authorities suspected that the Viesca raid was only the beginning. They had already rushed more troops to the border but, within twenty-four hours, the PLM launched another attack.

"Comrades!" hollered Jesús María Rangel, a veteran rebel, "the long-awaited hour has finally arrived! We will die or conquer freedom," at the start of an early morning raid on the town of Las Vacas on June 26.[12] For weeks, Rangel, Encarnación Díaz Guerra, and Antonio de Pío Araujo had been gathering guns and fighters from across Texas and Coahuila. Seventy-five men, most of whom were ranch hands and cotton pickers, met at a house in Del Rio at midnight on June 25 and, in small groups, headed to the river. Waiting for them at the border were more men with a box of guns. By 3 am on June 26, the fighters had crossed the river and were within 45 meters of the small military barracks at Las Vacas. Drawing from a battle report filed by Díaz Guerra, Práxedis Guerrero published an article that chronicled the raid.

The rebels split into three groups. The center flank was led by Benjamín Canales, a young fighter just twenty-five years old, but with military experience. Basilio Ramírez and Calixto Guerra led the left flank. Encarnación Díaz Guerra and Jesús María Rangel took the lead of the right flank. "We will fight for the justice of our cause," hollered Rangel, signaling the fighters to charge. Nearly one hundred soldiers were lying in wait in the tall grass around the barracks, but, as the PLM fighters charged, most of the soldiers stood up and fled. Benjamín Canales broke their line first, charging toward the barracks. According to Guerrero's account, "shots surrounded his fiery figure; his large and beautiful eyes, normally placid as those of a child, shone brightly. Amid the rain of steel, his classic profile stood out pure, virile, and magnificent, and his fight was brief: firing his carbine and crying 'Viva!' to freedom, he was approaching the entrance of the barracks when he received a dreadful bullet in the middle of his forehead—that beautiful forehead, where so many just aspirations and dreams of freedom had made their home, from which so many noble thoughts had taken flight. Benjamín died with his head destroyed and his arms extended. He would not live to see what he had wanted so much: freedom for Mexico."[13] The fighting continued.

Encarnación Díaz Guerra and his flank took heavy fire from a group of soldiers and quickly scattered back to the border. Rangel led his line in shooting into the back of the barracks. When the local police chief charged them, Rangel's line fired. Shot in the right arm and left leg, the police chief fell from his horse, screaming in pain. His men doubled back to drag him inside the barracks.

As day broke in Las Vacas, the fighting moved from the barracks to the main street. Dozens of men fell wounded and dead. "Dawn arrived," Guerrero reported, with "the sun . . . announc[ing] itself by tinting the horizon with a blood-colored gauze."[14] When a bullet severed Pedro Arreola's spine, he fell and, as the rebels later detailed, he "strove to reach the carbine that had fallen out of reach as he collapsed; a comrade approached him and placed the weapon in his failing hands. He smiled, attempting without success to place a new cartridge in the carbine's chamber; he asked about the fate of the struggle and through his tragic smile slowly slipped the final sentence of his rough philosophy: 'The cause will triumph; do not pay attention to me—one goat dying doesn't mean the herd will be lost.' "[15]

After five more hours of fighting, the battle slid into a stalemate of fatigue. Around noon, residents crept out of their homes to find their town pocked with bullet holes. There were streams of blood in the street and dead bodies everywhere. Corpses stiffened around the barracks. Jesús María Rangel made one last attempt at the barracks but got shot in the leg and had to retreat, his troop carrying dozens of wounded with them back across the border. They left more than twenty dead fighters and as many dead soldiers and police behind.

The Las Vacas raid cut the Díaz regime deeply. The death toll was large and the political fallout uncontrolled. Coded telegrams flew between Mexico City, Washington, DC, and Mexican consuls on the border as Mexican authorities scrambled to stop further attacks and quash doubts about the stability of the Díaz administration. Newspapers the world over wondered if Díaz would soon be booted from power. The *Houston Chronicle and Herald* predicted that the Viesca and Las Vacas raids signaled an armed revolt that "will likely tax the utmost resources of the [Mexican] federal government before it is quelled."[16]

Vice President Corral sent another statement to the Associated Press: "This whole trouble has been caused by three irresponsible agitators and anarchists who are at present residing in the United States. These men . . . recently appealed to certain of the criminal and ignorant element of the border states of Mexico, inciting them to raid certain designated towns for the purpose of robbing banks and Government offices under the plea that funds could be thus raised for the cause of an alleged revolution." But the Díaz regime had prevailed, he proclaimed. "In all other places, with the exception of Viesca and Las

Vacas, the plans miscarried. In the attack on the latter place 15 men were killed but no money was taken. The commander of the Mexican forces was shot twice in the arm. All of the raiders immediately fled back into Texas when repulsed," Corral claimed before declaring the regime's triumph. "The Government places absolutely no political significance or importance in these recent happenings, for the reason that not one of the participants is a representative citizen. . . . [T]hey were the poorest and most ignorant representatives of the lower class, who have been preyed upon by the designing charlatans in the United States. The outcome of the Viesca affair will be simple. These poor ignorant men without a leader will be hunted down in the wilds of Durango by Mexican troops. The Las Vacas affair, unfortunately, presents not so simple a solution, as the raiders are now in Texas and most of them claim protection on the plea that their offense was of a political nature and therefore non-extraditable . . . both governments will take up the entire matter. Everything is quiet at present, and the Government does not think a shadow of a chance for further trouble exists."[17]

While Corral hung a coat of falsehoods over the raids, Ricardo Flores Magón, still locked up in a Los Angeles jail, sent a statement to the press: "If this revolt against the Mexican authorities lasts three months it will result in the complete overthrow of the Mexican Government."[18] President Díaz ordered Enrique Creel back to Washington to manage the crisis while dispatching to the borderlands two troops of cavalry, two troops of infantry, and sixteen trainloads carrying four army regiments.[19] Thousands of Mexican troops occupied towns across northern Mexico, preparing to repulse any impending assaults. Creel also negotiated for the U.S. Department of War to station soldiers on the Texas border. President Roosevelt approved the request, personally directing troops to "effectively patrol the disturbed region and assist in apprehending any persons guilty of unneutral acts."[20] Meanwhile, the U.S. Marshal deputized 2,000 men in Texas to guard the border.[21]

The borderlands were on lockdown. Regardless, the PLM army struck again. This time, Práxedis Guerrero led the raid.

Since he left Los Angeles, Guerrero had traveled without rest across

Texas, Arizona, and New Mexico, distributing the battle plans and coordinating PLM fighters. He intended to lead a strike on Casas Grandes, but Mexican authorities had mobilized extra forces to guard the midsize city. With only twenty fighters and eleven guns, Guerrero rerouted his small detachment to the border town of Palomas, located about 100 kilometers west of Ciudad Juárez and just south of Columbus, New Mexico. Palomas was not strategically important but a fight there could draw soldiers and *rurales* west, allowing PLM fighters to cross the Texas border and attack larger cities, such as Ciudad Porfirio Díaz and even Ciudad Juárez. Plus, Palomas was guarded by only thirty soldiers. The odds were still against the rebels, but they were better in Palomas than in larger towns. Guerrero knew it was a risky campaign.

They crossed into Mexico on June 29, 1908. "The red dawn of Las Vacas had already shone, and Viesca, evacuated by the revolution, resounded still," wrote Guerrero of the hours before the attack.[22] In the darkness, they crept into Palomas "with their carbines held tightly and ready to fire, their *sombreros* pushed back, their steps cautious but firm, ears attentive to every sound and brows furrowed to concentrate the visual ray that fought with the blackness of the night." They tossed two homemade bombs at the customs house. No one was inside. They moved on to the army barracks, and were close enough to touch its adobe walls when "the battlements and rooftops showed, through the muzzle-flashes of rifles, the number of defenders." Soldiers shot at the outnumbered rebels "from above downward and from below upward," as Guerrero put it. Amid the shooting, he watched as Manrique "advanced toward the door of the barracks; fighting bare-chested two steps from the treasonous battlements spitting lead and steel, he fell, mortally wounded." Guerrero ran to him, but before he could reach the wounded man, he was shot twice: once in the foot and once in his left cheek, near his ear. Undeterred, Guerrero picked up Manrique and carried him to a covered location, where, while standing guard over the body of his dying friend, he continued to fight. By dawn, the gunfight was over. The rebels were bested and Manrique, fading in and out of consciousness, sipped his final breaths. "The horizon turned pale with the approaching sun, and Pancho [Manrique] grew pale, invaded by the death which advanced through the body that had been proud, agile, and reckless just a few hours before. The day began, blurring its paleness with that of the fading revolutionary star," Guerrero later wrote. His only option, if he wanted to survive, was to run, leaving Manrique behind. The rebels scattered into the dawn, a few fleeing across the border, the others running into the desert.[23]

Wounded, Guerrero and several of the fighters fled into the vast Chihuahuan Desert, south of the border, toward Casas Grandes, where they had planned to meet up with fifty other rebels to continue the fight. But the rebels got lost. For four days, with gangrene settling into his foot, Guerrero and the others wandered in the July heat, clutching their carbines. Slowly, the fighters peeled off in search of water. In Guerrero's words, "The group was defeated by that terrible Amazon of the desert. Thirst, a flame that embraces, a serpent that strangulates, an anxiety that makes one mad—the voluptuous companion of the restless and soft dunes. . . . Thirst, with the indescribable grimace of its caresses, burning the lips with its kisses, horribly drying out the tongue with its ardent breath, furiously scratching the throat."[24] By day four, he was alone. "In the distance," he saw "the mirage of a crystalline lake laughing at a thirsty man who dragged himself, clutching a carbine, impotent to fight against the wild Amazon of the desert, rabidly biting the ashen grass that provided neither shade nor juice."[25] He crawled toward the mirage of the glimmering lake, which, as he approached, dimmed into the smokestacks of a small mining camp. Playing the role of a lost miner, he inched into camp to request water. After drinking a bit and washing his wounds, he covered himself in mining dust and headed to the nearest town, Ciudad Guzmán, where he rested for a few days before boarding a train to Ciudad Juárez. By August, Guerrero was back across the border and planning the next raid. Finding him was one of the first assignments given to the U.S. Department of Justice's new police force, the Bureau of Investigation.

CHAPTER 23

The Bureau of Investigation

A T THE DAWN OF THE TWENTIETH CENTURY, THERE WERE only two federal law enforcement agencies in the United States, and their mandates were narrow. The U.S. Marshals supported the federal courts by serving writs and warrants, making arrests and holding prisoners, and so on. The U.S. Secret Service investigated counterfeit currency and, beginning in 1903, following the assassination of President McKinley, provided around-the-clock security for the president. What we know today as a massive federal law enforcement system—including Immigration and Customs Enforcement, the Drug Enforcement Agency, the Bureau of Alcohol, Tobacco, and Firearms, the FBI, the U.S. Marshals Service, the U.S. Secret Service, and more—was still in its infancy. In July 1908, President Theodore Roosevelt and U.S. attorney general Charles Bonaparte established the Bureau of Investigation, the forerunner of the FBI, within the Department of Justice. It was the Bureau's job to investigate violations of federal law.[1]

The Bureau was originally established because President Roosevelt wanted a federal police force to investigate land fraud. Large corporations had been buying up swaths of homestead plots intended for settlers operating small family farms. The corporations, mostly mining and lumber operations, then stripped the forests and poisoned streambeds with mine tailings. Roosevelt, a conservationist, was determined to stop them. Working through the Department of Justice, he contracted Secret Service agents to investigate. What the agents found was a system of conspiracies implicating everyone from individual plot-holders to major corporations to U.S. congressmen. When James B. Taw-ney, the chairman of the Senate Appropriations Committee, learned of the investigation and its findings, he did not censure his compro-mised colleagues. Instead, he attacked the Department of Justice for investigating the "private arrangements" of congressmen and accused it of becoming "an arm of the executive branch to spy on the other branches of government."[2] In Senator Tawney's view, Roosevelt's pro-gressive agenda of environmental conservation and anti-corruption investigations was executive-branch overreach tantamount to despo-tism. His colleagues agreed. In 1908, Congress adopted the Tawney Amendment, which prohibited the Secret Service from loaning officers to other federal agencies.

Roosevelt was never one to shy away from a political fight. Deter-mined to add the power of federal policing to his tool belt, he sat down with U.S. Attorney General Charles J. Bonaparte, the grand-nephew of Napoleon Bonaparte, an originator of the modern police state, to find another way to enforce federal law.[3] Poring over the Department of Justice's animating legislation, they found an appropriations clause authorizing the department to reserve funds for "the detection and prosecution of crimes." With this clause and at Roosevelt's direction, Bonaparte reallocated funds from the department's existing budget to establish a Bureau of Investigation and, thereby, expanded the federal government's police power.

Winning a power struggle with Congress and fighting land fraud in the West are the events that historians generally recognize as the inciting incidents in the establishment of the Bureau. The historical record shows that Roosevelt and Bonaparte quickly found other pur-poses for their new national police force. The Bureau was taking shape during the summer of 1908, just as the PLM army launched its raids on Las Vacas, Viesca, and Palomas, and then fled back across the bor-der. Bonaparte tasked at least two of the first nine Bureau agents with investigating and arresting *magonistas* involved in the raids.[4] To lead the investigation, he recruited Secret Service agent Joe Priest.[5] At first, the Department of State helped Bonaparte skirt the Tawney Amendment by paying for Priest's services. In 1909, Priest officially joined the Bureau. His title became "chief special agent of the Department of Justice, Bureau of Investigation." His mandate was "to be devoted entirely to the investigation of the neutrality matters on the Mexican border."[6] Indeed, with Agent Priest in the lead, crushing the nascent Mexican Revolution was one of the Bureau's very first assignments. And this work was meant to be covert. As Priest explained to the secretary of state, "I have always had the understanding that all this work should be kept from the public press."[7]

Collaborating with U.S. Marshals, the Secret Service, local police, county sheriffs, and others, Priest and his team of operatives began rounding up Junta members and PLM fighters, with a focus on those who had participated in or aided the 1908 raids. Thomas Furlong and Ambassador Creel fed them a steady stream of names and addresses parsed from stolen letters. After Priest's team arrested Antonio de Pío Araujo in Waco, the U.S. attorney for west Texas charged Araujo with violating the Neutrality Act for aiding the Las Vacas raid, using as evidence PLM letters stolen by Furlong's team. A judge sentenced Araujo to a fine of one dollar and two and a half years in Leavenworth Penitentiary.

Priest tracked Encarnación Díaz Guerra to a shack in Wilburton, Oklahoma. Accompanied by a U.S. Marshal, he crept up to the shack and broke down the door. Díaz Guerra reached for his gun but Priest got to him first, pistol-whipping him three times. He then hauled Díaz Guerra back to Texas, where, a few months later, a federal jury convicted him of violating the Neutrality Act and sentenced him to eighteen months in Leavenworth Penitentiary.[8]

They arrested Calixto Guerra, Tomás Sarabia, and Jesús María Rangel in San Antonio.[9] Priest found Guerra, who had participated in both the Jiménez and Las Vacas raids, in September 1908, after an informant called in with a tip.[10] In February 1909, he captured Sarabia and Rangel in a multi-agency raid on a small house in Laredito. Priest approached the house from the front, flanked by Lawrence H. Bates of the Secret Service and U.S. Marshals Fred H. Lancaster and T. H. Holloman. U.S. Marshal J. B. Dodson approached from the rear. Each officer carried two pistols and fifty rounds of ammunition. Crossing the open yard at the rear of the home, gun drawn, Marshal Dodson saw a woman sitting in the window. Although Dobson never saw her move, the woman, Mrs. Morantes, an active *foco* member who regularly provided shelter to La Junta and PLM fighters on the run, almost certainly alerted anyone inside that armed officers were approaching the house. When the officers stormed through the front and back doors, they found Jesús María Rangel and Tomás Sarabia sitting calmly with Mrs. Morantes and her young child.[11] The men surrendered without a fight. As Sarabia later explained in a statement issued from jail, "We have always anticipated the Bailiff's blow but we never feared for we knew that it had to come and that is why, when our persecutors surprised us, they found us calm and peaceful."[12] Before being taken to jail on charges of violating the Neutrality Act, Rangel asked to write two notes. The first was a letter to a friend in Waco, asking him to take care of his son. The other was a note he posted on the wall of the Morantes home: "*Somos revolucionarios*/We are revolutionists."[13] Rangel was sentenced to eighteen months in Leavenworth. Sarabia was released for lack of evidence.

By August 1909, Priest and his team of federal agents had rounded up dozens of *magonistas*, most of whom were convicted of violating the Neutrality Act for participating in or aiding the raid on Las Vacas. As Creel put it in a letter to the secretary of state, the Díaz regime was glad to see the U.S. government "take special pains . . . [and] all the measures necessary" to arrest these "agitators."[14] But Priest had not found Práxedis Guerrero, whom Mexican officials urged U.S. officials to arrest.

As early as July 29, 1908, the Mexican consul in El Paso had confirmed that Práxedis Guerrero was the leader of the Palomas raid. But Mexican authorities knew little about him. They did not know where he came from, where he lived, or what he looked like. Ignacio Mariscal, the secretary of foreign relations, pressed Mexican consuls across the borderlands to find a picture of Guerrero. Consul Elias in Tucson found a photo shop claiming to have once photographed him, but the shop burned down before he could secure the image. He reported that one informant was said to have made friends with a young woman who claimed to be Guerrero's lover, but the woman had not saved a photo of him.[15] Another informant, a minor government official from Mexico, claimed to know Guerrero, whom he described as a chubby and well-dressed womanizer with black hair and dark eyes. The informant either never knew Guerrero or was a PLM member knowingly throwing the spy off his trail, as Guerrero was a skinny, blond vegetarian who wore *huaraches* and wrote anarcho-feminist poetry about "revolutionary women." "You women, strong, just, sisters of the rebel slave and not the debased servants of feudal lords; you who have made your conscience independent when thousands of men still live in the fearful shadow of prejudice," he once wrote.[16] Based upon the informant's wildly inaccurate description, the consuls in the borderlands conducted surveillance in Mexican *colonias*, monitoring the movements of suspected *magonistas* and providing regular reports on who went to work and when and who left town and to where, all the while looking for a plump lothario dressed in a rich man's clothes.[17] All they found were the traces Guerrero left behind—handbills and boxes of ammunition.

Throughout 1909 and 1910, Guerrero worked on what he described as the "final campaign," which he hoped would do far more than oust Díaz.[18] As he explained, "I am not a mere political enemy of Díaz. I am an anarchist; I don't fight because I hate government, but for the love of a free humanity. . . . Our revolution must show the manner of liberating and not of governing."[19] Guerrero was going to fight for anarchy in Mexico.

To prepare for the long struggle ahead, Guerrero decided to return to Mexico to organize as many *focos* as possible. He left no record of where he went or whom he talked to, but historians believe he visited Veracruz, Puebla, Oaxaca, and other states in central and southern Mexico, laying out his plan for *focos* to independently rise up, raid Mexico City, and dig in for the final campaign. After traveling thousands of miles in just a few weeks, he returned home to Guanajuato, where he first visited Manrique's family. He told them the circumstances of Manrique's death: that Manrique had fought bravely and, as Guerrero himself learned after the battle was over, died bravely, too. Manrique was not yet dead when Guerrero fled Palomas, leaving Manrique behind, allowing Mexican soldiers to capture and interrogate him for names, addresses, any piece of intel that would help them close in on the PLM fighters before they could strike again. Manrique "remained incognito until death," coughing up nothing but a pseudonym, Otilio Madrid. It was a "sublime lie," Guerrero explained, which prevented the soldiers from identifying him or the other PLM fighters.[20]

After speaking with Manrique's family, Guerrero went to visit his own family. He arrived at night, taking precautions to not be seen, entering the hacienda through a back tunnel. When he appeared, his mother became frantic. Four and a half years had passed since she had seen the son who now stood before her, thin, indigent, and eerily calm. Over the course of three days, Guerrero explained his commitment to anarchism and the PLM movement. His mother worried that he would be killed in the fight against President Díaz. Guerrero, who knew he would be killed, tried to calm her by letting her know he had made peace with his chosen fate. Guerrero's family spent three days trying to convince him to change his path, but he just smiled and teased, "Of course you don't like anarchism because you are the bourgeoisie."[21] On the matter of violence, he explained that he believed in revolutionary violence, a form of violence he described as being "without hatred." "Hatred is not required to fight for freedom. Tunnels are dug without hatred, and dikes are made on rivers without it. Hatred isn't needed to wound the earth in order to plant grain. Despotism can be annihilated without hatred. One can embrace even the most violent act when it is needed for human emancipation," as he liked to put it.[22] When not speaking with his family about his new life, he spent time with the animals on the hacienda, calling them his "*viejos amigos*" (old friends).[23] Guerrero's mother gave up the argument, realizing she could do nothing more than keep her son alive as long as possible. When it was time for him to leave, she led the family in accompanying him to the train station in León, where she instructed his three brothers to escort him north to the border. When they arrived in Chihuahua City, Guerrero mailed his mother a letter: "The flowers arrived safely . . . I'll write again soon."[24] They all then continued to Ciudad Juárez. Before Guerrero crossed into the United States, his brothers, under instructions from their mother, pressed a wad of cash into his hand. He rejected it and crossed the border penniless and alone.

Guerrero returned to work immediately, visiting *focos* across the borderlands and meeting with American supporters everywhere from Kansas to San Francisco to south Texas. He also figured out how to keep *foco* members engaged with a new kind of journal. In El Paso, at the home of his friend William Lowe, he set up a small printing press and began cranking out a short, informal, intermittent publication called *Punto Rojo*. *Punto Rojo* was not a weekly like *Regeneración* or *Revolución*. It did not typically carry the long articles and exposés that had made those papers famous. *Punto Rojo*—translated by one scholar as "tracers," "flash points" by another—was more like a series of short prose pieces and one-liners. It was the Twitter feed of the printing-press era. In *Punto Rojo*, Guerrero published short quips that supporters could easily remember and pass along. "Beggar for freedom . . . beggar for bread . . . stop at once imploring and make demands instead. Stop waiting, and take!" he wrote.[25] "If you cannot be a sword, be lightning," he advised.[26] "It is better to die on one's feet than to live on one's knees," he prodded, citing an anarchist slogan.[27] He distributed free copies of *Punto Rojo* on the streets of El Paso and mailed copies to supporters across the borderlands. Soon, every issue of *Punto Rojo* was reaching 10,000 hands and thousands more hearts by word of mouth. As Consul Lomelí put it, Guerrero's words were reaching the masses and "increas[ing] the agitation."[28]

In May 1909, the Bureau of Investigation hired more agents, informants, and assistants to help Priest in the search for Práxedis Guerrero, whom U.S. and Mexican officials identified as "the present leader of the Mexican Revolutionists in Texas."[29] The U.S. Marshals sent an extra agent to El Paso with the exclusive charge of finding him.[30] But U.S. and Mexican authorities still lacked a photograph of Guerrero and could not find anyone who could or would identify him.

In November 1909, U.S. attorney general Bonaparte appointed a particularly ambitious consular official, Luther T. Ellsworth, to advise on the search for Guerrero and the *magonistas*. Ellsworth had sputtered in several careers before joining the consular service. He had run an unprofitable mine in Panama, served a stint as a schoolteacher, worked at a coal station, and assisted a master carpenter. By 1898, he was forty-four years old, divorced, and still searching for a vocation that would match his skills, interests, and ambition. After whipping votes for the Republican Party in his hometown of Cleveland, Ohio, Ellsworth won a small consular post in Colombia and made an immediate impression on his supervisors. He was enterprising, using a typewriter before most staff at the State Department adopted the new machine. He was organized, turning in meticulously typed dispatches and developing a new and improved filing system for the office. And, when transferred to improve operations at larger consular offices across Latin America, Ellsworth proved daring, perhaps even reckless, drawn to the front lines of insurgencies. In Venezuela, for example, when other staffers fled rebel fighting near the port town of Puerto Cabello, Ellsworth not only stayed behind but rode his bicycle out of the city into the hinterland to interview rebels, map their skirmishes with soldiers, and provide firsthand reports on the fighting. In 1904, after being transferred to the consular office in Cartagena, Colombia, Ellsworth relished the opportunity to participate in covert actions and gather intelligence about U.S. interests in the region.[31]

In January 1908, amid escalating U.S. efforts to crush the PLM, the Department of State transferred Ellsworth to the small town of Ciudad Porfirio Díaz, located on the border just south of Eagle Pass, Texas, and less than 40 miles from Jiménez, where the PLM first attacked back in 1906. Ellsworth eagerly accepted the position. A post in the borderlands seemed a good fit for a bilingual U.S. consular agent with a penchant for counterinsurgency work. Plus, Ellsworth's second wife had just left him and his only daughter had recently married. He was on his own and ready for another new start. He arrived in Ciudad Porfirio Díaz in early 1908, reorganized the office filing system, shook hands with Mexican officials across his district, and imagined himself quickly ascending the consular ranks in Mexico. He even wrote to the assistant secretary of state to nominate himself as the next consul general of Mexico. The suggestion was ignored. In June 1908, the PLM struck Las Vacas, a small town in Ellsworth's consular district. Ellsworth nominated himself to lead the investigation.

Ellsworth personally pursued the Las Vacas raiders rumored to be hiding in the mountains just south of the border. According to the detailed report he filed with the State Department, he and several U.S. customs inspectors entered Mexico and "went in the mountains . . . [for the] purpose of ascertaining real facts relative to the Revolutionists who were rendezvousing therein."[32] On their first day in the field, Ellsworth reported that they rode "for eight hours under a sun shedding terrific heat and without a particle of shade, we rode up and down the mountains, following this trail and that one, through a country famous for its wildcats with claws . . . meeting occasionally a sheep herder, herding sheep of a ranchman located many-many miles away, or a peon en route for the Rio Grande, or servants of the ranches in the interior, all of which I questioned, using the best in me, for the purpose of securing information as to the whereabouts of the Revolutionists and succeeding in discovering ardent sympathizers in them, too devout to the cause of Revolution to betray any of its members." The next day, they rode new trails but "we saw no indication of Revolutionists."[33] The trip left Ellsworth disappointed. He had wanted to rout the rebel hideout and catapult his career, but he found no trace of the *magonista* army. What Ellsworth did find were two wildcat claws, which he mailed to the secretary of state as evidence of the hard and dangerous journey he had endured.

Ellsworth stayed on the case, committing almost all of his time to tracking down *magonistas* north and south of the border. In November 1909, Stanley Finch, the director of the Bureau of Investigation, appointed Ellsworth a "special representative" to the Justice Department, to work alongside Agent Priest. Ellsworth relished the charge and delighted in having direct access to the Bureau's ciphers and secret encryptions, dashing off coded telegrams to Finch and receiving prompt replies. "Important matters here compel me to retain Quigley and Simons [code names] for the present," he wrote to Finch.[34] "Think it advisable that No. 20 be sent here at once," he later added.[35] Finch quickly replied, "Am advised number twenty will arrive at San Antonio to-night and secure lodgings at Elliott Flats unless intercepted at Depot and otherwise instructed."[36] Ellsworth was giddy with his new position in the world of American spycraft.

Meanwhile, Guerrero had gone into hiding in Houston. He rented a room under the name Gabriel Leal at the Hotel Louisiana and spent his days sending letters to *foco* leaders across the United States and Mexico: "The situation in Mexico is nearing its final outcome every day."[37]

In February 1910, U.S. Marshal Fred Lancaster found Guerrero at the Hotel Louisiana. How he did this is not clear in the historical record; perhaps he had followed Mrs. Morantes, the woman who had harbored Tomás Sarabia and Jesús María Rangel in San Antonio. Throughout their trial, Mrs. Morantes proved herself a loyal and unrepentant *magonista*, proclaiming her loyalties when she took the stand. "You are in sympathy with the revolutionists yourself, are you not?," asked the prosecuting attorney. "Yes, sir," she replied in English. "You would like to see President Díaz put out of the way?" he followed. "*Sí, Señor!*" she shouted in Spanish.[38] Throughout the trial, Mrs. Morantes also attended big-tent rallies organized to raise money for the *magonistas'* defense. "Expect from my lips no phrases sweetened with molasses, of a flowery and eloquent language," she exclaimed at one rally. "No, Gentlemen, my verbs shall be the candid words of a woman rebel and in her breast burns the sacred fire of rebellion against all that is despotic and tyrannical. . . . Díaz, the bandit, rose to power through fire and blood and through fire and blood will he descend."[39] After the trial, Mrs. Morantes had no intention of curtailing her support for the

PLM. U.S. agents also suspected her husband of supporting the cause, and, unable to locate him, questioned her about his whereabouts. "I don't know," she replied. "Maybe he don't want to live with me anymore." They did not believe her.[40]

Federal authorities continued to surveil Mrs. Morantes. U.S. Marshal Lancaster may have followed her all the way to Houston, where she checked into the Hotel Louisiana and reunited with her husband. Lancaster staked out the hotel and watched the couple meet in the lobby with a known PLM operative named S. T. Agis. Suspecting that other *magonistas* might be hiding out in the hotel, he organized a cross-agency raid. On February 12, 1910, Lancaster arrived at the hotel before 7 am and lingered outside, waiting for the other agents to arrive. Mr. Agis was up early and spotted him in front of the hotel; as Lancaster had been tracking PLM members across Texas, Mr. Agis recognized him and knew that his presence was not random. Agis ran. Lancaster followed. Agis flew up three flights of stairs to his room, where Guerrero was staying, and warned him of Lancaster's pursuit. Seconds later, Lancaster kicked in the door. As Guerrero later recalled in a letter to his sister, "I saw myself for a few moments in their hands, but taking advantage of their stupidity and cowardice I escaped through a window in my room."[41] He had quickly tied two sheets together and leapt out the third-story window as Lancaster arrived. The sheets ripped as soon as they "felt the weight of my body," he told his sister, and he fell onto the brick pavement below.[42] Though his back was injured, he shook off the fall and ran down the street as Lancaster watched from the window above. "Don't worry about me," Guerrero told his sister. "I am like an eagle that burnt its feathers crossing over the flames of a volcano. I feel them growing again, and I see from my retreat the space that will soon be mine."[43] Lancaster was left empty handed, except for a suitcase of Guerrero's letters, which he seized.

The U.S. government offered a $10,000 reward for Guerrero's capture.[44] Bounty hunters chased him across the borderlands, from California to Arizona to Texas. Priest and his men tracked him everywhere but never spotted him. In March 1910, Ellsworth woefully reported to the State Department, Guerrero "is a notorious revolutionist who is still at large along the border."[45]

Guerrero spent 1910 gathering guns and recruiting fighters for his final campaign, which he vowed would begin before the year's end. "This year is life or death," he wrote to PLM fighters across the borderlands.[46] Meanwhile, Porfirio Díaz made a series of political missteps that cracked the foundation of U.S. support for his rule. Into those cracks, the Mexican Cause unleashed a blistering political assault, ensuring that, when Guerrero's final campaign began, neither U.S. investors nor U.S. warships would move to protect the dictator.

CHAPTER 24

A Tremendous Shock to the American People

A ROUND 1908, PORFIRIO DÍAZ AND HIS FINANCE MINIS-
ter, José Yves Limantour, began curbing foreign control of the
Mexican economy.[1] To counter U.S. dominance in Mexico's oil industry, they made a generous land grant to Lord Cowdray of Britain, over
the interests of Edward Doheny and John D. Rockefeller's Standard
Oil.[2] The American tycoons took exception to this move against their
near monopoly. Similarly, the Díaz government passed a new mining law taxing foreign access to Mexico's subsoil resources. At a time
when U.S. investors controlled 75 percent of Mexico's mining industry, the law outraged American mining magnates, who threatened to
withdraw their money and cut off future investment.[3] According to
Daniel Guggenheim, "The new mining law is a most concrete example of the apparent desire on the part of the government of Mexico
to place an undue burden upon the capital which has already been
invested by citizens of this and other countries in Mexico, and which
will make it absolutely impossible in the future for such capital to be
invested in Mexico."[4]

Díaz and Limantour did not limit their moves to oil and mining. By
1910, they had quietly bought up enough stock to take control of the
Mexican National Railroad, effectively nationalizing a major segment
of the rail system. Such moves infuriated those who had come to expect
open, free, and even subsidized access to Mexico's land, labor, and natural resources. Clawing back control over Mexican industries did not

come without consequence. Like Daniel Guggenheim, powerful U.S. investors began to wonder if Díaz was their man in Mexico. For some, this was the beginning of the end of the Díaz regime.

Díaz simultaneously angered key players in the U.S. federal government, namely President Theodore Roosevelt and all those who supported the Roosevelt Corollary. Roosevelt had wanted to establish a permanent military base in Mexico, from which operations across Latin America could be staged. In 1909, the Roosevelt administration requested permission to build such a base in Baja California. Always sensitive to any hint of another U.S. invasion and still wary of Roosevelt's unilateral claim that the United States was to be the policeman of the Western Hemisphere, Díaz denied the request, conceding nothing more than a short-term lease with strict conditions. Ambassador Thompson tried to counsel Díaz toward compromise, but Díaz still refused to grant the United States a permanent military base. By 1910, Thompson had resigned his position with the State Department to return full-time to the railroad business. Díaz helped his old friend make this transition by approving Thompson's request to purchase the Pan-American Railway charter, putting Thompson in charge of building the longest railway in the Americas.[5] The officials who remained at the Department of State seemed almost indifferent to Díaz's fate. Some even wondered if it might be time for the old general to retire, making way for a new, more amenable partner south of the border.[6] As historian Frank McLynn puts it, "To Washington, Díaz now seemed like an ingrate; where previously they had cooperated with him and even deported his political enemies back to Mexico, now they made it clear that Díaz's enemies were free to use American soil as a base for their activities."[7]

The Department of State began to lay the groundwork for a post-Díaz Mexico. As early as 1907, Secretary of State Elihu Root visited Díaz and personally floated the idea of his retirement.[8] Ambassador Thompson followed up, encouraging Díaz to oversee a smooth transition of power while he still could. Díaz, after all, was seventy-seven years old and his health was declining. Backed by President Roosevelt and Secretary of State Root, Ambassador Thompson arranged for Díaz to give a rare interview to James Creelman, an American journalist famous for his role in helping William Randolph Hearst stoke the Spanish–American War and, thereby, allowing the U.S. to seize Puerto Rico, Guam, and the Philippines. Proofread by Thompson himself and published in *Pearson's Magazine* in March 1908, the Creelman interview read like a glowing obituary of the Díaz era. According to Creelman, Díaz was "the master and hero of modern Mexico."[9] He had steered the chaotic young republic "into [becoming] a strong, steady, peaceful, debt-paying and progressive nation." Of course, Creelman noted, Díaz had operated more like a monarch than a president. In Creelman's words, "For twenty-seven years he has governed the Mexican Republic with such power that national elections have become mere formalities. He might easily have set a crown upon his head." But Díaz had successfully remade Mexico and was now, finally, in 1910, ready to retire. According to Creelman, Díaz had repeatedly vowed during the interview, "No matter what my friends and supporters say, I will retire when my present term of office ends, and I shall not serve again. I shall be eighty years old then." Of course, it was a common promise for Díaz to make. One of his traditional stratagems for perpetual rule was to announce his retirement and then be ceremoniously drafted into running for reelection. Díaz soon walked back his retirement vow, stating that he had merely expressed to James Creelman his personal wish to step down from power. His wish had not been a political declaration. The journalist Filomeno Mata pressed the matter, publicly asking Díaz to clarify his intentions.[10] Díaz's reply was nonsensical: "The main topic, to which you refer is one which, in my opinion, should not be discussed just now, and if on a recent occasion I made a statement with respect to that subject, it was only the expression of a mere personal desire of mine. You will, therefore, not take it strange if, in answer to your request to be informed as to my resolution, I forbear to make it known seeing that so long a time has elapsed before the prospect time for manifesting it arrives."[11] In the ensuing months, Díaz's inner circle launched the familiar campaign to draft Díaz into running for president once more. Díaz agreed, sacrificing his personal will for the good of the nation, as he put it.[12] But it was too late. The consensus among historians of the Mexican Revolution is that the Creelman interview was a "cataclysmic error of judgement" by Díaz.[13] Orchestrated by the U.S. Department of State, conducted by a journalist famed for advancing U.S. imperial ambitions, and published in a popular U.S. magazine, the Creelman interview prepared the world to expect a transition of power in Mexico. This time, the PLM and a growing community of Mexican dissidents were ready to hold Díaz to his word. The only question was who would rule next.

Into the political opening created by the Creelman interview entered several potential successors. Enrique Creel was considered, but he was too deferential to Díaz to seriously challenge him once it was clear that Díaz would, in fact, run again. Vice President Ramón Corral may have hoped for the presidency, but he was too disliked to make a serious bid for the position. He was also dying of cancer.[14] Several campaign committees formed to support General Bernardo Reyes, but Díaz dispatched Reyes on an extended detail abroad, effectively ending his campaign. Díaz similarly isolated other potential contenders. In the end, only Francisco Madero mounted a serious challenge to Porfirio Díaz in the 1910 presidential election.

Madero was not a fierce political adversary. He was short, tender-hearted, and had a high-pitched wisp of a voice, none of which commanded attention. His own grandfather called his campaign against the Díaz regime "a microbe's challenge to an elephant."[15] But Madero was determined to run and willing to commit his fortune to the effort. According to one of his spirit advisers, "You have been chosen by your heavenly father to carry out a great mission on earth. . . . For this divine cause you will have to sacrifice everything material, everything of this world."[16]

To prepare himself for the campaign, Madero purified his body and mind by abstaining from sex for nearly a year, reducing his sleep, eating less, and reading more. He also began writing a book about Mexican history and politics, working out his thoughts about political corruption during the Porfiriato. When the spirit of Benito Juárez himself visited Madero and told him to use his book like a "sword of truth" against Díaz, Madero quickly finished the treatise in late 1909, sent it off for publication, and retreated into forty days and forty nights of biblical isolation.[17] When he emerged, he launched a national book tour and established the Anti-Reelectionist Party. At first, few people took him seriously, just as his grandfather had predicted. But slowly, Anti-Reelectionist Clubs began to form across the country; more and more people came to hear him speak. He strove for sincerity. The ghost of Benito Juárez had advised him, "You have to fight a shrewd, false, hypocritical man. You already know the antitheses you must use against him: against shrewdness, loyalty; against falsity, sincerity; against hypocrisy, candor."[18] People began to call Madero the "apostle of democracy."

By spring 1910, Madero and the Anti-Reelectionist Party had emerged as a credible political threat to the regime.[19] In the final weeks of the campaign, tens of thousands of supporters turned out to meet Madero at almost every stop. In response, Díaz's men banned public protests, issued an arrest warrant for Madero, and had members of Anti-Reelectionist Clubs arrested and impressed into the army. In one town, the mayor cut off the town's electricity when Madero's train arrived, forcing him to give his speech in the dark. But Madero's supporters arrived with torches to illuminate their candidate. In June 1910, as the election approached, Madero returned home to Monterrey, where, two weeks before voting was scheduled to begin, he was arrested for "insulting the president and fomenting rebellion."[20] Historians estimate that up to 60,000 arrests of Madero's supporters followed, and all oppositional newspapers were shuttered by government agents.[21] With Madero in jail, the election was held and the president's men tallied the votes, announcing that Díaz had won the election in a landslide, with 18,829 electoral votes to Madero's 221.

After the election, Madero was released on bail, although guards followed him everywhere. In October 1910, he escaped their surveillance and fled to Texas, where he began buying guns and planning an armed revolt. It was a radical shift for a man who had long held that Díaz could be defeated through the political process. He had supported the relaunch of *Regeneración* but never aided the PLM army. After the raid on Jiménez, Madero even chided the PLM for taking such action, telling a friend, "As you know perfectly well, I, too, reject the current state of affairs in our country, but we don't agree on how to remedy the situation. I have always believed that our struggle should occur within the limits set by the law, in the next elections. Everything induces me to believe that if we proceed energetically, we will triumph."[22] It was only after his rigged loss in the 1910 presidential election that Francisco Madero adopted the path of violence. Thanks to the work of the PLM, he found conditions ripe for revolution when he arrived in Texas. The PLM had been seeding insurrection for years in the borderlands and the PLM's Anglo-American allies had recently detonated a political bomb that created space for Mexico's revolutionaries to maneuver on U.S. soil.

Back in 1907, not long after Ricardo Flores Magón, Antonio Villarreal, Librado Rivera, and Lázaro Gutiérrez de Lara were arrested in Los Angeles, Job Harriman had invited his friend John Kenneth Turner to visit his clients at the Los Angeles County Jail. A socialist and a reporter, Turner interviewed the men for the local labor-leaning newspaper. Sitting across from the men in the visitors' room, he listened as they explained why the PLM had taken up arms against the Díaz regime. Díaz, they said, had "set aside the constitution . . . abolished civic rights . . . dispossessed the common people of their lands [and] converted free laborers into serfs, peons, and some of them even into—slaves."[23] As a socialist, Turner was inclined to believe most of what the men had to say about poor working conditions and civil rights violations in Mexico but, on the point of enslavement, he pushed back. "I scoffed. Bah!" he later recalled. "You mean 'wage slavery' . . . you do not mean chattel slavery," he said, accusing the men of hyperbole.[24] Flores Magón persisted. "Yes, slavery . . . chattel slavery. Men, women and children bought and sold like mules—just like mules—and like mules they belong to their masters. They are slaves."[25] Turner scoffed again: "Human beings bought and sold like mules in America! And in the twentieth century." But "if it's true, I'm going to see it," he declared, vowing to travel to Mexico to personally debunk or verify the PLM's claims.[26]

Turner spent the next few months learning Spanish and visiting the men in jail. Together, they planned his trip to Mexico. What should he see? Where should he go? They decided that he should venture into the Central Plateau and deep into southern Mexico, to the Yucatán, to where the Yaqui had been deported to work on henequen plantations. It was also decided that he could not go alone. He would need a guide, a translator, and a cover story to access places that a socialist journalist would never be allowed to enter. It was agreed that Lázaro Gutiérrez de Lara, who had just been released, would accompany him; they would pose as a prospective U.S. investor and his translator. Elizabeth Trowbridge funded the journey.

Turner and Gutiérrez de Lara left Los Angeles in August 1908. To slip the Furlong detectives and Bureau agents monitoring the Los Angeles *foco*, they dressed down as itinerant laborers and traveled, separately, by boxcar to El Paso, where they crossed into Mexico. They did not linger in northern Mexico, where Gutiérrez de Lara was well-known as an agitator from his years living and lawyering in Hiakim, but headed down to the Yucatán and into the Valle Nacional, where they visited with plantation owners, chatted with managers, and observed operations. When they returned, Turner wrote a series of articles confirming the PLM's claims of slavery in Mexico. He called the series "Barbarous Mexico" and had it published in *The American Magazine*, a national journal recently established by popular muckraking journalists including Ida Tarbell, Lincoln Steffens, and Ray Stannard Baker, gaining a new audience for the story that the PLM had been telling for years.

Published in October 1909, the first article, entitled "Slaves of the Yucatán," focused on the 15-million-acre plantation of Legario Molina, the governor of Yucatán and one of Díaz's closest allies, where deported Yaqui, local Maya, and even some Chinese contract laborers were held in various forms of debt servitude so profound that *hacendados* them-

selves referred to the workers as slaves—slaves whom they offered to
Turner for $1,000 per head. Turner reported that, during their charade
business trip to the plantation, "I was told that I could buy a man or a
woman, a boy or a girl, or a thousand of any of them, to do with them
exactly as I wished, that the police would protect me in my possession of those, my fellow beings."[27] If the workers resisted, they needed
only to be whipped, one of Molina's managers explained. "The Yaquis
are being exterminated, and exterminated fast."[28] Not only were they
exiled from their homes and their families, but the conditions in the
swampy henequen fields of the Yucatán were killing them outright.
"They are dying in a strange land, they are dying faster, and they are
dying alone, away from their families; for every Yaqui family sent to
the Yucatán is broken up on the way," Turner observed. He provided
a detailed report of a whipping he witnessed, when one morning a
worker was picked from the muster for a beating. One of the Chinese
workers was ordered to grab him by the wrists and hold him across his
back "in the manner of a tired child being carried by one of its elders."
Then, one of the managers, called a captain, whom Turner described
as "a deep-chested, hairy brute," reached into a bucket and "soused his
hands deep into the water within," pulling out "four dripping ropes,
each three feet long. The thick writhing things in the dim lamplight
seemed like four bloated snakes." The captain cocked the whip and
snapped it on the man's back. "The bloated snake swished through the
air and fell with a spat," in Turner's words. "The second blow fell,"
he continued, "and the third and the fourth. At the fourth the strong
brown skin broke and little pin-heads of crimson pushed themselves
out, burst, and started downward in thin tricklets. At the sixth the
glistening back lost its rigidity and fell to quivering like a jellyfish. At
the ninth a low whine, a whine somewhere in the depths of that Yaqui,
found its devious way outward and into the open." The lashing stopped
at fifteen blows. The Chinese worker was ordered to release his grip
and the Yaqui "tumbled in a limp heap to the ground. Five minutes
later the day's work on the farm had begun." The plantation needed

to produce for its top buyer: the American Harvester Company, which bought bundles of henequen to sell to Midwestern farms.[29]

Between November 1909 and February 1910, Turner published four more articles: "The Extermination of the Yaqui," "Over the Exile Road," "The Contract Slaves of the Valle Nacional," and "In the Valley of Death." Each article was widely read, unnerving Americans with similarly sensational and melodramatic exposés—a common style of investigative journalists at the time—of U.S. complicity in the brutality. In the words of Ethel Duffy Turner, the series delivered a "tremendous shock to the American people" that weakened popular support for the Díaz regime in the United States, especially among the era's influential cohort of middle-class reformers known as Progressives.[30] Indeed, some said "Barbarous Mexico" stung American Progressives like *Uncle Tom's Cabin* had once shocked Northern whites. As cotton, rice, and sugar produced by enslaved labor in the South powered the entire U.S. economy in the antebellum era, unfree Mexican labor produced key resources for the industrial and consumer economy at the opening of the twentieth century. Much of the nation's rubber, oil, copper, vanilla, cacao, hemp, and more arrived from south of the border.[31] Each text was an assault of sentiment, cutting away popular support for a once stable regime: chattel slavery in the South and the Porfiriato in Mexico.[32]

Building upon the popularity of the "Barbarous Mexico" series, the Mexican Cause convinced several members of the House of Representatives to hold a public inquiry into incidents of U.S. complicity in President Díaz's campaign against the PLM. Lázaro Gutiérrez de Lara was the first to testify, in June 1910. "I have been arrested five times in the United States without any evidence, and if you do not help . . . I will be arrested again and again until I am hanged," he stated. In particular, he chronicled how he had been arrested and detained in Los Angeles for extradition but kept in jail for 104 days—far beyond the forty-day cap for extradition cases. John Kenneth Turner spoke next, telling the story of Manuel Sarabia's kidnapping in June 1907. In Turner's words,

"This cherished idea of America being the cradle for political refugees and a place of safety did not seem to appeal to the [U.S.] Government."[33] John Murray followed. "May I sit down?" he asked. "I have a good deal to read here."[34] He read a detailed list of the numerous arrests of PLM members across Texas. Mother Jones was the last to speak. Refusing to sit, she stood before the committee and cautioned that Díaz's cross-border counterinsurgency campaign had become a direct threat to liberty in the United States. Díaz, she roared, was a "bloodthirsty pirate on a throne reaching across these lines and crushing under his feet the [U.S.] Constitution."[35]

The congressional hearing transformed the U.S. political landscape, souring support for the Díaz regime. By September, the *New York Times*, popular among Anglo-American elites, had run a full-page illustrated article describing labor relations in Mexico as "slavery" and condemning U.S. authorities for aiding Díaz's campaign against the PLM.[36]

Losing support among Progressives and some U.S. elites could not have come at a more dangerous time for Díaz. Not only had Francisco Madero arrived in the United States with sufficient personal funds to arm a revolt, but Práxedis Guerrero was at large in the borderlands, plotting what he hoped would be the PLM's final campaign. And Ricardo Flores Magón, Antonio Villarreal, and Librado Rivera were released from prison in August 1910. John Kenneth Turner, by then a celebrity journalist, met the men at the gates of the penitentiary in Arizona and personally escorted them by train to Los Angeles, where they were met by hundreds of cheering supporters. As the men climbed down from the train, the crowd whooped and hollered, tossing flowers in their path and offering them a heroes' return.[37]

After celebrating with the crowd, the three went their separate ways. Flores Magón and the Rivera family went to the Hotel Chapman. Villarreal went to stay with Lázaro Gutiérrez de Lara. The cheering crowd did not yet know that Flores Magón and Villarreal had had a falling-out. Historians surmise that their conflict boiled down to politics: Flores Magón was an anarchist, Villarreal was a socialist, and the men could not agree on what they were fighting for. As early as October 1908, while still in jail in Los Angeles, Flores Magón had written to his adopted daughter, Lucia, "Antonio is no longer a member of La Junta. . . . [He doesn't] share our ideals, that's all."[38] After leaving prison, the two men continued to work together, but the friendship they had once shared was over. John Kenneth Turner attempted to mediate the dispute, calling a meeting at his house, but the meeting turned "tempestuous" and Villarreal stormed out. He and Flores Magón never spoke directly again.[39]

By November 1910, the ranks of the Mexican exiles who had once worked together to end the Díaz regime had thinned considerably. Flores Magón had exiled Camilo Arriaga, Juana Belén Gutiérrez de Mendoza, and Elisa Acuña from the group. Santiago de la Hoz, Sara Estela Ramírez, and Modesto Díaz were dead. Juan Sarabia was in prison in Mexico, along with thousands of others. Antonio de Pío Araujo, Jesús María Rangel, and dozens of others were in prison in the United States. Lázaro Gutiérrez de Lara had always been careful to support the cause while maintaining his independence from La Junta. After his vicious disagreements with Flores Magón, Antonio Villarreal would soon break away from the group. And Manuel Sarabia was in Europe. After his last arrest, Elizabeth Trowbridge feared that his chronic tuberculosis would not allow him to survive another prison term. In love, she bailed him out of jail, asked him to marry her, and convinced him to flee to Europe with her. There, they distributed *Regeneración*, promoting the PLM cause in radical circles across the continent. But Flores Magón never forgave Sarabia for leaving (or for getting married). He did not speak of Manuel publicly again, and tried to ice him out of the PLM. Only Ricardo and Enrique Flores Magón, Práxedis Guerrero, Tomás Sarabia, and Anselmo Figueroa remained, all of whom were anarchists.

This small group worked long hours to relaunch *Regeneración*. Ethel Duffy Turner recalled these days as intense, but "the camaraderie in those days is unforgettable."[40] She worked in the front office, tapping on a portable typewriter, translating the rebels' words for the new English-language section of *Regeneración* she was editing. Next to her,

La Junta del PLM, c. 1910, showing Ricardo (seated) with Anselmo, Prax, Enrique, and Librado. But Prax's cutout image obscures someone, likely Antonio Villarreal, with whom Ricardo split in 1910.

Guerrero wrote a flurry of articles. In an article entitled "Something More," he laid out the stakes of the revolution to come, especially for the hundreds of thousands of Mexican immigrants in the United States who had fled "poverty, hunger, and abuse . . . in Mexico" only to find "shame, humiliation, and hunger" in the United States. He recounted the indignities they faced under Juan Crow: "the exclusion of Mexican children from the 'white' schools . . . the insulting 'No Mexicans Allowed' that slaps the eyes of our compatriots in certain stores or other public establishments in Texas . . . the violent insult of the racist mob or the abusive police that, inebriated with the savage spirit of Lynch, has bloodied its hands, taking the lives of the innocent and defenseless."[41] And conditions in the United States grew worse every day. Wages were being cut, rents were rising, and landowners were conspiring to put Mexican farmworkers "completely at the mercy of their masters."[42] As Guerrero put it, Juan Crow was "squeez[ing] industrial and agricultural workers of the Mexican race in this country in a terrible tourniquet."[43] He implored Mexican immigrants to stop living "between two hungers" and join the PLM army in the coming revolution.[44]

For those who feared or disagreed with an armed revolt, Guerrero wrote "The Means and the End," explaining his position on the use of violence: "We deplore such violence, and it disgusts us, but facing the dilemma of either remaining enslaved indefinitely or appealing to the exercise of force, we choose the passing horrors of armed struggle." But violence was, he wrote, more than expedient. It was also required to purge the masses of their own complicity in tyranny. As he put it, "Tyranny is the crime of collectivities that do not think for themselves, and it should be attacked as a social illness by means of revolution."[45]

With such writings, composed in the *Regeneración* office, Guerrero encouraged readers across the borderlands to take up arms not only against the Díaz regime but against all forms of tyranny, from the practices of capitalism to the systems of authority. He also called on his fellow PLM leaders to be ready to put down their pens and fight, insisting that force would be required to make La Junta's ideals a living reality. Without action, he wrote, "the conceptions of the human mind would be but a few wet matches in a moldy matchbox."[46] Without deeds, "the rebellion of conscience would be a cloud of smoke trapped in a nutshell, and the desire for freedom the useless flapping of the wings of an enchained, imprisoned eagle."[47] Without force, "all aspirations and ideals would spin in the minds of people like fallen leaves by the north wind." "I am Action," he declared.

Meanwhile, Flores Magón installed himself in a small corner office on the second floor where he spent days and nights writing, with the door open for friends to come and go. Behind this office was a small room, with the door always closed, where secret meetings were held. Here, La Junta laid new plans for revolt.[48] They announced their revolutionary intentions on the front page of *Regeneración*, which they began republishing on September 3, 1910: "Here we are, announcing war: with the torch of revolution in one hand, and the Program of the Liberal Party in the other. We are not whining messengers of peace. We are revolutionaries. Our ballots will be bullets fired by our rifles."[49]

Flores Magón still did not publicly declare his anarchist beliefs, but he published an article entitled "To the Proletarians," warning Mexicans to beware of a solely political revolution. "Political liberty requires as an adjunct another liberty to be effective, and that is economic liberty."[50] By October 1, he had emblazoned the anarchist motto "Land and Liberty!" on the front page of *Regeneración*. Emiliano Zapata made the phrase his battle cry, later explaining, some say, that "Land and Liberty!" was "what I wanted but I didn't know how to say it."[51]

A few weeks later, Francisco Madero released a manifesto from San Antonio, proclaiming himself Mexico's provisional president and calling for all Mexicans to join him in an armed revolt scheduled to begin at 6 pm on November 20, 1910. The rush to revolution was on. Díaz could not stop it. U.S. authorities hardly tried. The PLM was set to unleash Guerrero's final campaign. Madero's supporters were arming themselves on both sides of the border. But Madero's Anti-Reelection Party and Magón's PLM held very different visions for the revolution to come.

The PLM demanded both political and economic change. As anarchists, the remaining members of La Junta believed in the total abolition of capitalism, the state, and the church. A broader circle of PLM affiliates tended toward socialism, believing that the state needed to control the means of production and that taking control of government was the first step toward radical economic change. Many rank-and-file fighters and adherents were miners and migrant workers who simply wanted to see land redistributed and labor rights protected regardless of party, ideology, or faction. Despite their differences, they all demanded political and economic transformation.

Francisco Madero, on the other hand, had little interest in reforming Mexico's economic structure. Madero abhorred the political corruption endemic to Díaz's rule; he wanted to restore free and fair elections, break up the president's monopoly on political appointments, and fund public schools. But his economic reforms were largely limited to infrastructure investments, such as roads and irrigation. He did not plan a broad redistribution of land.[52] Flores Magón repeatedly warned his supporters of the substantive political differences between the PLM and Madero's Anti-Reelection Party. As he wrote in *Regeneración* in November 1910, "The Liberal Party [PLM] seeks political liberty, economic liberty by delivering to the people the lands illegally taken by the great landlords, an increase in wages and lessening of the hours of work, nullification of the influence of clergy and government in the home. The Anti-Reelectionist Party seeks only political liberty."[53] However, La Junta recognized Madero's call for revolt as an opportunity to be seized by the PLM, advising loyalists to join the uprising scheduled for November 20. "We will take advantage of the moment of confusion to rise up as Liberals," explained Flores Magón. "This does not mean that the junta recommends that you make common cause with the *maderistas* . . . just that Liberals take advantage of the special circumstances that will emerge in the country if the *maderistas* disturb public order."[54] They distributed this call to arms on the pages of *Regeneración* and encouraged every subscriber to read their instructions aloud to "your coworkers who do not know how to read . . . read them *Regeneración*."[55]

As the day of the uprising approached, a white farmer in Rocksprings, Texas, reported finding his wife, Effie Henderson, dead on their porch: one gunshot to her back, one to her head. That night, Henderson and his friends, joined by local law enforcement officers, formed a posse to find the killer. On November 3, 1910, they arrested a Mexican migrant laborer named Antonio Rodríguez. There was no evidence connecting Rodríguez to the murder, but there was a rumor circulating that he "was a member of the revolutionary faction which made an attack upon the garrison of Mexican troops at Las Vacas more than one year ago."[56] The sheriff booked him into the Rocksprings jail. A mob soon arrived, storming the jail and pulling Rodríguez from his cell. A mounted cowboy among them lassoed Rodríguez around the neck and dragged him to the edge of town, where "nearly every inhabitant of the town" had gathered around a sturdy mesquite tree prepared by "willing hands" with dry sticks and leaves at its base. Several men stepped forward to chain Rodríguez to the tree. The mob jeered him as "a can of kerosene was emptied" over his head until it soaked his clothes, his skin, and the kindling at his feet. A match was thrown and Rodríguez was burned alive. "In 30 minutes," wrote a local reporter, Antonio Rodríguez was dead.[57]

Jovita Idar, Pablo Cruz, and Mexican journalists across the borderlands reported the lynching of Antonio Rodríguez, blasting Anglo-American "barbarism."[58] In Los Angeles, Práxedis Guerrero raged on the pages of *Regeneración*, "Whites! Whites! . . . They burned a Mexican alive. . . . They formed a well-dressed, educated horde that was proud of its virtues and civilized; they were citizens and white 'men' of the United States." Anglo-American claims to "progress, civilization, culture, humanitarianism," he wrote, were little but "lies [that] turn to ash with the charred bones of Antonio Rodríguez. They are dead fantasies, asphyxiated by the pestilent smoke of the pyre of Rocksprings."[59] When these reports of "whiskey and sausage filled" Anglo-Americans burning a Mexican at the stake reached central Mexico, riots erupted.[60] Beginning in Mexico City, students and young people took aim at American-owned businesses, breaking windows and tearing down U.S. flags. For generations, since before the Mexican–American War (1846–48), dating back to the U.S. acquisition of Tejas (Texas), Mexicans had resisted Anglo-American incursions on their lands and lives. Rodríguez's murder was just the most recent assault. Enraged, Mexicans marched in the streets, accusing the Díaz regime of failing to protect Mexicans from Anglo-American aggression, at home and abroad. They chanted "Death to the Americans!" They stomped on U.S. flags. They set fire to the lobby of a Mexico City-based newspaper notorious for being friendly to U.S. interests in Mexico. Díaz smothered the riots with a swarm of arrests, but he could not break the firestorm of discontent. Newspapers across Mexico decried the murder of Antonio Rodríguez. Even the state-sponsored press covered the killing. The Catholic Church–sponsored paper *El País* demanded a national boycott of U.S. products. Filomeno Mata in Mexico City issued a public warning to the United States: "The day will arrive, whether you will it or not, in which the Mexican people will demand reparation for your insolent conduct, your lack of justice, and your ignominious work."[61] Díaz had him arrested but could not kill the story.

Concerned by Díaz's failure to hush the Mexican press, Henry Lane Wilson, the new U.S. ambassador to Mexico, called on the president. Unlike Thompson, the previous ambassador, Wilson was not Díaz's friend. He regarded Díaz as "infirm" and described his regime as full of old men "past their years of usefulness"; in his view, they were losing their grip on Mexico at a time when U.S. investments in the country had never been higher.[62] In a series of private meetings, Wilson lectured Díaz on "the great source of annoyance caused by the continued publication in *El País* of articles of a violent character, commenting on recent disturbances brought about by the lynching of Antonio Rodríguez."[63] Wilson insisted that Díaz "use his good offices towards suppressing these articles." According to Wilson's report to the secretary of state in Washington, Díaz "called his personal bodyguard and directed him to communicate with his private secretary at once and advise him that it was the President's desire that he send for the editor of *El País* and urge upon him the necessity of suppressing any further matter upon the above mentioned disturbances." Moreover, Díaz confirmed that "he had [already] given orders to the authorities of the whole Republic to act with the necessary energy to suppress any further agitation because of the Texas matter, and that if anything of the kind should happen again, those who participated in demonstrations would be dealt with all the severity of the law."[64]

The real problem, Díaz insisted, was "Francisco Madero and Ricardo Flores Magón." Flores Magón, who had been stirring up trouble for years, was in Los Angeles writing about the riots in Mexico as a "reaction against U.S. imperialism . . . against the engulf-and-devour politics of the U.S. government."[65] Madero, Díaz reported, was in Texas "openly buying arms and ammunition in the United States without being in the least molested by the authorities, and . . . unless the American Government prevents these men from making an open revolutionary propaganda against the Mexican Government and accumulating arms and ammunition a more serious disturbance might be expected."[66] Díaz wanted the U.S. government to arrest both men and charge them with violating the Neutrality Act. Wilson passed Díaz's request along to the Department of State, but federal authorities declined to intervene. They did not arrest Madero or Flores Magón, nor did they stop the gun-running across the border.[67] Díaz had lost U.S. protection, leaving him to stave off the revolution alone.

CHAPTER 25

The Revolution Begins

R EVOLUTIONS ARE HARD TO SCHEDULE. FRANCISCO MADERO
called for the Mexican Revolution to begin on November 20,
1910, at 6 pm, but not even he joined the fighting on time. He had
planned a symbolic raid on the border town of Ciudad Porfirio Díaz,
but the fighters who had promised to join him never arrived, leaving
him standing with his uncle and a handful of fighters on the bank
of the Rio Grande. He returned to San Antonio to make a new plan.
Soon, the PLM army began attacking Díaz's forces across northern
Mexico. Práxedis Guerrero led one of the first raids.

By December 1910, Guerrero was ready to fight. "We are going off
to a violent struggle without making violence our ideal and without
dreaming of the execution of our tyrants. . . . Our violence is not justice, it is simply a necessity," he announced in one of his final articles for
Regeneración.[1] Before leaving Los Angeles, he stopped by Ethel Duffy
and John Kenneth Turner's apartment to ask a favor. John was not
home; he was out buying guns to smuggle into Mexico for the PLM
army. With his head bowed and a small box in his hands, Guerrero
said, "If I don't return, Ethel, send this box to my sister." She agreed.
Placing the box on the table, he added, "I know I will not return."[2]
That evening, he took a train to El Paso. On his way to the station, he
stopped by the *Regeneración* office and offered a final challenge to the
PLM leaders, who had largely chosen to stay behind and continue writing rather than take up arms. In large letters on the window, he wrote,

"*¿Hombres?*" (Are you men?)[3] Lázaro Gutiérrez de Lara soon joined him. Antonio Villarreal followed. Ricardo and Enrique Flores Magón and Librado Rivera remained ensconced in Los Angeles.

In El Paso, Guerrero met with veterans of the previous PLM raids. Prisciliano Silva had recently been released from Leavenworth Penitentiary and was preparing for battle, along with more than twenty veterans of the Jiménez, Viesca, Las Vacas, and Palomas campaigns. They gathered guns, ammunition, and dynamite and left El Paso on the evening of December 19, hiking for two days through the mountains and deserts outside Ciudad Juárez until they arrived at the small railroad stop in Sapeyo, Chihuahua. In Sapeyo, they hijacked a train, disarmed the soldiers on board, and disembarked the passengers. After unhitching unnecessary cars, they forced the conductor to drive the train south as fast as possible. Along the way, they stopped to dig up tracks and destroy bridges behind them, denying federal forces at least one route of pursuit. By the time the train arrived in the town of Guzmán, they had burned four wooden bridges and dynamited one steel bridge. In Guzmán, a few more men joined the fighters before they split into two groups, with Guerrero at the head of thirty-two men and Prisciliano Silva, joined by Lázaro Gutiérrez de Lara, at the head of nineteen. Before they separated, they agreed to distinguish themselves from Madero's fighters by carrying a red flag emblazoned with "¡Tierra y Libertad!"[4]

On December 29, Guerrero's crew arrived at the small town of Janos to pick up supplies and recruit fighters. Janos was an old military colony where, back in the 1880s, Díaz had made one of the first large land grants to a survey company, displacing the entire town. Janos's families had been fighting for their land ever since.[5] Hoping that they would support the PLM fighters, Guerrero put a white flag in the barrel of a gun and sent Leonidas Vázquez into town to negotiate with the mayor. Vázquez presented their terms: if the mayor surrendered the town without a fight, no one would be hurt. If he did not, the fighters would attack. The mayor agreed to relinquish control the following morning. But it was a trick. As Guerrero and the fighters waited outside Janos, the mayor called for troops. Informed of his duplicity, Guerrero launched a quick attack, which began at 10 pm on December 29, 1910. The fighters rushed into the town yelling *"Viva el Partido Liberal!"* Residents shot at them from rooftops and houses lining the main street. After fifteen minutes, the PLM fighters had shot their way to the plaza and surrounded the military barracks. Two hours later, they had seized the barracks and captured the mayor as well as the local head of the *rurales*. But the victory was short-lived. Minutes later, five hundred mounted soldiers stormed into the town. In the dark of the night, hand-to-hand combat raged through the streets and alleys of Janos. Within minutes, dozens of rebels lay dead. Guerrero climbed onto a roof to gain a better view of the fight below. Standing there, with his rifle in his hand, he took a fatal bullet to the head. When they saw their leader fall, the surviving PLM army retreated, turning Janos over to government forces and leaving Guerrero's body behind.[6]

The death of Práxedis Guerrero was a major blow to the PLM. As one of his most tenacious biographers, Ward Albro, explains, "From 1907 to 1910 [while Flores Magón was in jail], Guerrero roamed the borderlands from California to Texas organizing, arming, encouraging, and physically leading *magonistas* into battle. One might question whether there would have been a Flores Magón movement without Guerrero's efforts."[7] Moreover, Guerrero had military experience and was willing to lead PLM fighters into battle, whereas Flores Magón, who had penned many of the words that inspired the insurgency, refused to join the action. Guerrero's death and Flores Magón's refusal to shift from word to deed—as well as his unpreparedness and incompetence as a military strategist—played major roles in the PLM's quick decline as the revolution accelerated in the months ahead.

After Guerrero's death, La Junta announced a half-baked plan to occupy the border town of Mexicali, Baja California, hoping that PLM forces could score an early win against Díaz's military before Madero could return to Mexico and claim leadership of the revolution. With few passable roads and no railroads connecting it to central Mexico, Baja California was largely isolated from the rest of Mexico, which

Mexican PLM soldiers in Baja California.

would make it difficult for Díaz's troops to respond quickly, as they had done in Janos and other locations.[8]

On January 29, 1911, a sleepy Sunday morning, Flores Magón ordered twenty fighters—mostly Mexicans but a few Anglos and African Americans, too—to liberate Mexicali in the name of the Partido Liberal Mexicano. In preparation for the raid, John Kenneth Turner took several wagonloads of guns and ammunition to a town near the border in boxes marked "agricultural implements."[9] A "gladiator" named Josefa Fierro smuggled the rifles across the border to Mexicali by hiding them in a baby carriage.[10] The PLM force arrived just before dawn, marched down the main street, and raised the red "¡Tierra y Libertad!" flag. Except for the jailer, who was killed in a scuffle, the town slept through the insurrection. When they awoke later that day, the citizens largely ignored the PLM occupation. They did not fight it. They did not agree to it. They paid no attention to the armed outsiders marching around town. However, in a technical sense, the PLM's occupation of Mexicali constituted the first seizure of territory from the Díaz regime.

A few weeks later, the governor of Baja California arrived with

*Josefina Fierro de Bright. Josefina was the daughter of Josefa Fierro,
an active* magonista *who smuggled guns into Mexico for the PLM's
1911 occupation of Baja California. Josefina grew up to become a
prominent Mexican-American civil rights activist, organizing with
the Congress of Spanish-Speaking People and the Sleepy Lagoon
Defense Committee.*

one hundred soldiers to oust the PLM. Overconfident, the governor
charged his soldiers across an open field toward a group of PLM fighters. Taking cover in a canal bed, the PLM strafed the soldiers. Dozens
fled or fell dead in the field. The governor was shot in the neck and carried away by his men. Wounded and humiliated, the governor and his
remaining soldiers retreated, defeated in battle by no more than twenty
poorly provisioned *magonistas*. The PLM declared its first major victory against Díaz's troops. But the achievement quickly crumbled.

In Flores Magón's mind, the PLM still only needed to light the spark
of revolt for the dispossessed to spontaneously rise up, throwing off the
chains of capitalism and replacing all forms of hierarchical governance

with mutualism and horizontal leadership. This had been the PLM's strategy at Jiménez, Acayucan, Viesca, Las Vacas, Palomas, and Janos. In each case, the PLM struck and the people did not revolt. So, too, in Mexicali. Local residents did not rush to the revolution. However, in the case of Mexicali, the small PLM band stuck around and was able to fight off the first wave of soldiers sent by the Díaz regime while an assortment of armed men from the United States rushed to the fight. Most of the men were members of the IWW, political brethren of the increasingly anarchist PLM. Others were an assortment of unemployed workers directed to Mexicali by none other than the popular writer Jack London, who, having learned about the PLM and their occupation from his friends in the Mexican Cause, took it upon himself to recruit soldiers for the campaign. In February 1911, London publicly issued the following letter to La Junta:

Dear, Brave Comrades of the Mexican Revolution: We socialists, anarchists, hobos, chicken thieves, outlaws, and undesirable citizens of the U.S. are with you heart and soul. You will notice that we are not respectable. Neither are you. No revolutionary can possibly be respectable in these days of the reign of property. All the names you are being called, we have been called. And when graft and greed get up and begin to call names, honest men, brave men, patriotic men and martyrs can expect nothing else than to be called chicken thieves and outlaws. So be it. But I for one wish there were more chicken thieves and outlaws of the sort that formed the gallant band that took Mexicali. I subscribe myself a chicken thief and revolutionist.[11]

Read aloud at a large labor rally in Los Angeles, London's letter provoked dozens of men into joining the revolt. Flores Magón ordered the fighters in Mexicali to welcome the new men into the fold, thinking that a shared spirit of insurgency might be the base of a revolutionary alliance. It was not. The PLM occupation of Mexicali descended into chaos.

The group of PLM fighters, IWW men (often called "wobblies"), and chicken thieves in Mexicali lacked the most basic of supplies, ranging from guns and bullets to flour and meat. When they asked La Junta to send supplies, Flores Magón sent two boxes of Peter Kropotkin's book *The Conquest of Bread*.[12] This almost comical gesture of ideological propaganda was an irrefutable sign of his inability to shift from ideas to deeds as the revolution began. In the end, he was an agitator, not a revolutionary. Without a quartermaster, the men in Mexicali fed themselves by raiding local farms, which alienated residents. Without clear leadership or a shared commitment to mutualism, they took to fighting one another. The tension tended to split along racial lines: the Mexican PLM fighters versus white wobblies and wanderers. More white men with unclear aims arrived daily, and general mayhem ensued. A member of the infamous Hatfield family turned up and, after an unrecorded altercation, shot a Mexican PLM fighter in the face.[13] There is no record of what the African American fighters thought of it all, just a photo documenting their participation in the campaign.

Amid this chaos, a wobbly named Stanley Williams took charge of a group of the white men in the camp and headed east to capture an additional town under the banner of the PLM. Williams and his crew seized the small town of Algodones but, as journalists in Mexico and the United States noted, the campaign was fully out of La Junta's control. Was this a PLM operation or a group of rogue Anglo-Americans laying claim to Mexican territory? La Junta asked John Kenneth Turner to go to Baja to try to clean up the mess. The mission failed. Turner described a mediation he convened with Williams and his lieutenants as "marked by loud talking and violent gestures."[14] Soon, the Mexican PLM fighters in Mexicali began deserting, leaving behind what amounted to a political disaster for La Junta: an armed Anglo-American occupation of Baja California under the flag of the PLM.

The disaster turned to farce when Richard Wells Ferris, a well-known promoter of carnivals and races from California, began placing ads in U.S. papers claiming that he would turn Baja California into a "sporting republic." Baja, he said, would soon be a land of leisure for

African American soldiers who joined the PLM Army in Baja California.

Anglo-Americans seeking the bawdy pleasures often banned north of the border: gambling, horse racing, prizefighting, and so on. Ferris's shenanigans did not amount to much, but his media bluster heightened suspicions about the PLM's campaign in Baja: were the armed white men patrolling the streets of Mexicali operating under the orders of La Junta, or were they the vanguard of an Anglo-American filibuster? Was this a Mexican revolution or another U.S. invasion?[15]

As the PLM campaign in Baja unraveled, Francisco Madero returned to Mexico and personally led a bold attack on Casas Grandes that won him the respect of insurgents across northern Mexico— most notably Pascual Orozco and Pancho Villa.[16] Prior to the revolution, Orozco had built a business in transportation, moving precious metals from mines to market. In this work, writes historian Friedrich Katz, Orozco became a "good rider and a good shot [and] a leader of extremely tough men."[17] He knew the terrain of Chihuahua far better than most. As early as 1907, Orozco had been drawn to politics. Local authorities reported him as reading *Regeneración* and showing an interest in the ideas of Ricardo Flores Magón. Upon Madero's call to revolution, Orozco organized his men into a fighting force. He quickly proved an able military chieftain who could move guerilla fighters surreptitiously and swiftly across difficult terrain.

Pancho Villa was an outlaw who had made his skills legal by setting up a transportation business. Like Orozco, Villa had headed squads of men moving mine and railroad materials across Chihuahua, before being recruited to the revolution by Madero's ally Abraham González. González knew Villa to be an able fighter. He did not expect Villa to rise into a leadership position. But within just a few months, Villa was raiding haciendas, stealing horses, throwing open jails, burning tax records, and generally harassing Díaz's troops across northern Chihuahua. *Hacendados* fled the region in fear of Villa's next strike, while government troops spread themselves thin trying to find him.[18]

Meanwhile, in the state of Morelos, not far from Mexico City, Emiliano Zapata had organized his neighbors into a small army of the dispossessed, ready to fight anyone who refused to honor their political autonomy and traditional claims to land. Since 1906, Zapata had been reading *Regeneración* and attending lectures and reading books on anarchism brought to Morelos by a local schoolteacher.[19] Driven by his community's claims to land and hunger for autonomy, Zapata and his followers, known as *zapatistas*, answered Madero's call to revolt, proudly carrying the banner of "Land and Liberty!" into battle. By April 1911, Madero, backed by Orozco and Villa, was popularly acknowledged as the leader of the revolutionary forces in the north, while Zapata became known as the "Supreme Chief of the Revolutionary Movement of the South."[20]

Squeezed by Madero's forces in the north and Zapata's indefatigable guerilla army in the south, and menaced by urban plots concocted by familiar insurgents such as Camilo Arriaga and Juana Belén Gutiérrez de Mendoza in Mexico City, Díaz's inner circle advised the president to appease the rebels with reform before they fought their way to the National Palace. On April 1, 1911, Díaz announced that he would not seek reelection again, that local elections would be protected from federal interference, and that some of the nation's largest estates would be broken up and the land redistributed. It was not enough. The revolutionists did not agree on much—Madero wanted political reform, while Zapata demanded land and autonomy—but they all agreed that they wanted Díaz's immediate resignation.

With Pancho Villa and Pascual Orozco at his side, Madero announced a plan to attack Ciudad Juárez. Seizing Juárez would put Madero in charge of Mexico's principal land port with the United States and thus its economic artery. It was a bold move which the PLM had been trying to pull off for years. Madero, Villa, and Orozco, leading 2,500 fighters, approached Juárez from the south, cutting telegraph lines, ripping up railroad tracks, and claiming towns along the way. By the time they reached the edge of the city, Díaz had dispatched emissaries to negotiate a ceasefire. Though nearly deaf, Díaz could hear the end of his regime approaching. With Juárez surrounded, he promised the immediate removal of federal troops from Sonora, Chihuahua, and Coahuila and the concession of fourteen governorships and four cabinet posts to the revolutionaries, as well as his firm commitment to no reelection. Madero agreed to the ceasefire and did not insist on Díaz's immediate removal from office. Villa and Orozco were furious. Without Madero's approval, they organized their forces to attack Juárez on May 7, 1911. Once the fighting began, Madero could not stop it.

The Battle of Ciudad Juárez was the definitive conflict in the revolution against Porfirio Díaz. Federal soldiers turned machine guns on the rebels. The rebels used dynamite to blow up army positions. Residents of El Paso rushed to the border, cramming onto rooftops and picnicking on the banks of the Rio Grande to see the battle.[21] Both the rebels and the soldiers were careful not to shoot across the border, which would provoke a U.S. intervention. Journalists reported the spectacle and the carnage, delighting at the drama of the *insurrectos* besting the Mexican Army. "We sat up there on the hill and saw the river oaks swarming with *insurrectos* moving into Juárez. They moved in no formation whatsoever, just an irregular stream of them, silhouettes of men and rifles. . . . They would fight for a while, and come back to rest, sleep and eat, returning refreshed to the front. The European-trained soldiers waved at this, tried to turn them back, to make everybody fight at one time. But that was not the way of these chaps from Chihuahua. They knew their business and they knew it well."[22] The Díaz regime surrendered on May 9, 1911. The Treaty of Ciudad Juárez required the immediate resignation of both Porfirio Díaz and Ramón Corral, impaneled an interim president, and stipulated that elections would be held within a few months. By the end of the month, the Díaz and Corral families had packed up and boarded a ship to France. The Porfiriato was over.

Porfirio Díaz lived the remainder of his life in exile. But he unleashed one last night of bloodshed before he left. On May 24, his final night in the National Palace, 75,000 people crammed into the Zócalo, Mexico City's central plaza, to celebrate his imminent departure. Díaz ordered the machine-gunners stationed on the roof of the palace and the riflemen on the roof of the cathedral to open fire. They killed 200 protestors and wounded at least 1,000 more.[23] The next morning, Díaz's old friend Victoriano Huerta, a drunkard general who had butchered dissidents and hunted Yaqui for the regime, marshaled two squadrons of soldiers to escort Díaz's train to Veracruz. Rebels attacked the train, but Huerta's men fought them off. On May 31, Díaz boarded a ship for France. He died in Paris in 1915 at the age of eighty-four.

With Díaz gone and an interim president in place, Madero turned to the business of running for president and laying plans for the future of Mexico. Acknowledging the role Ricardo Flores Magón had played in stirring the nation to revolt, Madero had, in the run-up to the revolution, proposed a Madero–Flores Magón government: Madero as president, Flores Magón as vice president.[24] Flores Magón rebuffed the offer and, as the revolution escalated, began to publicly berate Madero on the pages of *Regeneración*, calling him a "traitor to the cause of liberty" for suggesting that a new government could justly replace the Díaz regime.[25] In attacking Madero, Flores Magón began to reveal his commitment to anarchism. As he wrote in February 1911, "I am firmly convinced that there is not, and cannot be, a good government. They are all bad. . . . Government is tyranny, because it curtails the individual's free initiative, and the sole purpose it serves is to uphold a social system which is unsuitable for the true development of the human being. . . . I have no wish, therefore, to be a tyrant. I am a revolutionist, and a revolutionist I shall remain until I draw my last breath."[26] Madero was just seeking another form of oppression, he charged. "Mexicans, salvation is not the electoral ballot . . . death to Madero and the capitalist system! Long live Land and Liberty!" he roared from Los Angeles.

Despite Flores Magón's rancor, Madero still hoped to create a coalition party to rebuild Mexico. Soon after Díaz resigned, he dispatched Flores Magón's brother Jesús and Juan Sarabia to speak with him in person. The brothers had taken separate paths since Jesús left *Regeneración* in 1902. They had argued often but remained in contact, largely because of Jesús's willingness to weather his brother's criticisms. Juan Sarabia had only recently been released from San Ulua Prison. He and Ricardo Flores Magón had not seen each other since his arrest in 1906 but they had remained close, smuggling letters to each other over the years. The two emissaries had already agreed to support Madero's presidential campaign, as had Antonio Villarreal, Lázaro Gutiérrez de Lara, Elisa Acuña, Juana Belén Gutiérrez de Mendoza, and Camilo Arriaga. They wanted Flores Magón and the rest of La Junta remaining in Los Angeles to end the PLM occupation of Baja and join them in rebuilding Mexico.

Jesús Flores Magón and Juan Sarabia arrived in Los Angeles to meet with Ricardo and Enrique Flores Magón and Librado Rivera. After a brief greeting, they turned to the question at hand. Would Ricardo disband the PLM fighters in Baja? Would he recognize the emerging Madero administration? The answer was no: the anarchists in Los Angeles would settle for nothing less than immediate abolition of the state, private property, and the church. They would not bend their principles or delay their demands for anyone. "They would not listen to me. They asked impossible things. They hold to anarchistic ideas," as Jesús later explained.[27] Frustrated, the emissaries returned to Mexico City. When Madero learned that there was no possibility of an alliance with Flores Magón, his troops routed the remaining PLM fighters from Baja. By the end of June 1911, Ricardo Flores Magón and the *magonistas* had ceased to be a factor in the Mexican Revolution.

As the revolution moved on without him, Ricardo Flores Magón lashed out at everyone who he felt had betrayed him and compromised the ideals of the revolution. He publicly berated Juan Sarabia, calling him a Judas for supporting the Madero administration. "Juan Sarabia says he owes his freedom to Francisco I. Madero. Shut your filthy mouth, liar! Your freedom is owed to the Liberals who were the initiators of the movement which brought about the fall of Porfirio Díaz," he screeched. "The fall of Díaz has been written since Acayucan and Jiménez, since Las Vacas, Viesca, [and] Palomas.... Madero was a miserable creature who was able to take advantage of the extended agitations and sacrifices of the Liberals," he asserted.[28] When Juan Sarabia and Antonio Villarreal launched a new version of *Regeneración* in Mexico City, Ricardo smeared it, calling it "Degeneración." And he unleashed a barrage of personal attacks on Antonio Villarreal and Manuel Sarabia, whom he accused of being lovers: "We often surprised them in each other's arms, stroking one another's mustaches and hair."[29] When Villarreal did not respond, Flores Magón continued the attack. In one article, he wrote, "I have made serious charges against Antonio I. Villarreal. I have called him a pederast, an assassin, and many other things, yet he stays so calm. Why doesn't he answer? ... Silence does not exculpate; and in his case silence accuses him.... Everyone knows that he is silent because the accusations ring true. He is not a man but a ... pederast. Villarreal does not have a right to face any man. Villarreal should be spat upon by every man and woman."[30]

Fed up, Villarreal punched back, publishing an article that named Flores Magón a "blackmailer, swindler, coward, and a drunken pervert and scoundrel who shared his mistress with all men of bad taste."[31] The Idar family in Laredo agreed with this assessment, describing Flores

Magón and his remaining comrades as "socialist swindlers who with the money of thousands of reckless but honest workers gave themselves the grand life."[32] This assessment was too harsh. There is no evidence that Ricardo Flores Magón swindled his supporters to live a "grand life." However, as the historian Gabriela González puts it, "The Idar family was not prepared for the anarcho-syndicalist revolution heralded by the Magonistas."[33] They made their split with Ricardo Flores Magón clear in their newspaper. Many members of the Mexican Cause also split from him. Elizabeth Darling Trowbridge Sarabia, who had given her fortune to the PLM, lamented, "I cannot understand Magón's extraordinary and ridiculous behaviour. It is well enough to disagree with people but when it comes to such lies and foul language as he indulges in, that is another matter."[34] Ethel Duffy and John Kenneth Turner would continue to support the revolution in Mexico, but not at Flores Magón's side. Supporters peeled away.[35] Soon, only Enrique Flores Magón, Librado Rivera, and Anselmo Figueroa were left.

Juan Sarabia tried to mend his relationship with Flores Magón, publishing an open letter of "fraternal affection" to the man whom he still considered "the intimate friend, the good companion, the beloved brother," and for whom he had "lost nothing up to now of my esteem and affection, in spite of the many invectives that on every hand fall on your name." Sarabia explained the political conditions on the ground in Mexico. Madero had "won the adherence of all the Mexican people" and "the nation is satisfied. Weary of the dictatorship, they have overthrown it; avid for political liberties, they have won them, and they will not move a step further in the field of armed revolution to gain new conquests however just and beautiful they may be. I say here that the Nation will not follow along with you." In particular, Sarabia warned Flores Magón that Mexicans were not ready to fight for anarchy. "Your objective is anarchy, that is to say, the absolute free grouping of human beings, without private property, without government, without distinction of nationalities—without imposition of any kind, everyone working and distributing by mutual accord the products of the labor of all, constituting a society without privileges, without self-aggrandizement, or dissimilarities, a society based on brotherhood and love." Sarabia himself believed in that vision, but asked whether anarchy was "practicable in every situation and at every time?" Mexico, he explained, needed a period of education and evolution before anarchism could be adopted. Therefore, he advised Flores Magón—"my brother"—to "accept the situation created by the victorious revolution" and return to Mexico and help with the popular education campaign needed to forge its path to "social perfection and happiness."[36] Flores Magón refused, severing his brotherhood with Sarabia.

On a visit to Los Angeles, Mother Jones tried to address the ideological and personal rifts ripping the old friends and alliances apart. She and Job Harriman met with the two Flores Magón brothers and Rivera, but the meeting did not go well. As Mother Jones later recalled, they "charged everyone with being a traitor, but themselves." When she pressed, they continued to insist on an immediate end to all private property in Mexico. "We discussed the matter pro and con for an hour," she said, "but they believed only in direct action, the taking over of the lands." Harriman refused to offer them any further legal services and declared that he "wanted [nothing] more to do with them."[37] He soon left town to start a socialist commune called Rio de Llano on the outskirts of Los Angeles. Mother Jones returned a few months later for another meeting with the three men. Again, she encouraged them to join the new government in Mexico and help shape its agenda, pushing and pulling it from the inside toward more radical ends. They remained unmoved, prompting Mother Jones, one of the most radical voices in U.S. politics, to resolve, "I consider them one and all a combination of unreasonable fanatics, with no logic in their arguments."[38] The editor of *Appeal to Reason*, the leading socialist journal in the United States, called Flores Magón's intransigence "utterly impractical."[39]

In September 1911, Ricardo Flores Magón finally declared that he was an anarchist, making clear for the first time his true vision for the revolution in Mexico. Joined by Enrique Flores Magón, Librado Rivera, and Anselmo Figueroa, they reconstituted La Junta as an anarchist body, voided the 1906 PLM platform, and issued a new manifesto. The 3,000-word document declared that human freedom required the total abolition of the "dark trinity": private property, the state, and the church. "Abolishing [private property] means the annihilation of all political, economic, social, religious, and moral institutions that comprise the ambient within which free initiative and the free association of human beings are smothered," it began. "Without the principle of private property, there would be no reason for government, which is necessary solely for the purpose of keeping the disinherited within bounds in their quarrels or in their rebellions against those who hold social wealth; neither would there be reason for the church, whose only object is to strangle the innate human rebellion against oppression and exploitation through the preaching of patience, resignation and humility, and through quieting the call of the most powerful and fertile of instincts through immoral, cruel, and unhealthy penances; and so that the poor will not aspire to enjoying the good things of this earth . . . the church promises to the humble, to the most resigned, to the most patient, a heaven extending to infinity, beyond the stars one can see."[40]

Having declared a "solemn war upon Authority, Capital, and the Clergy," they urged Mexicans to join them by fighting against Madero and all those who sought to replace the Díaz regime with a new government. "Don't listen to the sweet songs from these sirens who want to take advantage of your sacrifices in order to establish a government, that is, a new dog to protect the interests of the rich," they warned. "On your feet everyone! . . . Expropriation must be carried out through blood and fire during the great course of this movement. . . ." Their instructions were simple: "Take possession" of "lands . . . agricultural implements . . . all the industries . . . mines, factories, workshops, foundries, cars, railways, ships, warehouses of all kinds and the houses" and take all mobile items to "a place easily accessible to all, where men and women of goodwill will take a careful inventory of everything that's been gathered in order to calculate how long these things will last . . . until the first harvest is taken from the fields and the order industries produce the first articles." In this process, no one need fear want, they promised, because "workers in different industries will come to a fraternal understanding among themselves on the management of production. In this manner, during the course of the movement, no one will lack anything, and the only ones who die of hunger will be those who don't want to work, with the exceptions of the old, the handicapped, and the children, who will have the right to the use of everything." Finally, they made their pitch to forestall what seemed to be all but guaranteed—that Francisco Madero would succeed Porfirio Díaz as president of Mexico. "Mexicans," they wrote, "if you want to be free, do not fight for any cause other than that of the Partido Liberal Mexicano. Everyone offers you political liberty after the triumph: the Liberals invite you to take the lands, the machinery, the means of transport, and the houses immediately, without waiting for anyone to give you all this, without waiting for some law to decree these things, because the laws are not made by the poor, but rather by the frock-coated bosses who guard well against making laws to the disadvantage of their own caste."[41] But Mexicans did not turn en masse to the PLM or its new anarchist manifesto. In October 1911, while Ricardo Flores Magón was promoting the manifesto in Los Angeles, Mexicans elected Francisco Madero as their next president.

Always a Rebel

BY 1915, RICARDO FLORES MAGÓN WAS A SICK MAN LIVING in a *jacal* on a commune located next to the city dump in the community of Edendale on the east side of Los Angeles. He spent his days taking care of chickens and publishing sporadic issues of *Regeneración* for a subscriber list that had dwindled to less than 2,000 people, mostly anarchists in Europe and a few diehard followers in Texas. The PLM was over. La Junta had long ago split, with the anarchist faction remaining in Los Angeles and the socialists returning to Mexico. But the Mexican Revolution they incited together was still underway.

The Madero administration did not last long. Madero, a forgiving man, allowed key members of the Díaz government to keep their jobs, including Díaz's trusted general, Victoriano Huerta, while filling open positions with his family and friends. In other words, Madero surrounded himself with friends and enemies while making little room for the allies who had fought to make him president. It was a recipe for mutiny. Madero also failed to redress the basic economic questions that had motivated so many Mexicans to join the fight. When he proposed only modest land and labor reforms, Emiliano Zapata, Pascual Orozco, and others charged him with betraying the revolution and turned their forces against him. Meanwhile, Díaz's old friends in the Madero administration circled the new president like birds of prey. In 1913, General Huerta and Díaz's nephew Félix ousted Madero from power and ordered him assassinated. Madero was shot dead on February 22, 1913.[1]

U.S. ambassador Henry Lane Wilson supported the coup. In fact, Huerta and Félix Díaz concocted their coup in Wilson's office. Huerta seized the presidency but he, too, was soon pushed from power as Mexico unraveled into a bloody civil war.[2]

The United States government made no secret of its efforts to stop the Mexican Revolution from impacting Anglo-American lands and lives on both sides of the border. The Immigration Service constructed the first ever border fence to hold back the surge of refugees.[3] It didn't work. More than one million Mexicans entered the United States during the revolution, establishing a wide foundation for future generations of Mexican Americans. Meanwhile, U.S. operatives provided arms to at least two counterrevolutionary movements in Mexico, and the U.S. military twice invaded Mexico, occupying the port city of Veracruz in 1914 and, in 1916, conducting a year-long search for Pancho Villa, known as the Punitive Expedition, after Villa raided the border town of Columbus, New Mexico. By 1917, the U.S. government had played a meaningful role in putting a new president, Venustiano Carranza, in power. Carranza, a senator from the Díaz era, was friendly to U.S. interests. During the worst of the fighting, he had proved willing to protect U.S. property and lives in Mexico. He had also helped to silence an echo of the *magonista* uprising in Texas.

In February 1915, U.S. Marshals in south Texas arrested a Mexican citizen named Basilio Ramos and found in his possession a code book, commission papers, and a document entitled "El Plan de San Diego," which called for non-whites to unite in revolution against "Yankee tyranny." In particular, El Plan de San Diego called for a "Liberating Army for Races & Peoples" to kill every white male over sixteen years old and to seize Texas, New Mexico, Arizona, Colorado, and California. The first lands to be seized were to be given to African Americans and Indigenous communities to build for themselves independent nations—sanctuaries—free of Anglo-American domination.

U.S. authorities generally dismissed El Plan de San Diego. Some called it a hoax.[4] A judge said that Ramos should be tried for lunacy rather than insurgency.[5] But on July 4, 1915, approximately fifty armed and mounted Mexicans crossed the border and executed three white men between Harlingen and Lyford, Texas, riding under the banner of El Plan de San Diego. A posse rode in pursuit, shooting two Mexicans for resisting arrest and hanging another. The attacks continued.[6]

Between July and November 1915, Mexicans and Mexican Americans in south Texas joined the insurgency, ripping up railroad tracks, derailing trains, burning bridges, and cutting down telegraph wires. They openly recruited African Americans and Japanese immigrants to their ranks. By October, their "Liberating Army for Races & Peoples" had raided five Texas towns and ranches, executing dozens of white men, wounding many more. White families fled south Texas en masse. The settlers were in retreat. Those who remained slept in fear, taking to their fields and rooftops with guns in their hands. In sum, El Plan de San Diego was one of the largest—and deadliest—uprisings against white settler supremacy in U.S. history.[7]

The reprisal was severe. In response to U.S. government demands, Venustiano Carranza arrested or killed anyone in Mexico suspected of participating in the raids.[8] The U.S. Army sent 4,000 troops into south Texas and placed all civilian lawmen under military orders while the Texas Rangers, backed by dozens of posses, made lists of "bad Mexican[s]" and went hunting.[9] Some called it a "war of extermination [that] will be carried on until every man known to have been involved with the uprising will have been wiped out."[10] The killings were indiscriminate, limited only by race. Fifteen Mexicans were found hanging near the railroad station in Ebenoza.[11] A U.S. Army patrol found another eleven bodies hanging near Lyford.[12] A reporter found the bodies of three men, all shot in the back, on the road near San Benito.[13] Corpses were everywhere. As one local paper put it, "The finding of dead bodies of Mexicans, suspected for various reasons of being connected with the troubles, has reached a point where it creates little or no interest."[14] By November 1915, at least 300 people, almost all of them Mexicans and Mexican Americans, had been killed in retaliation for El Plan de

"Texas Rangers with Dead Mexicans, 1915."

San Diego.[15] The final death toll will never be known. Local residents reported finding bodies for years, most with bullet holes in their skulls. Some scholars estimate that as many as 5,000 Mexicans and Mexican Americans were killed.[16] Historians of the Mexican American experience call this period "la Matanza"—the Massacre.

La Matanza is one of the least-known episodes of racial terror in U.S. history. Similarly, El Plan de San Diego is one of the least-known episodes of rebellion in U.S. history. The chronic marginalization of the Mexican American experience has held them both in the shadows of the American story. But El Plan de San Diego and La Matanza were major events in the three Rs of U.S. history: race, rebellion, and repression. Emboldened by the revolution in Mexico, armed bands of Mexican and Mexican American insurgents invited African Americans, Asians, and Indigenous people to join them in a mass insurgency against white supremacy in the United States. It took one of the largest massacres in U.S. history to stop them.

El Plan de San Diego was a legacy of the PLM. One of the uprising's principal leaders, Aniceto Pizaña, was a PLM adherent. Pizaña first met Ricardo Flores Magón in 1904, when he arrived in Laredo, and, over the years, they corresponded several times. Pizaña became a regular *Regeneración* subscriber, an early *foco* member, and, in time, a partisan supporter of the PLM's anarchist faction. He even named his youngest son Práxedis.[17]

Soon after the 1915 uprising began, a posse chased some of the riders to Pizaña's home. He escaped, but the posse arrested his wife and killed his son. Enraged, Pizaña became one of the uprising's leaders. He stamped "¡Tierra y Libertad!" on a handbill and distributed it across the Texas borderlands, inviting others to join him in fighting "*los gringos*."[18] "Enough of the suffering and scorn," he declared as he recruited a squad of fighters, including former PLM members. Together, these veterans of revolution in the borderlands launched some of the most devastating raids in south Texas.

Ricardo Flores Magón did not know anything about El Plan de San Diego or La Matanza until he read the reports in the newspapers. In 1915, in fact, he, his brother Enrique, Librado Rivera, and Anselmo Figueroa had just been released from prison once again. This time it was a two-year stint at the McNeil Island Penitentiary in Washington state, following a 1912 conviction for violating the U.S. Neutrality Act in aiding the PLM's 1911 raid in Mexicali. After they returned to Los Angeles, Figueroa died and the others started the commune in Edendale.

Ricardo Flores Magón, María Brousse, her daughter, Lucia, and Lucia's young son, Carlos, lived together on the commune, along with Enrique Flores Magón, Librado Rivera, their families, and a few other friends. Rivera was raising his two children on his own, as Conchita died of cancer sometime before 1915. They planted fruit trees, tended to a vegetable garden, and raised chickens. After several months of scrimping and saving, they put $100 down on an old printing press, which they installed in a stable and affectionately called "The Son of Guttenberg's First Tweak."[19] Beyond their daily chores, they were preoccupied with keeping *Regeneración* afloat. To cut costs, they bought paper on credit, fell behind on rent, and begged their remaining subscribers for donations. They rarely made enough. Sometimes the issues would pile up in the stable because they could not afford the postage to mail them out. "How can we go on? How?" wondered Enrique Flores Magón.[20] And his brother was often too sick to work.

Ricardo Flores Magón had struggled with bad lungs and deteriorating eyesight ever since his imprisonment in Belem. Living on the run or in prison had only exacerbated his chronic health problems. The recent interlude at McNeil Island had been difficult, and life on the commune wasn't much easier. As one of their friends put it, "poverty took root among them like a toothache."[21] His health only worsened as he began to show signs of diabetes.

When Ricardo Flores Magón and the others learned about El Plan de San Diego and La Matanza, they worked by candlelight in the stable with their old printing press to produce new issues of *Regeneración*. In a series of articles published in October 1915, they claimed the raiders as "compatriots" and exalted El Plan de San Diego as "a movement of legitimate defense by the oppressed against the oppressor . . . making themselves safe from the threats that people of our race are so frequently the victim of in this country."[22] Noting the reports of violent repression unfolding across south Texas—"the Mexican is killed wherever he is found," they wrote—they recommended that their readers take direct action in support of the raiders: "The ones who ought to be shot are THE RANGERS and the balance of fellows who are with them in their depredations."[23] It was not long before U.S. authorities swooped down on the commune, charging the Flores Magón brothers with sending "indecent" material through the mail. In June 1916, they were convicted, with the judge stating, "No one can read this article and not come to the conclusion that its every purpose was to incite, in the streets of Texas, where the paper is largely circulated, a state of insurrection against the Government, and against its people."[24] In effect, they were sentenced to prison for publishing their support of El Plan de San Diego.

Throughout the trial, Ricardo Flores Magón complained about his health. "I feel sick from diabetes. . . . I feel my brain is tired; physically I feel pretty bad, I have been sick for about five or six months," he wrote from the Los Angeles County Jail, where he was held throughout the trial because he could not post bail.[25] He complained so much that, upon his conviction, the judge decided to commute the sentences, letting both brothers go home. The judge likely expected them to return to the commune, where Ricardo Flores Magón would quietly die.

But he held on, writing a couple of plays and publishing occasional issues of *Regeneración*. Although sickly, he remained as combative as ever with his family and friends. In these years, he even split with Enrique. The brothers never publicly explained their disagreement, but the scholar Claudio Lomnitz suggests that at the root of it all was a wedge that Ricardo had driven between Enrique and his partner, Paula Carmona. When Paula eventually left Enrique, taking their children with her, the brothers stopped speaking to each other, even as they continued to live and work on the commune and after Enrique began a new family with María Brousse's niece Teresa Arteaga.[26]

In 1918, Ricardo and Enrique Flores Magón and Librado Rivera were arrested for violating the Espionage Act of 1917, which made it a felony to "obstruct the draft" and empowered the U.S. Postal Service to ban from the mail any publications deemed to foster disloyalty to the United States military or flag. Passed at the close of World War I, the Espionage Act and its successors, the Sedition and Immigration Acts of 1918, opened an era known as the Red Scare, when authorities beat back what they saw as the rise of Communism within the United States by smashing labor unions, arresting radicals, restricting immigration, and deporting non-citizen radicals. Eugene V. Debs, hundreds of wobblies, and many others were imprisoned. Emma Goldman and others were deported.

Amid the Red Scare, the crew at Edendale reprinted an article by Emma Goldman and issued a new manifesto, "Manifesto to the Anarchists of the entire World and to the Workers in General," both of which broadcast their unbroken commitment to anarchism. Pub-

Ricardo and Enrique Flores Magón at the
Los Angeles County Jail, circa 1916.

lished on March 16, 1918, their manifesto declared, "The death of the old society is close at hand, it will not delay much longer," and advocated for "the insurrection of all peoples against existing conditions," which U.S. authorities took to be a call for the overthrow of the federal government.[27] They also reprinted a defiant speech Ricardo Flores Magón gave to a local labor union, imploring the anarchists among them not to be cowed by the surging arrests. "We, the anarchists, cannot shut up: we shall not shut up. So long as injustice reigns, our voice shall be heard. . . . Go on you haughty overlords, swallow your order, for we, the anarchists, are not disposed to obey it; we cannot shut up, we will not shut up, and we shall speak. Cost what it may."[28] Federal authorities raided the commune and arrested most of its residents for violating the Espionage Act. María Brousse's case was dismissed, but the Flores Magón brothers and Rivera were tried and convicted. The U.S. district attorney hired none other than Emilio Kosterlitzky to translate the manifesto. When Huerta was overthrown as president, Kosterlitzky and a contingent of *rurales* had fled to the United States. Kosterlitzky settled in Los Angeles, where he found work with the Bureau of Investigation as a spy and translator.[29] Based upon Kosterlitzky's translations, Enrique Flores Magón was sentenced to three years in federal prison, Rivera was sentenced to fifteen years, and Ricardo Flores Magón was given the maximum sentence of twenty-one years. He called it "a sentence of life for a man as old and worn out as I am."[30]

The three men were sent to the federal penitentiary in Leavenworth, Kansas. There, Enrique Flores Magón avoided his estranged brother until one day Ricardo reached out, looking to reconnect. As Enrique explained in a letter to Teresa Arteaga, "The man before me was no longer the arrogant, aggressive, and haughty person." Instead, he looked to be "beaten, ashamed, [and] bearing a white flag."[31] Enrique conceded to what he called an "armistice," but their time together was short.

At Leavenworth, Ricardo Flores Magón's health continued to decline. He regularly complained about his "deteriorating eyesight, rheumatism, bad teeth and [an] ulcerated foot."[32] His lawyer applied for early release, arguing that his client was too ill to be held in confinement. The U.S. attorney general denied the request, stating, "The Justice Department has determined that the physical condition of Flores Magón is sufficiently normal so as to permit him to remain in confinement." Moreover, Flores Magón remained a "dangerous man" intent on spreading "seditious and revolutionary ideas."[33]

Within a year of arriving at Leavenworth, Flores Magón was nearly blind. As he told a friend in one of his final letters, "One fine day, that to me will be as dark as night . . . my eyes will not be able to guide my pen in the writing of those words which the humble loves and the proud detests. . . . My weapon—my pen—the only weapon I have ever wielded; the weapon that landed me here; the weapon that accompanied me through the infernos of a thirty years' struggle for what is beautiful, will be then as useless as a broken sword."[34] He visited the prison hospital often and regularly complained to friends that he was "poor, depressed, sick and nearly blind."[35]

Ricardo Flores Magón died at Leavenworth Penitentiary on November 23, 1922. Librado Rivera, one of his few remaining friends, believed that he was murdered, having heard a tussle coming from the direction of his cell the night he died. But most historians agree that he probably died from complications of diabetes.[36] He had been sick, untreated, and deteriorating for years.

Leavenworth officials returned Flores Magón's body to María Brousse in Los Angeles. The Mexican government had offered to repatriate the body, but she did not want to hand it over to state authorities. "We will not turn Ricardo's body into any government, only to the workers," as Enrique Flores Magón put it to the press.[37] Nor did she want to bury him in the United States, where she felt he had been so unjustly persecuted. While she considered what to do, the body began to decompose, so she had it embalmed and temporarily buried in Los Angeles. A few months later, Mexican railroad workers paid to have the body disinterred and transported to a grave in Mexico City. They draped red and black banners across the railroad car carrying the casket and, all along the route, supporters lined the track to honor Flores Magón's role in sparking the Mexican Revolution. In Mexico City, he was given a state funeral and his former comrade Antonio Díaz Soto y Gama, now a congressman, pronounced him the "precursor of the revolution, the true author of it, the intellectual author of the Mexican Revolution."[38] Ricardo Flores Magón had always been the most intrepid among the dissenters. As Díaz Soto y Gama said, the man hunted down for being "*el alma de todo*" was an agitator to the end: "Always a rebel, always unbending."[39]

When Enrique Flores Magón and Librado Rivera were released from prison, they were deported to Mexico, where they remained active in anarchist politics. Rivera died in a car crash in 1932. Enrique Flores Magón, who lived until 1954, dedicated much of his life to memorializing the roles he, Ricardo, and the others had played in inciting the revolution. He collected documents, wrote a book, gathered photo-

Ricardo Flores Magón's funeral.

graphs, and gave interviews. In 1945, he successfully lobbied to have his brother's body relocated to Mexico's Rotunda of Distinguished Men (later renamed the Rotunda of Distinguished Persons), a national cemetery established to honor leading figures in Mexican life, culture, and politics. It was a move that helped to secure the PLM's place in Mexican history.

The PLM's legacy was also secured by its leaders who returned to Mexico. Antonio Villarreal joined Madero's army. Following Madero's assassination, he led troops against Huerta, reached the rank of general, briefly served as the military governor of Nuevo León, and eventually became minister of agriculture, overseeing land reform projects during the left-leaning administration of Álvaro Obregón (1920–24). Camilo Arriaga served as secretary of the interior during the Madero administration and later joined the Obregón administration to work alongside Villarreal in implementing land reform. Juan Sarabia became a congressman during the Madero administration. He was imprisoned when Huerta took power but was later released and eventually directed a school for orphans. He died in 1920, at the age of thirty-eight, after years of struggling with tuberculosis. Manuel Sarabia and Elizabeth Darling Trowbridge Sarabia returned to Mexico to support the Madero administration, but fled to the United States after Huerta's coup. Sarabia soon died of tuberculosis, and Trowbridge died in poverty in a rented room in Brooklyn in the 1930s. Ethel Duffy Turner also moved to Mexico and went on to publish one of the most widely cited histories of the PLM. For her contributions to the revolution and its memorialization, the Mexican government paid her a pension until she died in 1969, in Cuernavaca. Lázaro Gutiérrez de Lara became a founding member of La Casa del Obrero Mundial, a radical labor organization based in Mexico City, and dedicated himself to agitating for the rights of Mexican workers. In 1918, while he was trying to revive labor organizing among miners in Sonora and Arizona, Venustiano Carranza ordered him killed. He was executed by firing squad in Sonora on January 18, 1918. They are all remembered in Mexico for their efforts to improve the lives of the impoverished and dispossessed.

Historians of the Mexican American experience have been chronicling the extraordinary PLM saga for decades, but so long as Latino voices and stories have been shunted to the sidelines of U.S. history, only the few students lucky enough to take specialized courses or those determined enough to engage in individual study have had the opportunity to learn what the PLM, and histories like theirs, can teach us. We have all paid a price for overlooking Latino history. Stripped from the narrative, Latinos in the United States are often cast as immigrants, outsiders, or newcomers to the American story, when, in fact, Mexico, Mexicans, and Mexican Americans, as well as other Latino communities, have long been major players in U.S. history.[40] The men and women who built the PLM were ordinary people: migrants, exiles, and citizens; farmworkers, sharecroppers, miners, and intellectuals. Most of all, they were rebels. Despite their internal disputes, they comprised an extraordinary political force. In the process of confronting the Díaz regime in Mexico, they rattled the workshop of U.S. empire, challenged the global color line, threatened to unravel the industrialization of the

American West, and fueled the rise of policing in the United States. Ultimately, the uprising they incited triggered a demographic revolution, giving birth to what is now the largest non-white population in the United States. Even after the PLM collapsed, their legacy inspired one of the most significant race rebellions—and massacres—in U.S. history. Some of the most powerful people on earth tried to suppress them and their story, but Ricardo Flores Magón and the *magonistas* altered the course of history, defining the world in which we live by defying the world in which they lived.

Appendix

REBEL PSEUDONYMS AND CODE NAMES

as compiled by the Furlong Secret Service Company

Antonio de Pío Araujo: *German Riesco, Moran, Axayacatl, Arcuijo, Cipriano, Emilio Bello, Charles Watson, Emilio Aceval, Joaquin B. Calvo, El Provisional*

Ricardo Flores Magón: *R. M. Caule, Benjamín, Raf, R. Escarega, Marcelo García, José H. Ruíz, Matilda Mota*

Enrique Flores Magón: *Luis*

Práxedis Guerrero: *Sempor Nihil, P. L. Mexicano*

Aarón López Manzano: *F. Oka, Mr. Foca, Manuel Ramírez*

Librado Rivera: *Leonel Guzman, John J. Cano*

Manuel Sarabia: *Sam Moret, Ramón Quevedo, A. García*

Tomás Sarabia: *Mario A. Bassat, Juan Suine, Tomas S. Labrada, Charles Keilingston, Henry Max Morton, Gaston N. Sperelli, Cuauhtemoc, Claudio Molltoni, Teodoro Sanders Teodoro Anderson*

Antonio I. Villarreal: *Verea, Anto, Esfinje*

ACKNOWLEDGMENTS

I FIRST LEARNED ABOUT RICARDO FLORES MAGÓN AND THE PLM in graduate school. Ever since, for more than twenty years, I have collected their story. The following researchers, mostly students, helped me along the way. In Mexico City, Marco Aguilar Ortega, Juan Manuel Salazar Pérez, Abraham Trejo Terreros, and Samantha Guadalupe Andrade Urdapilleta digitized files from the Archivo General de la Nación (AGN), the Archivo Histórico de la Secretaría de Relaciones en la Exterior (AHSRE), and the archive of La Casa de El Hijo del Ahuizote. A dear colleague, Professor Pablo Yankelevich, connected me with most of these gifted researchers. In Los Angeles, Stephanie Cajina, Linda Esquivel, Rebeca Martínez, Georgina Rodríguez, Michelle Servin, and Amanda Torres provided additional research assistance with the digitized files. The MacArthur Foundation as well as Darnell Hunt, Carla Pestana, David Yoo, Lorrie Frasure, Danielle Dupuy, and the Bunche and Million Dollar Hoods squads made it possible for me to have the time I needed to complete this book. Professors Mark Vestal and Chon Noriega as well as my son, Isaiah Lytle Hernández, a bibliophile, provided feedback on the book's introduction. The following colleagues provided feedback on an early draft of the entire book: Elliott Young, Natalia Molina, Devra Weber, and Ward Albro. Elliott's breadth of knowledge helped me to connect histories across time, borders, and communities. Natalia's wisdom—and arm-waving encouragement—pushed me to appreciate the sweep of the PLM tale.

Devra's expertise helped me to correct interpretive missteps. I love nerding out with Devra, delving deep into the PLM archival record together to revel in the extant record. Ward's encyclopedic knowledge of PLM history is astounding. A self-described "hillbilly from east Tennessee," Ward has worked the PLM archive for his entire career, dating back to when he attended night school in Texas in the 1960s. I reached out to Ward when I completed the first draft of this book. Although we had never met, Ward read the draft and spoke with me several times about his research on the PLM. I note Ward's intellectual generosity and vigor because I found it to be common in the world of *magonista* scholars. Based in Mexico, the United States, and around the world, *magonista* scholars are prolific, dogged, and generous, and bound by a determination to preserve PLM history. This book could not have been written without their library of labor, insight, and encouragement. This book also began as a chapter for my last book, *City of Inmates: Conquest, Rebellion, and the Rise of Human Caging in Los Angeles* (University of North Carolina Press, 2017). Brandon Proia was an excellent editor for that chapter. I am fortunate to be represented by Tanya McKinnon of McKinnon Literary. Tanya fought for this book and embraced me as its author. As long as she is in my corner, everything is going to be alright. My editors at W. W. Norton, Tom Mayer and Jon Durbin, sharpened my storytelling. Finally, thank you to my family and friends who listened to this story as I wrote it, and rewrote it, and wrote it all over again.

NOTES

ABBREVIATIONS:

ADRFM: *Archivo Digital de Ricardo Flores Magón, http://archivomagon.net/*

AEMEUA: *Archivo de la Embajada de México en los Estados Unidos de América, Archivo Histórico "Genaro Estrada," Acervo Histórico Diplomático de la Secretaría de Relaciones Exteriores, Mexico City*

CPD: *Colección Porfirio Díaz, Biblioteca Xavier Clavijero, Universidad Iberoamericana, Mexico City*

EDTA: *Ethel Duffy Turner Archive, Biblioteca Nacional de Antropología e Historia, Mexico City*

NARA: *National Archives and Records Administration, College Park, MD*

RG 59: *Numerical and Minor Files of the Department of State, 1906–10, microfilm, Internal Affairs of Mexico*

RG 60: *Records of the U.S. Department of Justice*

RG 84: *Records of the Foreign Service Posts of the Department of State, Consular Post Records, U.S. Department of State [Ciudad Porfirio Diaz (Piedra Negras) 1906–11]*

STP: *Silvestre Terrazas Papers, Bancroft Library, University of California, Berkeley*

Introduction: WE STAND BETWEEN

1. "Texas Town that Burned Mexican Is Not Worried," *San Antonio Light and Gazette*, November 14, 1910. For more on Rodríguez's murder and its legacy, see Monica Muñoz Martinez, *The Injustice Never Leaves You: Anti-Mexican Violence in Texas* (Cambridge, MA: Harvard University Press, 2018). For more on anti-Mexican violence in the U.S.–Mexico borderlands, see Nicole Guidotti-Hernández, *Unspeakable Violence: Remapping U.S. and Mexican National Imaginaries* (Durham, NC: Duke University Press, 2011); Nicholas Villanueva, Jr., *The Lynching of Mexicans in the Texas Borderlands* (Albuquerque: University of New Mexico Press, 2017). See also https://refusingtoforget.org/.

2. Travis Taylor, "Lynching on the Border: The Death of Antonio Rodríguez and the Rise of

Anti-Americanism during the Mexican Revolution," master's thesis, Angelo State University, 2012, 41–42.

3. Taylor, "Lynching on the Border," 49. See also William D. Carrigan and Clive Webb, "The Lynching of Persons of Mexican Origin or Descent in the United States, 1848 to 1928," *Journal of Social History* 37, no. 2 (Winter, 2003): 411–38.

4. Taylor, "Lynching on the Border," 60.

5. Taylor, "Lynching on the Border," 63.

6. Memo from Henry Lane Wilson, November 16, 1910, NARA, RG 59, M274, 812 series.

7. John Mason Hart, *Empire and Revolution: The Americans in Mexico since the Civil War* (Berkeley: University of California Press, 2002), 260.

8. William Schell, Jr., *Integral Outsiders: The American Colony in Mexico City, 1876–1911* (Wilmington, DE: Scholarly Resources, 2001), 113.

9. Evelyn Hu-DeHart, *Yaqui Resistance and Survival: The Struggle for Land and Autonomy, 1821–1910* (Madison: University of Wisconsin Press, 2016), 132.

10. Rodney D. Anderson, *Outcasts in Their Own Land: Mexican Industrial Workers, 1906–1911* (Ithaca, NY: Cornell University Press, 2008).

11. Frank McLynn, *Villa and Zapata: A History of the Mexican Revolution* (New York: Carroll & Graf, 2000), 8.

12. Memo from President Taft to Secretary of State Knox, 6:45 pm, November 10, 1910, NARA, RG 59, M274, 812 series.

13. Henry Lane Wilson, memo, November 15, 1910, NARA, RG 59, M274, 812 series.

14. Henry Lane Wilson, "Interview with the President," memorandum, November 16, 1910, NARA, RG 59, M274, 812 series.

15. Wilson, "Interview with the President."

16. Wilson, "Interview with the President."

17. Alan Knight, *The Mexican Revolution: Porfirians, Liberals, and Peasants,* vol. 1 (Lincoln: University of Nebraska Press, 1986), 75.

18. For more on Francisco Madero, see Enrique Krauze, *Mexico: Biography of Power: A History of Modern Mexico, 1810–1996* (New York: HarperPerennial, 1998), 245–73.

19. For a discussion of the composition of the *magonistas,* see W. Dirk Raat, *Los Revoltosos: Mexico's Rebels in the United States, 1903–1923* (College Station: Texas A & M University Press, 1981), 30–32. See also James D. Cockcroft, *Intellectual Precursors of the Mexican Revolution, 1900–1913* (Austin: University of Texas Press, 1968), 46.

20. Taylor, "Lynching on the Border," 96.

21. Taylor, "Lynching on the Border," 115.

22. "Lo que dice un colega honrado," *Regeneración,* March 7, 1901, ADRFM, http://archivomagon .net/wp-content/uploads/e1n29.pdf.

23. "Los amigos del Gral. Díaz," *Regeneración,* July 15, 1901, ADRFM, http://archivomagon.net/ wp-content/uploads/e1n46.pdf.

24. "Servants of foreigners" actually appeared in *El Hijo del Ahuizote,* which Flores Magón led after Mexico City authorities shut down *Regeneración* in 1903. Cockcroft, *Intellectual Precursors,* 113–14.

25. "Texas Town that Burned Mexican Is Not Worried," *San Antonio Light and Gazette,* November 14, 1910.

26. Matt Barreto and Gary M. Segura, *Latino America: How America's Most Dynamic Population Is Poised to Transform the Politics of the Nation* (New York: Public Affairs, 2014); Neil Foley, *Mexicans in the Making of America* (New York: Belknap Press, 2017); Charles Hirschmann, "Immigration and the American Century," *Demography* 42, no. 4 (November 2005): 595–620; George J. Sánchez, *Becoming Mexican American: Ethnicity, Culture, and Identity in Chicano Los Angeles, 1900–1945* (Oxford: Oxford University Press, 1995); John Tutino, ed., *Mexico and Mexicans in the Making of the United States* (Austin: University of Texas Press, 2012).

27. Francisco E. Balderrama and Raymond Rodríguez, *Decade of Betrayal: Mexican Repatriation in the 1930s,* revised edition (Albuquerque: University of New Mexico Press, 2006).

28. "From Ireland to Germany to Italy to Mexico: How America's source of immigrants has changed in the states, 1850 to 2013," Pew Research Center feature, September 28, 2015.

29. Jeffrey S. Passel, D'Vera Cohn, and Ana González-Barrera, "Net Migration from Mexico Falls to Zero—and Perhaps Less," Pew Research Center report, April 23, 2012.

30. William H. Frey, "The Nation Is Diversifying Even Faster Than Predicted, According to New Census Data," Brookings Institute report, July 1, 2020.

31. Dana Goldstein, "Two States, Eight Textbooks. Two American Stories," *New York Times*, January 12, 2020; Linda K. Salvucci, "Mexico, Mexicans and Mexican Americans in Secondary-School United States History Textbooks," *History Teacher* 24, no. 2 (1991): 203–22; Valerie Strauss, "Arizona's Ban on Mexican American Studies was Racist, U.S. Court Rules," *Washington Post*, August 23, 2017.

32. Darnell Hunt and Ana-Christina Ramón, *The Hollywood Diversity Report 2020: A Tale of Two Hollywoods*, UCLA Social Sciences Division, Institute of Labor Research and Education, 2021; Laura M. Jiménez and Betsy Beckert, "Diversity Baseline Study 2.0," blog.leeandlow.com, January 28, 2020; Elizabeth Méndez Berry and Mónica Ramírez, "How Latinos Can Win the Culture War," *New York Times,* September 2, 2020; Richard Jean So and Gus Wezerek, "Just How White Is the Book Industry," *New York Times*, December 11, 2020.

33. Roxanne Dunbar Ortiz, *An Indigenous People's History of the United States* (New York: Beacon Press, 2014). For more on settler politics and practices, see Patrick Wolfe, "Settler Colonialism and the Elimination of the Native," *Journal of Genocide Research* 8, no. 4 (December 2006): 387–409.

34. Alexander Saxton, *The Rise and Fall of the White Republic: Class Politics and Mass Culture in 19th-Century America* (New York: Verso, 2003).

35. Schell, *Integral Outsiders*, 137–57.

36. Hart, *Empire and Revolution*, 5. See also Gilbert González, *Culture of Empire: American Writers, Mexico, and Mexican Immigrants, 1880–1930* (Austin: University of Texas Press, 2003); Gilbert G. González, *Guest Workers or Colonized Labor? Mexican Labor Migration to the United States* (Boulder, CO: Paradigm, 2006); Greg Grandin, *Empire's Workshop: Latin America, the United States, and the Rise of the New Imperialism* (New York: Henry Holt, 2006).

37. Laura E. Gómez, *Manifest Destinies: The Making of the Mexican American Race* (New York: New York University Press, 2018); Natalia Molina, *How Race Is Made in America: Immigration, Citizenship, and the Historical Power of Racial Scripts* (Berkeley: University of California Press, 2014). For more on Juan Crow and its relationship to Jim Crow, namely its foundation in anti-Blackness, see Cecilia Márquez, "Juan Crow and the Erasure of Blackness in the Latina/o South," *Labor: Studies in Working Class History* 16, no. 3 (2019): 79–85.

38. Victor S. Clark, "Mexican Labor in the United States," *Bulletin of the Bureau of Labor*, no. 78 (Washington, DC: Government Printing Office, 1908), 496.

39. William D. Carrigan and Clive Webb, *Forgotten Dead: Mob Violence against Mexicans in the United States, 1848–1928* (Oxford: Oxford University Press, 2003); Villanueva, *The Lynching of Mexicans in the Texas Borderlands*.

40. Quoted in Taylor, "Lynching on the Border," 39-40.

41. Quoted in Taylor, "Lynching on the Border," 40.

42. Quoted in Taylor, "Lynching on the Border," 43–44.

43. W. E. B. Du Bois, *The Souls of Black Folk* (Chicago: A. C. McClurg and Co., 1903).

44. Gerald Horne, *Black and Brown: African Americans and the Mexican Revolution, 1910–1920* (New York: New York University Press, 2005). See also Christina Heatherton, "The Color Line and Class Struggle: The Mexican Revolution and Convergence of Radical Internationalism, 1910–1946," PhD dissertation, University of Southern California, 2012.

45. For more on domestic counterinsurgency within the continental United States, including Cointelpro, see Simon Balto, *Occupied Territory: Policing Black Chicago from Red Summer to Black Power* (Chapel Hill: University of North Carolina Press, 2020); Nelson Blackstock, *Cointelpro: The FBI's Secret War on Political Freedom* (New York: Pathfinder, 1988); José Angel Gutiérrez, *FBI Files on Mexicans and Chicanos, 1940–1980: The Eagle Is Watching* (Lanham, MD: Lexington Books, 2021); William Preston, *Aliens and Dissenters: Federal Suppression of Radicals, 1903–1933* (Cambridge, MA: Harvard University Press, 1963).

46. The following is a short list of the works on Ricardo Flores Magón and the *magonistas*. It is a list that draws broadly from U.S. and Mexican authors across time, documenting the deep and

broad effort to tell the *magonista* tale. Diego Abad de Santillán, *Ricardo Flores Magón: El apóstol de la revolución social Mexicana* (Mexico City: Centro de Estudios Históricos del Movimiento Obrero, 1978; reprint of 1925 edition); Ward S. Albro, *Always a Rebel: Ricardo Flores Magón and the Mexican Revolution* (Fort Worth: Texas Christian University Press, 1992); Ward S. Albro, *To Die on Your Feet: The Life, Times, and Writings of Práxedis G. Guerrero* (Fort Worth: Texas Christian University Press, 1996); Jacinto Barrera Bassols, *Correspondencia de Ricardo Flores Magón*, vol. 1, *1899–1918* (Mexico City: Consejo Nacional Para la Cultura y las Artes, 2000); Jacinto Barrera Bassols, ed., *Correspondencia de Ricardo Flores Magón, 1904–1912* (Puebla: Universidad Autónoma de Puebla, 1989); Chaz Bufe and Mitchell Cowen Verter, *Dreams of Freedom: A Ricardo Flores Magón Reader* (Oakland, CA: AK Press, 2005); Cockcroft, *Intellectual Precursors*; Ethel Duffy Turner, *Ricardo Flores Magón y el Partido Liberal Mexicano* (Mexico City: Comisión Nacional Editorial, 1984); Nathan Kahn Ellstrand, "Las Anarquistas: The History of Two Women of the Partido Liberal Mexicano in Early 20th Century Los Angeles," master's thesis, University of California, San Diego, 2011; Juan Gómez Quiñones, *Sembradores: Ricardo Flores Magón y el Partido Liberal Mexicano: A Eulogy and Critique* (Los Angeles: UCLA Chicano Studies Research Center Press, 1977); Gabriela González, *Redeeming La Raza: Transborder Modernity, Race, Respectability, and Rights* (Oxford: Oxford University Press, 2018); Claudio Lomnitz, *The Return of Comrade Ricardo Flores Magón* (New York: Zone Books, 2014); Chantal López and Omar Cortés, *El Partido Liberal Mexicano, 1906–1908* (Mexico City: Antorcha, 1986); Colin M. MacLachlan, *Anarchism and the Mexican Revolution: The Political Trials of Ricardo Flores Magón in the United States* (Berkeley: University of California Press, 1991); Benjamín Maldonado Alvarado, *La utopía de Ricardo Flores Magón: Revolución, anarquía, y comunalidad india* (Oaxaca: Universidad Autónoma de Oaxaca, 1994); Eugenio Martínez Núñez, *La vida heroica de Práxedis G. Guerrero* (Mexico City: Biblioteca del Instituto Nacional de Estudios Históricos de la Revolución Mexicana, 1960); Eugenio Martínez Núñez, *Juan Sarabia, apóstol y mártir de la Revolución Mexicana* (Mexico City: Biblioteca del Instituto Nacional de Estudios Históricos de la Revolución Mexicana, 1965); Pilar Melero, *Mythological Constructs of Mexican Femininity* (New York: Palgrave MacMillan, 2015), ch. 2; Emma Pérez, "A La Mujer: A Critique of the Mexican Liberal Party's Ideology on Women," in *Between Borders: Essays on Mexicana/Chicana History*, edited by Adelaida R. Del Castillo (Encino, CA: Floricanto Press, 1990), 459–82; Raat, *Revoltosos*; José C. Valadés, *El joven Ricardo Flores Magón* (Mexico City: Editorial Extemporáneos, 1983); Devra Anne Weber, "Wobblies of the Partido Liberal Mexicano: Reenvisioning Internationalist and Transnational Movements through Mexican Lenses," *Pacific Historical Review* 85, no. 2 (May 2016): 188–226.

47. For more on the museum La Casa de El Hijo del Ahuizote, see https://www.facebook.com/casadelahuizote/. The digital archive built by Professor Jacinto Barrera Bassols, Verónica Buitron Escamilla, and others is at archivomagon.net.

Chapter 1: If We're Not Careful

1. For more on the 1833 cholera epidemic in Mexico, see C. A. Hutchinson, "The Asiatic Cholera Epidemic of 1833 in Mexico," *Bulletin of the History of Medicine* 32, no. 1 (January–February 1958), 1–23; A. Llopis and J. Halbrohr, "Historical Background of Cholera in the Americas," *Epidemiological Bulletin* 12, no. 1 (1991): 10–12; Lourdes Márquez Morfín, "El cólera en la Ciudad de México en el siglo XIX," *Estudios demográficos y urbanos* 7, no. 1 (1992): 77–93; María del Pilar Velasco, "La epidemia del cólera de 1833 y la mortalidad en la ciudad de México," *Estudios demográficos y urbanos* 7, no. 1 (1992): 95–135.

2. The portrait of Porfirio Díaz's early life is drawn from the following sources: William H. Beezley, *Judas at the Jockey Club and Other Episodes of Porfirian Mexico* (Lincoln: University of Nebraska Press, 1987 [2018 edition]), 69–70; James Creelman, *Díaz: Master of Mexico* (New York: D. Appleton, 1916), 44; Carlos Tello Díaz, *Porfirio Díaz: Su vida y su tiempo: la guerra, 1830–1867* (Mexico City: Consejo Nacional para la Cultura y las Artes, 2015), 19–62; Paul Garner, *Porfirio Díaz: Profiles in Power* (Harlow, UK: Longman, 2001), 24–27; Ricardo Andrés Orozco Ríos, *Porfirio Díaz: La ambición y la patria*, tomo 1 (Mexico City: Lito-Grapo, 2015),

15–33; and, Mark Wasserman, *Everyday Life and Politics in Nineteenth Century Mexico: Men, Women, and War* (Albuquerque: University of New Mexico Press, 2000), 142–154.

3. For more on the *casta* system, see Ben Vinson III, *Before Mestizaje: The Frontiers of Race and Caste in Colonial Mexico* (New York: Cambridge University Press, 2018). For more on the Mexican War of Independence and post-revolution politics, see Peter Guardino, *Peasants, Politics, and the Formation of Mexico's National State: Guerrero, 1800–1857* (Palo Alto, CA: Stanford University Press, 1996); Timothy J. Henderson, *The Mexican Wars for Independence* (New York: Hill and Wang, 2009); Florencia Mallon, *Peasant and Nation: The Making of Postcolonial Mexico and Peru* (Berkeley: University of California Press, 1995); Elisa Servin, Leticia Reina, and John Tutino, eds., *Cycles of Conflict, Centuries of Change: Crisis, Reform, and Revolution in Mexico* (Durham, NC: Duke University Press, 2007); John Tutino, *From Insurrection to Revolution in Mexico: Social Bases of Agrarian Violence, 1750–1940* (Princeton: Princeton University Press, 1986); Eric Van Young, *The Other Rebellion: Popular Violence, Ideology, and the Mexican Struggle for Independence, 1810–1821* (Palo Alto, CA: Stanford University Press, 2001).

4. Theodore G. Vincent, *The Legacy of Vicente Guerrero, Mexico's First Black Indian President* (Gainesville: University Press of Florida, 2001).

5. For more on social and political conditions in nineteenth-century Mexico, see Mark Wasserman, *Everyday Life and Politics in Nineteenth Century Mexico: Men, Women, and War* (Albuquerque: University of New Mexico Press, 2000); Chris Frazer, *Bandit Nation: A History of Outlaws and Cultural Struggle in Mexico, 1810–1920* (Lincoln: University of Nebraska Press, 2006); Paul J. Vanderwood, *Disorder and Progress: Bandits, Police, and Mexican Development* (Wilmington, DE: Scholarly Resources, 1992); Paul J. Vanderwood, *The Power of God Against the Guns of Government* (Palo Alto, CA: Stanford University Press, 1998).

6. For more on the role of slaveholders and the Mexican–American War, see Kevin Waite, *West of Slavery: The Southern Dream of a Transcontinental Empire* (Chapel Hill: University of North Carolina Press, 2021).

7. For more on Manifest Destiny, expansion, and the racialization of Mexicans, see Laura E. Gómez, *Manifest Destinies: The Making of the Mexican American Race* (New York: New York University Press, 2018), and Reginald Horsman's classic study, *Race and Manifest Destiny: The Origins of American Racial Anglo-Saxonism* (Cambridge, MA: Harvard University Press, 1986).

8. Quoted in Gray Brechin, *Imperial San Francisco: Urban Power, Earthly Ruin* (Berkeley: University of California Press, 2006), 205.

9. Brechin, *Imperial San Francisco*, 205.

10. For more information on the Mexican–American War, see Brian DeLay, *War of a Thousand Deserts: Indian Raids and the U.S.–Mexican War* (New Haven: Yale University Press, 2008); Amy S. Greenberg, *A Wicked War: Polk, Clay, Lincoln, and the 1846 U.S. Invasion of Mexico* (New York: Knopf, 2012); Peter Guardino, *The Dead March: A History of the Mexican–American War* (Cambridge, MA: Harvard University Press, 2017); Timothy J. Henderson, *A Glorious Defeat: Mexico and its War with the United States* (New York: Hill and Wang, 2007).

11. Tello Díaz, *Porfirio Díaz*, 71–75.

12. Garner, *Porfirio Díaz*, 40.

13. Tello Díaz, *Porfirio Díaz*, 122.

14. Tello Díaz, *Porfirio Díaz*, 58.

15. Tello Díaz, *Porfirio Díaz*, 80–93.

16. Garner, *Porfirio Díaz*, 26.

17. Garner, *Porfirio Díaz*, 27.

18. "Indian Shepherd and the Austrian Duke," in Enrique Krauze, *Mexico: Biography of Power: A History of Modern Mexico, 1810–1996* (New York: HarperPerennial, 1998); William H. Beezley, *Mexico in World History* (New York: Oxford University Press, 2011).

19. Quoted in Garner, *Porfirio Díaz*, 28.

20. Tello Díaz, *Porfirio Díaz*, 137–47.

21. Tello Díaz, *Porfirio Díaz*, 144.

22. Quoted in Garner, *Porfirio Díaz*, 39. See also McNamara, *Sons of the Sierra*, 28–49.

23. Quoted in Michael Johns, *The City of Mexico in the Age of Díaz* (Austin: University of Texas Press, 1997), 98.

24. M. M. McAllen, *Maximilian and Carlota: Europe's Last Empire in Mexico* (San Antonio: Trinity University Press, 2014), 54.

25. For more on the Mexican debt crisis, see Steven C. Topik, "When Mexico Had the Blues: A Transatlantic Tale of Bonds, Bankers, and Nationalists, 1862–1910," *American Historical Review* 105, no. 3 (2000): 714–38.

26. McAllen, *Maximilian and Carlota*, 46–47.

27. McAllen, *Maximilian and Carlota*, 25.

28. McAllen, *Maximilian and Carlota*, 48–52.

29. McAllen, *Maximilian and Carlota*, 50.

30. McAllen, *Maximillian and Carlota*, 56. For more on U.S.–Mexico relations during the U.S. Civil War, see María Angela Díaz, "The Most Perfect Anarchy: Confederates Imagine the Southern Border," blog post, October 31, 2017, *Journal of the Civil War Era* website, https://www.journalofthecivilwarera.org/2017/10/perfect-anarchy-confederates-imagine-mexican-border; Don H. Doyle, *The Cause of All Nations: An International History of the American Civil War* (New York: Basic Books, 2015); Patrick Kelly, "The Lost Continent of Abraham Lincoln," *Journal of the Civil War Era* 9, no. 2 (2019): 223–48; William S. Kiser, "'We Must Have Chihuahua and Sonora': Civil War Diplomacy in the U.S.–Mexico Borderlands," *Journal of the Civil War Era* 9, no. 2 (2019): 196–222.

31. Samuel Kaplan, *Combatimos la tiranía* (Mexico City: Biblioteca del Instituto de Estudios Históricos de la Revolución Mexicana, 1958), 13–16.

32. Tello Díaz, *Porfirio Díaz*, 265. For another account of the Battle of Puebla, see McAllen, *Maximilian and Carlota*, 72–96.

33. Garner, *Porfirio Díaz*, 28.

34. Garner, *Porfirio Díaz*, 48–54.

35. Tello Díaz, *Porfirio Díaz*, 101.

36. McNamara, *Sons of the Sierra*, 80.

37. Tello Díaz, *Porfirio Díaz*, 141.

Chapter 2: ORDER AND PROGRESS

1. Some historians contest this story, finding no hard evidence that Díaz ever issued this order. Paul Garner, *Porfirio Díaz: Profiles in Power* (Harlow, UK: Longman, 2001), 87.

2. Quoted in Michael Johns, *The City of Mexico in the Age of Díaz* (Austin: University of Texas Press, 1997), 68.

3. Quoted in Charles A. Hale, *The Transformation of Liberalism in Late Nineteenth-Century Mexico* (Princeton: Princeton University Press, 2014), 34.

4. James D. Cockcroft, *Intellectual Precursors of the Mexican Revolution, 1900–1913* (Austin: University of Texas Press, 1968), 113.

5. Garner, *Porfirio Díaz*, 127–30.

6. Quoted in Garner, *Porfirio Díaz*, 104.

7. Pablo Piccato, *The Tyranny of Opinion: Honor in the Construction of the Mexican Public Sphere* (Durham, NC: Duke University Press, 2010), 174–85.

8. Paul J. Vanderwood, *The Power of God Against the Guns of Government: Religious Upheaval in Mexico at the turn of the Nineteenth Century* (Palo Alto, CA: Stanford University Press, 1998), 40.

9. Garner, *Porfirio Díaz*, 85.

10. Frank McLynn, *Villa and Zapata: A History of the Mexican Revolution* (New York: Carroll & Graf, 2000), 8.

11. Quoted in Garner, *Porfirio Díaz*, 81.

12. Alan Knight, *The Mexican Revolution: Porfirians, Liberals, and Peasants*, vol. 1 (Lincoln: University of Nebraska Press, 1986), 24–29.

13.   Paul J. Vanderwood, *Disorder and Progress: Bandits, Police, and Mexican Development* (Wilmington, DE: Scholarly Resources, 1992), 81.

14.   José Francisco Godoy, *Porfirio Díaz: President of Mexico, the Master Builder of a Great Commonwealth* (New York: G. P. Putnam's Sons, 1910), 98.

15.   Quoted in Garner, *Porfirio Díaz*, 75–76.

16.   Garner, *Porfirio Díaz*, 101–2, 143–44.

17.   James Creelman, *Díaz: Master of Mexico* (New York: D. Appleton, 1911), 369.

18.   Garner, *Porfirio Díaz*, 25 and 102.

19.   Quoted in Johns, *The City of Mexico in the Age of Díaz*, 68.

20.   For more on railroad development in Mexico prior to the Díaz regime, see Michael Matthews, *The Civilizing Machine: A Cultural History of Mexican Railroads, 1876–1910* (Lincoln: University of Nebraska Press, 2013), 4; Teresa Van Hoy, *A Social History of Mexico's Railroads: Peons, Prisoners, and Priests* (Lanham, MD: Rowman and Littlefield, 2008), 1–14.

21.   For more on railroads and U.S. expansion, see John Coatsworth, *Growth Against Development: The Economic Impact of Railroads in Porfirian Mexico* (DeKalb: Northern Illinois University Press, 1981); Manu Karuka, *Empire's Tracks: Indigenous Nations, Chinese Workers, and the Transcontinental Railroad* (Berkeley: University of California Press, 2019); Daniel Lewis, *Iron Horse Imperialism: The Southern Pacific of Mexico, 1880–1951* (Tucson: University of Arizona Press, 2007); Richard White, *Railroaded: The Transcontinentals and the Making of Modern America* (New York: Norton, 2011).

22.   John Mason Hart, *Empire and Revolution: The Americans in Mexico since the Civil War* (Berkeley: University of California Press, 2002), 1.

23.   Jason Ruiz, *Americans in the Treasure House: Travel to Porfirian Mexico and the Cultural Politics of Empire* (Austin: University of Texas Press, 2014), 5.

24.   Matthews, *The Civilizing Machine*, 40.

25.   Mark Wasserman, *Pesos and Politics: Business, Elites, Foreigners, and Government in Mexico, 1854–1940* (Palo Alto, CA: Stanford University Press, 2015), 61.

26.   Van Hoy, *A Social History of Mexico's Railroads*, 15–47.

27.   John Mason Hart, *Revolutionary Mexico: The Coming and Process of the Mexican Revolution* (Berkeley: University of California Press, 1997), 134.

28.   Hart, *Revolutionary Mexico*, 120–22. See also Ruiz, *Americans in the Treasure House*, 6.

29.   Hart, *Empire and Revolution*, 167–200.

30.   Mark Wasserman, *Capitalists, Caciques, and Revolution: The Native Elite and Foreign Enterprise in Chihuahua, Mexico, 1854–1911* (Chapel Hill: University of North Carolina Press, 1984), 27. For more on the Terrazas family, see Wasserman, *Capitalists, Caciques, and Revolution*, 26–70; Wasserman, *Pesos and Politics*, 34, 43–70; Jane H. Kelley, David A. Phillips, A. C. MacWilliams, and Rafael Cruz Antillón, "Land Use, Looting, and Archaeology in Chihuahua, Mexico: A Speculative History," *Journal of the Southwest* 53, no. 2 (2011): 185–86.

31.   Wasserman, *Pesos and Politics*, 43–53.

32.   Quoted in Ruiz, *Americans in the Treasure House*, 10. See also Hart, *Revolutionary Mexico*, 158.

33.   Quoted in Ruiz, *Americans in the Treasure House*, 15.

34.   Gray Brechin, *Imperial San Francisco: Urban Power, Earthly Ruin* (Berkeley: University of California Press, 2006), 200–241.

35.   John H. Davis, *The Guggenheims (1848–1988): An American Epic* (New York: Shapolsky, 1988).

36.   Wasserman, *Pesos and Politics*, 164. See also Davis, *The Guggenheims*.

37.   Wasserman, *Pesos and Politics*, 164. See also Kenneth Dale Underwood, "Mining Wars: Corporate Expansion and Labor Violence in the Western Desert, 1876–1920," PhD dissertation, University of Nevada Las Vegas, 2009, 125–28.

38.   Jessica Kim, Imperial Metropolis: Los Angeles, Mexico, and the Borderlands of American Empire, 1865–1941 (Berkeley: University of California Press, 2019), 70–72. See also Margaret Leslie Davis, The Dark Side of Fortune: Triumph and Scandal in the Life of Oil Tycoon Edward L. Doheny (Berkeley: University of California Press, 2001), 146.

39.   Hart, *Empire and Revolution*, 79.

40.   Wasserman, *Pesos and Politics*, 112–31.

41.   Wasserman, *Pesos and Politics*, 102–3.

42. Hart, *Revolutionary Mexico*, 47.
43. Hart, *Revolutionary Mexico*, 160.
44. Hart, *Revolutionary Mexico*, 141.
45. Hart, *Revolutionary Mexico*, 159. According to Ambassador Henry Lane Wilson, 75,000 U.S. citizens lived in Mexico in 1910. See "Investigation of Mexican Affairs," Preliminary Report and Hearings of the Committee on Foreign Relations, United States Senate, Pursuant to S. Res. 106, Directing the Committee on Foreign Relations to Investigate the Matter of Outrages on Citizens of the United States in Mexico, vol. 3, pt. 2, p. 2251.
46. William Schell, Jr., *Integral Outsiders: The American Colony in Mexico City, 1876–1911* (Wilmington, DE: Scholarly Resources, 2001), 115.
47. Hart, *Empire and Revolution*, 260.
48. Hart, *Empire and Revolution*, 169. See also Lawrence Cardoso, *Mexican Labor Emigration to the United States, 1897–1931* (Tucson: University of Arizona Press, 1980); George McBride, *The Land Systems of Mexico* (New York: American Geographical Society, 1923), 154.
49. Quoted in Hart, *Empire and Revolution*, 167.
50. Cardoso, *Mexican Labor Emigration*. See also Kelly Lytle Hernández, *Migra!: A History of the U.S. Border Patrol* (Berkeley: University of California Press, 2010), 25.
51. Cardoso, *Mexican Labor Emigration*, 2–5.
52. Hart, *Revolutionary Mexico*, 143.
53. Hart, *Revolutionary Mexico*, 144.
54. Hart, *Revolutionary Mexico*, 146.
55. Hart, *Revolutionary Mexico*, 133.
56. These quotes of praise are compiled in José Francisco Godoy, *Porfirio Díaz, President of Mexico, the Master Builder of a Great Commonwealth* (New York: G. P. Putnam's Sons, 1910). See also Thomas B. Davis, "Porfirio Díaz in the Opinion of His North American Contemporaries," *Revista de Historia de América*, January–December 1967, 79–116; Ruiz, *Americans in the Treasure House*, 65–101.

Chapter 3: DEN OF THIEVES

1. Patricia Romyna Báez Rentería, "Camilo Arriaga: una biografía política, 1862–1945," thesis, Colegio de San Luis, 2019, 86–87; James D. Cockcroft, *Intellectual Precursors of the Mexican Revolution, 1900–1913* (Austin: University of Texas Press, 1968), 64–70.
2. Dave Poole, *Librado Rivera: Anarchists in the Mexican Revolution* (Orkney, UK: Cienfuegos Press, 1979; digital edition East Sussex, TN: Christie Books, 2012). See also Cockcroft, *Intellectual Precursors*, 82–86.
3. Eugenio Martínez Núñez, *Juan Sarabia, apóstol y mártir de la Revolución Mexicana* (Mexico City: Biblioteca del Instituto Nacional de Estudios Históricos de la Revolución Mexicana, 1965). See also Cockcroft, *Intellectual Precursors*, 77–82.
4. Quoted in Pilar Melero, *Mythological Constructs of Mexican Femininity* (New York: Palgrave MacMillan, 2015), 78.
5. Cristina Devereaux Ramírez et al., *Occupying Our Space: The Mestiza Rhetorics of Mexican Women Journalists and Activists, 1875–1942* (Tucson: University of Arizona Press, 2015), 132.
6. Melero, *Mythological Constructs of Mexican Femininity*, 71.
7. Melero, *Mythological Constructs of Mexican Femininity*, 61–81. See also Devereaux Ramírez et al., *Occupying Our Space*, 132–60; Claudio Lomnitz, *The Return of Comrade Ricardo Flores Magón* (New York: Zone Books, 2014), 202; Ana Lau Jaiven, "La Participación de las mujeres en la Revolución Mexicana: Juana Belén Gutiérrez de Mendoza (1875–1942)," *Diálogos Revista Electrónica de Historia* 5, no. 1–2 (April–August 2005).
8. James Sandos, *Rebellion in the Borderlands: Anarchism and the Plan of San Diego, 1904–1923* (Norman: University of Oklahoma Press, 1992), 15.
9. Samuel Truett, *Fugitive Landscapes: The Forgotten History of the U.S.–Mexico Borderlands* (New Haven: Yale University Press, 2006), 13–32, 59. For more on economic development practices in

Sonora during the Porfiriato, see Miguel Tinker Salas, *In the Shadow of the Eagles: Sonora and the Transformation of the Border During the Porfiriato* (Berkeley: University of California Press, 1997).

10. Evelyn Hu-DeHart, *Yaqui Resistance and Survival: The Struggle for Land and Autonomy, 1821–1910* (Madison: University of Wisconsin Press, 2016), 105–6.

11. Hu-DeHart, *Yaqui Resistance and Survival,* 107.

12. Hu-DeHart, *Yaqui Resistance and Survival,* 140–41.

13. Knight, *The Mexican Revolution,* vol. 1, 13, 16. See also Gilbert M. Joseph, *Revolution from Without: Yucatán, Mexico, and the United States, 1880–1924* (Durham, NC: Duke University Press, 1988).

14. Hu-DeHart, *Yaqui Resistance and Survival,* 170–71.

15. Lomnitz, *The Return of Comrade Ricardo Flores Magón,* 130–31.

16. Jason Ruiz, *Americans in the Treasure House: Travel to Porfirian Mexico and the Cultural Politics of Empire* (Austin: University of Texas Press, 2014), 10.

17. Quoted in Cockcroft, *Intellectual Precursors,* 95.

18. Quoted in Lomnitz, *The Return of Comrade Ricardo Flores Magón,* 58.

19. José C. Valadés, *El joven Ricardo Flores Magón* (Mexico City: Editorial Extemporáneos, 1983), 13.

20. For an excellent review of the Flores Magón family in these years, see Lomnitz, *The Return of Comrade Ricardo Flores Magón,* 39–65.

21. T. Philip Terry, *Terry's Mexico: Handbook for Travellers* (Boston: Houghton Mifflin, 1909), 369. For more on public health in Mexico City during the Porfiriato, see Jonathan M. Weber, *Death Is All Around Us: Corpses, Chaos, and Public Health in Porfirian Mexico City* (Lincoln: University of Nebraska Press, 2019).

22. Paul J. Vanderwood, *The Power of God Against the Guns of Government: Religious Upheaval in Mexico at the Turn of the Nineteenth Century* (Palo Alto, CA: Stanford University Press, 1998), 159–84. See also Jesús Vargas Valdez, *Tomóchic: La revolución adelantada: Resistencia y lucha de un pueblo de Chihuahua con el sistema porfirista, 1891–1892* (Ciudad Juárez: Universidad Autónoma de Ciudad Juárez, 1994). The following novels by Luis Alberto Urrea also do an excellent job of placing Teresa's life within its historical context: *The Hummingbird's Daughter* (New York: Back Bay Books, 2005) and *Queen of America* (New York: Little, Brown, 2011).

23. Quoted in David Dorado Romo, *Ringside Seat to a Revolution: An Underground Cultural History of El Paso and Juárez: 1893–1923* (El Paso: Cinco Puntos Press, 2017), 24.

24. Quoted in Vanderwood, *The Power of God,* 277.

25. Quoted in Vanderwood, *The Power of God,* 282–83.

26. María Perales, "Teresa Urrea: Curandera and Folk Saint," in Vicki Ruiz and Virginia Sánchez Korrol, eds., *Latina Legacies: Identity, Biography, and Community* (Oxford: Oxford University Press, 2005). See also William Curry Holden, *Teresita* (Owing Mills, MD: Stemmer House, 1978).

27. Vanderwood, *The Power of God,* 148–49.

28. Lomnitz, *The Return of Comrade Ricardo Flores Magón,* 60.

29. Quoted in Lomnitz, *The Return of Comrade Ricardo Flores Magón,* 63.

30. See "Lugares, Calle de Santa Isabel," ADRFM, http://archivomagon.net/lugares/calle-de-santa-isabel/.

31. Valadés, *El joven Ricardo Flores Magón,* 17.

32. Valadés, *El joven Ricardo Flores Magón,* 17–18. For more on prostitution in Mexico City during the Porfiriato, see Katherine Bliss, *Compromised Positions: Prostitution, Public Health, and Gender Politics in Revolutionary Mexico City* (University Park: Pennsylvania State University Press, 2001), 1–62; James Alex Garza, *The Imagined Underworld: Sex, Crime, and Vice in Porfirian Mexico City* (Lincoln: University of Nebraska Press, 2007).

33. Valadés, *El joven Ricardo Flores Magón,* 17–18.

34. Quoted in Lomnitz, *The Return of Comrade Ricardo Flores Magón,* 83.

35. Lomnitz, *The Return of Comrade Ricardo Flores Magón,* 69–78.

36. Lomnitz, *The Return of Comrade Ricardo Flores Magón,* 69.

37. Cockcroft, *Intellectual Precursors,* 84. For more on anarchist thought in Mexico at the turn of the twentieth century, see John Mason Hart, *Anarchism and the Mexican Working Class, 1860–*

1931 (Austin: University of Texas Press, 1978); Sonia Hernández, "Chicanas in the US–Mexican Borderlands: Transborder Conversations of Feminism and Anarchism, 1905–1938," in *Promising Problem: The New Chicana/o History*, edited by Carlos Blanton (Austin: University of Texas Press, 2016); Sonia Hernández, *For a Just and Better World: Engendering Anarchism in the Mexican Borderlands, 1900–1938* (Champaign: University of Illinois Press, 2021). For more on culture and society in Mexico City during the Porfiriato, see William H. Beezley, *Judas at the Jockey Club and Other Episodes of Porfirian Mexico* (Lincoln: University of Nebraska Press, 2018).

38. Quoted in Peter Marshall, *Demanding the Impossible: A History of Anarchism* (Oakland, CA: PM Press, 2010), 319.

39. Quoted in Marshall, *Demanding the Impossible*, 324.

40. For more on the development of anarchist thought and politics, see Colin Ward, *Anarchism: A Very Short History* (Oxford: Oxford University Press, 2004); Marshall, *Demanding the Impossible*.

41. Manifesto of September 23, 1911, quoted in Chaz Bufe and Mitchell Cowen Verter, *Dreams of Freedom: A Ricardo Flores Magón Reader* (Oakland, CA: AK Press, 2005), 138.

42. Quoted in Lomnitz, *The Return of Comrade Ricardo Flores Magón*, 83.

43. Lomnitz, *The Return of Comrade Ricardo Flores Magón*, 83.

44. "Periódico independiente de combate," *Regeneración*, December 31, 1900, ADRFM, http://archivomagon.net/wp-content/uploads/e1n20.pdf.

45. "Club Liberal Regenerador 'Benito Juárez,'" *Regeneración*, December 23, 1900, ADRFM, http://archivomagon.net/wp-content/uploads/e1n19.pdf. See also Benjamín Maldonado Alvarado, *La utopía de Ricardo Flores Magón: Revolución, anarquía, y comunalidad india* (Mexico City: Universidad Autónoma de Oaxaca, 1994), 15.

46. "Periódico independiente de combate."

47. As quoted in Cockcroft, *Intellectual Precursors*, 96.

48. Quoted in Cockcroft, *Intellectual Precursors*, 97.

49. Ward S. Albro, *Always a Rebel: Ricardo Flores Magón and the Mexican Revolution* (Fort Worth: Texas Christian University Press, 1992), 12–13.

50. Cockcroft, *Intellectual Precursors*, 95. See also "Teatro de la Paz, San Luis Potosí," ADRFM, http://archivomagon.net/lugares/teatro-de-la-paz/.

Chapter 4: WE WON'T BE SILENCED

1. "Unámonos," *Regeneración*, March 7, 1901, ADRFM, http://archivomagon.net/wp-content/uploads/e1n29.pdf.

2. Quoted in Devra Anne Weber, "Wobblies of the Partido Liberal Mexicano: Reenvisioning Internationalist and Transnational Movements through Mexican Lenses," *Pacific Historical Review* 85, no. 2 (2016): 210.

3. Claudio Lomnitz, *The Return of Comrade Ricardo Flores Magón* (New York: Zone Books, 2014), 240–41. See also Weber, "Wobblies of the Partido Liberal Mexicano," 211.

4. Pablo Piccato, *The Tyranny of Opinion: Honor in the Construction of the Mexican Public Sphere* (Durham, NC: Duke University Press, 2010), 70, 162.

5. "Un cacique insufrible," *Regeneración*, March 31, 1901, ADRFM, http://archivomagon.net/wp-content/uploads/e1n32.pdf.

6. "A La Nación," *Regeneración*, March 31, 1901, ADRFM, http://archivomagon.net/wp-content/uploads/e1n32.pdf.

7. "Al Presidente de la República," *Regeneración*, April 15, 1901, ADRFM, http://archivomagon.net/wp-content/uploads/e1n34.pdf.

8. Michael Johns, *The City of Mexico in the Age of Díaz* (Austin: University of Texas Press, 1997), 52.

9. Johns, *The City of Mexico in the Age of Díaz*, 70. In lieu of a direct translation for *ratero*, which connotes a person regarded as a beggar, thief, and lowlife, often a migrant, I have chosen to use "tramp," a word in use in the United States during this era for migrants regarded as lazy, filthy, and prone to criminality.

10. Johns, *The City of Mexico in the Age of Díaz*, 55.

11. See "Cárcel de Belén" (Mexico City), ADRFM, http://archivomagon.net/lugares/carcel-de-belen/.

12. For more on Belem Prison, see James Alex Garza, *The Imagined Underworld: Sex, Crime, and Vice in Porfirian Mexico City* (Lincoln: University of Nebraska Press, 2007); Pablo Piccato, *City of Suspects: Crime in Mexico City, 1900–1931* (Durham, NC: Duke University Press, 2001).

13. Lomnitz, *The Return of Comrade Ricardo Flores Magón*, 107.

14. Quoted in Nicole Guidotti-Hernandez, *Archiving Mexican Masculinities in Diaspora* (Durham, NC: Duke University Press, 2021), 38.

15. Lomnitz, *The Return of Comrade Ricardo Flores Magón*, 218.

16. "La hierba maldita," *Regeneración*, June 7, 1901, ADRFM, http://archivomagon.net/wp-content/uploads/e1n41.pdf.

17. Samuel Kaplan, *Combatimos la tiranía* (Mexico City: Biblioteca del Instituto de Estudios Históricos de la Revolución Mexicana, 1958), 56–57.

18. Kaplan, *Combatimos la tiranía*, 54–58.

19. Lomnitz, *The Return of Comrade Ricardo Flores Magón*, 104.

20. Quoted in Chaz Bufe and Mitchell Cowen Verter, *Dreams of Freedom: A Ricardo Flores Magón Reader* (Oakland, CA: AK Press, 2005), 34.

21. Ana Luisa R. Martínez, "The Voice of the People: Pablo Cruz, El Regidor and Mexican American Identity in San Antonio, Texas, 1888–1910," PhD dissertation, Texas Tech University, 2003, 132.

22. James D. Cockcroft, *Intellectual Precursors of the Mexican Revolution, 1900–1913* (Austin: University of Texas Press, 1968), 102.

23. Inés Hernández Tovar, "Sara Estela Ramírez: The Early Twentieth Century Texas–Mexican Poet," PhD dissertation, University of Houston, 1984, 12. See also Emilio Zamora, "Sara Estela Ramírez: una rosa roja en el movimiento," in *Mexican Women in the United States: Struggles Past and Present*, edited by Magdalena Mora and Adelaida R. Del Castillo (Los Angeles: UCLA Chicano Studies Research Center, 1980).

24. "Discurso," *Regeneración*, August 31, 1901, ADRFM, http://archivomagon.net/wp-content/uploads/e1n52.pdf. For more on Antonio Díaz Soto y Gama, see Cockcroft, *Intellectual Precursors*, 71–77.

25. "Discurso."

26. "Amenazas de los caciques," *Regeneración*, September 15, 1901 ADRFM, http://archivomagon.net/wp-content/uploads/e1n54.pdf.

27. "Más sobre nuestra cafrería," *Regeneración*, October 7, 1901, ADRFM, http://archivomagon.net/wp-content/uploads/e1n57.pdf.

28. Cockcroft, *Intellectual Precursors*, 99–100.

29. Ward S. Albro, *Always a Rebel: Ricardo Flores Magón and the Mexican Revolution* (Fort Worth: Texas Christian University Press, 1992), 17.

30. Cockcroft, *Intellectual Precursors*, 103–5.

31. Cockcroft, *Intellectual Precursors*, 106–8.

32. Cockcroft, *Intellectual Precursors*, 103–8.

33. EDTA, file 552.

Chapter 5: THE CONSTITUTION IS DEAD

1. Quoted in José C. Valadés, *El joven Ricardo Flores Magón* (Mexico City: Editorial Extemporáneos, 1983), 23.

2. Quoted in James D. Cockcroft, *Intellectual Precursors of the Mexican Revolution, 1900–1913* (Austin: University of Texas Press, 1968), 108.

3. "Santiago de la Hoz," *Regeneración*, March 25, 1905, ADRFM, http://archivomagon.net/wp-content/uploads/e2n21.pdf.

4. "Santiago de la Hoz," *Regeneración*, March 25, 1905.

5. Valadés, *El joven Ricardo Flores Magón*, 25.

6. As quoted in Claudio Lomnitz, *The Return of Comrade Ricardo Flores Magón* (New York: Zone Books, 2014), 105.

7. Valadés, *El joven Ricardo Flores Magón*, 25.
8. As quoted in Cockcroft, *Intellectual Precursors*, 109.
9. Cockcroft, *Intellectual Precursors*, 109.
10. *El Hijo del Ahuizote*, March 1, 1903.
11. Cockcroft, *Intellectual Precursors*, 112.
12. Quoted in Alex Saragoza, *The Monterrey Elite and the Mexican State, 1880–1940* (Austin: University of Texas Press, 2014), 87.
13. Cockcroft, *Intellectual Precursors*, 112–13.
14. Cockcroft, *Intellectual Precursors*, 113. See also Saragoza, *The Monterrey Elite*, 88.
15. Lomnitz, *The Return of Comrade Ricardo Flores Magón*, xxvii–xxviii. See also Cockcroft, *Intellectual Precursors*, 113–14.
16. Quoted in Ana Lau Jaiven, "La participación de las mujeres en la Revolución Mexicana: Juana Belén Gutiérrez de Mendoza (1875–1942)," *Diálogos Revista Electrónica de Historia* 5, no. 1–2 (April–August 2005): 8.
17. Cockcroft, *Intellectual Precursors*, 112.
18. *El Hijo del Ahuizote*, April 19, 1903. Cockcroft, *Intellectual Precursors*, 113–14.
19. Samuel Kaplan, *Combatimos la tiranía* (Mexico City: Biblioteca del Instituto de Estudios Históricos de la Revolución Mexicana, 1958), 124.
20. Kaplan, *Combatimos la tiranía*, 127.

Chapter 6: THE BROWN BELT

1. Act of February 20, 1907 (34 Stat. 898).
2. Erika Lee, "Enforcing the Borders: Chinese Exclusion Along the U.S. Borders with Canada and Mexico, 1882–1924," *Journal of American History* 89, no. 1 (June 2002): 54–86. For more information about U.S. immigration control in the U.S.–Mexico borderlands at the dawn of the twentieth century, see Erika Lee, *At America's Gates: Chinese Immigration during the Exclusion Era, 1882–1943* (Chapel Hill: University of North Carolina Press, 2003); Julian Lim, *Porous Borders: Multiracial Migrations and the Law in the U.S.–Mexico Borderlands* (Chapel Hill: University of North Carolina Press, 2017).
3. Inés Hernández, "Sara Estela Ramírez: Sembradora," *Legacy: A Journal of American Women Writers* 6, no. 1 (Spring 1989): 13–26. See also Gabriela González, *Redeeming La Raza: Transborder Modernity, Race, Respectability, and Rights* (Oxford: Oxford University Press, 2018), 60–63. Sara Estela likely named her newspaper, *La Corregidora*, after Josefa Ortiz de Domínguez, a legendary female insurgent during Mexico's War for Independence against Spain. Ortiz de Domínguez's nickname was "La Corregidora."
4. Quoted in Aaron Johnson-Ortiz, "Exile & Utopia (1904–1906)," master's thesis, University of Michigan, 2010, 14. Available online at: http://www.magonista.net/book/printable_pdf/EXILE_UTOPIA.pdf.
5. Daniel D. Arreola, *Tejano South Texas: A Mexican American Cultural Province* (Austin: University of Texas Press, 2007), 47. See also John A. Adams, Jr., *Conflict and Commerce on the Rio Grande: Laredo, 1755–1955* (College Station: Texas A & M University Press, 2008); Armando C. Alonzo, *Tejano Legacy: Rancheros and Settlers in South Texas, 1734–1900* (Albuquerque: University of New Mexico Press, 1998); David Montejano, *Anglos and Mexicans in the Making of Texas, 1836–1986* (Austin: University of Texas Press, 1987).
6. At least thirty of these newspapers were PLM-related. See W. Dirk Raat, *Revoltosos: Mexico's Rebels in the United States, 1903–1923* (College Station: Texas A & M University Press, 1981), 38. See also Nicolas Kanellos, "Spanish Language Periodicals in the Early Twentieth Century United States," in *Protest on the Page: Essays on Print and the Culture of Dissent since 1865*, edited by James L. Baughman, Jennifer Ratner-Rosenhagen, and James P. Danky (Madison: University of Wisconsin Press, 2015).
7. Mark Reisler, *By the Sweat of Their Brow: Mexican Immigrant Labor in the United States, 1900–1940* (Westport, CT: Greenwood Press, 1976).

8.   For a list of items sold to fund trips north, see Victor S. Clark, "Mexican Labor in the United States," *Bulletin of the Bureau of Labor*, no. 78 (Washington, DC: Government Printing Office, 1908), 472.

9.   Emilio Zamora, *The World of the Mexican Worker in Texas* (College Station: Texas A & M University Press, 1993), 18.

10. For more on Mexican immigration to the United States in the early years of the twentieth century, see Rudolfo E. Acuña, *The Corridors of Migration: The Odyssey of Mexican Laborers, 1600–1933* (Tucson: University of Arizona Press, 2007); Lawrence A. Cardoso, *Mexican Emigration to the United States, 1897–1931* (Tucson: University of Arizona Press, 1980); Mario T. García, *Desert Immigrants: The Mexicans of El Paso, 1880–1920* (New Haven: Yale University Press, 1981); Reisler, *By the Sweat of Their Brow*; Moisés González Navarro, *Los extranjeros en México y los mexicanos en el extranjero, 1821–1970*, vol. 3 (Mexico City: Colegio de México, 1994); Camille Guérin-Gonzales, *Mexican Workers and the American Dream: Immigration, Repatriation, and California Farm Labor, 1900–1939* (New Brunswick, NJ: Rutgers University Press, 1994).

11. Cardoso, *Mexican Labor Emigration*, ch. 2.

12. 1910 U.S. Census, vol. 11: Mines & Quarries, General Report & Analysis (Washington, DC: Government Printing Office, 1914), 22 and 53; 1910 U.S. Census, vol. 6: Agriculture, Reports by States, Alabama to Montana (Washington, DC: Government Printing Office, 1914), 142; 1910 U.S. Census, vol. 7: Agriculture, Reports by States, Nebraska to Wyoming (Washington, DC: Government Printing Office, 1914), 626.

13. Cardoso, *Mexican Labor Emigration to the United States*; Reisler, *By the Sweat of Their Brow*.

14. Zamora, *World of the Mexican Worker in Texas*, 17.

15. For more on Native removal, race, and settler colonialism, see David Chang, *The Color of the Land: Race, Nation, and the Politics of Land Ownership in Oklahoma, 1832–1929* (Chapel Hill: University of North Carolina Press, 2010); Peter Cozzens, *The Earth Is Weeping: The Epic Story of the Indian Wars for the American West* (New York: Knopf, 2016); Brian DeLay, *War of a Thousand Deserts: Indian Raids and the U.S.–Mexican War* (New Haven: Yale University Press, 2008); Ben Madley, *An American Genocide: The United States and the California Indian Catastrophe, 1846–1873* (New Haven: Yale University Press, 2016); Pekka Hämäläinen, *The Comanche Empire* (New Haven: Yale University Press, 2008); Roxanne Dunbar Ortiz, *An Indigenous Peoples' History of the United States* (Boston: Beacon Press, 2014); Karl Jacoby, *Shadows at Dawn: A Borderlands Massacre and the Violence of History* (New York: Penguin Press, 2008); Jeffrey Ostler, *Surviving Genocide: Native Nations and the United States from the American Revolution to Bleeding Kansas* (New Haven: Yale University Press, 2019).

16. Benjamin Heber Johnson, *Revolution in Texas: How a Forgotten Rebellion and Its Bloody Suppression Turned Mexicans into Americans* (New Haven: Yale University Press, 2003), 7–37; Montejano, *Anglos and Mexicans*.

17. William D. Carrigan and Clive Webb, *Forgotten Dead: Mob Violence against Mexicans in the United States, 1848–1928* (Oxford: Oxford University Press, 2013). See also Nicholas Villanueva, Jr., *The Lynching of Mexicans in the Texas Borderlands* (Albuquerque: University of New Mexico Press, 2017).

18. Carrigan and Webb, *Forgotten Dead*, 17–18, 61–63.

19. For a chronological list of the killings, see Carrigan and Webb, *Forgotten Dead*, 179–38.

20. For more on Juan Crow conditions in the U.S.–Mexico borderlands prior to World War II, see Katherine Benton-Cohen, *Borderline Americans: Racial Division and Labor War in the Arizona Borderlands* (Cambridge, MA: Harvard University Press, 2009); William Deverell, *Whitewashed Adobe: The Rise of Los Angeles and the Remaking of its Mexican Past* (Berkeley: University of California Press, 2004); Reisler, *By the Sweat of Their Brow*; Laura E. Gómez, *Manifest Destinies: The Making of the Mexican American Race* (New York: New York University Press, 2018); Natalia Molina, *Fit to be Citizens? Public Health and Race in Los Angeles, 1879–1939* (Berkeley: University of California Press, 2006); Montejano, *Anglos and Mexicans*; Monica Perales, *Smeltertown: Making and Remembering a Southwest Border Community* (Chapel Hill: University of North Carolina Press, 2010).

21. Reisler, *By the Sweat of Their Brow*, 4.

22. Reisler, *By the Sweat of Their Brow*, 6.
23. Martha Menchaca, *Naturalizing Mexican Immigrants* (Austin: University of Texas Press, 2011).
24. Américo Paredes, *With a Pistol in His Hand: A Border Ballad and Its Hero* (Austin: University of Texas Press, 1958), 55–107.
25. Paredes, *With a Pistol in His Hand*, 71.
26. Quoted in F. Arturo Rosales, *Pobre Raza!: Violence, Justice, and Mobilization among Mexico Lindo Immigrants, 1900–1936* (Austin: University of Texas Press, 1999), 93.
27. Paredes, *With a Pistol in His Hand*, 84–86. See also María de Jesus Duarte, "Spaces of Law and Contestation: Mexican Immigrants and Consuls' Search for Justice in the United States during the Presidency of Porfirio Díaz," PhD dissertation, University of Indiana, 2012, 191.
28. González, *Redeeming La Raza*, 20.
29. González, *Redeeming La Raza*, 25.
30. González, *Redeeming La Raza*, 26–27.
31. Ana Luisa R. Martínez, "The Voice of the People: Pablo Cruz, El Regidor and Mexican American Identity in San Antonio, Texas, 1888–1910," PhD dissertation, Texas Tech University, 2003.
32. *El Regidor*, April 20, 1905. See also Martínez, "The Voice of the People," 114–16.

Chapter 7: SEND THE SECRET POLICE

1. *Laredo Times*, January 17, 1904, CPD, folder 1 (561).
2. Telegram from A. V. Lomelí to Ignacio Mariscal, January 16, 1904, AEMEUA, LE 270, exp. 3, p. 2.
3. Testimony by John Valis on January 22, 1920, for the "Investigation of Mexican Affairs," Subcommittee of the Committee of Foreign Relations, United States Senate, 66th Cong., 2nd Sess., vol. 9, December 1, 1919–June 5, 1920 (Washington, DC: Government Printing Office, 1920), 1199–225.
4. Letter from Juan A. Valls (John Valis) to Porfirio Díaz, January 17, 1904, CPD, folder 1 (561), document #1053/54.
5. Letter from Porfirio Diaz to Juan A. Valls (John Valis), January 24, 1904, CPD, folder 1 (561), document #1056.
6. Samuel Kaplan, *Combatimos la tiranía* (Mexico City: Biblioteca del Instituto de Estudios Históricos de la Revolución Mexicana, 1958), 129.
7. Letter from A. V. Lomelí to Ignacio Mariscal, February 8, 1904, AEMEUA, LE 270, exp. 3, pp. 4–5.
8. Letter from A. V. Lomelí to Ignacio Mariscal, February 8, 1904.
9. Letter from A. V. Lomelí to Ignacio Mariscal, February 8, 1904.
10. "Mexican Hall, Laredo, Texas," ADRFM, http://archivomagon.net/lugares/mexican-hall/.
11. Letter from A. V. Lomelí to Ignacio Mariscal, February 8, 1904.
12. Manuel González Oropeza, "Ignacio Mariscal," *Anuario Jurídico XVII* (Universidad Nacional Autónoma de México, 1990), 115–28.
13. Elliott Young, *Catarino Garza's Revolution on the Texas–Mexico Border* (Durham, NC: Duke University Press, 2004).
14. Letter from Ignacio Mariscal to Manuel Aspíroz, February 16, 1904, AEMEUA, LE 270, exp. 3 p. 1.
15. *Laredo Times*, March 6, 1904.
16. Benjamin Heber Johnson, *Revolution in Texas: How a Forgotten Rebellion and Its Bloody Suppression Turned Mexicans into Americans* (New Haven: Yale University Press, 2003), 62.
17. James D. Cockcroft, *Intellectual Precursors of the Mexican Revolution, 1900–1913* (Austin: University of Texas Press, 1968), 118.
18. Quoted in Claudio Lomnitz, *The Return of Comrade Ricardo Flores Magón* (New York: Zone Books, 2014), 201.
19. Quoted in Cockcroft, *Intellectual Precursors*, 118–19. For more on Sara Estela Ramírez, see Inés Hernández Tovar, "Sara Estela Ramírez: The Early Twentieth Century Texas–Mexican

Poet," PhD dissertation, University of Houston, 1984; Emilio Zamora, *The World of the Mexican Worker in Texas* (College Station: Texas A & M University Press, 1993), 104–15; "Sara Estela Ramírez: una rosa roja en el movimiento," in *Mexican Women in the United States: Struggles Past and Present*, edited by Magdalena Mora and Adelaida R. Del Castillo (Los Angeles: UCLA Chicano Studies Research Center, 1980).

20.   Ana Lau Jaiven, "La participación de las mujeres en la Revolución Mexicana: Juana Belén Gutiérrez de Mendoza (1875-1942)," *Diálogos Revista Electrónica de Historia* 5, no. 1–2 (April–August 2005): 5–6.

21.   Jaiven, "La Participación de las Mujeres," 6. Zamora, *World of the Mexican Worker*, 114.

22.   Quoted in Gabriela González, *Redeeming La Raza: Transborder Modernity, Race, Respectability, and Rights* (Oxford: Oxford University Press, 2018), 62.

23.   Kaplan, *Combatimos la tiranía*, 130.

24.   "Santiago de la Hoz," *Regeneración*, March 25, 1905, ADRFM, http://archivomagon.net/wp -content/uploads/e2n21.pdf.

25.   Ward S. Albro, *Always a Rebel: Ricardo Flores Magón and the Mexican Revolution* (Fort Worth: Texas Christian University Press, 1992), 24.

26.   Letter from Enrique Ornelas to Manuel Aspíroz, November 14, 1904, AEMEUA, LE 270, exp. 3, pp. 8–9.

27.   For more on the long arc of "The Ballad of Gregorio Cortez," see Américo Paredes, *With a Pistol in His Hand: A Border Ballad and Its Hero* (Austin: University of Texas Press, 1958).

28.   Albro, *Always a Rebel*, 120.

29.   Quoted in Cockcroft, *Intellectual Precursors*, 120.

30.   Mark Wasserman, *Pesos and Politics: Business, Elites, Foreigners, and Government in Mexico, 1854–1940* (Palo Alto, CA: Stanford University Press, 2015), 43–49.

31.   Enrique Krauze, *Mexico: Biography of Power: A History of Modern Mexico, 1810–1996* (New York: HarperCollins, 1998), 247.

32.   Krauze, *Mexico: Biography of Power*, 247–48.

33.   "Francisco I. Madero: The Apostle of Democracy," in Krauze, *Mexico: Biography of Power*, 245–73; Stanley R. Ross, *Francisco I. Madero: Apostle of Mexican Democracy* (New York: Columbia University Press, 1955).

Chapter 8: WE RETURN TO THE FIGHT

1.   Arnulfo Tovar, "San Antonio's Redlining and Segregation," *Methods of Historical Research*, Spring 2020, 1; Shannon Barker, "Los Tejanos de San Antonio: Mexican Immigrant Family Acculturation, 1880–1929," PhD dissertation, George Washington University, 1996, 61, 79; Kenneth Mason, *African Americans and Race Relations in San Antonio, Texas, 1867–1937* (New York: Garland, 1998). See also Arnoldo de León and Kenneth L. Stewart, *Tejanos and the Numbers Game: A Socio-Historical Interpretation from the Federal Censuses, 1850–1900* (Albuquerque: University of New Mexico Press, 1989), 88–89.

2.   The average wage for Mexican workers in Texas comes from table 3 in Emilio Zamora, *The World of the Mexican Worker in Texas* (College Station: Texas A & M University Press, 1993). Rent data for *corrales* on p. 12.

3.   Ana Luisa R. Martínez, "The Voice of the People: Pablo Cruz, El Regidor and Mexican American Identity in San Antonio, Texas, 1888–1910," PhD dissertation, Texas Tech University, 2003, 59.

4.   For more on Laredito, see Martínez, "The Voice of the People," 42–43; Elliott Young, "Red Men, Princess Pocahontas, and George Washington: Harmonizing Race Relations in Laredo at the Turn of the Century," *Western Historical Quarterly* 29, no. 1 (1998): 49–85.

5.   Greg Cantrell, "Our Very Pronounced Theory of Equal Rights to All: Race, Citizenship, and Populism in the South Texas Borderlands," *Journal of American History* 100, no. 3 (December 2013): 663.

6.   Cantrell, "Our Very Pronounced Theory"; Arnoldo de León, *In re Rodríguez: An Attempt at*

Chicano Disenfranchisement in San Antonio, 1896–1897 (San Antonio: Caravel Press, 1979); Ian F. Haney López, *White by Law: The Legal Construction of Race* (New York: New York University Press, 1996); Evelyn Nakano Glenn, *Unequal Freedom: How Race and Gender Shaped American Citizenship and Labor* (Cambridge, MA: Harvard University Press, 2002); Ariela S. Gross, *What Blood Won't Tell: A History of Race on Trial in America* (Cambridge, MA: Harvard University Press, 2008), 257–59; Laura E. Gómez, *Manifest Destinies: The Making of the Mexican American Race* (New York: New York University Press, 2018), 139–43; Martha Menchaca, *Naturalizing Mexican Immigrants: A Texas History* (Austin: University of Texas Press, 2011), 10; Gregory Rodríguez, *Mongrels, Bastards, Orphans, and Vagabonds: Mexican Immigration and the Future of Race in America* (New York: Vintage, 2007), 169.

7. de León, *In re Rodríguez*, 2.

8. For more on the history of race, immigration, and naturalization, see Martha S. Jones, *Birthright Citizens: A History of Race and Rights in Antebellum America* (Cambridge: Cambridge University Press, 2018); López, *White by Law*; Hiroshi Motomura, *Americans in Waiting: The Lost Story of Immigration and Citizenship in the United States* (Oxford: Oxford University Press, 2006); Kunal M. Parker, *Making Foreigners: Immigration and Citizenship Law in America, 1600–2000* (Cambridge: Cambridge University Press, 2015). For more on the racialization of Mexicans in the United States, see Martha Menchaca, *Recovering History, Constructing Race: The Indian, White, and Black Roots of Mexican Americans* (Austin: University of Texas Press, 2001).

9. Quoted in Cantrell, "Our Very Pronounced Theory," 676.

10. Samuel Kaplan, *Combatimos la tiranía* (Mexico City: Biblioteca del Instituto de Estudios Históricos de la Revolución Mexicana, 1958), 131.

11. José C. Valadés, *El joven Ricardo Flores Magón* (Mexico City: Editorial Extemporáneos, 1983), 43.

12. Martínez, "The Voice of the People," 60–63.

13. Martínez, "The Voice of the People," 123.

14. Martínez, "The Voice of the People," 123–24.

15. Quoted in Martínez, "The Voice of the People," 145.

16. Martínez, "The Voice of the People," 146.

17. Judith Berg Sobré, *San Antonio on Parade: Six Historic Festivals* (College Station: Texas A & M University Press, 2003). See also *Viva! Fiesta: San Antonio Pictorial Event Book* (San Antonio: *San Antonio Express–News*, 2009).

18. "Freedom of Mexico Duly Celebrated," *San Antonio Daily Light*, September 16, 1904.

19. "Mexican Consul Gets Promotion," *San Antonio Daily Light*, October 1, 1904.

20. Letter from Ignacio Mariscal to Manuel Aspíroz, October 25, 1904, AEMEUA, LE 270, exp. 3, pp. 5–6, 26.

21. Letter from Ignacio Mariscal to Manuel Aspíroz, October 25, 1904.

22. Letter from Ignacio Mariscal to Manuel Aspíroz, October 25, 1904.

23. "Regeneración," *Regeneración*, November 5, 1904, ADRFM, http://archivomagon.net/wp-content/uploads/e2n1.pdf.

24. "Los Cónsules mexicanos en los Estados Unidos," *Regeneración*, November 5, 1904, ADRFM, http://archivomagon.net/wp-content/uploads/e2n1.pdf.

25. "La Vicepresidencia de la República y el Porvenir de la Patria," *Regeneración*, November 12, 1904, ADRFM, http://archivomagon.net/wp-content/uploads/e2n2.pdf.

26. Alan Knight, *The Mexican Revolution: Porfirians, Liberals, and Peasants*, vol. 1 (Lincoln: University of Nebraska Press, 1986), 22.

27. "Porfirio Díaz no es la Patria," *Regeneración*, November 19, 1905, ADRFM, http://archivomagon.net/wp-content/uploads/e2n3.pdf.

28. Kaplan, *Combatimos la tiranía*, 135–39.

Chapter 9: WHAT I BELIEVE

1. Walter Johnson, "The Largest Human Zoo in World History: Visiting the 1904 World's Fair in St. Louis," *Lapham's Quarterly*, April 14, 2020. See also Walter Johnson, *The Broken Heart of America:*

St. Louis and the Violent History of the United States (New York: Basic Books, 2020). For more on the history of white supremacy, empire, and world's fairs, see Robert W. Rydell, *All the World's a Fair: Visions of Empire at American International Expositions, 1876–1916* (Chicago: University of Chicago Press, 1984). For a discussion of Mexico at the world's fairs, see Mauricio Tenorio-Trillo, *Mexico at the World's Fairs: Crafting a Modern Nation* (Berkeley: University of California Press, 1996).

2.   Henry W. Berger, *St. Louis and Empire: 250 Years of Imperial Quest and Urban Crisis* (Carbondale: Southern Illinois University Press, 2015). For more on Mexicans in St. Louis at the turn of the twentieth century, see David Gonzales, "Gateway to the East: An Exploration of St. Louis' Mexican History through the Built Environment," *Confluence*, Spring/Summer 2019, 30–41; Juan R. García, *Mexicans in the Midwest: 1900–1932* (Tucson: University of Arizona Press, 2003); Philip R. Mueller, "The Mexican Liberals in St. Louis: 1905–1906," master's thesis, Southern Illinois University at Carbondale, 1983.

3.   For more on the Villarreal family, see Ward S. Albro, "A Remarkable Family: Twentieth Century Mexico with the Villarreals," paper prepared for IX Reunión de Historiodadores Mexicanos y Norteamericanos (Mexico City, 1994), provided to the author by Ward Albro.

4.   "Información secreta que el agente N. N. de St. Louis, le dio al suscrito contestando al siguiente interrogatorio," STP, box 26, folder 7A. See also José C. Valadés, *El joven Ricardo Flores Magón* (Mexico City: Editorial Extemporáneos, 1983), 51.

5.   "'Regeneración' en St. Louis, Missouri," *Regeneración*, February 25, 1905, ADRFM, http://archivomagon.net/wp-content/uploads/e2n17.pdf.

6.   For more on the white working class and radical politics in St. Louis in the early twentieth century, see Johnson, *The Broken Heart of America*, 199–215.

7.   Emma Goldman, "What I Believe," *New York World*, July 19, 1908. For a closer look at sexuality and anarchist philosophy in the PLM movement, see Benjamin H. Abbott, "'That Monster Cannot Be a Woman': Queerness and Treason in the Partido Liberal Mexicano," *Anarchist Developments in Cultural Studies*, no. 1 (2018): 9–28.

8.   Ward S. Albro, *Always a Rebel: Ricardo Flores Magón and the Mexican Revolution* (Fort Worth: Texas Christian University Press, 1992), 30.

9.   "A La Mujer," *Regeneración*, September 24, 1910, ADRFM, http://archivomagon.net/wp-content/uploads/e4n4.pdf.

10.   "A La Mujer."

11.   Gabriela González, *Redeeming La Raza: Transborder Modernity, Race, Respectability and Rights* (Oxford: Oxford University Press, 2018), 51–81; Emma Pérez, "'A La Mujer': A Critique of the Partido Liberal Mexicano's Gender Ideology on Women," in *Between Borders: Essays on Mexicana/Chicana History*, edited by Adelaida R. Del Castillo (Encino, CA: Floricanto Press, 1990).

12.   For an analysis of gender ideology within the PLM, see González, *Redeeming La Raza*, 51–81; and Pérez, "'A La Mujer.'"

13.   "A La Mujer."

14.   "A La Mujer." For more on women and feminism in the *magonista* movement, see Nathan Kahn Ellstrand, "Las Anarquistas: The History of Two Women of the Partido Liberal Mexicano in Early 20th Century Los Angeles," master's thesis, University of California, San Diego, 2011; Sonia Hernández, "Chicanas in the US–Mexican Borderlands: Transborder Conversations of Feminism and Anarchism, 1905–1938," in *Promising Problem: The New Chicana/o History*, edited by Carlos Blanton (Austin: University of Texas Press, 2016); and Clara Lomas, "Transborder Discourse: The Articulation of Gender in the Borderlands in the Early Twentieth Century," *Frontiers: A Journal of Women Studies* 24, no. 2–3 (2003): 51–74. For more on the feminist movement in Mexico at this time, see Anna Macías, *Against All Odds: The Feminist Movement in Mexico to 1940* (Westport, CT: Greenwood Press, 1982). For more on women and anarchist politics in the era of the Mexican Revolution see, Sonia Hernandez, *For a Just and Better World: Engendering Anarchism in the Mexican Borderlands, 1900–1938* (Champaign: University of Illinois Press, 2021).

15.   Letter from Ricardo Flores Magón to Enrique Flores Magón and Práxedis Guerrero, June 13, 1908, ADRFM, http://archivomagon.net/obras-completas/correspondencia-1899-1922/c-1908/cor265/.

16.   Quoted in James D. Cockcroft, *Intellectual Precursors of the Mexican Revolution, 1900–1913* (Austin: University of Texas Press, 1968), 121.

17. Letter from Ricardo Flores Magón to Enrique Flores Magón and Práxedis Guerrero, June 13, 1908.

18. "Los derechos del trabajo," *Regeneración*, September 9, 1905, ADRFM, http://archivomagon.net/wp-content/uploads/e2n45.pdf.

19. "Propaganda católica," *Regeneración*, May 15, 1906, ADRFM, http://archivomagon.net/wp-content/uploads/e3n8.pdf.

20. "En pleno feudalismo," *Regeneración*, September 9, 1905, ADRFM, http://archivomagon.net/wp-content/uploads/e2n45.pdf.

21. "Camilo Arriaga no es Liberal," *Regeneración*, August 26, 1905, ADRFM, http://archivomagon.net/wp-content/uploads/e2n43.pdf.

22. Claudio Lomnitz, *The Return of Comrade Ricardo Flores Magón* (New York: Zone Books, 2014), 217.

23. "Camilo Arriaga no es Liberal."

24. Letter from A. M. Medino to Ricardo Flores Magón, August 1, 1907, AEMEUA, LE 294, exp. 10, pp. 27–28.

25. Ethel Duffy Turner, "Writers and Revolutionaries," interview conducted by Ruth Tieser for the University of California, Berkeley, 1967, 70–71, Bancroft Library Oral History Center, University of California, Berkeley. Available at https://californiarevealed.org/islandora/object/cavpp%3A13349.

26. Quoted in Benjamín Maldonado Alvarado, *La utopía de Ricardo Flores Magón: Revolución, anarquía, y comunalidad india* (Mexico City: Universidad Autónoma de Oaxaca, 1994), 29.

27. Francie R. Chassen-López, *From Liberal to Revolutionary Oaxaca: The View from the South, 1876–1911* (University Park: Pennsylvania State University Press, 2004), 452.

28. For a discussion of the various bolts of letters seized by U.S. and Mexican agents, see Jacinto Barrera Bassols, ed., *Correspondencia de Ricardo Flores Magón*, vol. 1, *1899–1918* (Mexico City: Consejo Nacional Para la Cultura y las Artes, 2000), 23–53.

29. Letter from M. E. Diebold to Ignacio Mariscal, February 17, 1909, AEMEUA, LE 942, pp. 280–90.

30. Quoted in Maldonado Alvarado, *La utopía de Ricardo Flores Magón*, 29–30.

31. Letter from Ricardo Flores Magón to Francisco I. Madero, March 5, 1905, in Barrera Bassols, ed., *Correspondencia*, vol. 1, 79.

32. Cockcroft, *Intellectual Precursors*, 129.

33. Valadés, *El joven Ricardo Flores Magón*, 67–77.

Chapter 10: CANANEA

1. Quoted in C. L. Sonnichsen, *Colonel Greene and the Copper Skyrocket: The Spectacular Rise and Fall of William Cornell Greene: Copper King, Cattle Baron, and Promoter Extraordinary in Mexico, the American Southwest, and the New York Financial District* (Tucson: University of Arizona Press, 1974), 185. For more on the PLM and the Cananea strike, see Ward S. Albro, *Always a Rebel: Ricardo Flores Magón and the Mexican Revolution* (Fort Worth: Texas Christian University Press, 1992), 23–43; Mario Aldana Rendón, *Manuel M. Diéguez y la revolución mexicana* (Zapopan: Colegio de Jalisco, 2006).

2. Teodoro Hernández, *Los precursores de la revolución* (México City: Instituto Nacional de Antropología e Historia, 1940), 24. Available at ADRFM, http://archivomagon.net/wp-content/uploads/2014/01/hernandez_teodoro_los_precursores_de_la_revolucion_1940.pdf. See also Lyle C. Brown, "Mexican Liberals and Their Struggle Against the Díaz Dictatorship," *Antología* (Mexico City: Mexico City College Press, 1956), 329.

3. Quoted in W. Dirk Raat, *Revoltosos: Mexico's Rebels in the United States, 1903–1923* (College Station: Texas A & M University Press, 1981), 119.

4. Katherine Benton Cohen, *Borderline Americans: Racial Divisions and Labor War in the Arizona Borderlands* (Cambridge, MA: Harvard University Press, 2009), 126–30, 202.

5. Eric L. Clements, "Pragmatic Revolutionaries?: Tactics, Ideologies, and the Western Federation of Miners in the Progressive Era," *Western Historical Quarterly* 40, no. 4 (2009): 449.

6. Clements, "Pragmatic Revolutionaries?," 448–49. See also George G. Suggs, Jr., *Colorado's War on Militant Unionism: James H. Peabody and the Western Federation of Miners* (Detroit: Wayne State University Press, 1972); Elizabeth Jameson, *All That Glitters: Class, Conflict, and Community in Cripple Creek* (Champaign: University of Illinois Press, 1998).

7. "Industrial Union Manifesto," Congress of Industrial Unions at Chicago, January 2, 3, and 4, 1905. Available at https://archive.iww.org/history/library/iww/industrial_union_manifesto/.

8. James McBride, "Gaining a Foothold in the Paradise of Capitalism: The Western Federation of Miners and the Unionization of Bisbee," *Journal of Arizona History* 23, no. 3 (Autumn 1982): 299–316.

9. C. L. Sonnichsen, "Colonel William C. Greene and the Strike at Cananea, Sonora, 1906," *Arizona and the West* 13, no. 4 (Winter 1971): 352–53.

10. Benjamín Maldonado Alvarado, *La utopía de Ricardo Flores Magón: Revolución, anarquía, y comunalidad india* (Mexico City: Universidad Autónoma de Oaxaca, 1994), 29.

11. Sonnichsen, "Colonel William C. Greene and the Strike at Cananea," 354.

12. Quoted in Sonnichsen, "Colonel William C. Greene and the Strike at Cananea," 345.

13. Sonnichsen, *Colonel Greene and the Copper Skyrocket*, 180.

14. Sonnichsen, *Colonel Greene and the Copper Skyrocket*, 9.

15. Sonnichsen, *Colonel Greene and the Copper Skyrocket*, 53–54.

16. Sonnichsen, "William C. Greene and the Strike at Cananea," 348.

17. Quoted in Sonnichsen, "William C. Greene and the Strike at Cananea," 348.

18. Hill Hastings, "Investigation of Reported Typhus Fever at La Cananea, Mexico," *Public Health Reports* (1896–1970) 17, no. 27 (July 4, 1902): 1550–51.

19. Quoted in Sonnichsen, "Colonel William C. Greene and the Strike at Cananea," 356.

20. D. L. Turner, "Arizona's Twenty-Four-Hour War: The Arizona Rangers and the Cananea Copper Strike of 1906," *Journal of Arizona History* 48, no. 3 (Autumn 2007): 269.

21. See also Samuel Truett, *Fugitive Landscapes: The Forgotten History of the U.S.–Mexico Borderlands* (New Haven: Yale University Press, 2006), 139.

22. Cornelius C. Smith, *Emilio Kosterlitzky: Eagle of Sonora and the Southwest Border* (Glendale, CA: Arthur Clark Company, 1979), 18. See also Truett, *Fugitive Landscapes*, 139–44.

23. Quoted in Turner, "Arizona's Twenty-Four-Hour War," 269.

24. Turner, "Arizona's Twenty-Four-Hour War," 270.

25. Quoted in Sonnichsen, "Colonel William C. Greene and the Strike at Cananea," 362.

26. Brown, "Mexican Liberals Against the Díaz Dictatorship," 338–41.

27. "Invasión del territorio nacional por tropas norteamericanas," *El Tiempo*, June 2, 1906.

28. Quoted in Raat, *Revoltosos*, 92.

29. Raat, *Revoltosos*, 106.

30. Raat, *Revoltosos*, 104–5.

31. Philip R. Mueller, "The Mexican Liberals in St. Louis: 1905–1906," master's thesis, Southern Illinois University at Carbondale, 1983, 37–39.

32. Quoted in Mueller, "The Mexican Liberals in St. Louis," 49.

Chapter 11: No Alarm in Mexico

1. "Hundreds Killed in War of Americans and Mexicans," *San Francisco Examiner*, June 2, 1906.

2. Evan Thomas, *The War Lovers: Roosevelt, Lodge, Hearst, and the Rush to Empire, 1898* (New York: Little, Brown, 2010).

3. John Mason Hart, *Empire and Revolution: The Americans in Mexico since the Civil War* (Berkeley: University of California Press, 2002), 180.

4. "Hundreds Killed in War of Americans and Mexicans."

5. "Yankees Chase the Mexicans Out of Cananea," *San Francisco Examiner*, June 3, 1906.

6. Broughton Brandenburg, "The War Peril on the Mexican Border," *Harper's Weekly* 50 (August 25, 1906): 1198–201.

7. Brandenburg, "The War Peril on the Mexican Border."

8. Mark Wasserman, *Pesos and Politics: Business, Elites, Foreigners, and Government in Mexico, 1854–1940* (Palo Alto, CA: Stanford University Press, 2015), 136.

9. "Frontier Fakers Busy," *Los Angeles Times*, September 5, 1906.

10. "No War with Mexico," *Los Angeles Times*, July 22, 1906. See also W. Dirk Raat, *Revoltosos: Mexico's Rebels in the United States, 1903–1923* (College Station: Texas A & M University Press, 1981), 99.

11. "No War with Mexico."

12. "No War with Mexico."

13. "The Outside Securities," *New York Times*, August 7, 1906.

14. "President a Celebrant: Mexico's Chief Executive Helps on Fourth," *Los Angeles Times*, July 22, 1906.

15. "President a Celebrant."

16. "Diaz Will Protect Foreigners in Mexico," *New York Times*, July 22, 1906.

17. "Strike Settled by Díaz," *New York Times*, August 16, 1906.

18. "Strike Settled by Díaz."

19. "Diaz Smashes Union Octopus," *Los Angeles Times*, August 23, 1906.

20. Rafael de Zayas Enríquez, *Porfirio Díaz* (New York: D. Appleton, 1908), 223.

21. Zayas Enríquez, *Porfirio Díaz*, 217.

22. Zayas Enríquez, *Porfirio Díaz*, 226.

23. Zayas Enríquez, *Porfirio Díaz*, 227–28.

24. Zayas Enríquez, *Porfirio Díaz*, 229.

25. Zayas Enríquez, *Porfirio Díaz*, 236.

26. Zayas Enríquez, *Porfirio Díaz*, 232.

27. Zayas Enríquez, *Porfirio Díaz*, 233.

28. Zayas Enríquez, *Porfirio Díaz*, 231–33. For more on the Zayas Enríquez report, see Lyle C. Brown, "Mexican Liberals and Their Struggle Against the Díaz Dictatorship," *Antología* (Mexico City: Mexico City College Press, 1956), 345; James D. Cockcroft, *Intellectual Precursors of the Mexican Revolution, 1900–1913* (Austin: University of Texas Press, 1968), 35.

29. Twelfth Census of the United States (1900): Sheet 8, Enumeration District 44, First Ward, Lincoln, Lancaster County, Nebraska.

30. William Schell, Jr., *Integral Outsiders: The American Colony in Mexico City, 1876–1911* (Wilmington, DE: Scholarly Resources, 2001), 117.

31. Schell, *Integral Outsiders*, 113–36.

32. Schell, *Integral Outsiders*, 149.

33. Schell, *Integral Outsiders*, 145.

34. President Theodore Roosevelt, Annual Message to Congress, December 6, 1904. See Schell, *Integral Outsiders*, 137–49.

35. Schell, *Integral Outsiders*, 145–49.

36. Quoted in Philip R. Mueller, "The Mexican Liberals in St. Louis: 1905–1906," master's thesis, Southern Illinois University at Carbondale, 1983, 38.

37. Mueller, "Mexican Liberals in St. Louis," 38.

38. Mueller, "Mexican Liberals in St. Louis," 39.

39. Raat, *Revoltosos*, 111.

40. Julia Rose Kraut, *Threat of Dissent: A History of Ideological Exclusion and Deportation in the United States* (Cambridge, MA: Harvard University Press, 2020), 49–55.

41. Raat, *Revoltosos*, 111.

42. Raat, *Revoltosos*, 111.

43. Brown, "Mexican Liberals Against the Dictatorship," 344.

44. "Goodman House, 73rd Street, El Paso, Texas," ADRFM, http://archivomagon.net/lugares/7-3rd-st/.

45. "Goodman House, 73rd Street, El Paso, Texas."

46. Glenn Dumke, "Douglas, Border Town," *Pacific Historical Review* 17, no. 3 (August 1948): 283–98.

47. Letter from Antonio Maza to Ignacio Mariscal, September 20, 1906, AEMEUA, LE 1241(2), pp. 113–17.

48. Letter from Antonio Maza to Ignacio Mariscal, September 20, 1906.

49. Letter from Antonio Maza to Ignacio Mariscal, September 20, 1906.

50. Joseph F. Park, "The 1903 'Mexican Affair' at Clifton," *Journal of Arizona History* 18, no. 2 (1977): 119–48; Philip J. Mellinger, *Race and Labor in Western Copper: The Fight for Equality, 1896–1918* (Tucson: University of Arizona Press, 1995).

51. Rachel St. John, *Line in the Sand: A History of the Western U.S.–Mexico Border* (Princeton University Press, 2011), 104.

52. Letter from George Webb to Commissioner General of Immigration, September 22, 1906, AEMEUA, LE 1241(3), pp. 172–75.

53. "Rebel Leaders Thrown into Prison," *Los Angeles Examiner*, September 5, 1906.

54. For IWW propaganda, see Raat, *Revoltosos*, 45.

55. See newspaper clippings from *Hamburger Nachrichten* in AEMEUA, LE 1241(2), pp. 109–10.

56. Letter from Balbino Davalos to Ignacio Mariscal, September 5, 1906, AEMEUA, LE 285, exp 6, pp. 1–3.

57. Letter from Balbino Davalos to Ignacio Mariscal, September 5, 1906.

58. Quoted in Raat, *Revoltosos*, 113.

59. Letter from Albert Leal to Ignacio Mariscal, September 14, 1906, AEMEUA, LE 1241, pp. 83–84.

60. Mueller, "Mexican Liberals in St Louis," 40. See also "Denies Story of Revolt," *New York Times*, September 8, 1906; "Denies Tale of Revolution," *San Francisco Chronicle*, September 8, 1906; untitled article beginning "Daniel Guggenheim, President of the American Smelting and Refining Company was asked yesterday for his opinion of the supposed anti-American spirit developing in Mexico," *New York Times*, September 12, 1906.

61. Raat, *Revoltosos*, 100.

62. Raat, *Revoltosos*, 114. See also "Mexican Junta Leaves St. Louis; Now in Europe," *St. Louis Globe Democrat*, September 13, 1906.

63. Raat, *Revoltosos*, 100.

64. Quoted in Mueller, "Mexican Liberals in St. Louis," 57. See also Brown, "Mexican Liberals Against the Díaz Dictatorship," 350–53.

65. "Mexicans Celebrate," *Los Angeles Times*, September 23, 1906. For more on Mexican Independence Day celebrations during the final years of the Porfiriato, see Rafael Tovar y de Teresa, *De la paz al olvido: Porfirio Díaz y el final de un mundo* (Mexico City: Penguin Random House Grupo Editorial, 2018), 56–115.

66. Raat, *Revoltosos*, 101.

Chapter 12: SEND FIVE DOLLARS FOR THE MACHINE

1. For more on the 1906 PLM Platform, see Ward S. Albro, *Always a Rebel: Ricardo Flores Magón and the Mexican Revolution* (Fort Worth: Texas Christian University Press, 1992), 44–56. See also Chaz Bufe and Mitchell Cowen Verter, *Dreams of Freedom: A Ricardo Flores Magón Reader* (Oakland, CA: AK Press, 2005), 131–34.

2. Quoted in Albro, *Always a Rebel*, 45.

3. Grace Delgado, *Making the Chinese Mexican: Global Migration, Localism, and Exclusion in the U.S.– Mexico Borderlands* (Palo Alto, CA: Stanford University Press, 2012); Evelyn Hu-DeHart, "Racism and Anti-Chinese Persecution in Sonora, Mexico, 1876–1932," *Amerasia* 9, no. 2 (1982): 1–27; Robert Chao Romero, *The Chinese in Mexico, 1882–1940* (Tucson: University of Arizona Press, 2010); Jason Oliver Chang, *Chino: Anti-Chinese Racism in Mexico, 1880–1940* (Champaign: University of Illinois Press, 2017); Elliott Young, *Alien Nation Chinese Migration in the Americas from the Coolie Era through World War II* (Champaign: The University of North Carolina Press, 2014).

4. Jacinto Barrera Bassols, "Ricardo Flores Magón, de la xenofobia popular al internacionalismo proletario," in *Xenofobia y xenofilia en la historia de México: siglos XIX y XX: Homenaje a Moisés González-Navarro*, edited by Delia Salazar Anaya (Mexico City: Segob, 2006), 433–48.

5. Quoted in Christina Heatherton, "University of Radicalism: Ricardo Flores Magón and Leavenworth Penitentiary," *American Quarterly* 66, no. 3 (Fall 2014): 576.

6. Albro, *Always a Rebel*, 55.

7. Frank McLynn, *Villa and Zapata: A History of the Mexican Revolution* (New York: Carroll & Graf, 2000), 43.

8. Letter from Ricardo Flores Magón to Crescencio Villarreal Márquez, June 16, 1906, AEMEUA, LE 855, p. 33.

9. Letter from León Cárdenas to Ricardo Flores Magón, June 29, 1906, STP, box 26, folder 2B.

10. Letter from Ancelmo Velarde to Ricardo Flores Magón, September 15, 1906, STP, box 27, folder 9B. See also letter from Ancelmo Velarde to Ricardo Flores Magón, September 11, 1906, AEMEUA, LE 294, exp. 1, pp. 1–6.

11. Letter from Rafael Valle top Ricardo Flores Magón, September 18, 1906, AEMEUA, LE 294, exp. 1, p. 16.

12. Letter from Sixto to Ricardo Flores Magón, September 19, 1906, AEMEUA, LE 294, exp. 1, pp. 18–19.

13. For "gladiators," see Claudio Lomnitz, *The Return of Comrade Ricardo Flores Magón* (New York: Zone Books, 2014), xxxiii.

14. Memo from Antonio Villarreal and Ricardo Flores Magón, August 31, 1906, "re: commission of Javier Guitemea (also referred to as Javier Buitemea)," NARA, RG 60, box 713, file 90755, entry 112. For more on Yaqui involvement with the PLM, see Evelyn Hu-DeHart, *Yaqui Resistance and Survival: The Struggle for Land and Autonomy, 1821–1910* (Madison: University of Wisconsin Press, 2016), 188–90.

15. Justin Akers Chacón, *Radicals in the Barrio: Magonistas, Socialists, Wobblies, and Communists in the Mexican American Working Class* (Chicago: Haymarket, 2018), 274–77; Devra Anne Weber, "Keeping Community, Challenging Boundaries: Indigenous Migrants, Internationalist Workers, and Mexican Revolutionaries, 1900-1920," in *Mexico and Mexicans in the Making of the United States*, edited by John Tutino (Austin: University of Texas Press, 2012), 208–35.

16. Quoted in Weber, "Keeping Community, Challenging Boundaries," 224.

17. Numerous copies of this letter were sent to soldiers at the National Palace and guards at Ulua Prison. They can be found in AEMEUA, LE 294, exp. 4.

18. Letter from Ricardo Flores Magón to Crescencio Villarreal Márquez, June 16, 1906, AEMEUA, LE 855, p. 33.

19. Letter from Ricardo Flores Magón to Rafael Rembao and Silvina Rembao de Trejo, August 21, 1906, AEMEUA, LE 294, exp. 4, pp. 7–8.

20. Letters from Francisco I. Madero to Crescencio Villarreal Márquez, August 17 and 24, 1906, AEMEUA, LE 855, p. 53, 66. For "anti-patriotic," see James D. Cockcroft, *Intellectual Precursors of the Mexican Revolution, 1900–1913* (Austin: University of Texas Press, 1968), 159.

21. Letter from Francisco I. Madero to Crescencio Villarreal Márquez, August 17, 1906, AEMEUA, LE 855, p. 66. For "insulting everyone," see Cockcroft, *Intellectual Precursors*, 122.

22. "Juana B. Gutiérrez de Mendoza," *Regeneración*, June 15, 1906, ADRFM, http://archivomagon .net/wp-content/uploads/e3n10.pdf. See also Lomnitz, *The Return of Comrade Ricardo Flores Magón*, 203, 222.

23. Letter from Ricardo Flores Magón to Bruno Treviño, August 18, 1906, NARA, RG 60, box 713, file 90755, entry 112.

24. Letter from Ricardo Flores Magón to Bruno Treviño, August 18, 1906.

25. EDTA, file 49.

26. José C. Valadés, *El joven Ricardo Flores Magón* (Mexico City: Editorial Extemporáneos, 1983), 67–77.

27. "General Instructions for Revolution," AEMEUA, LE 294, exp. 10, pp. 3–8.

28. Noam Chomsky, *On Anarchism* (New York: New Press, 2013), 19–20.

29. Letter from Ricardo Flores Magón to Antonio Balboa, September 7, 1906, STP, box 26, folder 6.

30. "Márquez Is Talkative on Junta's Plans," *San Antonio Daily Express*, December 23, 1906.

31. Juan Mora-Torres, *The Making of the Mexican Border: The State, Capitalism, and Society in Nuevo Leon, 1848–1910* (Austin: University of Texas Press, 2001), 69.

32. Arredondo's friend Dimas Domínguez played a central role in establishing the PLM *foco* in

Jiménez. William Stanley Langston, "Coahuila in el Porfiriato, 1893–1911: A Study of Political Elites," PhD dissertation, Tulane University, 1980, 195–96.

Chapter 13: THE JIMÉNEZ RAID

1. Depositions filed by Miguel Cárdenas, November 17 1906. See AEMEUA, LE 854, pp. 7–24.
2. "Story of the Jimenez Raid is Developed," *San Antonio Daily Express*, December 19, 1906.
3. "Story of the Jimenez Raid is Developed."
4. "Story of the Jimenez Raid is Developed."
5. "Deposition of the Collector of Revenue," September 29, 1906, AEMEUA, LE 854, pp. 199–207.
6. "A La Nación," as translated by Chaz Bufe in Chaz Bufe and Mitchell Cowen Verter, *Dreams of Freedom: A Ricardo Flores Magón Reader* (Oakland, CA: AK Press, 2005), 129–31. U.S. authorities also translated a copy of the proclamation for Arredondo's deportation hearing in January 1907. See AEMEUA, LE 304, exp. 8, pp. 40–67. For the original text, see AEMEUA, LE 294, exp. 10, pp. 2–3.
7. Translated copy of the proclamation available in AEMEUA, LE 304, exp. 8, pp. 59–61.
8. Hearing in the Case of Juan José Arredondo, January 6, 1906, AEMEUA, LE 304, exp. 8, pp. 40–67.
9. William Stanley Langston, "Coahuila in el Porfiriato, 1893–1911: A Study of Political Elites," PhD dissertation, Tulane University, 1980, 191–94.
10. Langston, "Coahuila in el Porfiriato," 195–96.
11. "Arredondo Tells of His Revolution," *San Antonio Daily Express*, January 1, 1907.
12. "Márquez Is Talkative on Junta Plans," *San Antonio Daily Express*, December 25, 1906.
13. "Developments Are Few in Trial for Extradition," *San Antonio Daily Express*, December 21, 1906.
14. "Bandits Take Village Near Rio Grande," *San Antonio Daily Express*, September 28, 1906.
15. Depositions filed by Miguel Cárdenas, November 17, 1906, AEMEUA, LE 854, pp. 17–24. See also certified copy of proceedings, AEMEUA, LE 854, P. 185–207.
16. W. Dirk Raat, *Revoltosos: Mexico's Rebels in the United States, 1903–1923* (College Station: Texas A & M University Press, 1981), 129.
17. PLM *focos* also launched smaller attacks on towns in Veracruz and Tamaulipas. The *focos* marshaled an estimated 1,000 fighters, but the uprisings were quickly suppressed by federal forces. See Ward S. Albro, *Always a Rebel: Ricardo Flores Magón and the Mexican Revolution* (Fort Worth: Texas Christian University Press, 1992), 63–64. See also Bufe and Verter, *Dreams of Freedom*, 52–53; James D. Cockcroft, *Intellectual Precursors of the Mexican Revolution, 1900–1913* (Austin: University of Texas Press, 1968), 148.
18. Hearing in the Case of Juan José Arredondo, January 6, 1906, AEMEUA, LE 304, exp. 8, pp. 40–67.

Chapter 14: SOMETHING UNUSUAL

1. See Philip R. Mueller, "The Mexican Liberals in St. Louis: 1905–1906," master's thesis, Southern Illinois University at Carbondale, 1983, 62–63. See also W. Dirk Raat, *Revoltosos: Mexico's Rebels in the United States, 1903–1923* (College Station: Texas A & M University Press, 1981), 133–42.
2. For more on this history, see Ahilan Arulanantham and Michael Tan, "Is It Constitutional to Lock up Immigrants Indefinitely," *ACLU: Speak Freely* blog, March 5, 2018; Kelly Lytle Hernández, *City of Inmates: Conquest, Rebellion and the Rise of Human Caging in Los Angeles, 1771–1965* (Chapel Hill: University of North Carolina Press, 2017), 64–91; Erika Lee, *At America's Gates: Chinese Immigration during the Exclusion Era, 1882–1943* (Chapel Hill: University of North Carolina Press, 2003); Mae Ngai, *Impossible Subjects: Illegal Aliens and the Making of Modern America* (Princeton: Princeton University Press, 2004).
3. Torrie Hester, "Deportability and the Carceral State," *Journal of American History* 102, no. 1

(June 2015): 141–51. See also Adam Goodman, *The Deportation Machine: America's Long History of Expelling Immigrants* (Princeton: Princeton University Press, 2020), 29.

4. Board of Special Inquiry hearings for Bruno Treviño, Carlos Humbert, and Genaro Villarreal, September 4, 1906 (Nogales, Arizona), AEMEUA, LE 1240(2), pp. 146–48.

5. Statement of Luis García before the Board of Special Inquiry, at Tucson, Arizona, September 10, 1906, AEMEUA, LE 1241, pp. 18–19.

6. Letter from George Webb to Commissioner General of Immigration, September 22, 1906, AEMEUA, LE 1241(3), pp. 172–75.

7. Letter from George Webb to Commissioner General of Immigration, September 22, 1906.

8. Letter from George Webb to Commissioner General of Immigration, September 22, 1906.

9. Letter from George Webb to Commissioner General of Immigration, September 22, 1906.

10. Letter from J. L. B. Alexander to George Webb, September 14, 1906, AEMEUA, LE 1241(2), pp. 130–31.

11. Quoted in Raat, *Revoltosos*, 140.

12. Raat, *Revoltosos*, 141–42.

13. Letter from Ramón Corral to Enrique Creel, October 9, 1906, STP, box 26, folder 7A. See also Jacinto Barrera Bassols, ed., *Correspondencia de Ricardo Flores Magón*, vol. 1, *1899–1918* (Mexico City: Consejo Nacional Para la Cultura y las Artes, 2000), 25.

14. Letter from Ramón Corral to Ignacio Mariscal, September 5, 1906, AEMEUA, LE 1240, p. 62.

15. Coded telegram from Ignacio Mariscal to Mexican Embassy in Washington, DC, September 7, 1906, AEMEUA, LE 1240, pp. 66–68.

16. Letter from Lázaro Puente to his son, September 17, 1906, AEMEUA, LE 1241(2), pp. 132–33. See also Raat, *Revoltosos*, 140.

17. "6 Mexican Agitators—From Tucson Jail—in Rurales Clutches," *Tucson Citizen*, October 4, 1906.

18. "6 Mexican Agitators."

19. "Rurales Were Waiting for the Insurgents," *Bisbee Daily Review*, October 10, 1906.

Chapter 15: The Death of Juan José Arredondo

1. "Arredondo Tells of His Revolution," *San Antonio Daily Express*, January 1, 1907.

2. Statement and Report, undated, AEMEUA, LE 854, pp. 50–52.

3. "Mexicans Are Discharged by Commissioner," *San Antonio Daily Express*, January 6, 1907.

4. Julia Padierna Peratta and Bruce Zagaris, "Mexico–United States Extradition and Alternatives: From Fugitive Slaves to Drug Traffickers—150 Years and Beyond the Rio Grande's Winding Courses," *American University International Law Review* 12, no. 4 (1997): 519–627. For recent work on enslaved persons escaping to freedom in Mexico, see Alice L. Baumgartner, *South to Freedom: Runaway Slaves to Mexico and the Road to the Civil War* (New York: Basic Books, 2020); Sarah E. Cornell, "Citizens of Nowhere: Fugitive Slaves and Free African Americans in Mexico, 1833–1857," *Journal of American History* 100, no. 2 (September 2013): 351–74; James David Nichols, *The Limits of Liberty: Mobility and the Making of the Eastern U.S.–Mexico Border* (Lincoln: University of Nebraska Press, 2018).

5. Statement and Report, undated, AEMEUA, LE 854, pp. 50–52.

6. Statement and Report, undated.

7. Telegram from Robert T. Neil to John Robinson, November 20, 1906, AEMEUA, LE 854, p. 65.

8. "Developments Are Few in Trial for Extradition," *San Antonio Daily Express*, December 21, 1906.

9. "Rodríguez Mayor of Jiménez Tells of Raid," *San Antonio Daily Express*, December 20, 1906.

10. "Arredondo Tells of His Revolution."

11. "Arredondo Tells of His Revolution."

12. "To Read Papers," *San Antonio Daily Light*, December 28, 1906.

13. "Mexicans Are Discharged by Commissioner."

14. "Members of Liberal Party Form a Junta," *San Antonio Daily Express*, January 7, 1907.

15. Telegram from Enrique Ornelas to Ignacio Mariscal, January 5, 1907, AEMEUA, LE 854, pp. 233–35.
16. Statement by Inspector Brown, January 20, 1907 (Inspector Brown's statement is incorrectly dated as 1906 in the original record), AEMEUA, LE855(2), p. 100.
17. Letter from Enrique Creel to Elihu Root, March 28, 1907, NARA, RG 60, box 713, file 90755, entry 112.
18. Letter from Francisco de P. Villasana to Enrique Creel, March 24, 1907, AEMEUA, LE 299, exp. 4, pp. 71–74.
19. Letter from Francisco de P. Villasana to Enrique Creel, March 24, 1907.
20. "Revolutionists Seek Safety in Texas," *El Paso Herald*, May 24, 1907.
21. Letter from Antonio de Pío Araujo ("Riesco") to Tomás Sarabia in San Antonio, May 24, 1907, AEMEUA, LE 299, exp. 7, p. 12.
22. Letter from Antonio de Pío Araujo ("Riesco") to Tomás Sarabia, May 19, 1907, AEMEUA, LE 299, exp. 7, p. 6.
23. Letter from Ricardo Flores Magón to Tomás Sarabia ("Henry Max Morton"), May 25, 1907, AEMEUA, LE 299, exp. 7, p. 20.
24. Letter from Ricardo Flores Magón to Tomás Sarabia ("Henry Max Morton"), May 25, 1907.
25. Letter from Aarón López Manzano to Manuel Sarabia, May 22, 1907, AEMEUA, LE 299, exp. 7, p. 32. See also letter from Tomás Sarabia to Ricardo Flores Magón, May 31, 1907, AEMEUA, LE 299, exp. 7, p. 21.

Chapter 16: THE DEAD LETTER OFFICE

1. Letter from M. E. Diebold to Enrique Creel, November 26, 1906, AEMEUA, LE 285, exp. 7, pp. 97–98. See also Claudio Lomnitz, *The Return of Comrade Ricardo Flores Magón* (New York: Zone Books, 2014), 218.
2. "Informe general del cónsul sobre revoltosos mexicanos," February 17, 1909, AEMEUA, LE 942, p. 280.
3. Kerry Seagrave, *Wiretapping and Electronic Surveillance in America, 1862–1920* (Jefferson, NC: MacFarland, 2014), 98; Andrew Thiesing, *Made in USA: East St. Louis, the Rise and Fall of an Industrial River Town* (St. Louis: Virginia Publishing, 2003); William Hunt, *America's Sherlock Holmes: The Legacy of William Burns* (Lanham, MD: Lyons Press, 2019).
4. Hunt, *America's Sherlock Holmes.*
5. Hunt, *America's Sherlock Holmes.*
6. Thomas Furlong, *Fifty Years a Detective*, facsimile of 1912 edition (Charleston, SC: Nabu Press, 2011), 138.
7. Furlong, *Fifty Years a Detective*, 148.
8. Letter from R. M. Fulton to W. L. Morsey, November 6, 1906, AEMEUA, LE 285, exp. 7, p. 57.
9. Letter from Balbino Davalos to Miguel Diebold, November 10, 1906, AEMEUA, LE 285, exp. 7, pp. 38–41.
10. Letter from Balbino Davalos to Ignacio Mariscal, November 9, 1906, AEMEUA, LE 920, pp. 143–152.
11. Winifred Gallagher, *How the Post Office Created America* (New York: Penguin, 2016); Devin Leonard, *Neither Snow nor Rain: A History of the United States Postal Service* (New York: Grove Press, 2016).
12. Gallagher, *How the Post Office Created America*, 41.
13. United States Postal Service, "First Post Offices by State," https://about.usps.com/who-we-are/postal-history/first-post-offices.pdf. For more on the U.S. Post and western expansion see Cameron Blevins, *Papers Trail: The U.S. Post and the Making of the American West* (Oxford: Oxford University Press, 2021).
14. Gallagher, *How the Post Office Created America*, 29–62, 182, 191.
15. United States Postal Service, "Texas: Dates That First Rural Routes Were Established at Post Offices Through 1904," https://about.usps.com/who-we-are/postal-history/first-rfd-texas.pdf.

16. United States Postal Service, "Arizona: Dates That First Rural Routes Were Established at Post Offices Through 1904," https://about.usps.com/who-we-are/postal-history/first-rfd-arizona.pdf.

17. Gallagher, *How the Post Office Made America*, 75–77.

18. Leonard, *Neither Snow nor Rain*, 53–58.

19. Letter from Balbino Davalos to Ignacio Mariscal, November 9, 1906, AEMEUA, LE 920, p. 149.

20. Letter from Balbino Davalos to Ignacio Mariscal, p. 150.

21. W. Dirk Raat, *Revoltosos: Mexico's Rebels in the United States, 1903–1923* (College Station: Texas A & M University Press, 1981), 126–27.

22. Letters from M. E. Diebold to Enrique Creel, November 15, 20, and 26, 1906, AEMEUA, LE 285, exp. 7, pp. 75–76, 91, 94–95. See also letter from Thomas Furlong to M. E. Diebold, November 23, 1906, AEMEUA, LE 285, exp. 7, p. 93.

23. Letter from Thomas Furlong to M. E. Diebold, November 30, 1906, AEMEUA, LE 921, p. 145; Letter from M. E. Diebold to Ignacio Mariscal, November 30, 1906, AEMEUA, LE 921, pp. 142–44. See also Jacinto Barrera Bassols, *Correspondencia de Ricardo Flores Magón*, vol. 1, *1899–1918* (Mexico City: Consejo Nacional Para la Cultura y las Artes, 2000), 39–40. For examples of seized letters from Chicago, San Antonio, and El Paso, see LE 304, exp. 8, pp. 1–4.

24. Furlong, *Fifty Years a Detective*, 139. For reference to the suitcases of letters, see Jacinto Barrera Bassols, ed., *Correspondencia de Ricardo Flores Magón*, vol. 1, *1899–1918* (Mexico City: Consejo Nacional Para la Cultura y las Artes, 2000), 27.

25. Letter from Furlong Secret Service Company to Enrique Creel, February 13, 1907, AEMEUA, LE 304, exp. 8, p. 13.

26. Letter from Tomás Sarabia to Ricardo Flores Magón, July 2, 1907, AEMEUA, LE 299, exp. 7, p. 77.

27. Letter from M. E. Diebold to Enrique Creel, November 26, 1906, AEMEUA, LE 285, exp. 7, pp. 97–98. Consul Diebold worked hard trying to crack *magonista* codes; see letter from M. E. Diebold to Enrique Creel, March 5, 1907, AEMEUA, LE 299, exp. 4, p. 8.

Chapter 17: WE KNEW HIS WHEREABOUTS CONTINUOUSLY

1. Letter from M. E. Diebold to Ignacio Mariscal, November 1, 1906, AEMEUA, LE 920, pp. 63–65.

2. Sanders report embedded in letter from Thomas Furlong to M. E. Diebold, November 10, 1906, AEMEUA, LE 920, pp. 114–16.

3. Letter from M. E. Diebold to Ignacio Mariscal, November 15, 1906, AEMEUA, LE 920, p. 168.

4. "America Is Just, Mexican Declares," *St. Louis Republic*, December 1, 1906.

5. U.S. Congress, House Committee on Rules, Providing for a Joint Committee to Investigate Alleged Persecutions of Mexican Citizens by the Government of Mexico: Hearings on H.J.R. 201, 61st Cong., 2nd Sess., 35.

6. "Four Mexicans Indicted for Alleged Libel," *St. Louis Post–Dispatch*, December 1, 1906.

7. Furlong, *Fifty Years a Detective*, facsimile of 1912 edition (Charleston, SC: Nabu Press, 2011), 144.

8. For one list of Antonio de Pío Araujo's many pseudonyms and codenames, see Furlong, *Fifty Years a Detective*, 138–39. See also, "Lista de los nombres que se menciona en parte de la correspondencia de los llamados revolucionarios," AEMEUA, LE 304, exp. 8, pp. 68–76. The list in the book/appendix is a combination of both of these sources.

9. Letter from Antonio de Pío Araujo ("Germán Riesco") to Tomás Sarabia ("Tomás Labrada"), January 25, 1907, AEMEUA, LE 923, p. 22. See also letter from Antonio de Pío Araujo ("Germán Riesco") to Tomás Sarabia ("Tomás S. Labrada"), January 26, 1907, AEMEUA, LE 299, exp. 8, pp. 17–19.

10. Letter from Antonio de Pío Araujo to Ricardo Flores Magón, February 10, 1907, AEMEUA, LE 299, exp. 8, p. 32. See also memos from José F. Godoy to department of state, November 16 and 18, 1907, AEMUEA, LE 929, pp. 340–41.

11. "Rurales Take 50 Rebels in Battle," *St. Louis Globe–Democrat*, June 28, 1908.

12. Letter from Antonio de Pío ("Germán Riesco") to Tomás Sarabia ("Tomás S. Labrada"), January 26, 1907, AEMUEA, LE 299, exp. 8, p. 19.

13. Letter from Ignacio J. Mendiola ("R. L. Braden") to Antonio Araujo ("Riesco"), February 26,

1907, AEMEUA, LE 299, exp. 8, p. 56; Letters from Pascual Rodríguez to Aniceto Moreno, February 9 and 11, 1907, LE 299, exp. 8, p. 38–39; Letter from Ignacio Mendiola to Tomás Sarabia ("T. S. Labrada"), February 19, 1907, LE 299, exp. 8, p. 44; Letter from Ignacio Mendiola to Antonio de Pío Araujo ("G. Riesco"), February 19, 1907, LE 299, exp. 8, p. 45.

14. Ricardo Flores Magón ("R. M. Caule") to Manuel Sarabia ("Chamaco"), February 20, 1907, AEMEUA, LE 299, exp. 8, p. 55.

15. Letter from Librado Rivera ("Leonel") to Tomás Sarabia ("M. A. Bassat"), April 28, 1907, AEMEUA, LE 925, pp. 37–38. See also letter from Tomás Sarabia ("Cuahtemoc"[sic]) to Antonio de Pío Araujo, May 3, 1907, AEMEUA, LE 925, p. 33–34.

16. Letter from Librado Rivera ("Leonel") to Tomás Sarabia ("M. A. Bassat"), April 28, 1907.

17. Letter from Librado Rivera ("Leonel") to Tomás Sarabia ("M. A. Bassat"), April 28, 1907.

18. Letter from Librado Rivera ("Leonel") to Tomás Sarabia ("M. A. Bassat"), April 28, 1907.

19. Letter from Conchita Rivera to Librado Rivera, July 3, 1907, AEMEUA, LE 299, exp. 7, p. 93.

20. Letter from Conchita Rivera to Librado Rivera, July 3, 1907.

21. Letter from Irenia G. Vda. de Rivera to Librado Rivera, June 20, 1907, AEMEUA, LE 299, exp. 7, pp. 93–94.

22. Letter from Irenia G. Vda. de Rivera to Librado Rivera, June 20, 1907.

23. Letter from Severa Chavez de López to Aarón López Manzano, April 9, 1907, AEMEUA, LE 925, p. 2.

24. Two letters from Aarón López Manzano ("F. Oka") to Tomás Sarabia ("Tomás S. Labrada"), April 25, 1907, AEMEUA, LE 925, pp. 12–13.

25. Letter from Aarón López Manzano to Tomás Sarabia, April 25, 1907, LE 925, p. 13.

26. Letter from Tomás Sarabia ("Henry") to Manuel Sarabia, May 5, 1907, AEMEUA, LE 925, p. 54.

27. Letter from Aarón López Manzano to Manuel Sarabia, May 22, 1907, AEMEUA, LE 299, exp. 7, p. 32.

28. Letter from Thomas Furlong to Enrique Creel, April 29, 1907, AEMEUA, LE 304, exp. 9, pp. 55–56.

29. Letter from Thomas Furlong to Enrique Creel, April 29, 1907.

30. Letter from Thomas Furlong to Enrique Creel, April 29, 1907.

31. Letter from Aarón López Manzano to Tomás Sarabia, May 22, 1907, AEMEUA, LE 299, exp. 7, p. 32.

32. Letter from Aarón López Manzano ("Martin S. Blanco") to Jesús María Rangel, June 12, 1907, AEMEUA, LE 299, exp. 7, p. 33.

Chapter 18: The Kidnapping of Manuel Sarabia

1. Report from L. C. H. (Chicago) to Thomas Furlong, January 15, 1907, AEMEUA, LE 304, exp. 8, p. 1.

2. Report from L. C. H. (Chicago) to Thomas Furlong, January 15, 1907.

3. Letter from Ignacio Mariscal to Enrique Creel, March 25, 1907, AEMEUA, LE 299, exp. 4, p. 32. Letter from Ignacio Mariscal to Enrique Creel, March 6, 1907, AEMEUA, LE 299, exp. 4, p. 14.

4. Letter from Arturo Elias to Enrique Creel, March 6, 1907, AEMEUA, LE 299, exp. 4, pp. 12–13.

5. Letter from Manuel Sarabia to Antonio de Pío Araujo, June 8, 1907, AEMEUA, LE 299, exp. 7, pp. 48–49.

6. Manuel Sarabia, "How I Was Kidnapped: part 1," *International Socialist Review* 9 (May 1909).

7. Sarabia, "How I Was Kidnapped: part 1."

8. Manuel Sarabia, "How I Was Kidnapped: part 2," *International Socialist Review* 9 (May 1909).

9. Ward S. Albro, *Always a Rebel: Ricardo Flores Magón and the Mexican Revolution* (Fort Worth: Texas Christian University Press, 1992), 83.

10. U.S. Congress, House Committee on Rules, Providing for a Joint Committee to Investigate Alleged Persecutions of Mexican Citizens by the Government of Mexico: Hearings on H.J.R.

201, 61st Cong., 2nd Sess., 8–14, 90–93. See also W. Dirk Raat, *Revoltosos: Mexico's Rebels in the United States, 1903–1923* (College Station: Texas A & M University Press, 1981), 46–47.

11. Mother Jones, *The Autobiography of Mother Jones*, edited by Mary Field Parton (Chicago: Charles Kerr, 1925), 138.

12. David M. Struthers, *The World in a City: Multiethnic Radicalism in Early Twentieth-Century Los Angeles* (Urbana: University of Illinois Press, 2019), 98–99.

13. U.S. Congress, House Committee on Rules, Providing for a Joint Committee to Investigate Alleged Persecutions of Mexican Citizens, 90–93. See also Raat, *Revoltosos*, 46–47.

14. "Denounces Douglas Affair," *El Paso Herald*, July 5, 1907.

15. "Sarabia, Member of Mexican Junta, Is Free," *St. Louis Globe–Democrat*, July 3, 1907.

16. "Returned to American Soil," *San Francisco Chronicle*, July 13, 1907.

Chapter 19: El Alma de Todo

1. "Gain the Purpose," *Galveston Daily News*, June 2, 1907.

2. "Mexican Revolution for Revenue Only," *Arizona Republican*, January 6, 1907.

3. "Mexican Consul Issues Statement," *St. Louis Globe–Democrat*, January 6, 1907.

4. Jacinto Barrera Bassols, ed., *Correspondencia de Ricardo Flores Magón*, vol. 1, *1899–1918* (Mexico City: Consejo Nacional Para la Cultura y las Artes, 2000), 28.

5. Barrera Bassols, ed., *Correspondencia*, vol. 1, 35.

6. Mark Wasserman, *Capitalists, Caciques, and Revolution: The Native Elite and Foreign Enterprise in Chihuahua, Mexico, 1854–1911* (Chapel Hill: University of North Carolina Press, 1984), 5.

7. Mark Wasserman, *Pesos and Politics: Business, Elites, Foreigners, and Government in Mexico, 1854–1940* (Palo Alto, CA: Stanford University Press, 2015), 34.

8. Wasserman, *Pesos and Politics*, 31.

9. Letter from James G. Griner to Enrique Creel, May 2, 1907, AEMEUA, LE 299, exp. 5, pp. 3–4.

10. Letter from Enrique Creel to Rodolfo Valles, October 27, 1906, STP, box 26, folder 2B.

11. Letter from Enrique Creel to Ramón Corral, October 4, 1906, STP, box 26, folder 7A.

12. Eugenio Martínez Núñez, *Juan Sarabia, apóstol y mártir de la Revolución Mexicana* (Mexico City: Biblioteca del Instituto Nacional de Estudios Históricos de la Revolución Mexicana, 1965), 89-91. See also James D. Cockcroft, *Intellectual Precursors of the Mexican Revolution, 1900–1913* (Austin: University of Texas Press, 1968), 149; Philip R. Mueller, "The Mexican Liberals in St. Louis: 1905–1906," master's thesis, Southern Illinois University at Carbondale, 1983, 61.

13. For more on the aborted Juárez raid, see W. Dirk Raat, *Revoltosos: Mexico's Rebels in the United States, 1903–1923* (College Station: Texas A & M University Press, 1981), 132–33.

14. Letter from Enrique Creel to Ramón Corral, October 30, 1906, STP, box 26, folder 7A.

15. Letter from Ricardo Flores Magón ("R. M. Caule") to Antonio Villarreal, February 13, 1907, AEMEUA, LE 294, exp. 10, pp. 14–15. See also letter from S. Montemayor to Enrique Creel, October 22, 1906, STP, box 27, folder 11B.

16. Letter from S. Montemayor to Enrique Creel, October 22, 1906.

17. Ward S. Albro, *To Die on Your Feet: The Life, Times, and Writings of Práxedis G. Guerrero* (Fort Worth: Texas Christian University, 1996), 26. See also Ward S. Albro, *Always a Rebel: Ricardo Flores Magón and the Mexican Revolution* (Fort Worth: Texas Christian University Press, 1992), 67.

18. As quoted in Albro, *Always a Rebel*, 69.

19. Quoted in Martínez Núñez, *Juan Sarabia*, ch. 6. See also Albro, *Always a Rebel*, 71.

20. Martínez Núñez, *Juan Sarabia*, ch. 7.

21. Albro, *Always a Rebel*, 73–75.

22. Albro, *Always a Rebel*, 75.

23. Martínez Núñez, *Juan Sarabia*, ch. 7. Lauro Aguirre printed and distributed a copy of Sarabia's defense speech in his El Paso-based newspaper *La Reforma Social*, available in AEMEUA, LE 299, exp. 10, pp. 1–8.

24. As translated and quoted in Claudio Lomnitz, *The Return of Comrade Ricardo Flores Magón* (New York: Zone Books, 2014), 197.

25. As quoted in Raat, *Revoltosos*, 37.
26. Raat, *Revoltosos*, 37.
27. Martínez Núñez, *Juan Sarabia*, ch. 7.
28. Telegram from Francisco Mallen to Mexican Embassy in Washington, DC, November 11, 1906, AEMEUA, LE 285, exp. 10, p. 22.
29. Quoted in Lomnitz, *The Return of Comrade Ricardo Flores Magón*, 308.
30. Letter from Francisco Mallen to Enrique Creel, November 20, 1906, STP, box 26, folder 7A.
31. Albro, *Always a Rebel*, 71.
32. Letter from Thomas Furlong to Enrique Creel, January 21, 1907, AEMEUA, LE 299, exp. 8, pp. 8–10. See also letter from Antonio Lozano to Enrique Creel, March 2, 1907, AEMEUA, LE 295, exp. 1, pp. 79–80.
33. Letter from Thomas Furlong to Enrique Creel, January 21, 1907.
34. Letter from Thomas Furlong to Enrique Creel, January 21, 1907.
35. Letter from Thomas Furlong to Enrique Creel, January 21, 1907.
36. Letter from Thomas Furlong to Enrique Creel, January 21, 1907.
37. Letter from Thomas Furlong to Enrique Creel, January 21, 1907.
38. Letter from Manuel Sarabia ("Sam Moret") to Tomás Sarabia ("Tomás Labrada"), January 24, 1907, AEMEUA, LE 299, exp. 8, p. 17.
39. Ethel Duffy Turner, *Ricardo Flores Magón y el Partido Liberal Mexicano* (Mexico City: Comisión Nacional Editorial, 1984), 114.
40. Letter from Manuel Sarabia ("Sam Moret") to Tomás Sarabia ("Tomás Labrada"), January 24, 1907.
41. Quoted in Lomnitz, *The Return of Comrade Ricardo Flores Magón*, 198.
42. Letter from Ricardo Flores Magón ("R. M. Caule") to Antonio Villarreal, February 13, 1907, AEMEUA, LE 294, exp. 10, pp. 14–15.
43. Letter from Ricardo Flores Magón ("R. M. Caule") to Manuel Sarabia ("Sam Moret"), March 25, 1907, AEMEUA, LE 299, exp. 8, pp. 151–52.
44. Letter from Ricardo Flores Magón to Manuel Sarabia, March 25, 1907.
45. Letter from Ricardo Flores Magón to Manuel Sarabia, March 25, 1907.
46. Letter from Ricardo Flores Magón to Ignacio J. Mendiola, June 12, 1907, AEMEUA, LE 925, p. 191.
47. William David Estrada, *The Los Angeles Plaza: Sacred and Contested Space* (Austin: University of Texas Press, 2008); George Sanchez, *Becoming Mexican American: Ethnicity, Culture, and Identity in Chicano Los Angeles, 1900–1945* (New York: Oxford University Press, 1993); David M. Struthers, *The World in a City: Multiethnic Radicalism in Early Twentieth-Century Los Angeles* (Urbana: University of Illinois Press, 2019); Mark Wild, *Street Meeting: Multiethnic Neighborhoods in Early Twentieth-Century Los Angeles* (Berkeley: University of California Press, 2005).
48. Letter from Antonio Lozano to Ignacio Mariscal, July 27, 1907, AEMEUA, LE 927, pp. 2–5, and letter from Antonio Lozano to Ignacio Mariscal, August 10, 1907, AEMEUA, LE 927, pp. 109–11; "agente secreto" is in a letter from Antonio Lozano to Ignacio Mariscal, November 20, 1907, AEMEUA, LE 929, p. 378.
49. Letter from Ricardo Flores Magón to D. Eulalio Trevino, July 17, 1907, AEMEUA, LE 299, exp. 7, p. 110.
50. Letter from Antonio de Pío Araujo to Ricardo Flores Magón, August 2, 1907, AEMEUA, LE 299, exp. 7, p. 129.
51. Letter from Tomás Sarabia ("Henry") to Manuel Sarabia, August 6, 1907, AEMEUA, LE 299, exp. 7, p. 130.
52. Letter from Tomás Sarabia ("Henry") to Manuel Sarabia, August 6, 1907.
53. Ángeles Mendieta Alatorre, *La mujer en la Revolución Mexicana* (Mexico City: Instituto Nacional de Estudios Históricos de la Revolución Mexicana, 1961).
54. Quoted in "Murder Plotting Letters Found on the Mexican Revolutionists," *Los Angeles Times*, September 19, 1907.
55. Lomnitz, *The Return of Comrade Ricardo Flores Magón*, 228.

56. Letter from María Brousse to Ricardo Flores Magón, September 17, 1908, ADRFM, http://archivomagon.net/obras-completas/correspondencia-1899-1922/c-1908/cor267/.

57. Letter from Lucia Norman to Ricardo Flores Magón, September 25, 1908, ADRFM, http://archivomagon.net/obras-completas/correspondencia-1899-1922/c-1908/cor269/.

58. "Nip Revolutionists in Los Angeles Den," *Los Angeles Times*, August 24, 1907.

59. Coded telegram from M. E. Diebold to Enrique Creel, August 21, 1907, AEMEUA, LE 927, pp. 94–95.

60. "Makes Heroes of the Accused," *Los Angeles Times*, August 27, 1907.

61. Letter from Antonio Lozano to Ignacio Mariscal, August 12, 1907, AEMEUA, LE 927, p. 91.

62. Thomas Furlong, *Fifty Years a Detective* (St. Louis, 1912), facsimile of 1912 edition (Charleston, SC: Nabu Press, 2011), 143. See also Colin M. MacLachlan, *Anarchism and the Mexican Revolution: The Political Trials of Ricardo Flores Magón in the United States* (Berkeley: University of California Press, 1991), 20.

63. "Nip Revolutionists in Los Angeles Den."

64. Quoted in Nicole Guidotti-Hernández, *Archiving Mexican Masculinities in Diaspora* (Durham, NC: Duke University Press, 2021), 49.

65. "Nip Revolutionists in Los Angeles Den."

66. "Información secreta que use el agente N. N. de St. Louis, Missouri, le dio al suscrito contestando al siguiente interrogatorio," STP, box 26, folder 7A. See also José C. Valadés, *El joven Ricardo Flores Magón* (Mexico City: Editorial Extemporáneos, 1983), 51.

67. Cockcroft, *Intellectual Precursors*, 24.

68. Jessica Kim, *Imperial Metropolis: Los Angeles, Mexico, and the Borderlands of American Empire, 1865–1941* (Chapel Hill: University of North Carolina Press, 2019), 70.

69. "Fairygarden for Diners," *Los Angeles Times*, August 30, 1907.

70. "Fairygarden for Diners."

71. "Senor Creel in Honored," *Los Angeles Herald*, August 30, 1907.

Chapter 20: THE UNITED STATES VS. RICARDO FLORES MAGÓN

1. Job Harriman, "How I Became a Socialist," *Comrade* 8, no. 1 (May 1902): 170.

2. Harriman, "How I Became a Socialist," 170.

3. Errol Wayne Stevens, "Two Radicals and Their Los Angeles: Harrison Gray Otis and Job Harriman," *California History* 86, no. 3 (2009): 44–64, 69–70.

4. Stevens, "Two Radicals."

5. Letter from Consul Lozano to Enrique Creel, March 2, 1907, AEMEUA, LE 295, exp. 1, pp. 79–80.

6. "Makes Heroes of the Accused," *Los Angeles Times*, August 27, 1907.

7. "Partido Socialista Internacional," *Revolución*, September 14, 1907.

8. "Fighting for Their Liberty," *Los Angeles Times*, August 29, 1907.

9. "Liberty Denied Them," *Los Angeles Times*, August 30, 1907.

10. Letter from José Godoy to Ignacio Mariscal, August 29, 1907, AEMEUA, LE 927, pp. 275–76.

11. Letter from Oscar Lawler to Charles Bonaparte, September 12, 1907, NARA, RG 60, box 713, file 90755, entry 112.

12. "Las intrigas de Porfirio," *Revolución*, September 21, 1907.

13. Letter from Enrique Creel to John Foster, March 4, 1907, AEMEUA, LE 299, exp. 4, p. 27.

14. Letter from Ignacio Mariscal to Enrique Creel, March 21, 1907, AEMEUA, LE 299, exp. 4, pp. 58–59.

15. Letter from Enrique Creel to Elihu Root, March 6, 1907, LE 299, exp. 4, pp. 22–31.

16. Letter from Elihu Root to Charles Bonaparte, April 11, 1907, NARA, RG 60, box 713, file 90755, entry 112.

17. Letter from Charles Bonaparte to Charles Boynton, April 13, 1907, NARA, RG 60, box 713, file 90755, entry 112.

18. Letter from Oscar Lawler to Charles Bonaparte, September 12, 1907, NARA, RG 60, box 713, file 90755, entry 112.
19. José C. Valadés, *El joven Ricardo Flores Magón* (Mexico City: Editorial Extemporáneos, 1983), 84.
20. Letter from Donald Barker to Enrique Creel, September 21, 1907, AEMEUA, LE 929, pp. 268.2–71. See also letter from Donald Barker to Enrique Creel, October 17, 1907, AEMEUA, LE 929, pp. 268-268.1.
21. Letter from Oscar Lawler to Charles Bonaparte, September 12, 1907, NARA, RG 60, box 713, file 90755, entry 112.
22. "Excitable Mob Cheers Reds," *Los Angeles Times*, October 17, 1907.
23. Letter from Enrique Creel to J. L. B. Alexander, September 3, 1907, NARA, RG 60, box 713, file 90755, entry 112.
24. Letter from Ricardo Flores Magón to Gabriel Rubio, July 27, 1906, NARA, RG 60, box 713, file 90755, entry 112.
25. Letter from J. L. B. Alexander to Charles Bonaparte, September 10, 1907, NARA, RG 60, box 713, file 90755, entry 112.
26. Letter from Donald Barker to Enrique Creel, September 21, 907, AEMEUA, LE 929, pp. 268.2–71.
27. Letter from Enrique Creel to J. L. B. Alexander, September 3, 1907, NARA, RG 60, box 713, file 90755, entry 112.
28. Letter from Antonio Lozano to Ignacio Mariscal, December 3, 1907, AEMEUA, LE 304, exp. 11, pp. 23–25.
29. Letter from Ricardo Flores Magón to María Brousse, September 20, 1908, ADRFM, http://archivomagon.net/obras-completas/correspondencia-1899-1922/c-1908/cor268/.
30. As quoted in Ward S. Albro, *Always a Rebel: Ricardo Flores Magón and the Mexican Revolution* (Fort Worth: Texas Christian University Press, 1992), 95.
31. Quoted in Andrew Grant Wood, "The Death of a Political Prisoner: Revisiting the Case of Ricardo Flores Magón," *A Contracorriente: una revista de estudios latinoamericanos* 3, no. 1 (2005): 44.
32. Letter and receipt from Arturo Elias to Ignacio Mariscal, March 10, 1910, AEMEUA, LE 952, pp. 116–18.
33. Quoted in Wood, "Death of a Political Prisoner," 45.
34. Wood, "Death of a Political Prisoner," 45.

Chapter 21: The People's Cause

1. Eugenio Martínez Núñez, *La vida heroica de Práxedis G. Guerrero* (Mexico City: Biblioteca del Instituto Nacional de Estudios Históricos de la Revolución Mexicana, 1960), 31–36.
2. Quoted in Ward S. Albro, *Always a Rebel: Ricardo Flores Magón and the Mexican Revolution* (Fort Worth: Texas Christian University Press, 1992), 53.
3. For more on Manuel Vázquez and his travels with Guerrero, see *Weaving the Past: Journey of Discovery*, documentary film, dir. Walter Dominguez, 2014.
4. Quoted in Ward S. Albro, *To Die on Your Feet: The Life, Times and Writings of Práxedis G. Guerrero* (Fort Worth: Texas Christian University Press, 1996), 13.
5. Claudio Lomnitz, *The Return of Comrade Ricardo Flores Magón* (New York: Zone Books, 2014), 258.
6. As translated by Albro in *To Die on Your Feet*, 13. See also Martínez Núñez, *La vida heroica de Práxedis G. Guerrero*, 40.
7. As translated by Albro in *To Die on Your Feet*, 13.
8. Martínez Núñez, *La vida heroica de Práxedis G. Guerrero*, 42.
9. Quoted in Albro, *To Die on Your Feet*, 33.
10. Letter from Ysidro Romero to Ignacio Mariscal, September 12, 1906, AEMEUA, LE 1241, pp. 26–27.
11. Albro, *To Die on Your Feet*, 30.
12. Letter from Ricardo Flores Magón to Práxedis Guerrero, July 14, 1906, ADRFM, http://archivomagon.net/obras-completas/correspondencia-1899-1922/c-1906/cor89/.
13. Martínez Núñez, *La vida heroica de Práxedis G. Guerrero*, 84. See also letter from Ricardo Flores

Magón to Práxedis G. Guerrero, September 6, 1906, ADRFM, http://archivomagon.net/obras
-completas/correspondencia-1899-1922/c-1906/cor111/.

14. David Poole, "The Anarchists and the Mexican Revolution, Part 2: Práxedis Guerrero (1882–
1910)," *Anarchist Review* 4 (1978): 3.

15. Devra Anne Weber, "Wobblies of the Partido Liberal Mexicano: Reenvisioning Internationalist
and Transnational Movements through Mexican Lenses," *Pacific Historical Review* 85, no. 2
(2016): 188–226.

16. Henry Huntington was Collis Huntington's nephew and inherited his rail system in Los Angeles. See Charles Wollenberg, "Working on El Traque: The Pacific Electric Strike of 1903,"
Pacific Historical Review 42, no. 3 (August 1973): 358–69.

17. Quoted in Wollenberg, "Working on el Traque," 365.

18. David M. Struthers, *The World in a City: Multiethnic Radicalism in Early Twentieth-Century Los
Angeles* (Urbana: University of Illinois Press, 2019), 74.

19. There is an extensive historiography of Mexican labor and labor organizing in the United States.
The following texts are focused on the Los Angeles area during the early twentieth century:
William David Estrada, *The Los Angeles Plaza: Sacred and Contested Space* (Austin: University
of Texas Press, 2008); Matt Garcia, *A World of Its Own: Race, Labor, and Citrus in the Making of
Greater Los Angeles, 1900–1970* (Chapel Hill: University of North Carolina Press, 2001); Vicki
Ruiz, *Cannery Women, Cannery Lives: Mexican Women, Unionization, and the California Food
Processing Industry, 1930–1950* (Albuquerque: University of New Mexico Press, 1987); Devra
Anne Weber, *Dark Sweat, White Gold: California Farm Workers, Cotton, and the New Deal*
(Berkeley: University of California Press, 1994).

20. Struthers, *The World in a City*, 44. See also Nicolás Kanellos, "Spanish Language Anarchist
Periodicals in the Early Twentieth Century United States," in *Protest on the Page: Essays on Print
and the Culture of Dissent Since 1865*, edited by James L. Baughman, James P. Danky, and Jennifer Ratner-Rosenhagen (Madison: University of Wisconsin Press, 2015), 59–84.

21. Quoted in Nicole Guidotti-Hernández, *Archiving Mexican Masculinities in Diaspora* (Durham,
NC: Duke University Press, 2021), 58.

22. Guidotti-Hernández, *Archiving Mexican Masculinities*, 49.

23. Guidotti-Hernández, *Archiving Mexican Masculinities*, 49–50.

24. Quoted in Guidotti-Hernández, *Archiving Mexican Masculinities*, 57.

25. For more on the early partnership between Paula Carmona and Enrique Flores Magón, see
Guidotti-Hernández, *Archiving Mexican Masculinities*, 49–64.

26. John Kenneth Turner, *Barbarous Mexico* (Chicago: H. Kerr, 1911), 9–11.

27. For more on John Murray, see W. Dirk Raat, *Revoltosos: Mexico's Rebels in the United States,
1903–1923* (College Station: Texas A & M University Press, 1981), 49; Lomnitz, *The Return of
Comrade Ricardo Flores Magón*, 26–28; Struthers, *The World in a City*, 68, 72–74.

28. Quoted in Lomnitz, *The Return of Comrade Ricardo Flores Magón*, 30.

29. Lomnitz, *The Return of Comrade Ricardo Flores Magón*, 30.

30. Patricia Loughlin, "In Search of Capable Allies: Frances Nacke Noel and Women's Labor
Activism in Los Angeles," *Southern California Quarterly* 82, no. 1 (2000): 61–74.

31. Lomnitz, *The Return of Comrade Ricardo Flores Magón*, xli–xlii.

32. Ethel Duffy Turner, *Ricardo Flores Magón y el Partido Liberal Mexicano* (Mexico City: Comisión
Nacional Editorial, 1984), 151.

33. Duffy Turner, *Ricardo Flores Magón*, 145.

34. Quoted in Lomnitz, *The Return of Comrade Ricardo Flores Magón*, 20–21.

35. Quoted in Lomnitz, *The Return of Comrade Ricardo Flores Magón*, 21.

36. Money for guns: Lomnitz, *The Return of Comrade Ricardo Flores Magón*, 142.

37. Duffy Turner, *Ricardo Flores Magón*, 151.

38. Letter from Tomás Sarabia to Manuel Sarabia, September 9, 1907, AEMEUA, LE 299, exp. 7,
pp. 164–65.

39. Lomnitz, *The Return of Comrade Ricardo Flores Magón*, 72.

40. Práxedis G. Guerrero, *I am Action: Literary and Combat Articles, Thought, and Revolutionary
Chronicles*, translated by Javier Sethness-Castro (Chico, CA: AK Press, 2018), 143.

41. Duffy Turner, *Ricardo Flores Magón*, 152.
42. Guerrero, *I am Action*, 24.
43. EDTA, file 59.
44. Letter from Donald Barker to Antonio Lozano, November 18, 1907, AEMEUA, LE 929, pp. 348–348.1.
45. *Revolución*, October 12, 1907.
46. EDTA, file 59. See also "His Bombast Evaporated," *Los Angeles Times*, January 9, 1908, and "Trying to Free de Lara: Habeas Corpus Proceedings in Behalf of Mexican Revolutionist—New Complaint May Be Filed," *Los Angeles Times*, December 24, 1907.
47. "Ink Slinging Leads to Jail," *Los Angeles Times*, January 15, 1908.
48. Albro, *To Die on Your Feet*, 35–37.
49. Jacinto Barrera Bassols, ed., *Correspondencia de Ricardo Flores Magón*, vol. 1, *1899–1918* (Mexico City: Consejo Nacional Para la Cultura y las Artes, 2000), 42–43.
50. Letter from Ricardo Flores Magón to María Brousse, October 11, 1908, ADRFM, http://archivomagon.net/obras-completas/correspondencia-1899-1922/c-1908/cor272/. This translation is from Nathan Kahn Ellstrand, "Las Anarquistas: The History of Two Women of the Partido Liberal Mexicano in Early 20th Century Los Angeles," master's thesis, University of California, San Diego, 2011, 25.
51. Letter from Ricardo Flores Magón to María Brousse, September 25, 1908, ADRFM, http://archivomagon.net/obras-completas/correspondencia-1899-1922/c-1908/cor269/. This translation is from Ellstrand, "Las Anarquistas," 25.
52. Letter from Ricardo Flores Magón to María Brousse, September 25, 1908.
53. Letter from Lucia Norman to Ricardo Flores Magón, September 17, 1908, ADRFM, http://archivomagon.net/obras-completas/correspondencia-1899-1922/c-1908/cor267/. See also Kelly Lytle Hernández, *City of Inmates: Conquest, Rebellion and the Rise of Human Caging in Los Angeles, 1771–1965* (Chapel Hill: University of North Carolina Press, 2017), 123.
54. Duffy Turner, *Ricardo Flores Magón*, 157. See also Ethel Duffy Turner, "Writers and Revolutionaries," interview conducted by Ruth Tieser for the University of California, Berkeley, 1967, 70–71, Bancroft Library Oral History Center, University of California, Berkeley, 111–12. Available at https://californiarevealed.org/islandora/object/cavpp%3A13349. For more on the life of Ethel Duffy Turner see, Rosario Margarita Vasquez Montaño, "Ethel Duffy Turner: una biografía política e intelectual desde la frontera, 1885–1969," PhD dissertation, El Colegio de México, 2019.
55. Duffy Turner, *Ricardo Flores Magón*, 158.

Chapter 22: AN ATTEMPT TO PRECIPITATE A GENERAL DISTURBANCE

1. Práxedis Guerrero, "Viesca," *Regeneración*, September 17, 1910. As translated in Práxedis G. Guerrero, *I am Action: Literary and Combat Articles, Thought, and Revolutionary Chronicles*, translated by Javier Sethness-Castro (Chico, CA: AK Press, 2018), 129. Available at ADRFM, http://archivomagon.net/wp-content/uploads/e4n3.pdf. See also "The Death of Heroes," *Regeneración*, September 3, 1910, ADRFM, http://archivomagon.net/wp-content/uploads/e4n1.pdf.
2. Guerrero, "Viesca."
3. Guerrero, "Viesca."
4. Eugenio Martínez Núñez, *La vida heroica de Práxedis G. Guerrero* (Mexico City: Biblioteca del Instituto Nacional de Estudios Históricos de la Revolución Mexicana, 1960), 140.
5. Martínez Núñez, *La vida heroica de Práxedis G. Guerrero*, 134–35.
6. "Attack by Bandits Is Determined" *[San Antonio?] Daily Express*, June 27, 1908, clipping in AEMEUA, LE935; Letter from David Thompson to U.S. Secretary of State, June 26, 1908, NARA, RG 59, 8183, part 1.
7. "Revolutionary movements": letter from Alvin Aldee to President Theodore Roosevelt, June 29, 1908; "an attempt to precipitate a general disturbance": memo from David Thompson to U.S.

Secretary of State, June 26, 1908, and letter from Acting Attorney General Hoyt to U.S. Secretary of State, June 27, 1908. All in NARA, RG 59, 8183, part 1.

8. "Díaz will Kill Mexican Rebels; Troops Amassing," *St. Louis Republic*, June 28, 1908.

9. Unsigned telegram, likely from A. V. Lomelí to Ignacio Mariscal, June 18, 1908, AEMEUA, LE 935, p. 1.

10. Jacinto Barrera Bassols, ed., *Correspondencia de Ricardo Flores Magón*, vol. 1, *1899–1918* (Mexico City: Consejo Nacional Para la Cultura y las Artes, 2000), 43.

11. Letter from Leocadio Treviño to Sr. N., June 24, 1908, AEMEUA, LE 935, p. 94.

12. Práxedis Guerrero, "Las Vacas," *Regeneración*, September 10, 1910, ADRFM, http://archivomagon.net/wp-content/uploads/e4n2.pdf. As translated in Guerrero, *I am Action*, 123.

13. Guerrero, "Las Vacas," in *I am Action*, 124.

14. Guerrero, "Las Vacas," in *I am Action*, 122.

15. Guerrero, "Las Vacas," in *I am Action*, 125.

16. "Jiminez [sic] Is Captured by the Insurgents: Mexico Border Appears to Be Ablaze with a Formidable Revolution," *Houston Chronicle and Herald*, June 28, 1908.

17. "Scores Killed in Battles in North Mexico," *St. Louis Post–Dispatch*, June 28, 1908.

18. "Outbreak Will Be Serious," *San Antonio Daily Express*, June 29, 1908.

19. "Troops Arrive in C. P. Díaz," *San Antonio Daily Express*, June 28, 1908.

20. Telegram from Wilbur J. Carr to Luther T. Ellsworth, June 30, 1908, NARA, RG 84, vol. 29.

21. "Rebels Alarm the Mexican Government," *San Francisco Call*, June 28, 1908.

22. Guerrero, "Las Vacas," in *I am Action*, 122–28.

23. Práxedis Guerrero, "Palomas," *Regeneración*, September 10, 1910, ADRFM, http://archivomagon.net/wp-content/uploads/e4n2.pdf. As translated in Guerrero, *I am Action*, 133–36.

24. Guerrero, "Palomas."

25. Guerrero, "Palomas."

Chapter 23: The Bureau of Investigation

1. For more on the early history of the FBI, see Rhodri Jeffreys-Jones, *The FBI: A History* (New Haven: Yale University Press, 2007); Willard M. Oliver, *The Birth of the FBI: Teddy Roosevelt, the Secret Service, and the Fight over America's Premier Law Enforcement Agency* (Lanham, MD: Rowman and Littlefield, 2019), 171; Tim Weiner, *Enemies: A History of the FBI* (New York: Random House, 2013), 10–12.

2. Oliver, *Birth of the FBI*, 153.

3. For more on Napoleon I and the modern police state, see Michael Sibalis, "The Napoleonic Police State," in *Napoleon and Europe*, edited by Philip G. Dwyer (London: Routledge, 2001), 79–94.

4. The Bureau began with nine "permanently hired" agents." See Oliver, *Birth of the FBI*, 171–72. For the hiring of agents by the Bureau of Investigation to work what they called the "neutrality cases," see memos from Charles Bonaparte to Secretary of State, July 7 and 27, 1908, and letter from Luther T. Ellsworth to Assistant Secretary of State, August 14, 1908, both in NARA, RG 59, file 8183, part 1. For record of Special Agent Donaghy, see letter from U.S. Attorney Charles Boynton to Charles Bonaparte, April 23, 1909, NARA, RG 60, box 713, file 90755, entry 112.

5. In 1909, Priest provided the Secretary of State with an extensive review of his work on the neutrality cases since July 1908. See letter from Joseph Priest to U.S. Secretary of State, enclosed in dispatch from Luther T. Ellsworth to Assistant Secretary of State, September 30, 1909, NARA, RG 84, vol. 29.

6. Letter from Joseph Priest to U.S. Secretary of State, enclosed in Ellsworth dispatch.

7. Letter from Joseph Priest to U.S. Secretary of State, enclosed in Ellsworth dispatch.

8. "Revolutionary Attitude Shown in Guerra's Capture," *San Antonio Express*, December 1, 1908.

9. Letter from Joseph Priest to U.S. Secretary of State, enclosed in Ellsworth dispatch.

10. "Confesses Plot to Overthrow Díaz Government," *San Antonio Daily Express*, October 3, 1908; for Priest's account of the arrest of Calixto Guerra, see letter from Joseph Priest to U.S. Secretary of State, enclosed in Ellsworth dispatch.

11. "Capture of Colonel Rangel and Thomas Sarabia," letter from Luther T. Ellsworth to Assistant Secretary of State, August 11, 1909, NARA, RG 84, vol. 29.

12. Statement of Tomás Sarabia, October 8, 1909, NARA, RG 84, vol. 29.

13. "Stored Arms Are Taken by Officers," clipping from unnamed San Antonio newspaper sent from Luther Ellsworth to Assistant Secretary of State, August 11, 1909, NARA, RG 84, vol. 29.

14. Letter from Enrique Creel to Secretary of State, July 11, 1908, NARA, RG 59, 8183, part 1.

15. Albro, *To Die on Your Feet*, 48; Letter from Arturo Elias to Ignacio Mariscal July 29, 1908, AEMEUA, LE 939, pp. 78–81.

16. Práxedis Guerrero, "Revolutionary Women," *Regeneración*, January 11, 1913, ADRFM, http://archivomagon.net/wp-content/uploads/e4n123.pdf. As translated in Práxedis G. Guerrero, *I am Action: Literary and Combat Articles, Thought, and Revolutionary Chronicles*, translated by Javier Sethness-Castro (Chico, CA: AK Press, 2018), 108–9.

17. Letter from Arturo Elias to Ignacio Mariscal, July 29, 1908, AEMEUA, LE 938, pp. 78–81.

18. Manifesto by Práxedis Guerrero, published in *La Estrella* in August 1909 by Club Leona Vicario of San Antonio, NARA, RG 84, vol. 29.

19. Quoted in Albro, *To Die on Your Feet*, 53. See also Eugenio Martínez Núñez, *La vida heróica de Práxedis G. Guerrero* (Mexico City: Biblioteca del Instituto Nacional de Estudios Históricos de la Revolución Mexicana, 1960), 173–74.

20. Práxedis Guerrero, "Palomas," *Regeneración*, September 10, 1910, ADRFM, http://archivomagon.net/wp-content/uploads/e4n2.pdf. As translated in Guerrero, *I am Action*, 133–36.

21. Martínez Núñez, *La vida heróica de Práxedis Guerrero*, 52.

22. Quoted in Claudio Lomnitz, *The Return of Comrade Ricardo Flores Magón* (New York: Zone Books, 2014), 259.

23. Martínez Núñez, *La vida heroica de Práxedis Guerrero*, 53.

24. Martínez Núñez, *La vida heroica de Práxedis Guerrero*, 55.

25. Práxedis Guerrero, "Beggar," *Punto Rojo*, August 29, 1909. As translated in Guerrero, *I Am Action*, 30.

26. Guerrero, *I Am Action*, 113.

27. Guerrero, *I Am Action*, 115.

28. Letter from A. V. Lomelí to Ignacio Mariscal, August 16, 1909, AEMEUA, LE 947, pp. 335–36.

29. Letter from Charles Boynton to Charles Bonaparte, April 23, 1909, NARA, RG 60, box 713, file 90755, entry 112. "Leader of Mexican revolutionists": Letter from Luther T. Ellsworth to Assistant Secretary of State, September 30, 1909, NARA, RG 84, vol. 29.

30. Letter from Manuel Cuesta to Ignacio Mariscal, July 29, 1909, AEMEUA, LE 947, p. 282.

31. For more on Ellsworth's career and character, see Dorothy Pierson Kerig, *Luther T. Ellsworth: U.S. Consul on the Border during the Mexican Revolution* (El Paso: Texas Western Press of the University of Texas at El Paso, 1975).

32. Letter from Luther T. Ellsworth to Assistant Secretary of State, August 3, 1908, NARA, RG 84, vol. 29.

33. Letter from Luther T. Ellsworth to Assistant Secretary of State, August 3, 1908. See also Kerig, *Luther T. Ellsworth*, 20; Letter from Luther T. Ellsworth to Assistant Secretary of State, June 30, 1908, NARA, RG 59, Roll 594, 8183.

34. Telegram from Luther T. Ellsworth to Stanley Finch, November 16, 1909, NARA, RG 84, vol. 33.

35. Telegram from Luther T. Ellsworth to Stanley Finch, November 18, 1909, NARA, RG 84, vol. 33.

36. Telegram from Stanley Finch to Luther T. Ellsworth, November 22, 1909, NARA, RG 84, vol. 33.

37. Letter from Práxedis Guerrero to M. L. Escamilla, January 2, 1910, AEMEUA, LE 952, p. 122.

38. "Sarabia to Go Before Federal Grand Jury," *San Antonio Express*, September 1, 1909.

39. Enclosure in a letter from Luther T. Ellsworth to Assistant Secretary of State, March 19, 1910, NARA, RG 60, box 713, file 90755, entry 112.

40. "Sarabia to Go Before Federal Grand Jury."
41. Quoted in Albro, *To Die on Your Feet*, 57.
42. Quoted in Albro, *To Die on Your Feet*, 58.
43. Quoted in Albro, *To Die on Your Feet*, 58. See also Martínez Nuúñez, *La vida heroica de Práxedis G. Guerrero*, 183–84.
44. Albro, *To Die on Your Feet*, 59.
45. Letter from Luther T. Ellsworth to Assistant Secretary of State, March 17, 1910, NARA, RG 60, box 713, file 90755, entry 112.
46. Letter from Práxedis Guerrero ("P. L. Mexicano") to "Compañeros," January 1, 1910, AEMEUA, LE 952, p. 68.

Chapter 24: A Tremendous Shock to the American People

1. Mark Wasserman, *Pesos and Politics: Business, Elites, Foreigners, and Government in Mexico, 1854–1940* (Palo Alto, CA: Stanford University Press, 2015), 1–30.
2. John Mason Hart, *Empire and Revolution: The Americans in Mexico since the Civil War* (Berkeley: University of California Press, 2002), 156–57. See also Frank McLynn, *Villa and Zapata: A History of the Mexican Revolution* (New York: Carroll & Graf, 2000), 23.
3. Wasserman, *Pesos and Politics*, 132.
4. Wasserman, *Pesos and Politics*, 17.
5. Eric Rutkow, *The Longest Line on the Map: The United States, the Pan-American Highway, and the Quest to Link the Americas* (New York: Scribner, 2019), 114–17.
6. McLynn, *Villa and Zapata*, 23.
7. McLynn, *Villa and Zapata*, 23.
8. William Schell, Jr., *Integral Outsiders: The American Colony in Mexico City, 1876–1911* (Wilmington, DE: Scholarly Resources, 2001), 151.
9. James Creelman, "President Díaz: Hero of the Americas," *Pearson's Magazine* 19, no. 3 (March 1908).
10. "President Díaz Makes Statement on Rumors of Coming Candidacy," *Mexican Herald*, October 28, 1908.
11. "President Díaz Makes Statement on Rumors of Coming Candidacy."
12. Quoted in Alan Knight, *The Mexican Revolution: Porfirians, Liberals, and Peasants*, vol. 1 (Lincoln: University of Nebraska Press, 1986), 48.
13. Knight, *The Mexican Revolution*, vol. 1, 49.
14. Jesús Luna, "The Public Career of Don Ramón Corral," PhD dissertation, North Texas State University, 1973.
15. Knight, *The Mexican Revolution*, vol. 1, 59.
16. Quoted in Enrique Krauze, *Mexico: Biography of Power: A History of Modern Mexico, 1810–1996* (New York: HarperCollins, 1998), 251.
17. McLynn, *Villa and Zapata*, 28.
18. Quoted in Krauze, *Mexico: Biography of Power*, 251.
19. Knight, *The Mexican Revolution*, vol. 1, 74.
20. Knight, *The Mexican Revolution*, vol. 1, 75.
21. Knight, *The Mexican Revolution*, vol. 1, 75.
22. Quoted in Claudio Lomnitz, *The Return of Comrade Ricardo Flores Magón* (New York: Zone Books, 2014), 255.
23. John Kenneth Turner, *Barbarous Mexico* (Chicago: H. Kerr, 1911), 11.
24. Turner, *Barbarous Mexico*, 11.
25. Turner, *Barbarous Mexico*, 11.
26. Turner, *Barbarous Mexico*, 11.
27. John Kenneth Turner, "Slaves of the Yucatán," *American Magazine* 68 (October 1909).
28. Turner, *Barbarous Mexico*, 37.

29. Turner, "Slaves of the Yucatán."
30. Quoted in Shelley Streeby, *Radical Sensations: World Movements, Violence, and Visual Culture* (Durham, NC: Duke University Press, 2013), 119.
31. Lomnitz, *The Return of Ricardo Flores Magón*, 121.
32. The comparison to *Uncle Tom's Cabin* is in Streeby, *Radical Sensations*, 132–33. Claudio Lomnitz found that "the writer Ernest Gruening compared [*Barbarous Mexico*] to Thomas Paine's writings on the American Revolution"; see Lomnitz, *The Return of Comrade Ricardo Flores Magón*, xli.
33. U.S. Congress, House Committee on Rules, Providing for a Joint Committee to Investigate Alleged Persecutions of Mexican Citizens by the Government of Mexico: Hearings on H.J.R. 201, 61st Cong., 2nd Sess., 89.
34. U.S. Congress, House Committee on Rules, Providing for a Joint Committee to Investigate Alleged Persecutions of Mexican Citizens, 49.
35. Mother Jones, Testimony before the House Committee on Rules, Joint Resolution 201, Providing for a Joint Committee to Investigate Alleged Persecutions of Mexican Citizens by the Government of Mexico: Hearings [61st Cong., 2nd Sess.]," in *Mother Jones Speaks: Collected Writings and Speeches*, edited by Philip Foner (New York: Monad Press, 1983), 370–72.
36. "How We Pull Diaz's Chestnuts Out of the Fire," *New York Times*, August 7, 1910. For an analysis of the *New York Times* as an elite publication catering to the Wall Street investor class, see Michael Schudson, *Discovering the News: A Social History of American Newspapers* (New York: Basic Books, 1978).
37. EDTA, file 191.
38. Quoted in Lomnitz, *The Return of Comrade Ricardo Flores Magón*, 296.
39. EDTA, file 191.
40. Ethel Duffy Turner, *Ricardo Flores Magón y el Partido Liberal Mexicano* (Mexico City: Comisión Nacional Editorial, 1984), 205.
41. Práxedis Guerrero, "Something More," *Regeneración*, September 3, 1910, ADRFM, http://archivomagon.net/wp-content/uploads/e4n1.pdf. As translated in Práxedis G. Guerrero, *I am Action: Literary and Combat Articles, Thought, and Revolutionary Chronicles*, translated by Javier Sethness-Castro (Chico, CA: AK Press, 2018), 45.
42. Guerrero, "Something More," 46–47.
43. Guerrero, "Something More, 47–48."
44. Guerrero, "Something More, 48."
45. Práxedis Guerrero, "The Means and the End," *Regeneración*, November 5, 1910. Available at http://archivomagon.net/wp-content/uploads/e4n10.pdf. As translated in Guerrero, *I am Action*, 91–92.
46. Práxedis Guerrero, "Soy la Accion," *Regeneración*, September 17, 1910, ADRFM, http://archivomagon.net/wp-content/uploads/e4n3.pdf. As translated in Guerrero, *I am Action*, 53–54.
47. Guerrero, *I am Action*, 53–54.
48. Duffy Turner, *Ricardo Flores Magón*, 206.
49. Quoted from *Regeneración* in Martínez Núñez, *La vida heróica de Práxedis Guerrero*, 196. Translated in Lomnitz, *The Return of Comrade Ricardo Flores Magón*, 255.
50. Quoted in Ward S. Albro, *Always a Rebel: Ricardo Flores Magón and the Mexican Revolution* (Fort Worth: Texas Christian University Press, 1992), 119.
51. Benjamín Maldonado Alvarado, *La utopía de Ricardo Flores Magón: Revolución, anarquía, y comunalidad india* (Oaxaca: Universidad Autónoma de Oaxaca, 1994), 52.
52. Friedrich Katz, *The Life and Times of Pancho Villa* (Palo Alto, CA: Stanford University Press, 1998), 52–53; Knight, *The Mexican Revolution*, vol. 1, 55–59, 70–77; Enrique Krauze, "Francisco I. Madero: The Apostle of Democracy," in Krauze, *Mexico: Biography of Power*, 245–73; McLynn, *Villa and Zapata*, 25–32.
53. Martínez Núñez, *La vida heroica de Práxedis G. Guerrero*, 215. See also James D. Cockcroft, *Intellectual Precursors of the Mexican Revolution, 1900–1913* (Austin: University of Texas Press, 1968), 176; James A. Sandos, *Rebellion in the Borderlands: Anarchism and the Plan de San Diego, 1904–1923* (Norman: University of Oklahoma Press, 1992), 26; Diego Abad de Santillán, *Ricardo Flores Magón: El apóstol de la revolución social mexicana* (Mexico City: Centro de Estudios Históricos del Movimiento Obrero Mexicano, 1978), 65–66.

54. Martínez Núñez, *La vida heroica de Práxedis G. Guerrero*, 215.

55. Untitled article, *Regeneración*, October 1, 1910, ADRFM, http://archivomagon.net/wp-content/uploads/e4n5.pdf.

56. "Texas Town that Burned Mexican Is Not Worried," *San Antonio Light and Gazette*, November 14, 1910.

57. Monica Muñoz Martínez, *The Injustice Never Leaves You: Anti-Mexican Violence in Texas* (Cambridge, MA: Harvard University Press, 2018).

58. "Barbarismos," *La Crónica*, November 12, 1910.

59. Práxedis Guerrero, "Whites, Whites," *Regeneración*, November 19, 1910, ADRFM, http://archivomagon.net/wp-content/uploads/e4n12.pdf. As translated in Guerrero, *I am Action*, 100–103.

60. "Whiskey and sausage filled": quoted in "Sonora Paper Berates Yankees," *San Antonio Light and Gazette*, November 26, 1910.

61. Translated and reprinted in "Flaming Editorials that Stirred Mexican Mobs," *San Antonio Light and Gazette*, November 13, 1910.

62. Testimony by Henry Lane Wilson, Preliminary Report and Hearings of the Committee on Foreign Relations, United States Senate, Pursuant to S. Res. 106, Directing the Committee on Foreign Relations to Investigate the Matter of Outrages on Citizens of the United States in Mexico, vol. 3, part 2, p. 2254.

63. Henry Lane Wilson, memo, November 16, 1910, NARA, RG 59, M274, 812 series.

64. Henry Lane Wilson, memo, November 16, 1910.

65. Ricardo Flores Magón, "The Repercussions of a Lynching," *Regeneración*, November 12, 1910, ADRFM, http://archivomagon.net/wp-content/uploads/e4n11.pdf. As translated by Chaz Bufe in Chaz Bufe and Mitchell Cowen Verter, *Dreams of Freedom: A Ricardo Flores Magón Reader* (Oakland, CA: AK Press, 2005), 198-201.

66. Henry Lane Wilson, memo, November 16, 1910, NARA, RG 59, M274, 812 series.

67. Henry Lane Wilson, telegram, November 18, 1919, NARA, RG 59, M274, 812 series.

Chapter 25: THE REVOLUTION BEGINS

1. Práxedis Guerrero, "El medio y el fin," *Regeneración*, November 5, 1910, ADRFM, http://archivomagon.net/wp-content/uploads/e4n10.pdf. As translated in Claudio Lomnitz, *The Return of Comrade Ricardo Flores Magón* (New York: Zone Books, 2014), 259.

2. Ethel Duffy Turner, *Ricardo Flores Magón y el Partido Liberal Mexicano* (Mexico City: Comisión Nacional Editorial, 1984), 207.

3. Lomnitz, *The Return of Comrade Ricardo Flores Magón*, 264.

4. Eugenio Martínez Núñez, *La vida heróica de Práxedis G. Guerrero* (Mexico City: Biblioteca del Instituto Nacional de Estudios Históricos de la Revolución Mexicana, 1960), 222–26.

5. Friedrich Katz, *The Life and Times of Pancho Villa* (Palo Alto, CA: Stanford University Press, 1998), 19. See also Lance R. Blyth, *Chiricahua and Janos: Communities of Violence in the Southwest Borderlands, 1680–1880* (Lincoln: University of Nebraska Press, 2012).

6. Martínez Núñez, *La vida heroica de Práxedis G. Guerrero*, 227–37; Ward S. Albro, *To Die on Your Feet: The Life, Times and Writings of Práxedis G. Guerrero* (Fort Worth: Texas Christian University Press, 1996), 65–66.

7. Albro, *To Die on Your Feet*, 138.

8. Lowell L. Blaisdell, *Desert Revolution: Baja California, 1911* (Madison: University of Wisconsin Press, 1962), 34–35.

9. W. Dirk Raat, *Revoltosos: Mexico's Rebels in the United States, 1903–1923* (College Station: Texas A & M University Press, 1981), 56–57.

10. Gabriela González, *Redeeming La Raza: Transborder Modernity, Race, Respectability and Rights* (Oxford: Oxford University Press, 2018), 77. See also Devra Anne Weber, "Wobblies of the Partido Liberal Mexicano: Reenvisioning Internationalist and Transnational Movements through Mexican Lenses," *Pacific Historical Review* 85, no. 2 (2016): 188–227.

11. Quoted in Blaisdell, *Desert Revolution*, 42.

12. Blaisdell, *Desert Revolution*, 46.
13. Blaisdell, *Desert Revolution*, 74.
14. Quoted in Blaisdell, *Desert Revolution*, 76.
15. Blaisdell, *Desert Revolution*, 57–69.
16. Katz, *The Life and Times of Pancho Villa*, 93.
17. Katz, *The Life and Times of Pancho Villa*, 62–63.
18. Katz, *The Life and Times of Pancho Villa*, 107–8.
19. On Zapata and anarchism, see Frank McLynn, *Villa and Zapata: A History of the Mexican Revolution* (New York: Carroll & Graf, 2000), 43.
20. For more on Emiliano Zapata, see Samuel Brunk, *Emiliano Zapata!: Revolution and Betrayal in Mexico* (Albuquerque: University of New Mexico Press, 1995); John Womack, Jr., *Zapata and the Mexican Revolution* (New York: Vintage, 1968).
21. Charles H. Harris III and Louis R. Sadler, *The Secret War in El Paso: Mexican Revolutionary Intrigue, 1906–1920* (Albuquerque: University of New Mexico Press, 2009); David Dorado Romo, *Ringside Seat to a Revolution: An Underground Cultural History of El Paso and Juárez: 1893–1923* (El Paso: Cinco Punto Press, 2005).
22. Quoted in Katz, *Life and Times of Pancho Villa*, 110.
23. McLynn, *Villa and Zapata*, 105.
24. Duffy Turner, *Ricardo Flores Magón*, 215–18.
25. Quoted in Ward S. Albro, *Always a Rebel: Ricardo Flores Magón and the Mexican Revolution* (Fort Worth: Texas Christian University Press, 1992), 129.
26. Quoted in Peter Marshall, *Demanding the Impossible: A History of Anarchism* (Oakland, CA: PM Press, 2010), 512.
27. "Magonistas Ask Impossibilities," *El Paso Herald*, June 20, 1911.
28. EDTA, file 257.
29. Quoted in Lomnitz, *The Return of Comrade Ricardo Flores Magón*, 311.
30. Quoted in Emma Pérez, T*he Decolonial Imaginary: Writing Chicanas into History* (Bloomington: Indiana University Press, 1999), 64.
31. James A. Sandos, *Rebellion in the Borderlands: Anarchism and the Plan de San Diego, 1904–1923* (Norman: University of Oklahoma Press, 1992), 38.
32. Quoted in González, *Redeeming La Raza*, 62–63.
33. González, *Redeeming La Raza*, 63.
34. Quoted in Lomnitz, *The Return of Comrade Ricardo Flores Magón*, 309.
35. Lomnitz, *The Return of Comrade Ricardo Flores Magón*, 305.
36. EDTA, file 263.
37. Quoted in Raat, *Revoltosos*, 59.
38. Sandos, *Rebellion in the Borderlands*, 38. See also letter from Mother Jones to Manuel Calero, October 25, 1911, in Mary Harris Jones, *The Correspondence of Mother Jones*, edited by Edward M. Steel (Pittsburgh: University of Pittsburgh Press, 1985), 97–100.
39. Quoted in Blaisdell, *Desert Revolution*, 184.
40. Chaz Bufe and Mitchell Cowen Verter, *Dreams of Freedom: A Ricardo Flores Magón Reader* (Oakland, CA: AK Press, 2005), 138–44.
41. Bufe and Verter, *Dreams of Freedom*, 138–44.

Conclusion: Always a Rebel

1.   For overviews of the Mexican Revolution, see Adolfo Gilly, *The Mexican Revolution* (New York: New Press, 2005); Alan Knight, *The Mexican Revolution*, vols. 1 and 2 (Cambridge: Cambridge University Press, 1986); Friedrich Katz, *The Life and Times of Pancho Villa* (Palo Alto, CA: Stanford University Press, 1998); Elena Pontiatowska, *Las Soldaderas: Women of the Mexican Revolution* (El Paso: Cinco Puntos Press, 2006).
2.   For more on foreign entanglements in the Mexican Revolution, see Friedrich Katz, *The Secret War in Mexico: Europe, the United States and the Mexican Revolution* (Chicago: University of

Chicago Press, 1981). For a closer look at U.S. involvement in the Mexican Revolution, see "The Mexican Revolution and the United States in the collections of the Library of Congress," online exhibit, https://www.loc.gov/exhibits/mexican-revolution-and-the-united-states/.

3. For more on the U.S.–Mexico border fence, see Rachel St. John, *Line in the Sand: A History of the Western U.S.–Mexico Border* (Princeton: Princeton University Press, 2011); Mary Mendoza, "Unnatural Border: Race and Environment at the U.S.–Mexico Divide," PhD dissertation, University of California, Davis, 2015; Mary Mendoza, "Fencing the Line: Race, Environment, and the Changing Visual Landscape at the U.S.–Mexico Divide," in *Border Spaces: Visualizing the U.S.-Mexico Frontera*, edited by Katherine G. Morrissey and John-Michael Warner (Tucson: University of Arizona Press, 2018).

4. Benjamin Heber Johnson, *Revolution in Texas: How a Forgotten Rebellion and Its Bloody Suppression Turned Mexicans into Americans* (New Haven: Yale University Press, 2003), 72–74.

5. Johnson, *Revolution in Texas*, 74.

6. James A. Sandos, *Rebellion in the Borderlands: Anarchism and the Plan of San Diego, 1904–1923* (Norman: University of Oklahoma Press, 1992), 87.

7. Johnson, *Revolution in Texas*, 2.

8. Johnson, *Revolution in Texas*, 106–7.

9. Johnson, *Revolution in Texas*, 109. Several prominent Mexican Americans attempted to intervene. Among them was José T. Canales, who would go on to hold a series of public hearings on the violence perpetrated by the Texas Rangers (see 169–75).

10. Johnson, *Revolution in Texas*, 108.

11. Johnson, *Revolution in Texas*, 115.

12. Johnson, *Revolution in Texas*, 115.

13. Johnson, *Revolution in Texas*, 118.

14. Quoted in James A. Sandos, *Rebellion in the Borderlands: Anarchism and the Plan de San Diego, 1904–1923* (Norman: University of Oklahoma Press, 1992), 98.

15. Sandos, *Rebellion in the Borderlands*, 109; Johnson, *Revolution in Texas*, 3.

16. Johnson, *Revolution in Texas*, 119–20.

17. Johnson, *Revolution in Texas*, 62.

18. Sandos, *Rebellion in the Borderlands*, 94–95.

19. Claudio Lomnitz, *The Return of Comrade Ricardo Flores Magón* (New York: Zone Books, 2014), 442.

20. Quoted in Lomnitz, *The Return of Comrade Ricardo Flores Magón*, 443.

21. Quoted in Lomnitz, *The Return of Comrade Ricardo Flores Magón*, 443.

22. Quoted in Johnson, *Revolution in Texas*, 132.

23. Sandos, *Rebellion in the Borderlands*, 126.

24. Sandos, *Rebellion in the Borderlands*, 138.

25. Quoted in Andrew Wood Grant, "Death of a Political Prisoner: Revisiting the Case of Ricardo Flores Magón," *A Contracorriente: una revista de estudios latinoamericanos* 3, no. 1 (2005): 47.

26. Lomnitz, *The Return of Comrade Ricardo Flores Magón*, 463–71.

27. As translated in Chaz Bufe and Mitchell Cowen Verter, *Dreams of Freedom: A Ricardo Flores Magón Reader* (Oakland, CA: AK Press, 2005), 145–46. See also Colin MacLachlan, *Anarchism and the Mexican Revolution: The Political Trials of Ricardo Flores Magón in the United States* (Berkeley: University of California Press, 1991), 81.

28. Quoted in MacLachlan, *Anarchism and the Mexican Revolution*, 90.

29. "Russian Born Soldier of Fortune Thrived in West," *Los Angeles Times*, December 18, 2005. For more on Kosterlitzky's exile in the United States, see Cornelius C. Smith, Jr., *Emilio Kosterlitzky: Eagle of Sonora and the Southwest Border* (Glendale, CA: Arthur H. Clark Company, 1970), 233–87.

30. Letter from Ricardo Flores Magón to Gus Teltsch, December 15, 1920, quoted in Paul Avrich, *Anarchist Portraits* (Princeton: Princeton University Press, 1988), 210.

31. Quoted in Lomnitz, *The Return of Comrade Ricardo Flores Magón*, 478.

32. Wood, "Death of a Political Prisoner," 51.

33. Wood, "Death of a Political Prisoner," 55.

34. Quoted in Lomnitz, *The Return of Comrade Ricardo Flores Magón*, 472.
35. Wood, "Death of a Political Prisoner," 53.
36. Dave Poole, *Librado Rivera: Anarchists in the Mexican Revolution* (Orkney, UK: Cienfuegos Press, 1979; digital edition East Sussex, TN: Christie Books, 2012).
37. Quoted in Lomnitz, *The Return of Comrade Ricardo Flores Magón*, 495.
38. Quoted in Sandos, *Rebellion in the Borderlands*, 170.
39. Quoted in MacLachlan, *Anarchism and the Mexican Revolution*, 105.
40. Vicki Ruiz, "Nuestra América: Latino History as United States History," *Journal of American History* 93, no. 3 (December 2006): 655–72.

ILLUSTRATION CREDITS

104   Courtesy of the Library of Congress.

107   Courtesy of the Archivo Histórico de la Secretaría de Relaciones Exteriores, Mexico City.

127   Courtesy of Southern Methodist University, DeGoyler Library.

146   Courtesy of the Archivo Histórico de la Secretaría de Relaciones Exteriores, Mexico City.

183   PLM code key courtesy of the Archivo Histórico de la Secretaría de Relaciones Exteriores, Mexico City; coded letter courtesy of the Archivo Histórico de la Secretaría de Relaciones Exteriores, Mexico City.

188   SECRETARIA DE CULTURA.-INAH.-SINAFO F.N.-Mex. Reproduction authorized by the Instituto Nacional de Antropología e Historia.

197   Courtesy of the George Grantham Bain collection at the Library of Congress.

211   Courtesy of the Instituto Nacional de Antropología e Historia.

216   Courtesy of the Library of Congress.

230   Courtesy of the Instituto Nacional de Antropología e Historia.

236   Courtesy of the Bancroft Library, University of California, Berkeley.

282   Courtesy of the San Diego History Center.

283   Courtesy of the Department of Special Collections, Stanford University Libraries.

286   Courtesy of the San Diego History Center.

300   Courtesy of the Robert Runyon Photograph Collection, di_04323, The Dolph Center for American History, The University of Texas, Austin.

304   Courtesy of the Special Collections at Charles E. Young Research Library, University of California, Los Angeles.

307   Courtesy of the Instituto Nacional de Antropología e Historia.

INDEX

Page references in *italics* indicate illustrations.